Taking Darwin Seriously

Michael Ruse

Taking Darwin Seriously

A Naturalistic Approach to Philosophy

Basil Blackwell

© Michael Ruse 1986

First published 1986

Basil Blackwell Ltd
108 Cowley Road, Oxford OX4 1JF, UK

Basil Blackwell Inc.
432 Park Avenue South, Suite 1505,
New York, NY 10016, USA

British Library Cataloguing in Publication Data

Ruse, Michael
   Taking Darwin seriously: a naturalistic
approach to philosophy.
   1. Philosophical anthropology
   I. Title
   128   BD450
ISBN 0-631-13542-1

Library of Congress Cataloging in Publication Data

Ruse, Michael.
   Taking Darwin seriously.

   Bibliography: p.
   Includes index.
   1. Evolution–Philosophy.   I. Title.
QH371.R77 1986   575.01′62   85-15094
ISBN 0-631-13542-1

Typeset by Oxford Publishing Services, Oxford
Printed in Great Britain by TJ Press Ltd, Padstow

For Lizzie, with love

Contents

Plato . . . says in Phaedo that our
imaginary ideas arise from
the preexistence of the soul,
are not derivable from
experience. – read monkeys
for preexistence.
(Charles Darwin, 1837)

Preface

On 19 March 1981 the then Governor of the State of Arkansas signed
into law Act 590 of 1981, known as the Balanced Treatment for
Creation-Science and Evolution-Science Act. This act required of the
biology schoolteachers in the State that, if they were to deal with
evolutionary hypotheses in their classes, then they had also to deal
equally with that subject which its supporters call Creation-science, and
which is better known to the rest of us as the Book of Genesis. If a
teacher told students that many people believe that organic life
developed slowly down through the ages from simple forms, and
perhaps even that life itself grew out of inert minerals, then that teacher
had also to tell the students that many people believe in a miraculous
creation of fully fledged life, which occurred but a few thousand years
ago.

At once, the American Civil Liberties Union swung into action,
opposing the law. The United States' constitution carefully separates
Church and State – too many Americans fled from State-backed religious
persecution in Europe – and the courts have interpreted this to mean
that you cannot teach religion of any kind in State-supported schools.
The case had to be made that Creation-science is not genuine science but
dogmatic fundamentalist religion, and to this end the ACLU assembled
a team of expert witnesses, including theologians, scientists and
educators. I am a historian and philosopher of science, and I was asked
to join the team because, in the past decade, I had written extensively
both on the nature of contemporary evolutionary biology, and on the
history of the emergence of biology from its pre-scientific past. I was to
show the difference between science and non-science, how evolutionary
ideas fit the former and Creationism the latter, and why it would be a
distortion of history to say that evolutionism was really an 'atheistic

religion' which had conquered the true religion of Christianity.

The ACLU won a smashing victory. After a two-week trial in December 1981, on 5 January 1982 US District Court Judge William R. Overton turned back the balanced treatment law, arguing in a withering judgment that Creation-science is a travesty of scholarship, designed solely to slip one particular brand of reactionary religion into school curricula (Overton, 1982). The forces of reason may not have won the war, but they won that battle decisively, and I feel thrilled and proud to have been part of it (Ruse, 1982a).

But I do not write about the Arkansas Creation Trial complacently, trying to inflate my own ego. Rather, I set it as a background, showing why it was that I was led to write this book. As you can imagine, one of the chief things that opposing counsel tries to do when faced with an expert witness is to destroy that witness's credibility and authority. In the trial, the State attorney general was forced to defend the law, and his lawyers spent much time trying to show that the ACLU witnesses were hostile to true religion, with but a shaky grasp on the foundations of morality. This was not a particularly easy task, since several of the witnesses were ordained clergymen. I myself got away fairly lightly, mainly I think because I send my children to private Anglican schools. The Church of England may not be much of a religion in the eyes of many Arkansas residents, but anyone who pays to have his children taught about the Bible cannot be all bad.

It is one thing to duck and weave your way through the sparring of a cross-examination in court. It is quite another to speak from a properly thought-out philosophy of nature and of life. In the months after the trial, because of the questions which had been asked – questions which I had never truly asked myself – I grew to realize that at least my Creationist opponents had a sincerely articulated world picture. I had nothing. Even though I had been a professional philosopher for twenty years, I still had no settled thoughts on the foundations of knowledge or of morality. When asked about ethical claims by opposing counsel, I had airily replied, 'I intuit them as objective realities.' God only knows what that means. Fortunately, it was sufficiently pompous sounding that no one cared to follow it up, although the attorney general did give me a long, hard, chilly stare.

Where does one start to try to develop a consistent and satisfying philosophical system? How does one find a basis for epistemology, the question of knowledge, and ethics, the question of morality? Perhaps the Creationists were right. If you reject the belief that we were made on the Sixth Day, literally in God's image, and think rather that we are modified monkeys, then this should make some difference to the way you approach knowledge and morality. And yet I knew, historically and philosophically, that most previous excursions into 'evolutionary episte-mology' and 'evolutionary ethics' leave much to be desired. Indeed, through the years I have myself criticized them severely (in somewhat well-trodden ways).

Nevertheless, I have now come to see that our biological origins do make a difference, and that they can and should be a starting-point for philosophy today. I do not pretend that a total cleansing of the Augean stables is required. I once read a book where the author opened by hoping that he was not saying anything original. I am not that self-effacing, but I do agree that philosophical progress occurs through a building on past achievements, rather than by breaking entirely with what has gone before. I shall in fact show that the philosophy I now advocate has deep roots in the past – roots which, when uncovered, help us to understand our position today. But I do most insistently argue that evolutionary biology must be brought right up front in philosophical discussion. In particular, we must begin with Charles Darwin's theory of evolution through natural selection. In every sense of the word, the time has come to take Darwin seriously.

I would like to think that this book will be of interest to philosophers and biologists, and perhaps also to others. For this reason, I have deliberately written it in a non-technical way, trying to be readable to students of more than one specialized discipline. Donald Campbell once said that projects such as these have to be attempted 'by marginal scholars who are willing to be incompetent in a number of fields at once' (1977, p. 9). That about says it all. Because I am trying to be inter-disciplinary, those of you with specialized knowledge in one area or another will probably find some parts of this book somewhat pedantic. Please remember that these parts are not written for you. Of course, if you find the whole of the book pedantic, then none of the book was written for you.

A brief synopsis is as follows: the first chapter deals generally with scientific thinking about origins, concentrating particularly on modern evolutionary thought. I distinguish three claims: about the fact of evolution, about the course of evolution, and about the mechanisms of evolution. Much concerned with mechanisms, I present and discuss the modern version of Darwin's theory of evolution through natural selection, the dominant paradigm today. Defending it against a number of attacks, which seem continually to be made, my aim is to show that neo-Darwinism is good tough science, which should command the respect of all.

The second and third chapters are primarily critical, clearing the way for the main arguments to follow. I look first at the usual way in which epistemology is related to evolution, concentrating (with previous writers) on the way in which claims to scientific knowledge are related to evolution. I argue that such ways are at best illustrative and at worst downright misleading. Then, I go on to consider analogous attempts to put ethics on an evolutionary footing. I show that, historically, they have sometimes been a lot more reasonable than critics allow, but that ultimately all such efforts collapse. If they are not impaled on points of logic, then they fail to do justice to modern science. Yet, although critical, I do want to emphasize that my discussions, in these chapters on evolutionary epistemology and evolutionary ethics, are far from totally negative. I appreciate the spirit in which such work has been done, and moreover I use my critiques as an opportunity to tease out important features both of scientific knowledge and of moral reasoning. These are features to which any adequate philosophy must do justice.

In the fourth chapter, to prepare for a fresh philosophical assault, I take up the question of human biological nature and evolution. Because mine is a *naturalistic* approach to philosophy, this empirical discussion is very important indeed. Our origins are traced, comparison is made with non-human animals, and then the findings are related to what is known about the present state of humankind. The evolution of language is taken as a model for the full understanding of our biological nature. This leads us into an exposition and discussion of new extensions of Darwinian evolutionary theory, particularly as they address the ways in which human thought and action generally reflect our evolutionary past.

The next two chapters are the heart of the book. In the fifth chapter, I see how our present biological understanding of *Homo sapiens* has important implications for what we can claim to know, and how we can know that which we know. In particular, I argue that knowledge is shaped and informed by our evolutionary past. The mind is not a *tabula rasa*, and this crucially affects perceptions, reasoning, and the consequences we would draw. Turning to the history of philosophy, I suggest that the true philosophical father of neo-Darwinian epistemology is David Hume. Armed with this awareness, we can move to apply our findings to some of the problems which have engaged philosophers, both past and present. Problems discussed include those of scepticism and realism.

The sixth chapter brings us once again to morality. I argue that now, at last, we are able adequately to mesh evolution and ethics. We can see that our simian nature does not plunge us into a world of Hobbesian brutishness or Tennysonian strife: 'nature red in tooth and claw'. Thanks to newly discovered models of social interaction, the human biologist can give backing to an ethics which is realistic, in the best sense of the term. Again the name of Hume arises, when it is shown that Darwinism points to just the kind of ethics based on human feelings as is espoused in the *Treatise of Human Nature*. I argue also that such an evolutionary-based ethics can withstand the attacks of those who oppose any naturalistic approaches to morality, and can indeed incorporate many of the important insights of modern moral philosophy.

Finally, in a brief conclusion, I try to quell the doubts of those who fear that no new approach to philosophy could be quite as wonderful as I claim it is. If nothing else, let me assure you that I deserve no special merit. At most, I am a lucky person in the right place at the right time, caught between a rapidly forward-moving biological science and a state of philosophy ripe for a new impetus.

My debts are many, to institutions and to individuals. Above all, I must thank the John Simon Guggenheim Memorial Foundation for support. As a Canadian, I am particularly in debt to this private American foundation, since my own government funding agency felt compelled to bow to the fervent critical prayer of a well-known opponent of the application of Darwinism to humankind. Also, more than usually, I am indebted to my home institution, the University of Guelph, which backed me, even though I had no claim on its support. The Museum of Comparative Zoology of Harvard University gave me entry to, and full use of, all its facilities, particularly libraries.

Edward O. Wilson has been a friend, guide and critic. In this book, I admire him, agree with him, and differ from him. Ours is a very happy relationship, personally and professionally. Payment is also owed to Bert Hölldobler, the other leader of the Social Insects Laboratory at Harvard. As a working empirical scientist, he exposed my ideas to close scrutiny, even though he did not always show the deep sympathy for grandiose metaphysical systems that one might have expected from one who hails from Germany. Like everyone else writing in this field, I owe an incredible debt to Donald Campbell. His enthusiasm is infectious and his magnificent bibliographies halve the scholar's task. Our agreements, in spirit and in fact, are far more than anything in the following pages may suggest.

Little did I think some twenty years ago at the University of Rochester, when Jeffrie Murphy was a very successful student of Kant and I a very unsucccessful student of anything, that our intellectual paths would cross today. I am happy to acknowledge my debt to his recent thinking about ethics, especially in his *Evolution, Morality, and the Meaning of Life*. And thanks must go to all the others who read earlier portions of this work, argued with me, ate and drank with me, and who showed that a meaningful, happy life is the other side to the evolutionary coin; especially Robert Paul Wolff, Abner Shimony, Alex Rosenberg, Richard Sens, Ernst Mayr, Michael Bradie, Sarah Hrdy, and John and Pat Matthews.

1

The Biological Background

In dealing with evolution, I make a three-part division (Ruse, 1984b). I separate the actual *fact* of evolution from the particular *path* of evolution, and both of these from the *theory* of evolution, which is about causes or mechanisms. Clearly, any such division as this is somewhat artificial. You could hardly have a path of evolution without its being a fact, and mechanisms which take us nowhere are surely not all that evolutionary. Nevertheless, the division does help in the task of exposition, and does correspond roughly to separate parts of the evolutionary enterprise. In this chapter, I aim only to provide a background to what is to come. Deliberately, I say little specifically about our own species, reserving discussion of this until a later chapter.

The fact of evolution

By 'evolution' I mean the natural unfolding and change of organisms down through the generations, from earlier forms, widely different (Ruse, 1979a). Some, including most scientists today, would extend the term to cover the natural development of life from non-life (Fox and Dose, 1977). I am happy to do this, although such initial events do not really interest me here. For the purposes of this book, I shall understand the term to refer to development from common ancestors. At the earliest point, these were presumably relatively few in number. Strictly, this final claim starts to push us towards thoughts about the path of evolution, but it is convenient to include it in the sense of 'fact'.

Evolution is an idea with a long history, stretching back in some form or another to the Greek atomists, or even before (Goudge, 1973). However, the rise of Judaeo-Christian religion, with the Creation-story of Genesis, led to a long dormant period. But, by the early part of the nineteenth century, many were arguing for some version of organic evolution, which was generally taken to be a special aspect of that general unfurling which governs the whole universe. Well-known evolutionists included Erasmus Darwin, Charles Darwin's grandfather, and the French invertebrate palaeontologist, Jean Baptiste de Lamarck (Mayr, 1982; Bowler, 1984).

It was the publication of the *Origin of Species* in 1859 which changed evolution from fanciful speculation to established fact. Not a few have pointed out that Darwin never actually used the word 'evolution' in the *Origin*; but this is something of a quibble. The last word of the text is 'evolved', and Darwin unambiguously uses his own phrase 'descent with modification' where we would use our term 'evolution'. The latter term, indeed, was only just then coming into general use. We need fear no undue anachronisms in relying on our own language.

Darwin's argument is solid, and is that used by evolutionists today. It is important that we understand it fully, for there are still many who think there is something a little uncertain about the very fact of evolution. One hears that 'evolution is only a theory [whatever that means], not a fact [whatever that means]'. Apparently, this scepticism about the status of evolution itself was one shared by that most influential of modern philosophers, Ludwig Wittgenstein (Burret, 1967, p. 26). Little wonder then that he thought Darwinian theory irrelevant to philosophical enquiry.

Darwin was influenced methodologically by the British philosopher of science William Whewell (Ruse, 1975a). Drawing on his perception of Newtonian mechanics, Whewell argued that the best kind of science tries to bring many disparate areas of enquiry under one unifying principle. This integration, which Whewell termed a 'consilience of inductions', works two ways. On the one hand, the unifying principle throws explanatory light on the various sub-areas. On the other hand, the sub-areas combine to give credence to the unifying principle. Indeed, argued Whewell, you can thus have confidence in the truth of the principle, even without direct sensory evidence. Much as in a law-court, where one assigns guilt indirectly through circumstantial evidence, so in science you move beyond speculation indirectly through its circumstantial evidence (Whewell, 1840; Kitcher, 1981).

Whewell was surely right in arguing this. At least, he was surely right in arguing that in science, as elsewhere, the best kind of reasoning is taken to involve consiliences. It is a method used constantly in science, and a mark that the work has been well done. Convergence on a common principle convinces us that we have moved beyond coincidence. 'It just couldn't be chance.' Most recently, it is a consilience which recommends to geologists the new theory of plate tectonics (Ruse, 1981c).

Darwin endorsed Whewell's ideas entirely, and the *Origin* offers a textbook example of a consilience. There are many different areas in biology. There is the study of the geographical distribution of organisms: biogeography. There is the study of the form of organisms and of relations between them: comparative anatomy. There is the investigation into the early forms of organisms and their development: embryology. There is the question of the fossil record: palaeontology. And much more. It was Darwin's genius to show that knotty problems in all of these areas of biology fall away before the explanatory hypothesis of evolution (figure 1.1).

Conversely, this unifying idea is supported by all of the various biological sub-disciplines. Thus, in biogeography, oceanic islands pose a puzzle. Why on the Galapagos archipelago, for instance, do we find different species of finch, mocking bird, and tortoise, from island to island, within sight of each other? Why does this happen when, on the South American mainland, one single species might roam the length, from steamy jungle to frigid desert? Obviously, because ancestors came to the Galapagos and then evolved, cut off from their fellows. In

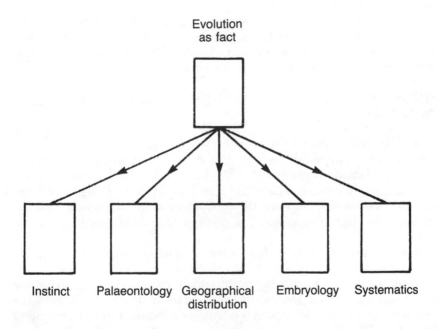

Figure 1.1 The structure of Darwin's argument for the fact of evolution. The fact explains and unifies claims made in the subdisciplines (only some of which are shown), which latter in turn yield the 'circumstantial evidence' for the fact itself.

comparative anatomy, homologies pose a puzzle. Why do we get isomorphism between the bones of the arms and hand of man, the fore-leg of horse, the wings of bird and of bat, the flipper of whale, and the paw of mole? Why do we get these, despite the very different uses to which these limbs are put? Because of descent from common ancestors. In embryology, virtually everything poses puzzles. Why are the embryos of man and dog indistinguishable, when the adults are so very different? Because they have a common evolutionary origin (figures 1.2 and 1.3).

Then, reversing the thread of thought, Darwin argued that the Galapagos finches, the fore-limb homologies, the identical embryos, are the fingerprints, the bloodstains, the broken alibis, of evolution. Gathering together all the wide evidence, the case for evolution is thus made overwhelming. It is 'beyond reasonable doubt'. Moreover, modern evolutionists agree in this with Darwin, simply following his method and adding yet more strands of evidence. For instance, recently molecular biology has opened up dramatic new veins of support. The essential macromolecules of life speak no less eloquently about the past than does any other level of the biological world (Futuyma, 1983; Kitcher, 1983a).

One conclusion only is tenable. Evolution may be almost entirely unseen. But it is a fact, and a well-established fact, no less than that Henry VIII's daughter Elizabeth was Queen of England, and that a heart beats within my breast.

The path of evolution

Most people when asked why they believe in evolution, reply: 'Because of the fossils.' The same goes for the critics, who concentrate almost entirely on palaeontology (Gish, 1973; Halstead, 1984). Supporters and critics commit the same fallacy. As you should now realize, the fossil record is not the only, or even the most significant, item in the case for descent. The fact of evolution is distinctively established by *all* the evidence.

But this is not to deny that fossils, the remains of dead organisms, do have a special role in our understanding of organic history, for it is they that tell us much about the path which life has taken, from the beginnings up to the present. It may surprise you to learn that the essential outlines of this path were mapped before Darwin published (Bowler, 1976). Not only that, the cartographers were ardent anti-evolutionists, keen to demonstrate God's creative miraculous powers! They discovered that, in the beginning somewhere back in the mists of time, there was not the full diversity of life which exists today. They discovered also that such diversity, involving mighty complex forms,

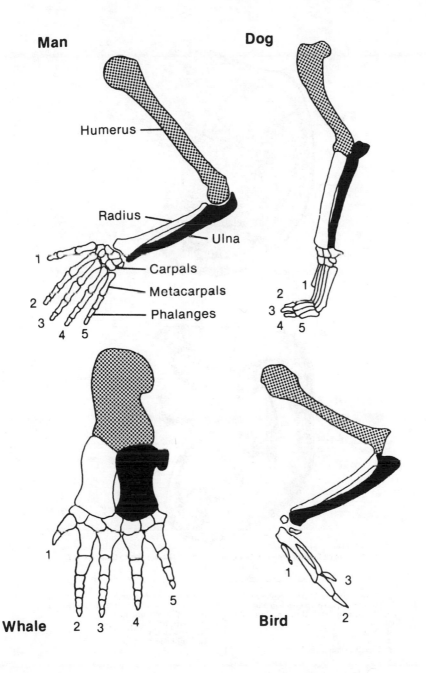

Figure 1.2 Homology between the fore-limbs of several vertebrates. Numbers refer to digits. (Adapted with permission from Dobzhansky *et al.*, 1977, p. 41.)

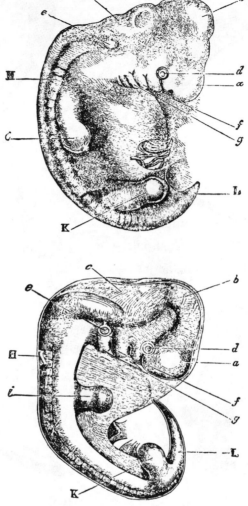

Fig. 1. Upper figure human embryo, from Ecker. Lower figure that of a dog, from Bischoff.

a. Fore-brain, cerebral hemispheres, &c.
b. Mid-brain, corpora quadrigemina.
c. Hind-brain, cerebellum, medulla oblongata.
d. Eye.
e. Ear.
f. First visceral arch.

g. Second visceral arch.
H. Vertebral columns and muscles in process of development.
i. Anterior } extremities.
K. Posterior }
L. Tail or os coccyx.

Figure 1.3 Comparison of human and canine embryos. Why are they so similar if man and dog have not descended from a joint ancestor? (From Darwin's *The Descent of Man*, 1871.)

first appeared gradually, down through the passage of years. And, much to their own amazement, non-evolutionary palaeontologists working before the *Origin* found that life's history had not been one uninterrupted drive to the present, but had involved multiple branchings. Moreover, dead-ends or extinctions occur far more often than do successes. Truly, it is a tree which is the appropriate metaphor for the history of life, not a ladder (figures 1.4–1.6 and tables 1.1 and 1.2).

Without the fossils, we would know little of life's history. Even today, where there are major gaps in the record, it is often difficult to do more than speculate about probable paths, or 'phylogenies'. But it has always been recognized that other parts of biology play significant roles in uncovering the past. In particular, comparative studies – previously primarily of anatomy, but more and more today of organic macromolecules – tell us much about the way living beings meandered down through the eons (Ayala and Valentine, 1979; Futuyma, 1979). Also, as has long been realized, embryology is a powerful tool in puzzling out the past. The old notion that 'ontogeny recapitulates phylogeny' (i.e. that the history of the individual compresses the history of its group) has long been discarded in its original form. Darwin always kept it at arm's length (Ospovat, 1981). Nevertheless, from pre-evolutionary days on, it has been realized that the child is the father of the man. Deeper relations are revealed in the early stages of life than can be seen through adult forms. Think of how much more telling is the human/dog embryo comparison than anything appearing in the mature animals (Russell, 1916; Gould, 1977).

The most important thing that we now know – what the Victorians did not know – is precisely when everything happened. Thanks to radiometric dating, and other physico-chemical techniques, we can confidently put the age of the Earth at about 4,500 million years. Life began some 3,500 million years ago, but it was not for another 3,000 million years that forms outside the simple cellular level began to proliferate (Cloud, 1974). Mammals first appeared 200 million years ago. Nevertheless, until the dinosaurs died out, some 60 million years ago, mammals remained small and insignificant. Since then, they have flourished mightily, as all who have eyes to see can tell (Valentine, 1978).

One question is asked again and again about the course of evolution. Is it progressive? Do things, in some way, get better? This is hardly a silly question. Non-evolutionists were quite convinced that the fossil record shows progression. And evolutionists have usually allowed that, in respects, the record certainly seems this way (Bowler, 1976; Rudwick, 1972). Given only simplicity at the start of the fossil record and complexity evolving out of it, what more natural than to suppose that the simple is in some way 'primitive', and that the complex 'advanced'? How much more natural this all seems when the advanced just so

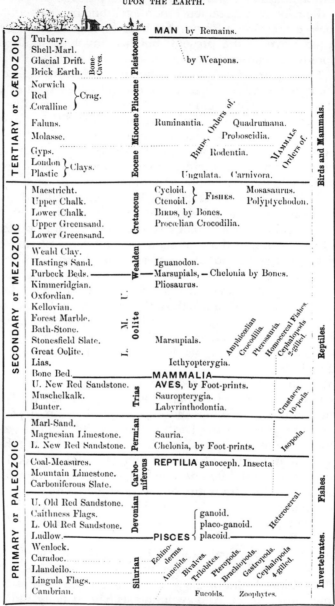

Figure 1.4 The animal fossil record, as known at the time of the *Origin*. As explained in the text, by this time all serious scientists, including non-evolutionists, realized that the history of life was not a single progressive rise, but involved much branching. (From Richard Owen, *Paleontology*, 1861.)

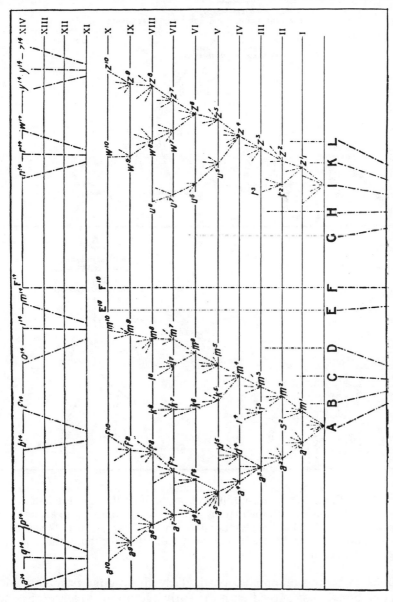

Figure 1.5 In the *Origin*, Darwin gave this figure showing how he thought of evolution as a (branching) tree of life.

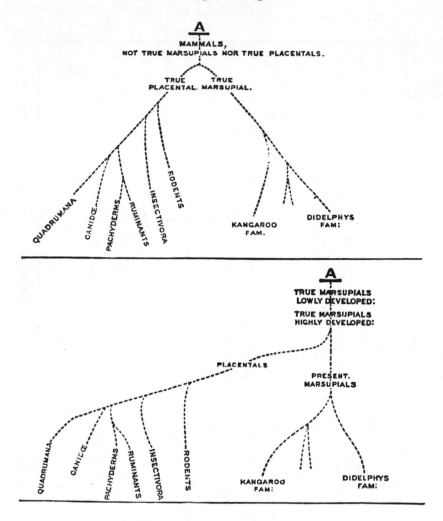

Figure 1.6 Although Darwin said little about how he thought life had actually evolved, he did think about the matter, as these illustrations, from a letter to the geologist Charles Lyell (23 September 1860), well show. In each sketch, *A* is a (hypothetical) ancestor. Notice that Darwin seems to have thought of change as being fairly gradual.

happens to be the mammals, particularly the higher primates. More than one person has agreed with the early evolutionist Herbert Spencer (1852) that the apotheosis of the evolutionary climb is a being very much like himself.

We cannot answer completely questions about progression without talk of mechanisms. But it can at once be said that, whatever comfort progressionists may draw from the record, it does at the same time pose severe problems for such would-be interpreters. Most particularly, the branching which is the most striking feature of the record raises the question of where all the supposed progression is leading to. Today, all

Table 1.1 Major Events in the History of the Earth

Events in biosphere	Time (billions of years)	Events in planetary environment		
Permian–Triassic extinctions	0.22		(Plate tectonics)	
First well-mineralized skeletons	0.57			
First body fossils	0.70			
First metazoans?	1.0			Free oxygen in atmosphere
Possible early eukaryotes	1.3			
		Cranial sediment, chiefly oxidized		
Possible early eukaryotes	1.91		(Plate tectonics probable)	
		Most branded iron formations		
	2.21			
(Prokaryotes becoming diverse)				
		Cratonal sediment, chiefly unoxidized		
Oldest dated fossils (prokaryotic autotrophs)	3.31	Rocks chiefly granitic and gneissic, sediments extensive	(Global tectonics unlike present)	Chiefly anoxic atmosphere, probably reducing
	3.81	Oldest dated rocks Record not known		
	4.61	Origin of Earth		

Prokaryotes have cells without nucleii, whereas eukaryotes have cells with nucleii. Metazoans are multicellular organisms. (Adapted with permission from Cloud, 1974.)

Table 1.2 Major Events in the Evolution of a Multicellular Life

Millions of years ago	Era	Period		Epoch	Events
	Cenozoic	Quaternary		Pleistocene	Evolution of man
0	Cenozoic	Tertiary		Pilocene Miocene Oligocene Eocene Paleocene	Mammalian radiation
50					
100	Mesozoic	Cretaceous			Last dinosaurs First primates First flowering plants
150	Mesozoic	Jurassic			Dinosaurs First birds
200	Mesozoic	Triassic			First mammals Therapside dominant
250	Paleozoic	Permian			Major marine extinction Pelycosaurs dominant
300	Paleozoic	Carbo-niferous	Pennsylvanian		First reptiles
			Mississippian		Scale trees, seed ferns
350	Paleozoic	Devonian			First amphibians Jawed fishes diversify
400	Paleozoic	Silurian			First vascular land plants
450	Paleozoic	Ordovician			Burst of diversification in metazoan families
500	Paleozoic	Cambrian			First fish First chordates
550					
600	Precambrian	Ediacaran			First skeletal elements
650	Precambrian				First soft-bodied metazoans First animal traces (coelomates)

It is interesting to compare this with Owen's corresponding 1861 picture (figure 1.4). The older picture stands up surprisingly well. (Adapted with permission from Valentine, 1978 © Scientific American Inc.)

sorts of organisms thrive: big and small, fast and slow, prolific and slow breeding, simple and complex. Which of these is to be taken as the real end point of evolution? Progress implies getting better or truer in some way: yet much of the history of life belies this claim. Consider the reptiles. Today's representatives are piddling little creatures compared to the dinosaurs, which were neither so clumsy nor so gormless as popular myth would have it. Of course, you might want to argue that warm-bloodedness or a large brain is the sign of progress. But the nasty suspicion arises that you are reading into the fossil record your own idea of progress, which you then triumphantly extract.

There are, indeed, good reasons for treating very warily simple statements of the chief physical evidence for claims about progression. Although the evolutionist must agree that, by anyone's criteria, the very earliest forms would have been simpler than today's forms, very rapidly the picture becomes muddied. Comparing mammal and fish, the icthyologist George Williams writes: 'In some respects, such as brain structure, a mammal is certainly more complex than any fish. In other respects, such as integumentary histology, the average fish is much more complex than any mammal. What the verdict after a complete and objective comparison would be is uncertain' (1966, p. 43). All in all, the conclusion has to be that palaeontology does not, in itself, thrust some notion of an upward progressive climb of life upon you. More on this topic shortly.

Before leaving this direct look at the path of evolution, there is one other matter which must be touched on. As nearly everyone seems now to know, recently a group of evolutionists – primarily palaeontologists –

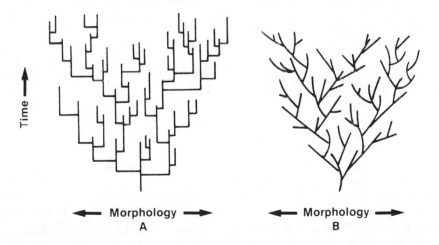

Figure 1.7 The saltationary or 'punctuated' model (A) and the Darwinian or 'gradualistic' model (B) compared.

Figure 1.8 The most famous fossil of them all: the Berlin *Archaeopteryx*, found in 1877 in Bavaria. Note the feathers.

has argued vigorously that, unlike the traditional picture of gradual phylogenetic change, the course of evolution has been jerky. You go along for a while without much happening, and then suddenly you get a switch from one form to another. There are gaps between different fossils (see Eldredge and Gould, 1972; Gould and Eldredge, 1977; Stanley, 1979; and figure 1.7)

It is important to appreciate what is *not* being claimed here. No one is saying that the gaps are so significant as to put the fact of evolution in doubt. There are bridging fossils between virtually all of the major classes of organisms. The best known case is that of Archaeopteryx, the bird/reptile, which is the mid-point of a series of fossils attesting to evolution (Feduccia, 1980, and figures 1.8 and 1.9) Likewise, the transition from reptile to mammal is particularly well documented (Luria, Gould and Singer, 1981). What is being suggested is that most

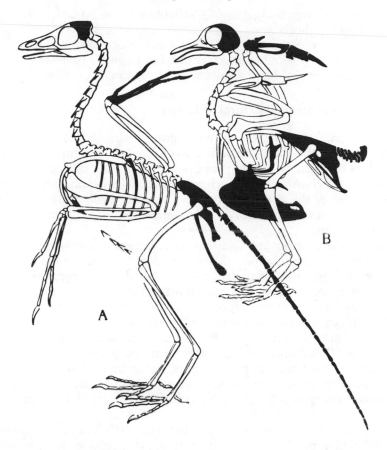

Figure 1.9 Figure 1.8 shows that *Archaeopteryx* has (bird-like) feathers, but now compare *Archaeopteryx* (A) against a modern bird (B, in this figure, a pigeon). Like a reptile, but unlike a bird, *Archaeopteryx* has teeth, a small brain, separate digits on the forelimbs, no breast-bone, and a tail. It is, therefore, a perfect intermediate. (Reproduced with permission from Colbert, 1969 © Lois Darling.)

change occurs rapidly, in short intervals, rather than gradually all of the time.

Paradoxically, although this is a thesis which is much linked to the fossil record, it is becoming apparent that the record is less than helpful in deciding its veracity. Gradualists argue, with some justification, that too much is lost from the history of life – that gaps might just represent incomplete fossilization – for one to say definitively what really happened (Kellogg, 1975, 1983; Gingerich, 1976, 1977). Final decisions must be made at the level of mechanisms. As we shall see, the jerky interpretation of the fossil record is indeed allied to a new theory of evolution, one supposing jumps ('saltations'), the so-called theory of 'punctuated equilibria'.

Obviously, in eschewing talk of causal processes, we have now reached a point of diminishing returns. Let us now, therefore, turn to mechanisms, the third and final aspect of organic evolution.

The theory of evolution: natural selection

In the *Origin*, Darwin did not just argue for the fact of evolution (as noted, he said little about the path of evolution), he put forward a theory to explain it. In particular he proposed a major new causal mechanism to account for change. This mechanism, *natural selection*, persists today as the centre of the dominant causal picture of evolutionary thinking, and thus the modern theory is properly known as 'Darwinism' (or neo-Darwinism).

Darwin started from the fact that all organisms, plants and animals, have a potential for great population increase. Yet, given food and space constraints, this potential can never be fully realized. There will consequently be a 'struggle for existence'. As Darwin made very clear, this phrase, which he took from the conservative clergyman and social theorist Thomas Robert Malthus (1826), should not be understood in a strictly literal sense. It may well be that organisms battle in a bloody fashion, but they could (perhaps often) compete in more subtle ways, as (say) when one organism proves more fertile than its fellows. Darwin noted also that the struggle must be for reproduction more even than for existence. There is little point in being Superman if Kryptonite has reduced your sperm-count to zero.

Taking into consideration the fact that not all that are born can or do survive and reproduce, Darwin then drew attention to the natural variation which occurs throughout the organic world – plants and animals differ in size, weight, speed, hardiness, and so forth. He argued that, on average, we should expect the winners in the struggle (the 'fit') to differ from the losers, and that this winning will be in part a function of the winners' distinctive features. Given that this differential between winners and losers occurs that sufficiently often, the cumulative effect will be evolutionary. Drawing on the analogy of the animal and plant breeders' skill at transforming through picking desired forms, Darwin christened his new mechanism 'natural selection'. Later he allowed an alternative term (invented by Spencer), 'survival of the fittest'.

I want to make three points about selection. They are crucially important to our understanding of the evolutionary process, and today perhaps have more significance than at any time since the *Origin*. First, it must be recognized that Darwin did not simply want to explain the evolution of organisms. He wanted to explain why they are as they are. And in his judgement of what organisms are, Darwin showed the solid influence of his own training in the niceties of natural theology (standard fare at Cambridge when Darwin was an undergraduate). He took the salient feature of all organisms to be the fact that they seem *as if designed*. Organisms work or function. They have 'adaptations', features like hands and eyes and leaves and roots, which help them to survive and reproduce. They seem end-directed or 'teleological' (Limoges, 1970; Ruse, 1979a; Ospovat, 1981).

Pre-evolutionists took adaptations as clear evidence of God the Designer. Darwin argued that natural selection, unaided, can do the job. Organisms function simply because those that did better than others survived and reproduced. However, note that although Darwin thus gave a natural explanation of the supposed teleology of biology, in one crucial respect he broke from the religious understanding of organic adaptation. For Darwin, adaptation is all very much a relative thing. There is no question of actually setting out a blue print of perfection before you start, which is presumably what God did or could have done. You work with the variation at hand, and the winner is that which does better than its fellows.

This means that, in respects, evolution through selection is very much a string and sealing wax operation. You cobble together what you have at hand, building on the point where you are now, rather than going back to the beginning. (This is why Creationist stories of intricate adaptations tend to backfire. Why did God not do it all in a simpler way?) Also, you must appreciate that selection is indifferent to absolutely perfect functioning. It is only comparatively better functioning which counts. Darwin noted that the eye, although a marvellous organ, could have been better designed.

The second point follows on the first. Evolution demands a constant supply of new variations, of 'raw stuff'. Otherwise, one will soon run to identical forms. Darwin himself had little idea about the causes and nature of new organic variation – in a moment, we will see that this is where major advances have been made since his day – but on one matter he was adamant, as are modern-day Darwinians: all such new variation must be 'random', in the sense that it appears without respect for organisms' present needs. A new variation, as like as not, will harm its possessor, rather than help it. It is selection which is the creative element in evolution. Nothing else. Because of this, Darwin (and his successors) felt that the crucial new variations in evolution had to be very small. Large changes (saltations or 'sports') would invariably move an organism too far out of adaptive focus.

Third, there is the matter of the units of selection. What exactly is it that is selected? What is it that wins or loses in the struggle for survival and reproduction? In an argument that is much appreciated by today's biologists, Darwin argued that it must be the individual organism. It cannot be the group – be this population or species or whatever – to which the organism belongs. The struggle occurs at all levels, within and without breeding groups, and the ends of adaptations thus reflect ultimately to the benefit of the individual possessors. Darwin argued that if this were not so, evolution simply would not work. You do not get variations preserved and selected, no matter how much they may benefit the group, if they prove burdensome or costly to the possessor. To use today's terminology, Darwin was an 'individual selectionist' rather than 'group selectionist'. Precisely why he took this stand will be explained shortly (Ruse, 1980a).

The theory of evolution: modern genetics

Much has happened to evolutionary theory since the appearance of the *Origin*. But, as just noted, the main conceptual move on Darwin's ideas has been with respect to the question of variation (Mayr, 1982; Ruse, 1982c; Maynard Smith, 1975; Dobzhansky *et al.*, 1977). It is now recognized that the key concept in the understanding of organic features is the so-called 'gene', today identified as referring to long chain-like molecules of deoxyriboneucleic acid (DNA), carried on the chromosomes, at the centre of cells, those units which make up all living organisms (Ayala and Kiger, 1984). The genes make organisms what they are: tall or short, black or white, animal or plant. They are the factors of heredity, passed on from generation to generation. And, occasionally, they change spontaneously, 'mutate', thus making the building blocks of evolution. Darwin was right. The change at the physical level (the 'phenotype'), caused by change at the genetic level (the 'genotype'), has no relation to organic needs.

Fortunately, genes get passed on within groups of interbreeding organisms (populations) in identifiable ways, and this means that evolutionists can get a theoretical handle on the forces causing change (Li, 1955; Lewontin, 1974). Consequently, 'population genetics' is now that core part of modern evolutionary theory from which causal understanding flows (Ruse, 1973a; Sober, 1984). It is still argued, with Darwin, that natural selection is the dominant factor. Today, given our new understanding of the genes, evolution is often now directly thought of as changes in gene ratios. However, ultimately, of course, what really matters is change at the physical, phenotypic level, and it is this primarily that sets up new selection pressures.

One crucial point of undertanding has been brought out by genetics. This is that selection can maintain and hold variation within a population, as well as cause ongoing genetic change. A simple situation where this might occur comes in the case of selection for rarity. Suppose one has alternative genes ('alleles') in a group, that these cause black and white forms respectively, and that the chief selective 'pressure' comes from a predator, which nevertheless has to learn to recognize its prey. At first, most of the population carries black-causing genes, and thus the predator happily munches away on black forms, scarcely noticing the whites. What happens, obviously, is that the white forms get more common and the black forms less so, until finally the predator realizes what is happening, and changes its diet to white-causing gene carriers. Eventually, it can be shown, you will get a *balance* in a population between black- and white-causing genes. And this is a balance which is a function of selection, rather than despite it (Dobzhansky, 1970; Futuyma, 1979; Ayala and Valentine, 1979).

There are other similar mechanisms, some of which depend directly on the ways in which genes express themselves at the phenotypic level. What this all means is that, in a natural population at any time, thanks to selection, you generally have masses of variation to draw upon. The consequence is that, should a new need be imposed upon a group – for instance, a change in environmental conditions – there is no need to wait around for suitable new mutatins. Already there is a stockpile of variation on which to draw, some of which will probably do the job.

I cannot overemphasize the importance of this point. Probably the major lack of credibility of Darwinism today is incomprehension that random variations, generally harmful to their owners, could yet add up to full-blown adaptations (Popper, 1972; 1974). The sole reason for this lack of understanding and sympathy is ignorance of modern biology. Perhaps a little analogy will help to drive this point home. Suppose you were asked to write an essay on civil wars, and you found yourself in one of two possible situations. On the one hand, you are on an island, and your sole reading matter comes by post from the Book-of-the-Month Club. On the other hand, you are a student at Harvard, with all of its libraries open to you. Obviously, the second possibility is going to make much easier the writing of the essay. Rarely, if ever, will the book club send you anything relevant. But, while it is true that not even Harvard has every book on every subject, if you cannot find a suitable volume on the English civil war, then you will find one on Spain, and if not on Spain then on America. Something exactly analogous is true of biology. The ignorant think that Darwinism is caught in the Book-of-the-Month Club situation; but in reality, what Darwinism supposes is that every population has its own card to the Harvard library system (Ruse, 1982c).

Note, however – to pick up a point left over from earlier – that none of this says anything supportive of progressionism. In fact, we can now see that you cannot be a true Darwinian and a biological progressionist of any genuine kind whatsoever. The building blocks of evolution are functionally random, and the essentially non-directed nature of the process is in no way affected by selection gathering variations within groups. Given a need, the option taken to satisfy it is a function of what you have at hand, rather than what the perfect answer would be. This conclusion corresponds to what happens at the phenotypic level. Many of the most successful adaptations started life in some other role, and then were converted to their present tasks.

Moreover, there is nothing in selection itself which encourages progressionism. What counts is reproduction, here and now and in the immediate future. If the simpler, less intelligent form can do it better – and it often can – then so be it. Venereal diseases clearly have the biological edge on the great apes. Sexuality, surely one of the most 'advanced' of features, is often discarded by highly successful life-forms. That the history of life shows a supposed rise in complexity in some forms is no more than a contingent consequence of the fact that the world filled up, and so new options required new adaptations. Biologically, we might all collapse back down again. And, as we saw earlier, 'complexity' is itself a somewhat value-impregnated term. Some of the 'humblest' organisms are remarkably complex, and conversely. (Analogously, the jet-powered plane is much more 'advanced' than the propeller-driven plane, and yet much simpler; Williams, 1966, p. 50.)

Darwinism is antithetical to progressionism. Conferring a somewhat dubious honour, although no doubt one which he would have appreciated, I shall refer to biological progressionism as 'Spencerism' (see especially Spencer, 1857). Pessimistically, I do not expect that I have yet fully convinced my non-biological readers of the point I am making. I shall refer to progressionism later, and one of my aims will be to show why it has such a pervasive hold on the human intellect. If logic cannot convince you, perhaps psychology can.[1]

Good science?

Not only does evolution in itself invite comment, often critical, but Darwinism in particular draws detractors (for instance, Macbeth, 1971; Taylor, 1983). I suppose it is because it is a fascinating subject, with obvious, deliciously scandalous implications for ourselves. Also, fatally for the peace of Darwinians, their theory's main outline is not clothed in abstruse mathematics, making it incomprehensible to all but the *cognoscenti*. Be this as it may, even those basically favourable to the fact of evolution usually qualify their enthusiasm by allowing that there is something a little odd about the theory of evolution, either in structure or in the methodology it invokes. By 'odd' in this context is generally meant: 'not like physics and chemistry' (Smart, 1963).

---

[1] The denial is of biological progress. I am not denying the validity of any notion of 'progress'. Since I got a micro-computer, my typing skills have progressed significantly. A major theme in this book is how we can get other forms of progress, despite the lack of any biological progress.

Like so much to do with Darwinian evolutionary theory, a great deal that is said in this vein is based more on imagination than on reality. We have already encountered the key importance of consilience in biological thought. Demonstrating the fact of evolution, this supports and permeates all theorizing. In this respect, there is nothing peculiar about evolutionary science. More specifically, Darwinians experiment and observe in nature no less than do other scientists, and with no less success (Ruse, 1969; 1973a). It is true that no one can predict the future evolution of the elephant's nose, nor, if one could, would anyone be around to check. But there are lots of fast-breeding organisms on which you can do studies. Fruit-flies (*Drosophila*) have long been a favourite subject (figure 1.10). Putting these flies in cages and running selection

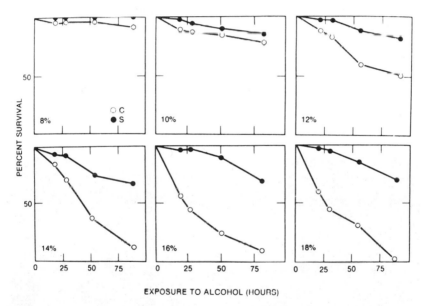

EXPOSURE TO ALCOHOL (HOURS)

Figure 1.10 Populations of a certain species of fruit-fly, *Drosophila melanogaster*, which live around breweries and wineries have a far higher alcohol tolerance than do their teetotaller species mates. Could selection have caused this? The diagrams show the percentages of *Drosophila melanogaster* flies which survive exposure to alcohol concentrations. Two strains were tested: those selected for alcohol tolerance (S), and those not selected (C). One can see a drastic difference in survival rates, especially as the alcohol concentration (given in lower left of graphs) gets greater. (Adapted with permission from McDonald *et al.*, 1977). What is particularly nice about this experiment is that the flies chosen for study were taken from non-alcohol containing habitats. Thus, they not only show the potentiality of selection, they support the Darwinian's key claim that many variations always exist within populations, held there by selection, and that these can be used as needed. The original flies had never needed alcohol-tolerance variations. Such variations certainly did not come into being, nor were they held in populations, because they might be wanted.

experiments is indeed artificial; but is it any more so than what happens in physics laboratories? I doubt it.

One venerable critical chestnut (dating from the days of Darwin's great supporter, Thomas Henry Huxley, no less) is that selection will always remain essentially unproven until the day that someone makes new species – populations breeding inwardly, but reproductively isolated from all others (Huxley, 1893). Darwinian evolutionists have never quite conceded the fairness of this demand. There is lots of other evidence, both of the effect of selection and of its importance in making new species: 'speciation' (Lewontin, 1974). Fortunately, further debate is otiose. There are now several cases of good species having been created artificially. And more cases reported where, in living memory, speciation has happened naturally (Jones, 1981).

There is massive support elsewhere, through the great biological consilience, not merely for the fact of evolution, but for the mechanism of natural selection. In every corner of the biological world, we encounter adaptations of all kinds, attesting to the power and influence of Darwin's central causal evolutionary force. My favourite example, one which I am sure will appeal to my fellow philosophers, is that of the trilobite eye. Selection discovered the most efficient lenses several hundred million years before Descartes (Clarkson and Levi-Setti, 1975, and figures 1.11 and 1.12)

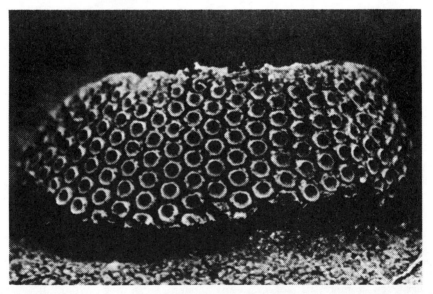

Figure 1.11 Trilobites are long-extinct marine invertebrates, whose ecological niche is today taken by crabs and like creatures. They had very complex eyes, using a large number of lenses. This is a much-magnified photograph of such a trilobite eye. (Reproduced with permission from Clarkson and Levi-Setti, 1975).

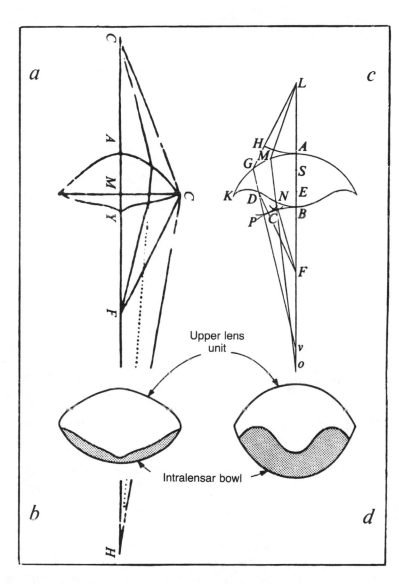

Figure 1.12 How does one design a lens which avoids spherical aberration? In the seventeenth century, René Descartes (upper left) and Christian Huygens (upper right) discovered the shape of the required lenses. However, as the lower diagrams (cross-sections of two trilobite eyes) show, nature had beaten them by a long time. The trilobite intralensar bowls are needed for sharp focusing because the trilobite eyes functioned in water. (Reproduced with permission from Clarkson and Levi-Setti, 1975).

It is sometimes said that Darwinism is inevitably flawed, because natural selection is a bogus mechanism. Supposedly, selection is little more than a redescription of the phenomena or an outright tautology. All it states is that the fittest survive, and by definition the fittest are the survivors (Manser, 1965; Peters, 1976). For three reasons, however, this objection is altogether too slick. First, selection depends vitally on the squeeze brought on by the population explosion. If it is not the case that more organisms are being born than can survive and reproduce, then there can be no selection.

Second, selection depends equally vitally on the claim that, on average, the winners in the struggle will differ from the losers, and that the win/loss result stems from those very distinguishing differences. If being black does not protect against predators, then there is no selection. Third, the claim is that features bringing success or failure in one case, will bring like results in like cases. Without this systematic feature, no science of evolution would be possible. But since it does obtain, as do the other claims of selection, and since they are all clearly empirical, the genuinely scientific worth of natural selection is secure (Caplan, 1977; Mills and Beatty, 1979).

There is yet one final objection that must be considered, and then we can be done. Critics claim that natural selection in the hands of Darwinians is a little bit too powerful. It is argued that there is nothing for which the enthusiast will not provide a 'just so' adaptationist story. Hence, one ends up with a Panglossian metaphysical pseudo-scientific picture of the world, where everything happens for the adaptive best because of natural selection. There is no counter-evidence a Darwinian would consider. Either that, or plausible alternatives are rigorously excluded or ignored (Lewontin, 1977; Gould and Lewontin, 1979).

No doubt, as in most such claims, there is some truth in these charges. Did not the Newtonians likewise see gravitational attractions everywhere? However, the fact that some supporters become besotted by a theory is not to say that the theory is irrevocably compromised. As it happens, no one wants to claim that every aspect of an organism is adaptive, and thus directly under the control of selection. For instance, there is today great interest in the molecular dimension to organisms. It seems quite plausible that much which happens at that level altogether escapes the effects of selection (Kimura, 1983). If this be so, no Darwinian would feel threatened.

As far as the methodological practice of seeking and supposing adaptations at the phenotypic level is concerned, this is admitted and defended. Experience has shown, again and again, that the most unlikely looking features are adaptive (Cain, 1979). It is a standing joke that, within a week of a supposed counter-example being identified, strong evidence for its adaptive nature will be uncovered. Heuristically, supposing strange features have adaptive value is a good policy. You do not find gravitational forces by giving up before you begin (Kuhn, 1962). Nor yet do you find adaptations.

Likewise, the way selection is treated is defended. Preferring individual selection to a group stance is not a blind following of Darwin's footsteps. Theoretically, as Darwin himself fully recognized, it is very difficult to see how a feature could benefit a group if it were a burden to its possessor (Williams, 1966). A rival not thus burdened (i.e. with only self-serving variations) would be favoured by selection. And this would be true to the extent that the self-server would wipe out the group-server, before the value of the group features could be felt. As you might imagine, since it is always fun to attack orthodoxy, many theoretical models have been devised, supposedly showing how group selection could work. But since the special circumstances which these models necessarily suppose are so special, it is thought unlikely that their instantiation ever would be more than a relatively rare occurrence (Brandon and Burian, 1984).

What about the charge of ignoring potential rivals? This question has particular pertinence today, for (as noted) there is now an active rival to Darwinism. The theory of punctuated equilibria supposes that the (claimed) jerky nature of the fossil record is a true reflection of what actually happened (Eldredge and Gould, 1972; Stanley, 1979). There are saltations, or saltation-like phenomena, which are at the heart of significant evolutionary change. Let us take this theory as representative of all alternatives to Darwinism. This seems fair to do, since its main supporters, most particularly Stephen Jay Gould, want to strike right at natural selection, arguing that its importance has been much over estimated. They argue that there is nothing like so tight a fit between organisms and their environment, as is supposed by Darwinism. The major changes of evolution occur suddenly, without much regard for adaptation, and then selection enters in to work on the fine tuning (Gould, 1980a; 1982a).

Unfortunately, close scrutiny of the writings of punctuated equilibria supporters reveals an obfuscating fogginess, precisely at those very central points where theoretical clarity is most demanded. Specifically, one wants to know something of the nature of the saltations supposedly causing all of the important change. Sometimes, it is suggested that the random effects of having just a small founder population for a new group will cause fairly rapid evolution. If any large group has lots of variation held within it by selection, then a small number of founders will necessarily be somewhat atypical (there is no 'type'), and this could cause quick and significant biological change (Eldredge and Gould, 1972). But this is an idea which has already been worked out by conventional Darwinians, so from this perspective punctuated equilibria is hardly a radical alternative to orthodoxy. (See Mayr, 1963, for more on the 'founder principle', and Lande, 1980, for a critique.)

In some other places, it is suggested that the sudden changes might involve major new instantaneous variations, produced in turn by 'macromutations' (Gould, 1980a). The trouble is that there is not the slightest evidence for such changes or their causes, and much that counts against them. Apart from anything else, to ask a very old question, if an organism carries a massive new change, transforming it from its parents, where is it going to find a mate with which to found a new species? If these changes are rare, which presumably they must be since we do not get new species in each generation, the totally new form is liable to perish reproductively unrequited (Dobzhansky, 1951).

Recently, Gould and others have been pulling back somewhat. It is now argued that the change is rapid, but not that sudden. Perhaps the jumps in the fossil record represent events lasting in the order of 50,000 years (Gould, 1982b). But the response now becomes: 'Who ever denied this kind of change?' Not the orthodox Darwinian, who points out that you can pack a lot of generations into 50,000 years, and that selection can thus have great effects (Stebbins and Ayala, 1981). No Darwinian has ever said that evolution must always go uniformly and that it can never go in fits and starts, these being controlled by various external factors. Certainly not Darwin himself.

The general attack on natural selection also seems ineffectual. It is claimed that the general engineering problems encountered in putting together a functioning organism set all sorts of constraints on the power of selection (figure 1.13). Furthermore, selection has to work with what is at hand, rather than creating new features. Thus, here also we are going to lose perfect, from-the-ground-up adaptation. However, this is surely what Darwinians have argued all along, and indeed was properly made a central feature of the exposition above. Punctuated equilibria supporters frequently point to the four-limbedness of vertebrates as an example of an organic feature without purpose (Gould and Lewontin, 1979). But no Darwinian wants to argue that the number four must today necessarily have special significance for vertebrates (and six for insects, and so forth).

In fact, there were early vertebrates which did not have four limbs, and our ancestors probably settled on their number for highly adaptive reasons. With four limbs, two fore and two aft, you can control your rise and fall in a fluid medium. The principle is that which dictates the four-wingedness of aeroplanes today. Since the early ancestral vertebrates were fish, living in that ubiquitous fluid medium, water, a good adaptive explanation for the original number of vertebrate limbs is readily forthcoming. That we have such a number today is a legacy of our past, and the fact that there was apparently no overriding reason for (or, perhaps, possibility of) change (Maynard Smith, 1981).

Figure 1.13 One of the spandrels of St Mark's (in Venice). It exists as a matter of architectural necessity, to keep the building up! That it can be used for decoration is a by-product. Gould and Lewontin argue that many Darwinians commit a fallacy akin to thinking the decoration the primary purpose. They feel that many things in the organic world, which seem as if they have an immediate function (like decoration), are in fact essentially non-adaptive by-products of the overall 'architectural' or 'engineering' constraints of a working organism. (Reproduced with permission from Gould and Lewontin, 1979).

Conclusion

Enough has been said. My interest is not in polemics, but in presenting Darwinism as a viable, defensible approach to the problems of evolution. I am afraid that because the issues strike so close to home, charges of 'prejudice' will forever be hurled. It will be argued (or implicitly assumed) that nothing could make plausible the Darwinian case for evolution through selection, and that consequently there must be other, hidden, less reputable reasons for its appeal. Certainly, it has been suggested that the theory of natural selection is more a reflection of Darwin's Victorian political views than of the course of life: '. . . a quintessential product of the bourgeois intellectual revolution' (Levins and Lewontin, 1985, p. 3; see also Young, 1971). Anyone who travels with Darwin must do so because of social and class sympathies – 'pervasive political bias' – rather than from pure scientific conviction (Gould, 1979, p. 9; see also Rose, 1982; Lewontin, Rose and Kamin, 1984).

This is not an entirely silly objection. To be honest, certain of Darwin's comments about our own species are precisely what you might expect from the grandson of a highly successful leader of the Industrial Revolution (Josiah Wedgwood). But I suspect that as far as the central mechanism of selection is concerned, this worry of crypto-capitalist bias is misplaced. Darwin's emphasis on gradual microchange does not stem from a fear of political revolutions. Apart from anything else, Darwin does not deny that, from a broader perspective, the course of evolution may be uneven. As noted, Darwin's insistence of the smallness of each individual step in the evolutionary process comes from the simple fact that he could not see how large, sudden change could preserve the adaptive fit between organisms and their environment (Ruse, 1979a). Furthermore, this is the reasoning most influential with today's Darwinians, the vast majority of whom are far from being immediate beneficiaries of unbridled capitalism.

I suspect that much of the current controversy surrounding Darwinism is an artefact of human nature; attacks on the dominant position, particularly a position with implications about human beings, are more newsworthy than agreements. Also, commentators on science, like philosophers, naturally (and properly) are attracted to areas of disagreement. But, because controversy is fun, it does not follow that attacks on the majority view necessarily strike right home. In the case of Darwinism, this caution is particularly applicable. We have a good causal theory, complementing our knowledge of the fact and path of evolution. And that is enough.

We are now ready to turn, in an informed way, to philosophical questions. Let us therefore do this at once.

2

Evolutionary Epistemology

There are two questions which must be faced by any reflective human being – any human being who thinks *philosophically*. What can I know? What should I do? The problem of knowledge, or 'epistemology'. The problem of morality, or 'ethics'.

For nearly 2,000 years, for those of us in the West, answers to both of these questions were defined and guaranteed within the Judaeo-Christian world picture. Knowledge comes through our God-given powers of reason and observation. It is to be set against the historical background revealed by the Sacred Texts, and it would be incompatible with His Goodness were we to be in constant error about everything. Morality comes through our God-given power of choice between good and ill. It is to be set against the moral background revealed by the Sacred Texts, and it is given meaning by God's great sacrifice in the person of the crucified Christ.

This secure vision of life came apart for many reasons, but the prime factor was the development and rise of modern science. Both Luther and Calvin warned of the dangers of heliocentrism, even before Copernicus published. If it is the earth which does the moving, then the sun can hardly have stopped for Joshua, as we read in the Old Testament. Thus the Bible cannot be literally true, and hence doubt is thrown on the story of Creation, not to mention the Ten Commandments and Jesus' directives for his followers (Kuhn, 1957).

Scientists were not out to destroy religion and its underpinning of philosophical understanding. Copernicus was an ordained member of the Church of Rome and died secure in his faith. The greatest scientist of them all, Isaac Newton, spent more time and effort on interpretation of the Book of Revelation than on the mysteries of the physical universe (Westfall, 1981). Nevertheless, after the Middle Ages, the increasing triumphs of physics, of biology, of geology, and of others, made the foundations of traditional belief ever more insecure. And these foundations were further weakened by developments in other quarters, most directly within science-influenced philosophy itself. By the time of the nineteenth century, even theologians were joining in the chorus, as they tried to understand the Bible less as the Divine Word of God, and more as the human-recorded history of an intensely religious people, the Jews, and of their supposed Messiah, Jesus of Nazareth (Benn, 1906).

But even in 1850, the *coup de grâce* to the traditional way of thought had not yet been delivered. To most people, secular philosophies seemed incomplete and unsatisfying. Moreover, for all of the problems with traditional religious thought, without the supposition of a Divine Being, some matters were quite baffling. In particular, the intricacies of organisms – their adaptations – spoke definitively against blind chance (Ruse, 1975b). People were not necessarily Christians. Some were deists – believers in an unmoved Mover – and of like persuasions. But, with few exceptions, there was at least a vague belief in something more. Indeed, at the end of his *Dialogues Concerning Natural Religion*, (1779), perhaps even that arch-critic of traditional religious thought, David Hume, equivocated on this point. He could see all of the problems with the notion of God as Designer, but he could not see clearly the way to an alternative.

The coming of evolution, of Darwinism in particular, altered all of that. Now, for the first time, one could confidently suspend belief in any kind of God. The natural development of organisms explains everything, most especially adaptation. Even if you did not want to become a full-blown atheist, you could become what Darwin's already-mentioned supporter, T. H. Huxley, labelled an 'agnostic', neither believer nor disbeliever (Huxley, 1900). However, excluding or distancing God in this fashion raises with some urgency the major problems of philosophy. If God (perhaps) does not exist, wherein lie the guarantees of knowledge and of truth? Possibly all is subjective illusion. If God does not exist, wherein lies the force of morality? Why should we not do precisely what we please, cheating and lying and stealing, to serve our own ends? Dry answers by philosophers aiming for purely secular answers tended not to convince.

Evolution destroyed the final foundations of traditional belief. To many people, it was evolution that would provide the foundations of a new belief-system. Evolution would lead to a deeper and truer understanding of the problems of knowledge. Evolution would lead to a deeper and truer understanding of the nature of morality. Thus were born (what are now known as) 'evolutionary epistemology' and 'evolutionary ethics'.

It is these secular philosophies which are the focus of this book. I trust the reader is aware that in setting up the apparent dichotomy between religion and evolution, as I have just done, I am making a historical point about how many people thought in the middle and late nineteenth century. There were then those (as there still are many) who were both Believers and evolutionists. Moreover, I do not pretend that if your philosophy is not God-based, then it must necessarily be evolution-based. It is significant, however, that in the nineteenth century we start to see the rise of philosophies which, as it were, try to get over the death of God. Evolutionism apart, one thinks of existentialism (starting point: if God does not exist, then all things are permitted), and Marxism (explicitly materialist).

Parenthetically, Anglo-Saxon philosophy strikes me generally as being hollow – that is, ignoring those many Catholic thinkers who work away happily, as though Copernicus and Darwin had never existed. We practitioners have an obsession with technical problems for their own sake, and frequently deny that traditional philosophical questions are meaningful. (If you doubt me, read A.J. Ayer's *Language, Truth and Logic* – still a strong seller.) It is argued that empirical science is where the action occurs, and philosophers should simply ease the way of its acolytes. Of course, I exaggerate. There is much good philosophy still going on, addressing traditional issues. And, as you will learn, I myself wonder wherein lies the meaning of certain traditional philosophical claims. I shall, however, argue later that much modern work is radically incomplete (perhaps 'without anchor' is a better term), and needs Darwinism to put it into full and proper perspective.

For now, I want to look at the work of others who take evolutionary biology as their philosophical starting-point. Specifically, I want to look at traditional approaches to evolutionary epistemology and evolutionary ethics. These will be the topics of this and the next chapter, respectively. Although I am sympathetic to the spirit of both attempts, and think them a lot more interesting and fruitful than many would allow, I conclude that, as traditionally conceived, ultimately they fail. Moreover, I argue that thus construed they are beyond repair. There is something fundamentally wrong with all such attempts to bring evolution to bear on the problems of philosophy. However, criticism for criticism's sake is not my game. I hope to extract positive findings, which will prove crucial to my later constructive arguments.

Evolution as analogy

Let us begin by sketching out the basic initial moves which an evolutionary approach to epistemology – the theory of knowledge – might be expected to make. This is to cheat somewhat. I know already what people have in fact asked and answered. So discussion at this point is structured with this knowledge in mind. However, the intellectual sleight of hand is warranted, because we can thus lay out a general, informative background of what is going on, before we turn to specific contributions – whose merits can then be better evaluated. Like most writers on the subject, I shall restrict discussion to study of *scientific* knowledge, assuming that it is better to concentrate first on one specific area of human inquiry, rather than trying to answer everything at once. (An invaluable survey of traditional evolutionary epistemology is given in Campbell, 1974.)

The key to organic evolution is continuous, natural development. Organisms do not just appear, as it were. Rather, they exist in succession, with one form unfolding by a connected chain of reproduction from other forms. Monad to house sparrow, at the extremes of time. The most obvious evolutionary approach to knowledge (i.e. scientific knowledge) thus presumably seeks and emphasizes what it takes to be the likewise developmental nature of such knowledge. It notes and stresses how important claims do not just appear out of nowhere, but have antecedents which lead up to them, and which are themselves part of a continuity leading to further ideas. Thus, it suggests that knowledge is a dynamic phenomenon, and (unless you subscribe to an evolutionism which has a fixed end point) something which will be forever ongoing. Any major contribution to science, like that of Copernicus, came out of its past. It did not suddenly miraculously appear in the mind of a Polish cleric, one day early in the sixteenth century. Nor was it the last word. It was something on which succeeding scientists could and did build.

Already we have clues to the form such an evolutionary approach to knowledge will take. Most importantly, the central relationship is going to be one of *analogy*. Scientific claims are not organisms. Copernicus' hypothesis that the earth goes round the sun rather than vice versa is not (and never was) a living being, like a member of the species *Canis lupus* (wolf) or some such thing. Nor, obviously, did such a hypothesis ever pretend to be an organism. Hence, if we speak of the development or evolution of astronomy, we cannot be speaking literal biological language, as when we speak of the evolution of the birds from the reptiles. What we are rather saying is that the development of astronomy is in some crucial (i.e. noteworthy) respects like the organic evolution of the birds from the reptiles.

Now, since we are apparently working with an analogy, we can at once go on to ask an important question of any such an evolutionary approach to science as is being proposed. We can and must ask: what is the point of the analogy, that is to say, what is the analogy supposed to do? In an analogy, we are comparing two things which are in some sense similar (and in some sense different, otherwise we would at once have a total identity). The question which arises is: why bother?[1]

To answer this question, let us spell things out in a little more detail. You have two things, M and N, and you are comparing them; striking an analogy between them. M has a number of properties which you note: $a_1, \ldots a_n$. You find that N has the same properties. Now you realize, if you did not already know, that M has property b. You argue analogically that N likewise has property b. Straightaway, you can start to see one important use of an analogy. It has stimulated you into thinking – into exploring some of the properties of N. Quite possibly you never knew or even dreamed about the fact that N had property b. In other words, the analogy has led to a *discovery*. Let us speak of this as 'analogy-as-heuristic'.

Note that this heuristic use of analogy, that which occurs in the context of discovery, asks little of an analogy in itself. It is, after all, merely scaffolding, which can in principle come down once your building is complete. The similarities between the two things (M and N) being compared may be great, or they may be small. Additionally, the phenomenon from which you are arguing analogously (M) may or may not be something which, in its own right, commands respect or attention. For instance, the chemist Kekulé, discovered the circular nature of the benzine ring from imagining a snake swallowing its tail (Findlay, 1948). Were a herpetologist to complain that snakes never swallow their tails, the objection would rightly be dismissed as irrelevant. The tail-swallowing image was just a crutch that could be thrown away, once the idea of a circular benzine molecule had been grasped.

This is all very well, but of course now Kekulé (like anyone using an analogy-as-heuristic) had to go away and find evidence for his hunch. He had to find some *support* or justification. This does suggest that perhaps sometimes, if not in the benzine ring case, you might hope to get more from an analogy than suggestive insights. You might, indeed, hope to get some confirmatory evidence for the conclusion towards which you are directed. Let us speak here of the hope for 'analogy-as-justification'.

As you should expect, like everything in life, since you are asking more of your analogy, you have to be prepared to put more in. The analogy is no longer dispensable scaffolding. I suspect that the implicit reasoning at issue here goes somewhat along the following lines: M

---

[1] The notion of analogy is much discussed, primarily because it is so central to Catholic thought. Supposedly we know of God through analogy. He is not literally a (human) father, but he has father-like qualities. Our needs here are fairly simple. Clear and brief is Salmon (1973). Also, most informative is Hesse (1966), and, as always, John Stuart Mill (1884) has a good strong statement of the chief pertinent issues. An insightful recent discussion is Weitzenfeld (1984).

suggests that any object (or whatever) with properties $a_1 \ldots a_n$ has property b. (Possibly, you have independent evidence for this claim.) N has $a_1 \ldots a_n$. Therefore, we can conclude that N has b. And not merely that N so happens to have b, but that it *must* have b. Quite obviously in this case, as opposed to the analogy-as-heuristic, the truth of that from which you are arguing is vitally important. If M does not exist, or does not have properties a_1 through a_n, or does not have b, or if N does not have properties a_1 through a_n, your analogy-as-justification (in its present form) collapses. Your general statement is unsupported, or N is not an instance of it.

I hasten to point out that rarely, if ever, do you spell out to yourself exactly what your general middle statement might be, if indeed you recognize that there is such a one. That is why I spoke of 'implicit' reasoning. As you might expect, there is controversy about whether an analogy really does presuppose a hidden general premise. For clarity in exposition, I will assume that it does – but nothing essential to my main argument rests on its real existence.

Also, do note that this middle statement, hypothetical or otherwise, does not have some special unique nature. In principle, there are many which would do, depending on how you chose a_1 through a_n. Here the notion of 'relevance' or 'centrality' becomes important. Given any two objects, you can always find common properties. The Eiffel Tower and Pythagoras' theorem have the common property of being referred to in this sentence. The properties $a_1, \ldots a_n$ must be relevant to b. They must be the sorts of things that make you think that having b must follow. Conversely, remember that in analogy you are comparing things which are different in certain respects. M and N are not absolutely identical. Thus, in drawing conclusions, you need to avoid relevant dissimilarities. Your general statement has a *ceteris paribus* clause. If M has property c and N does not, but possession of c seems vital to inferring b, no matter how many as you may have, your analogy-as-justification fails.

In a way, in analogy-as-justification you are trying to eliminate the analogy. You are trying to show that, despite differences, in crucial relevant ways the things being compared are identical. Hence, their having the concluding property (b) follows deductively from the general premise. It would be presumptuous for us to object if people want to stress this point, or for us to complain if this gets reflected into the language they use. Just remember in what follows, that if I point to someone insisting that he is presenting no analogy but an identity (or if he insists he is making a literal claim), this will probably fall under what I am speaking of analogy-as-justification.

Also, although this is of less concern to us here, I am not pretending that analogy-as-heuristic and analogy-as-justification are absolutely different. In fact, I suspect that in real life there is a spectrum of strengths of arguments, with people happy to get as much as they can from analogies. I would certainly not want to claim that the process of scientific discovery is totally unreasonable, implying that analogy-as-heuristic is only for crazy folk. There may not be a formal logic of discovery; but, equally, great findings do not come by chance, to the totally undisciplined mind (Hanson, 1958; Nickles, 1980a, 1980b).

Darwin, incidentally, gives us a beautiful case of an analogy working in both of our ways. He was led to natural selection through study of artificial selection. Breeders work fantastic transformations, as they pick or select the types they want (figure 2.1). These successes inspired Darwin to seek a like process in nature (Ruse, 1975c). Here we have an analogy functioning heuristically, as Darwin reasoned from pigeons and turnips and sheep and cattle to what he thought was going on all the time in the wild. Then, when Darwin began to put together the evidence for natural selection in the *Origin,* he brought forward artificial selection in support (Ruse, 1973b; 1975a). And he went on so doing. He pointed out that breeders select for adult forms, and that consequently embryos of varieties very different are often quite similar. Analogously, natural selection's acting only on adult forms accounts for the fact that the embryos of very different species show significant similarities (Darwin, 1859, pp. 439–50).

Pertinently, after the *Origin* was published, Darwin's critics attacked the analogy by claiming that artificial selection shows that you can never cross specific boundaries (pig into cow), and Darwin responded that the evidence from breeding is that the potentiality for change is indefinite (Ruse, 1979a, especially chapter 8). This all fits in with the above-explained logic of analogy-as-justification. No one objected to the fact that Darwin himself had been led to natural selection through artificial selection, or protested that such a leap was impossible. This fits in with what we have just learned of analogy-as-heuristic.

No more exposition or illustration is needed. Here it is enough to stress that there do seem to be the two main uses of analogy, discovery and support.

> The cases in which analogical evidence affords in itself any very high degree of probability, are ... only those in which the resemblance is very close and extensive; but there is no analogy, however faint, which may not be of the utmost value in suggesting experiments or observations that may lead to more positive conclusions. (Mill, 1884, p. 368)

Relating the theoretical discussion back to the question of evolutionary epistemology, a number of points emerge. The most important point clearly revolves around just how you are going to use the analogy between the development or evolution of organisms and the supposed development or evolution of (scientific) knowledge. If you are simply in the business of discovery, then you can treat the analogy in a fairly

Figure 2.1 The power of artificial selection is well shown by the different varieties of pigeon. (These pictures come from Charles Darwin's *The Variation of Animals and Plants Under Domestication*.)

cavalier manner. But the trouble is then that, although you may throw illuminating light on science, you will probably fail to solve the very problems you set out to solve – about the nature of scientific knowledge, its underlying justification, and so forth. At best you have a collection of stimulating ideas, which you must then go off and validate independently. If independent chemical analysis had not shown that the benzine ring really is circular, who would remember Kekulé's name today?

However, if you are in the business of justification, then one assumes that you hope to find something about the real nature and support for knowledge, just as biology yields something of the real nature and existence of organisms. In which case, you must treat the analogy much more seriously. You are hoping to transfer some of the legitimacy of our knowledge of organic evolution across to the understanding of scientific knowledge, its development and nature. You are hoping, indeed, to wring answers to questions about the nature and status of scientific knowledge that traditional approaches have failed to extract. Presumably, in the light of the divisions made in the last chapter, you are hoping to learn something about the actual fact of science being evolutionary, something about the paths that science's development takes, and, most crucially, something about the causes lying behind scientific change. No doubt, as in the case of organisms, this will tell much about the actual status of science. Why is it as it is? What keeps it going?

Enough of background presentation. Let us now turn to actual excursions into evolutionary epistemology. To focus discussion, deliberately I will concentrate on work which takes the organic-change/scientific-change analogy seriously, namely that which aims for an analogy-as-justification. Without such a restriction, we shall be led through the broadest of surveys, forced to look at much work with but the faintest relevance to our enquiry. The people now to be discussed believe that that which goes on in the world of organisms is sufficiently like that which goes on in the world of science, that study of the former leads to direct knowledge about the latter. Of course, if they fail to make this strong case, there is still much potential for exploitation of the analogy-as-heuristic. Even if we do not get all we want, we need not come away empty handed.

Herbert Spencer and the law of progress

Even before the *Origin* appeared, there were those who tried to draw links between organisms and science, arguing that what occurs to the former serves as a justificatory analogical model for an understanding of what occurs to the latter. One who argued this way was that indefatigable Victorian generalist and optimist, Herbert Spencer (1857). He argued that in organic nature, and indeed everywhere else, we see a 'law of progress', which takes the form of complexity arising from simplicity, or more precisely (as he put it) of heterogeneity arising from homogeneity. Simple organic forms are forever evolving into diverse, complex forms. We go from a uniform sameness to a set of interconnected but different components. 'It is settled beyond dispute that organic progress consists in a change from the homogeneous to the heterogeneous' (p. 3). Analogously, argued Spencer, we have progress from simple to complex in other spheres, including that of scientific knowledge.

[W]e might trace out the evolution of Science; beginning with the era in which it was not yet differentiated from Art, and was, in union with Art, the handmaid of Religion; passing through the era in which the sciences were so few and rudimentary, as to be simultaneously cultivated by the same philosophers; and ending with the era in which the genera and species are so numerous that few can enumerate them, and no one can adequately grasp even one genus. (p. 29)

From remarks I made in the last chapter, you might well imagine that I have more-than-serious reservations about whether Spencer's ideas in themselves can lead to conclusions of lasting value. But let us look at the ideas with a straight face, even though this is never entirely an easy matter when dealing with one so full of his self-worth as Spencer. We shall find this policy pays dividends in its own right, and is moreover an excellent way of getting our epistemological feet wet, before we turn to more recent writers.

Start with the fact of evolution. In the organic world, we have continuous natural change from one form to another. Do we indeed have continuous natural change in the world of science, from one form (presumably, one theory or equivalent) to another? This is at the heart of Spencer's position, as I have suggested it is at the hearts of all traditional approaches to evolutionary epistemology. Without this, we have no analogy-as-justification. We really do not have an analogy-as-much-else, either. You might think, however, that here, at least, we can give Spencer the case, virtually without argument. Copernicus led to Kepler and Galileo, who led to Newton, who led (eventually) to Einstein. If this is not evolution, what is?

But not everyone would grant Spencer even this much. The distinguished historian of the Copernican revolution, Thomas Kuhn, argues (1962) that scientists get committed to and work within conceptual frameworks: 'paradigms'. He argues further that there are sharp, absolutely discontinuous breaks at times of revolution, when one paradigm is thrown over for another. Looking at a number of transitions, Kuhn claims that we get chasms which quite preclude evolutionary interpretation, and that people on different sides of revolutions see the world in different ways. And, happily relying as much on sociology as on logic, he argues that unless we adopt a discontinuous theory of change, we quite fail to explain the bitterness and controversy which breaks out between disputants at times of transition. Reasonable people, talking of the same things, ought to have found a meeting point.

As you can imagine (if you did not already know), much has been written about Kuhn's vision of scientific history, and of this virtually all has been critical (see, for instance, Lakatos and Musgrave, 1970). However, with Kuhn I would agree that most such criticisms miss the point. It matters not how subtle may be the logical points you make, if you fail to address that matter which was at stake in the first place, namely what is the actual phenomenology of scientific change? Is it continuous or not? Nevertheless, taking Kuhn on his own terms, it is hard to see that his thesis really does tell us about science and its change.

Consider Darwin's achievement in the *Origin*, a revolutionary work if ever anything was, and certainly one which led to all kinds of nastiness and invective. We have already seen how much he took from his non-evolutionary predecessors – artificial selection, the Malthusian struggle, the branching fossil record, the facts of embryology, the importance of thinking functionally, the methodology of consilience, to name but some items. And the list could be much extended. I have not even mentioned Charles Lyell, the geologist, and how his way of looking at the inorganic world in natural terms influenced Darwin to look likewise at the organic world (Rudwick, 1972; Wilson, 1972). The story is one of links and continuity, all of the way.

Analogously, after the *Origin*, we have seen continuity to the present, not sharp, unbridgeable breaks. Most particularly, we have the binding chain furnished by the central mechanism of natural selection (Mayr, 1982). Thought about this mechanism has evolved somewhat, especially in the way that attention is now focused on its consequences for the units of heredity, the genes (Sober, 1984). And yet there is strong continuity, most obviously in the ongoing emphasis on individual returns (Williams, 1966). Adaptation, benefitting the possessor, is as central a part of evolutionary theory today as it was more than a century ago.

Indeed, the more one looks into the Darwinian revolution, the more one starts wondering wherein lies Darwin's originality and genius. He came out of the past, and went into the future. The case for Darwin's importance can and must be made in the use he made of his materials. Nor does it seem very convincing to mount a last-ditch stand for Kuhn by denying the continuity of the revolution, in claiming that shared terms conceal significant differences. That, for instance, Darwin's 'consilience' was not really the 'consilience' of a non-evolutionist like Whewell. Darwin got the notion from Whewell, he intended to use that very notion, and he was recognized by himself and others as having done so (Ruse, 1975d). It simply is not reasonable to dispute the continuous, evolutionary nature of the Darwinian revolution.

Furthermore, I would want to turn Kuhn's important sociological point right on its head. The nastiness came, not because people were talking at total cross-purposes, about entirely different things; but precisely because they were talking of the same things. Those scientists lagging in the revolution resented those ahead in the revolution, because the latter were picking up on the former's points and making such different use of them. The most bitter difference in the Darwinian controversy was between the anatomist Richard Owen and the always-pugnacious T.H. Huxley. Owen was apoplectic over the way in which Huxley took all of his (Owen's) findings and ideas, turned them about, and used them for the cause of evolution. Almost literally, Owen did not know whether to excoriate the Darwinians as followers of Satan, or to sue for plagiarism on grounds that he had thought of everything first (Ruse, 1979a, especially chapters 6 and 9).

The Darwinian revolution was one of change with continuity. And, without making a dogmatic statement, the same goes elsewhere in science. Certainly, none of the better-known cases of scientific change differs one tittle from Darwin's case. Kuhn is wrong on this point, and Spencer is right. The fact of science is evolutionary. (Of course, I am making a dogmatic statement. But it can be backed by many other examples, as I and others have shown in geology (Kitts, 1974; Frankel, 1981; R. Laudan, 1981; Ruse, 1981c); as Richard Westfall (1971) has shown quite brilliantly in mechanics; and as Kuhn-the-historian (1957) shows most fully in the case of astronomy!)

Next, we have the path of evolution. Here, I fear that Spencer's position starts to run into trouble, particularly if we take (as he would insist that we do take) the organic change/scientific change analogy in a justificatory sense. Spencer argues that organic evolution is progressive, and in his idiosyncratic way gives a special meaning to 'progressive', as heterogeneity arising from homogeneity. But whatever else may be, we can categorically state that organic evolution is not progressive, either in a conventional sense of getting better or some such thing, or in a special Spencerian sense (if this be genuinely different).

The falsity of the conventional sense has been seen in the last chapter, and talk of 'homogeneity' and 'heterogeneity' helps matters not a bit. In the well-known evolution of the horse, we get a reduction in the number of toes from four to one. The latter is surely a more homogeneous state than the former (Simpson, 1951, 1953, and figure 2.2). Analogously, many asexual organisms were previously sexual (Mayr, 1963; Williams, 1975). Again we have the heterogeneous going to the homegeneous. I must stress how common an occurrence this is. It cannot be dismissed by the Spencerian as a freak of nature. And, more generally, as Darwinians we can see that it could never be a genuine law of organic nature that heterogeneity comes from homogeneity. The whole point about natural selection is that it is opportunistic. If the simpler will do, then so be it.

This spells the end of the strong case Spencer is trying to build from organic change (as he sees it) to scientific change. His picture of organic change is wrong. Therefore no analogy can persuade us that this is the way scientific change is and must be. But we can always fall back for a while on the weaker analogy-as-heuristic. It may surprise you to learn that I do not think this an entirely futile exercise. Stimulated by Spencer's claims, I want to seize favourably on the notion of progress in

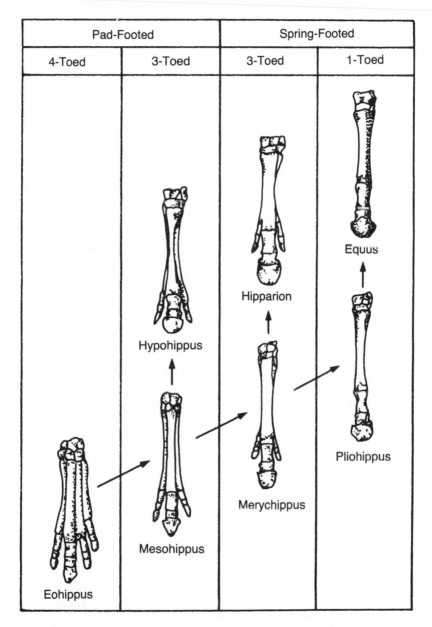

Figure 2.2 Perhaps the most famous aspect of horse evolution, from the four-toed eohippus (*Hyracotherium*) to the modern one-toed horse (*Equus*). (Adapted with permission from Simpson, 1951.)

science. Spencer is right in suggesting that there is something seemingly directional about the history of science. Where he goes wrong is in trying to generalize this insight to the rest of the world, or in pretending that it can be inferred in some manner from the nature of organic change.

An idea is not proof, and much will have to be said on this subject to make it convincing. All I want to do now is to sow the seeds in your mind. Consider, for instance, the Copernican revolution (taking a point which Kuhn emphasizes). The Ptolemaic geocentric theory was replaced by the heliocentric theory. And because of this, all sorts of things hitherto inexplicable became 'obvious'. Most significantly what had always seemed like an arbitrary division of the planets into 'inferior' (always seen near to the Sun) and 'superior' (wander through the heavens) suddenly became explicable: the inferior planets are closer to the Sun than the earth, and the superior planets are further away. Given also that related phenomena also fell into place – why, for instance, the superior planets only retrogress when they are in opposition to the Sun – it seems reasonable to assert that Copernicus' theory represents a move forward. It represents *progress*. Of course, no less than Spencer it is incumbent upon me to tell you what I mean by 'progress' at this point. Simply stating, without argument (as yet), I mean that Copernicus was a little closer to the truth – a real, independent, objective mapping of the world – than Ptolemy and his supporters. The planets really do go around the Sun.

Similarly, in the recent geological revolution. There was progress when it was realized that the continents move, and that they do this by slipping around the surface of the globe on big plates rather than by ploughing like ships through oceans of solid rock (Cox, 1973). We now know something about the real world which was not known some fifty years ago. Moreover, because of this, we can now explain many hitherto strange facts. Why Africa and South America fit together. Why the Himalayas are so tall. Why San Francisco has earthquakes. Why there are rifts in the oceans. Why the animals of Australia are so odd. And much more (Hallam, 1973 and figure 2.3).

Note what I am claiming, and more particularly what I am not claiming. I am not saying that every scientific change is progressive. It was not. Darwin, for instance, was told by the physicists of his day that he had allowed himself altogether too much time in the first edition of the *Origin* (Burchfield, 1975). What neither he nor they knew was that their estimates were way too low, because they did not know of the heat-producing properties of radioactive decay. The earth is very old – enough for the leisurely process of natural selection. But, dutifully, Darwin set about speeding everything up. He moved all sorts of false mechanisms more prominently to the fore. This was hardly progress. (This is why you should always read the first edition of the *Origin*.)

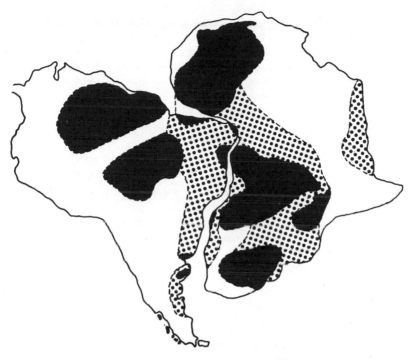

Figure 2.3 The matching of age provinces between Africa and South America. Black areas are at least 2,000 million years old; stippled areas, more than 600 million years old. The broken line marks the dated contact that extends from the vicinity of Accra, Ghana, to that of São Luis, Brazil. (Reproduced with permission from Marvin, 1973.)

Also, I do not pretend to have established, in some God-guaranteed way, that progress does actually occur in science. My point is that, as we commonly think, progress has occurred in science. Indeed, I would say that scientific development is our touchstone for progress. Furthermore, 'progress' signifies that our beliefs are getting closer to a true mapping of a real, objective world 'out there', independent of our whims and wishes. This may all be a pipe-dream. The crux is that this is what we think. Perhaps we are all caught in an illusion. At some stage we shall have to consider this possibility. For now, I will rest with appearances, although in fairness I would suggest that if you think that the progress of science is illusory, there is some obligation upon you to show why this is so.[2]

---

[2] One who would argue against such progress is Larry Laudan (1977, 1981). However, as you will now see, I tie scientific progress tightly to the creation of ever-stronger consiliences, and as Hardin and Rosenberg (1982) have shown, Laudan's historical examples fall before this point.

I have gone this far with Spencer. Now let me pull back sharply. Spencer argues that progress involves the growth of heterogeneity from homogeneity. This is just not true of organic evolution. Equally, it is not an essential ingredient of scientific progress. Indeed, I would go so far as to turn Spencer on his head, arguing that the most significant progress in science occurs precisely when we pick simplicity out of complexity, homogeneity out of heterogeneity. Most crucially, as we have seen in the Darwinian case, advance comes when disparate, hitherto-unconnected elements are brought together, under one unifying hypothesis. Then we feel convinced that we are onto something, meaning that our hypothesis absolutely must be true about some part of reality – 'true' meaning telling it like it really is. 'When the explanation of two kinds of phenomena, distinct and not apparently connected, leads us to the same cause, such a coincidence does give a reality to the cause, which it has not while it merely accounts for those appearances which suggested the supposition' (Whewell, 1840, 2, 285). I argue, therefore, that while Spencer may be right about progress in science, he is quite wrong about the form such progress takes. I shall have more to say about this point shortly.

Given the collapse of Spencer's hopes of providing a strong bond between organic change and scientific change, and the now-diminishing value of his views from a heuristic standpoint, there is no need here to linger over his claims about the third aspect of evolution, namely that dealing with causes or mechanisms. In fact, although Spencer did support natural selection (even discovering it independently and writing on it before Darwin, not to mention coining the term 'survival of the fittest'), it was never primary in his mind (Spencer, 1852). He relied much more heavily on so-called Lamarckism, the old notion that features can be acquired through environmental stress by adults, and then transmitted directly to offspring. The long neck of the giraffe, the callused bottom of the ostrich, and the massive arms of the blacksmith are supposed exemplifications (Burkhardt, 1977).

This view is quite false. It goes against everything we know about genetics and cytology (the science of the cell). Every supposed case of Lamarckism can be explained away, without recourse to special *ad hoc* hypotheses (Ruse, 1982c). Thus, no analogy-as-justification can be based on it, and I think by now the heuristic value of Spencer's ideas are coming to an end. Inasmuch as Lamarckism leads to progression (which Lamarck himself thought), we have covered the matter; and for the rest, we would be better occupied in looking at more recent theories.

Yet, as we do so, I hope you will agree with me that, dated though Spencer's ideas may be, they have proven a good foil for starting to develop our own ideas. In the next chapter, I shall likewise use Spencer to start the exploration of evolution and morality.

Stephen Toulmin's Darwinian model

Obviously we are not going to get very far unless we introduce Darwinism – specifically natural selection – into our analogy making. Certainly nothing approaching justification is going to be possible. As it happens, Spencer was not the only nineteenth century evolutionary epistemologist, and it will come as no surprise to learn that those who were closer in spirit to Darwin's work did try to make use of selection in understanding the nature of scientific change.

How does one use natural selection as an analogy for the process of scientific change? The move is fairly obvious. Theories (or that which you take as your basic unit of scientific knowledge) engage in an intellectual struggle for existence, and the 'fitter' succeed. Thus Copernicus' theory beat out Ptolemy's; at the beginning of the nineteenth century, the wave theory of light beat out the particle theory; and, more recently, the geological theory of plate tectonics proved significantly fitter than the old static world view. Huxley, whom we shall later see as a strong opponent of Darwinism in ethics, endorsed this view of science.

> Now the essence of the scientific spirit is criticism. It tells us that whenever a doctrine claims our assent we should reply, Take it if you can compel it. The struggle for existence holds as much in the intellectual as in the physical world. A theory is a species of thinking, and its right to exist is coextensive with its power of resisting extinction by its rivals. (Huxley, 1893, p. 229)

But it is one thing casually to suggest an analogy between organisms and science. Many have done this at one level or another (Campbell, 1974). It is another to develop and exploit it to the full, trying to take it to the level of justification. The honours for the most fully articulated Darwinian evolutionary analogical model along these lines should go to a contemporary philosopher, Stephen Toulmin (1967, 1972). Consequently, it is his work that I shall take as the prime exemplar of this approach. He is explicit about wanting to push the analogy through, beyond insight (discovery), to justification.

> In talking about the development of natural science as 'evolutionary', I [am not] employing a mere *façon de parler*, or analogy, or metaphor. The idea that the historical changes by which scientific thought develops frequently follow an 'evolutionary' pattern needs to be taken quite seriously; and the implications of such a pattern of change can be, not merely suggestive, but explanatory. (Toulmin, 1967, p. 470)

Toulmin's approach is straight-forward. Ideas or concepts are invented by scientists. These are introduced into the pool of science. There they stand, in the journals and books and seminars, ready to do battle for their own existence and worth. If they do better than their rivals, in some sense, they remain. Otherwise, they get modified or rejected. Successful concepts are thus fitter than unsuccessful concepts. Toulmin is careful to point out that the 'fitness' of any particular concept is not a quantity to be measured on some absolute fixed scale; particularly not some absolute scale telling only of approximation to objective reality. Solving a problem better than others might be a cause for success. However, success might be linked to sociological or philosophical reasons, such as fitting in with values taken seriously by a particular (dominant) scientific group. For instance (to use an example of my own), even though Newtonian gravitational forces solved certain problems better than Cartesian physics, they were rejected by Cartesians because they violated prohibitions against occult forces acting at a distance (Westfall, 1971).

Summing up, Toulmin writes as follows:

> Science develops . . . . as the outcome of a double process: at each stage, a pool of competing intellectual variants is in circulation, and in each generation a selection process is going on, by which certain of these variants are accepted and incorporated into the science concerned, to be passed on to the next generation of workers as integral elements of the tradition.
>
> Looked at in these terms, a particular scientific discipline – say, atomic physics – needs to be thought of, not as the contents of a textbook bearing any specific date, but rather as a developing subject having a continuing identity through time, and characterized as much by its process of growth as by the content of any one historical cross-section... Moving from one historical cross-section to the next, the actual ideas transmitted display neither a complete breach at any point – the idea of absolute 'scientific revolutions' involves an over-simplification – nor perfect replication, either. The change from one cross-section to the next is an *evolutionary* one in this sense too: that later intellectual cross-sections of a tradition reproduce the content of their immediate predecessors, as modified by those particular intellectual novelties which were selected out in the meanwhile – in the light of the professional standards of the science of the time. (1967, pp. 465–6)

Helpfully, also, he gives us a diagram showing how he thinks the course of a (fictitious) science would appear from afar (figure 2.4). (Recently, Toulmin, 1981, reaffirmed his faith in this position. Others sympathetic to the general approach include Rescher, 1977; Richards, 1977; Hull, 1983; Bechtel, 1984; and Bradie, 1986.)

The analogy considered: the fact of evolution

Let us now see how well Toulmin's ideas withstand scrutiny. First, there is the question of evolution as fact. It has been agreed already that we

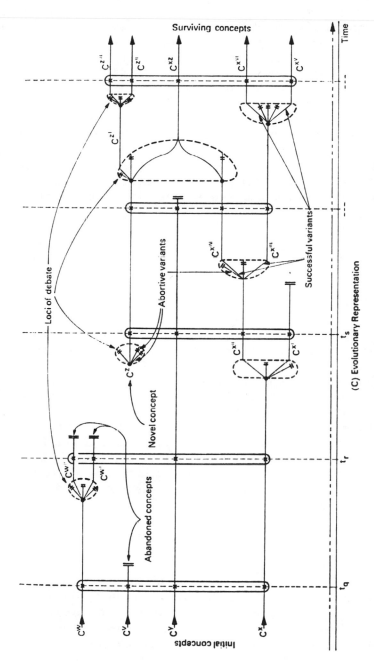

Figure 2.4 Stephen Toulmin's model of the evolution of science. (Reproduced with permission from Toulmin, 1972.)

can properly speak of scientific change as being evolutionary in this sense. Toulmin helps us to realize what an important point this is. Indeed, through his presentation of the evolutionary analogy in modern terms, we can get much greater insight into the nature of science than Spencer's views yielded. Remember, today the fact of evolution refers not merely to changing phenotypes, but to changes in gene ratios within populations or species.[3] And these gene ratios are themselves distributed in different genotypes – Michael Ruse's, Herbert Spencer's, Stephen Toulmin's. This means that, even in principle, at one point in time, it is virtually impossible to pick out the typical organism within a group (Mayr, 1969). Thanks to the balance and related hypotheses, all organisms will be different. No unique set of necessary and sufficient genes define species membership. The fact of evolution, therefore, translates as a change in unique collections drawn from shared pools of genes.

Thinking about this fact with reference to the organic change/scientific change analogy, leads you to realize that a very similar situation obtains in science (Hull, 1983). Change consists in the transition between unique collections of concepts, held by individual scientists, where such concepts are drawn from shared pools. This may seem implausible to you, particularly if your knowledge of science has come through textbooks and other secondary sources, which specialize in giving a sanitized, standard view of theories. You might think that a Newtonian is a Newtonian is a Newtonian. But, the contrary is true, and is no fringe phenomenon. Virtually no two scientists believe exactly the same things, no matter how closely they may be identified with the same position or school. Moreover, the differences are often far from trivial.

Consider, by way of example, the case of Darwinism just after the *Origin* (Ruse, 1979a, especially Chapter 8). If ever there was an identifiable theory or position – held and promulgated by the tightest of sociological groups – this was it. And yet: Darwin believed in natural selection for most phenomena, was a strong individual selectionist, and applied his theory to humankind. The co-discoverer of natural selection, Alfred Russel Wallace was even more of a selectionist than Darwin, was a group selectionist, but pulled back when it came to humankind. Huxley was a fanatical evolutionist, completely convinced of humankind's natural origin, and yet not overly impressed by selection. And so the story goes. What more natural than to think of each individual Darwinian as a kind of intellectual genotype, collectively making up that species known as 'Darwinism'? And then, perhaps, new genotypes are formed, containing many but not quite

---

[3] I willingly admit what I cannot deny, that as the *theory* of evolution has changed through the years, so also has our understanding of the *fact* of evolution. Moreover, these two changes, not to mention our knowledge of the *path* of evolution, are interconnected.

all of the original ideas. Thus, the position known as 'Darwinism' evolves down to the present. I assure those readers who are not themselves evolutionary biologists that today there is no less diversity within the group.

Thus far, the analogy pays dividends. It is hardly yet strong enough to support reasoned conclusions about the nature of science, but it does draw attention to an aspect of the scientific enterprise that is simply unknown to most people, especially non-scientists.

The analogy considered: the path of evolution

We come to the second aspect of evolution: the path taken by organisms down to the present. At once, all seems to fall apart, at least as far as analogy-as-justification is concerned, for those very reasons that stymied Spencer's efforts. Admittedly, unlike Spencer, we now know that organic evolution is not progressive, so we will not make the mistake of arguing from false premises. But, known or unknown, this is irrelevant to the main point: organic evolution is really not progressive, whereas scientific evolution is apparently progressive. It is obviously true that such scientific progress is not of a Spencerian homogeneity-developing-into-heterogeneity type. I have suggested that it is a growing awareness of the true nature of reality. But, this is of little help to the would-be defender of the strong analogy. Whatever the nature of scientific progress may be, it is a nature missing from the world of organisms. Thus, all hopes of a justificatory argument are smashed.

Not so fast! Toulmin knows all of this. Nevertheless, he is sure that the strong case can yet be forged. We have obviously got to rethink the whole question of progress, both in nature and in science. And, when we do, the analogy-as-justification seems far more hopeful. On the one hand, while it is indeed true that organic evolution shows no genuine progress – a notion missing from the fossil record and entirely repudiated by Darwinian theory – no one can deny that it shows a quasi-progress: microbe to man. Else, why did the pre-evolutionists seize on this fact, and why is it such a pervasive notion even unto this day, among evolutionists and non-evolutionists alike?

On the other hand, one should look very suspiciously at claims about scientific progress, particularly inasmuch as we supposedly advance towards knowledge of ultimate objective reality. Virtually every scientific theory in the past, including those for which the greatest claims have been made, has come crashing down. Where is phlogiston theory today? Where is Newtonian mechanics as a true description of reality, even though in the nineteenth century its supporters were prepared to argue that it is logically necessary (Whewell, 1840)? Or (if I might be allowed to offer a recent example of my own), consider the sad tale of Charles Lyell's geology (1830-3). His 'uniformitarian' thesis, namely that normal laws and processes can account for all geological phenomena, has been considered a watershed, since it was first expounded in the first volume of his *Principles of Geology* in 1830. Its influence on Darwin has been noted, not to mention its being the guiding inspiration for generations of earth scientists. Moreover, Lyell and followers have taken uniformitarianism in a strong sense. Not only must all effects come through unbroken law, but extra-terrestrial phenomena must be excluded. Explicitly, Lyell prided himself on avoiding 'catastrophes' – he could do all 'without help from a comet, or any astronomical change' or so forth (Lyell, 1881, 1, p. 262).

And yet, today we are told that mass extinctions, particularly that ending the dinosaurs, come from the dust clouds caused by comets striking the earth (Alvarez, 1980). So much for Lyell. Even if this case proves false, the principle is sound, and the point is made. Scientific progress is essentially illusory. Ptolemy's ideas are at best like triblobites. Copernicus' ideas are like dinosaurs. And Einstein's ideas are like mammals. This is not to say that there is anything essentially wrong with either trilobites or dinosaurs. But, they were not the ultimate, and neither were Ptolemy or Copernicus. Or mammals and Einstein, for that matter.

The evolutionary analogy in the strong sense is right back on track. And it would be coy to pretend, before we get to explicit discussion of causes, that we cannot see where it is headed, and what ultimate conclusions one might hope to draw from the analogy. They are those which we have already seen given by Toulmin, in his own words. Organisms survive because they 'work' better than others. No more. No less. The same will be true of scientific theories. They will survive because they 'work' better than others. No more. No less. Moreover, their natures will be governed by the need to survive in the jungle of science. Everything will be geared to utility. As it contingently happens, you get a kind of seeming-progress in both the organic and the scientific worlds.

You might complain that you find this all a bit odd and threatening. Such a scenario is not at all how you envisioned the end of science. But Toulmin can rightly respond that oddness and threat are hardly decisive criteria in intellectual discussion. Darwin's views on the fossil record were odd and threatening, yet they properly prevailed. That the evolutionary analogy will push us to accept conclusions which we never dreamed were true is to its credit, not debit.

Unfortunately, however, while it is indeed true that we should not reject Toulmin's position simply because it pushes us towards new perspectives, serious problems remain. More must be said about the path of scientific change and its putative essential identity with the path of organic change. There are at least two major differences, which again put the analogy-as-justification programme in jeopardy.

First, there is *hybridism*. In the organic world, particularly in the world of plants, it sometimes happens that two separately evolving lines come together, reproductive barriers collapse, and the organisms concerned now form one evolving unit (Grant, 1981). However, this can happen only between closely related lines. Beyond a certain point, hybridism is impossible. We humans share 99 per cent of our genes with chimpanzees, and yet we cannot hybridize with them. As a consequence, in basic respects, hybridization is not a major evolutionary factor and it is essentially a falling back to earlier positions. [4]

In science, as already shown in both this and the last chapter, the equivalent process to organic hybridization has a very different status. Scientific blending occurs when disparate subjects are brought together in one consilient theory. Sometimes the thus-joined subjects are not that far apart. But sometimes, as in great revolutions, the connected areas come from widely separated parts of science. Joining embryology and biogeography, as Darwin did in the *Origin*, is the scientific equivalent of hybridizing elephants and mice. The difference is that Darwin did it, whereas nature does not and cannot.

This is not a trivial point. Hybridization points to significant difference between the course of organisms and the course of science – a difference so central that one doubts whether the analogy-as-justification can ever really succeed. The great emphasis in the path of Darwinian organic evolution is on fanning out, like branches of a tree. That is a major reason why talk of progression fails. The great emphasis in the path of scientific evolution is on bringing together, like roots of a tree. That is a major reason why talk of progression seems appropriate, and why we think that such progression is directed towards an understanding of objective reality. (You will have noticed in his illustration that Toulmin does seem to acknowledge, and even stress, the importance of hybridization. But you will see that he is really talking about evolution within an interbreeding group, like a species. His joining is therefore akin to sexual intercourse and the production of jointly parented offspring. I am talking of real hybridism, between separate groups.)

Extinction causes no less difficulty for Toulmin's thesis. In organic evolution, total extinction (i.e. leaving no descendants) is not an occasional side phenomenon. It is the invariable fate of every group, usually sooner rather than later (Raup and Stanley, 1978). Moreover, for every group that leaves descendants, there are many more that do not. We mourn the dodo and the passenger pigeon. Did you know that we are approaching the rate when one species, *every hour*, will go extinct (Wilson, 1984)? The most successful of groups leave no living repre-

---

[4] There are special cases of hybridism in plants, where complete sets of chromosomes from members of different species combine in one new-type offspring. But Toulmin does not rely on such cases, nor is it easy to see how they could really help him.

sentatives. In the course of hundreds of millions of years, there were literally thousands of species of trilobite. None survives. The dinosaurs ruled the earth for 150 million years. They are gone, and if indeed the birds descended from them, it was through a minor line (Feduccia, 1980).

Thinking causally, this extinction is precisely what one expects from a mechanism like natural selection. But this is not the main point here, for we are focussing on paths. What counts now is that extinction of this kind and frequency is simply not a mark of the course of science. It is true that theories go 'extinct'. Ptolemy's, for instance. Pre-Darwinian creationism, for another. And the static, pre-plate tectonics, geological world picture. But it is rare for a theory that has endured successfully for a while to vanish without a trace. None of these did. Nor, incidentally, has Lyell's uniformitarianism, for all of its present troubles with comets. Indeed, the new catastrophists use very Lyellian techniques to make their case against him. The geology of the *Principles* is far from totally extinct (Ruse, 1981c).

Rather than total extinction, we find that parts tend to get incorporated into the successors. These incorporations obviously are the facts on which we have made the case for scientific evolution. However, more than this. The incorporated parts then tend to get incorporated into the successors' successors, and so *ad infinitum*. I do not assert that theories never vanish entirely. Nevertheless, it does seem that science is cumulative in a way that the organic world is not. There are no trilobite genes today. There are important elements of pre-evolutionary biology in modern Darwinian theory. The focus on adaptation, for instance. And the recognition of the importance of homologies. Moreover, one expects that any successor to Darwinism will likewise acknowledge and incorporate these elements. A major reason why many view punctuated equilibria theory with mistrust is precisely because it does not pay sufficient attention to them, most especially adaptation (Turner, 1984). In fairness, I add that the neo-saltationists have never denied the existence of adaptation. But they do claim that it is not as important as neo-Darwinians think.

More generally, one cannot imagine that the major theories of modern science will ever go completely – Einsteinian astronomy, quantum mechanics, molecular biology. Their predecessors, on which they are built, did not, so why should they? Molecular biology, for instance, took in and expanded the discoveries, factual and theoretical, of the Mendelian geneticists (Schaffner, 1969, 1976; Ruse, 1976). No doubt this part of biology will, in turn, be developed; but, does anyone seriously think that the double helix (and its importance) will be totally scrapped? Here again, then, we seem to have a difference between organic change and scientific change, and again the difference seems to point to progression in one case and not the other. (Before you object that inability to imagine major theories going extinct is no definitive proof, I will grant this as a point of logic, which will have to be taken up at some point. I am talking now of the way we think about science.)

Looking at the path of scientific change as compared to the path of organic change, the conclusion is that they are still far apart. The rehabilitation programme, sketched at the beginning of this section, was not enough.[5]

The analogy considered: the cause of evolution

Finally, there is the third aspect of evolution, that to do with causes. Here, if anywhere, we should be able to find the real reason why the analogy-as-justification seems to be crumbling, and whether there is ever to be any hope of drawing a significant parallel between organic change and scientific change.

It is in the causal context that the natural-selection analogy comes into full play. The units of science fight for supremacy, just as do the units of life. A theory with a sun-centred universe is fitter than a theory with an earth-centred universe. A theory with elliptical planetary orbits is fitter than a theory with circular planetary orbits. A theory with sideways moving continents is fitter than a theory where the continents stay put, or merely move up and down. Copying biology, we can glean new insights by considering the exact nature of the units of selection (Brandon and Burian, 1984). Presumably, just as the genes confer fitness on the individual, which latter does the actual battling in the struggle of life, so the parts confer fitness on the whole theory, which latter is judged in the struggle of science. However, in both cases, ultimately it is in terms of the components by which evolution is judged.

Before we get to the questions bothering us, note how neatly this (causal) aspect of the evolutionary analogy draws attention to one significant point of similarity between organic and scientific change – a point which is too frequently ignored in discussions of science. Nothing happens without good reason. In particular, change occurs only when a 'problem' arises (Popper, 1972; Laudan, 1977). A population of insects (say) is suddenly faced with a new predator. This sets off selection pressures and (one hopes) an adaptive response. The population must find a 'solution', for instance new camouflaging colouration or a distinctively unpleasant odour or taste. Analogously

[5] I stress again that in using terms like progression, objective, and truth, I am following common-sense perceptions of what is the case. Against Toulmin, when a scientist has what he/she judges to be a good explanation, he/she thinks the explanation has some objective merit – indeed, this is probably the standard for all else. I will later raise the question of whether we can really use terms like objective, and so forth.

in science. Its practitioners do not go into their laboratories on Monday mornings and then explain the world – any part of the world. Science is stimulated by problems – Why are there homologies? – and this sets up intellectual responses which attempt to solve them. The winners thus are 'adapted' to the problems set before them. Fish are adapted to the problems of a watery environment. Comparative anatomy is adapted to the problems of homology.

Thus far, all is well with the evolutionary analogy. We seem to be learning something important about the true nature of science. However, natural selection is only one side to modern causal thinking about organic change. Also to be considered is the variation on which selection works. For organisms, this is (in large part) variation held in populations by selection, but ultimately coming from mutation of genes. Here, I believe, we do come to the heart of the matter. The essential difference between organic variation and scientific variation is the real reason why the organic change/scientific change analogy can never be more than an insightful metaphor (Cohen, 1973; Thagard, 1980). And why, indeed, we think scientific change is progressive in a way organic change is not. But let me not simply state my belief as fact. Rather, let us look, through examples, at the 'raw stuff' of organisms as opposed to the 'raw stuff' of science.

For organisms, a hypothetical case will do. Take a population of white insects, surviving and reproducing quite happily. Within the group there is variation, but nothing is changing. Along comes a predator which starts picking off the insects. One highly likely result is that they will all get eaten, and that will be the end of them. Certainly, if the external threat were inorganic (a flood, for instance) that would be most probable. Another possibility is that the 'problem' will go away. So many get eaten that the predator starves. Or the other major option is that the population responds and changes. But there is no unique or guaranteed change. It is all a matter of what you have in the group at the time – and nothing which is there came expressly in order to deal with white-insect-eating predators. Whatever happens will be makeshift. The organisms might turn black. They might turn poisonous. They might, simply, fly away. There is no special direction to the response.

Now let us turn to science and the nature of its variations, taking the actual case of the problem posed by the Galapagos birds and tortoises in the 1830s. (figure 2.5). When Darwin came on the scene, there was already an explanation held by scientists for such animals as these. Ultimately, their form had been designed and made flesh by the Creator. Then the animals had made their way to the islands. You may object that one should not use the word 'scientific' in this context, because there were subtle arguments to show that, for the initial appearance of such animals, science demands that non-natural causes be invoked (Ruse, 1975b). But this is a trivial matter, for my interest is in

Testudo microphyes, **Isabela I.**   *Testudo abingdonii,* **Pinta I.**

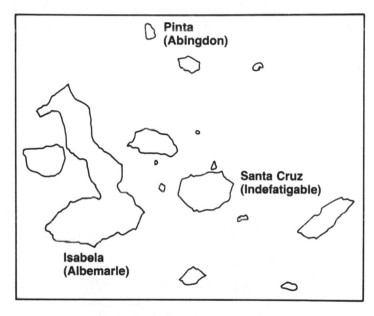

Testudo ephippium, **Santa Cruz I.**

Figure 2.5 Three different tortoises from three different islands of the Galapagos. (Adapted with permission from Dobzhansky *et al.,* 1977.)

the growth of human understanding. If we are now talking of the growth of science from that which we would not now normally call science, then so be it. In any case, our focus is on the undoubtedly scientific variations introduced by Darwin.

There were difficulties with the conventional answer. How was it that we get all of the different species on the different islands, when the South American mainland has so few of the respective pertinent forms? However the explanation persisted, it had merits (it explained adaptation), and (most significantly) it gave scope for more research. You could spend a lifetime studying and experimenting with such undoubtedly empirical phenomena as ocean currents, seed dispersal, and bird-flight speeds. Charles Lyell (1830-3), for one, was much interested in natural methods of transportation to oceanic islands.

Enter Charles Darwin. He was unhappy with the prevailing situation. How could each island of the Galapagos have indigenous species, when the South American mainland fared so poorly? Because of past influences (reading his grandfather's writings, working as a Lyellian geologist, and so forth), Darwin slipped over to evolutionism (Sulloway, 1979b). Then, for eighteen long months, he worked frenetically – observing, talking, reading – to find a mechanism. He toyed with Lamarckism, but it would not fully explain adaptation. The wax in one's ear, bitter in order to discourage insects, seems hardly the result of habit (de Beer *et al.*, 1960-7, C, p. 174).

Next, drawing on his background (his Wedgwood relatives were much into animal breeding), Darwin realized that artificial selection is the key to domestic change. Slowly he saw that a form of selection transferred to nature would satisfy his need to explain adaptation (Ruse, 1975c). But how to get the process to work? Finally, a systematic search through literature brought Darwin to Malthus, and he realized that in this cleric's conservative doctrine – state help is pointless, because a struggle always ensues – lay the force to make a natural form of selection effective. 'Population is increase at geometrical ratio in FAR SHORTER time than 25 years – yet until the one sentence of Malthus no one clearly perceived the great check amongst men' (de Beer *et al.*, 1960-67, D, p. 135). Consequently, 'One may say there is a force like a hundred thousand wedges trying [to] force every kind of adapted structure into the gaps in the oeconomy of nature. or rather forming gaps by thrusting out weaker ones' (D, p. 135).

Now this drawn-out act of discovery by Darwin strikes me as being anything but a chance process of mutation. And the application of the discovered product, evolution through selection, to such problems as the Galapagos island animals is anything but the drawing on an already-existing black variation, or poisonous variation, or get-the-hell-out-of-here variation. The scientific variation is one which was explicitly thought up by Darwin, and designed not merely to beat out the competition, but to do the job properly. After all, unlike the insects, before Darwin set to work there was no threat to the Creationist explanation that it would go extinct. Darwin did not only want to win (although he was sensitive to the delights of that). He wanted to be right. And after he had bound up his ideas in a consilience, Darwin thought he was right. 'I must freely confess, the difficulties and objections are terrific; but I cannot believe that a false theory would explain, as it seems to me it does explain, so many classes of facts' (Darwin, 1887, 1, p. 455).

I am not saying absolutely that Darwin was right – that would be to assume more than has been proven. But clearly, there is something very different going on in the discovery-of-selection case from the avoidance-of-predator case. The science is being moulded or directed according to certain perceived ends of the scientist, in a way quite unlike that which occurs in organic evolution. The science is being aimed towards what the scientist hopes is a true reflection of objective reality. The old ideas are then dropped, not because they are worse than the new ideas, but because they are perceived to be wrong.

What does this all mean? It means that the variations of science are directed in a way that the variations of nature are not. Of course, we have all heard of chance discoveries, like Alexander Fleming's finding the power of penicillin (which may or may not be true). However, in the vast majority of cases new scientific ideas appear to order, because they are needed. Thus, at its heart, scientific evolution differs from organic evolution. You could not have a more central or relevant point of dissimiliarity. The 'natural selection' of science is now seen to be far less significant. Darwin said it all: 'The view that each variation has been providentially arranged seems to me to make natural selection entirely superfluous, and indeed takes the whole case of the appearance of new species out of the range of science' (Darwin and Seward, 1903, 1, p. 191).

Heuristically insightful though the organic change/scientific change analogy may be, because of the difference in variations it collapses at the level of justification. Scientific evolution is not Darwinian. There is no warrant for concluding that the status of science is the status of organisms. We do not have to accept as proven fact that scientific theories exist only in so far as they have beaten out all others. Nor, remembering the discussion of the last chapter, do we have to accept that science exhibits Darwin's relativized notion of adaptation (Ospovat, 1981).

Contrary to all of this Darwinism, the picture which is starting to emerge, and for which a number of plausible arguments have now been adduced, is that science is progressive. It moves towards an understanding of reality. 'Unfashionable as it may be to say so, we really do have a better grasp of biology today than any generation before us, and if further progress is to be made it will have to start from where we now stand' (Maynard Smith, 1982, p. 42). This means, therefore, that inasmuch as a scientific theory is 'adapted' to the problems before it, this must be understood in terms of right and wrong, rather than simply in terms of the relative notion of doing better than any other. We do not have to accept that scientific-theory adaptation merely reduces to being better than competitors, rather than being objectively good in its own right.

But these conclusions are too important to let pass without notice. We must give traditional evolutionary epistemologists a chance to respond. Concluding this chapter, I shall let them do just that.

Donald Campbell's Darwinian variations

There are two ways in which you can try to remedy the disanalogy between scientific variation and organic variation. You can try to show that the new elements of science do not really constitute a counter-example to Darwinism. Or you can try to show that, in some way, organic variations are or simulate directed variations. Donald Campbell (1974a,b) takes the first alternative, and, building on this, Karl Popper (1972, 1974) takes the second also.

Campbell, a distinguished social psychologist, is an enthusiastic supporter of the Darwinian analogy. Appreciating that the question of variation cannot be ignored, he draws on his own professional expertise to suggest that the variations of science are truly no less random than are the variations of nature. 'A blind-variation-and-selective-retention process is fundamental to all inductive achievements, to all genuine increases in knowledge, to all increases in fit of system to environment' (1974a, p. 421). How can this be so, for as Campbell recognizes, new scientific variants do certainly seem to be directed towards the solution of the problem at hand – that is, directed towards the right answer as perceived by the scientist?

Campbell's move is to put the discussion one step back. He argues that, by the time an idea does get into science, it is *already* directed or quasi-directed. However, the process by which the idea itself is produced required randomness and selection. Thus, take the work of James Watson and Francis Crick (1953), showing that the correct model of the DNA molecule is a double helix – two long strands twisted around each other. (This is my example.) The introduction of the model into science was not random. The idea of a double helix answered certain problems, directly. But the process of arrival at the model itself required a profusion of random ideas and checking. Internally, what happened here is what always happens. You throw up a number of chance ideas in your mind, run through them, pitching out all that you do not want to keep, and retaining the best. Here, we have a crucial Darwinian process at work. Then you announce your solution.

This sounds like a terribly drawn-out process. Did millions of ideas have to be produced before Watson and Crick hit on the double helix? (They tell us, in fact, that they did try a number of ideas – but not an infinite number; Watson, 1968). Campbell (1974b) anticipates this question, arguing that obviously by now (i.e. in today's state of human evolution) discoveries are not entirely random: 'I recognize the practical value of heuristic principles' (p. 152). According to Campbell, the crucial point is that, although most discoveries are hardly random today, the guiding principles themselves did once appear through random variation. 'I regard these [principles] as partial, general knowledge of a domain, already achieved through a trial and error of heuristics, and of highly corrigible truth value' (p. 152). And, in any case, the principles are only guides. Any fresh discovery will still require going blindly beyond what we know today. 'If one is expanding knowledge beyond what one knows, one has no choice but to explore without the benefit of wisdom (gropingly, blindly, stupidly, haphazardly)' (p. 142). In short, the new variations in science are indeed random, in some ultimate sense.

This is a plausible-sounding way out of a difficult problem. You will learn later that in proposing selection-caused principles which guide our thinking, I believe Campbell has grasped something very important about human knowledge. However, as an attempt to patch up traditional evolutionary epistemology, Campbell's suggestions fail.

First note that even if Campbell's position were entirely correct and successful, he would locate the supposedly Darwinian element in science at the wrong point to save the organism/science analogy, as it is usually conceived. Campbell argues that the Darwinian process in science occurs in the production of variations, *before* they get into the public pool of science. By the time Watson and Crick published their model (1953), expectedly it had a directed look about it, because by then the 'blind-variation-and-selective-retention process' was finished. But in the world of organisms, it is these just-appearing-in-public variations which are random. No one says they are uncaused; however, conversely, no one says they are themselves the product of selection. The variations are the raw stuff of selection. Thus, even if Campbell were right, the grand analogizing of someone like Toulmin – seeing public ideas or theories clashing in an intellectual struggle – makes science no more genuinely Darwinian than before.

Second, Campbell's position succeeds only because of an unnoted confusion, namely that between something being unknown and something being 'haphazard' (or its discovery being haphazard or random). Before one starts an enquiry, presumably the answer – the desired intellectual variant – is unknown. (Campbell says this is an analytic truth.) But this is not to say that when the answer, definite or putative, appears, it is haphazard. Darwin tried out different ideas to explain evolution – including an extended form of Lamarckism. However, neither these, nor the first groping thoughts about natural selection ('Whether species may not be made by a little more vigour being given to the chance offspring who have any slight peculiarity of structure, hence seals take victorious seals, hence deer victorious deer, hence males armed and pugnacious all order'; de Beer *et al.*, 1960-7, C, p. 61), strike me as haphazard or random. They are inadequate. They need revision. And so forth. But that is another matter. Against Campbell, I would suggest that, in Darwin's work, as in other classic tales of discovery like Kepler's, one sees a dedicated alert mind, probing into the unknown in a systematic way (Hanson, 1958). Even the mistakes are directed.

Third, note that the success of Campbell's suggestion would demand a price. Although the point in the scientific process where selection supposedly occurs has been shifted, you are now back to one idea being played off against another. You run through a number of supposedly random ideas in your mind. You choose the one which works best. At least, that is what you do if you are being genuinely Darwinian. Absolute or objective or non-relative truth goes out of the window. What works best is what counts. Of course, as pointed out earlier in this chapter, you might accept or even welcome this conclusion. Someone like Toulmin (as well as Kuhn) would. But now you are obligated to explain (or, rather, explain away) all the progressive-like marks of science. If it is not progressive, why is 'hybridization' so important in science, and 'extinction' so rare?

As a matter of fact, Campbell is no relativist. He believes in a real world and in the possibility of science edging up to knowledge of it. But even if he breaks with true Darwinism, and relinquishes the notion of ideas fighting between themselves for supremacy, as long as Campbell stays with any essentially random process of discovery/invention of new ideas, it is very difficult to see how this could be made compatible with hope of finding the right or true answer. The American pragmatist Charles Sanders Peirce pointed this out a hundred years ago.

> How was it that man was ever led to entertain a true theory? You cannot say it happened by chance, because the possible theories, if not strictly innumerable, at any rate exceed a trillion – or the third power of a million; and therefore the chances are too overwhelmingly against the single true theory in the twenty or thirty thousand years during which man has been a thinking animal, ever having come into any man's head. (Peirce, 1931-5, v, p. 614) [6]

[6] This passage is quoted by Skagestad (1978). The convergence between Skagestad's title and mine is coincidental.

In other words, variations in nature and variations in science still differ, so long as you accept the progressive nature of the latter and not the former. Hence, we have not yet seen reasons to resuscitate the organic change/scientific change justificatory analogy, and even if we could, all the problems about the apparently progressive nature of science would remain.

Karl Popper and the revision of Darwinism

Could we possibly have the biology wrong? Suppose that, in some way, the variations of nature are, if not genuinely directed, then at least pseudo-directed. This is the supposition of Karl Popper (1972, 1974), who tries to keep aloft a number of the apparently conflicting ideas being discussed in this chapter, and who finds he can best do this by putting pressure on claims commonly made about the process of organic evolution.

Popper's thinking about organic evolution is very much at one with his general, well-known thoughts on science (Popper, 1959, 1962). He starts with the basic assertion that the only genuine way of making inferences is deductively, that kind of reasoning where the truth of the conclusion is contained in the truth of the premises. He has no time at all for so-called 'inductive reasoning', where you go from particulars to general statements – from incomplete evidence to definitive claims. He denies, therefore, that the mark of science is, as is often claimed, a reliance on induction – a going from observations of particulars to universal laws of nature.

However, Popper is no sceptic. He too would distinguish science from all else. He argues that the difference between science and pseudo-science (whether this latter is religion or astrology or whatever) lies in the fact that the former, and only the former, lays itself open to check against the empirical world. Real science is falsifiable. Newton's theory of gravitational attraction, the most successful scientific theory ever, had to be dropped when the facts told against it. Falsifiability is a deductive form of reasoning. A general statement can be disproved by a particular negative instance, even though no number of positive instances will ever inductively confirm it.

Popper sees falsifiability, his 'criterion of demarcation' between science and non-science, as leading straight to a Darwinian view of the growth of science. 'It is not meant metaphorically' (1972, p. 261). The scientist throws up wild hypotheses about the world – 'bold conjectures' – and then tries to knock them down, refute them, against the empirical evidence. This is a never-ending process, with success a transient, temporary phenomenon. Like organisms, theories are here today, gone tomorrow. But as with organic evolution, out of all of this chaos and randomness grows order.

> [T]he growth of our knowledge is the result of a process closely resembling what Darwin called 'natural selection'; that is *the natural selection of hypotheses*: our knowledge consists, at every moment, of those hypotheses which have shown their (comparative) fitness by surviving so far in their struggle for existence; a competitive struggle which eliminates those hypotheses which are unfit. (Popper, 1972, p. 261, his italics)

However, at this point Popper runs into a conceptual road-block, for although enthused by the Darwinian nature of his philosophy, he refuses to compromise his independent belief that there is a real world, and that science shows a progressive advance towards the understanding of it. Such a view fits in with our common sense thinking.

> However one may look at this, there are excellent reasons for saying that *what we attempt in science is to describe and (so far as possible) explain reality*. We do so with the help of conjectural theories; that is, theories which we hope are true (or near the truth), but which we cannot establish as certain or even as probable. . . .
> There is a closely related and excellent sense in which we can speak of 'scientific realism': the procedure we adopt involves (as long as it does not break down, for example because of anti-rational attitudes) success in the sense that our conjectural theories tend progressively to come nearer to the truth; that is, to true descriptions of certain facts, or aspects of reality. (Popper, 1972, p. 40, his italics)

If you accept a real world and the progressive move of scientific understanding towards it, what is to be done about the kinds of objections I have raised about the impossibility of being a genuine Darwinian about science? In fact, I think, even Popper has some qualms about how strong a link can really be drawn between scientific change and organic change, for he does acknowledge that a main factor making us believe in the progressive nature of science is the way that its branches hybridize, as opposed to the ever-dividing way of organic evolution (Popper, 1972, p. 264).

Never to be daunted, Popper is still convinced that scientific change is truly exactly analogous to the change which occurs within organic groups. Of course, as one who disparages all but deductive reasoning, Popper is hardly that enthused by analogies *per se*, particularly if they are used for support. But analogy-as-justification really only works when you have two phenomena actually subsumed beneath the same general principles. In other words, as allowed earlier in this chapter, the analogy ends as identity, which is what Popper seeks. He argues that change in the world of science is identically similar to change in the world of organisms.

Part of Popper's case rests on a feeling that the variations of science are far more random than most people recognize. Indeed, Popper believes that in this respect they match the randomness of the variations of nature. Given his conviction that the only genuine kind of reasoning is deductive reasoning, Popper (1970) has long argued to the impossibility of a logic of scientific discovery. (And this, despite the irony of his having published a book with those very words as a mistranslation of the original title.) Hence, there is, at heart, bound to be something non-directed about scientific variants. Ultimately, one has to see them as lacking any essential design or end-directedness. They are fortuitous, very much in the way that the variants of organic evolution are fortuitous.

However, obviously, in thus aligning the variants of science with the variants of organisms, Popper does little to convince you of the directed nature of science – of its journey towards an understanding of reality. If anything, Popper has poured water all over the altar of progress. It is time for the philosopher to match the scientist's bold conjectures, and, to his credit, this is something Popper is never loathe to do. He argues (as noted above) that, despite the fundamental non-directed nature of the variants of evolution, all forms of Darwinism, scientific and organic, demand quasi-directed variations to function adequately!

In science, Popper relies on arguments akin to Campbell's. Directedness comes from a kind of internal selection process. Initial randomness, and the impossibility of a logic of scientific discovery, are thus made compatible with seeming directedness. But what of the organic world? Here also the Darwinian needs directed variations, and the scientist is simply kidding himself if he thinks he can do without them. The Darwinian theory of evolution as applied to organisms is incomplete. It must be supplemented. Otherwise, you cannot explain the intricacies of adaptation.

> The real difficulty of Darwinism is the well-known problem of explaining an evolution which *prima facie* may look *goal-directed*, such as that of our eyes, by an incredibly large number of very small steps; for according to Darwinism, each of these steps is the result of a purely accidental mutation. That all of these independent accidental mutations should have had survival value is difficult to explain. (Popper, 1972, pp. 269-70)

Biological theory has to be strengthened by supposing some special kinds of mutations which cause significant variations. These variations must be at least quasi-directed, bringing enough change for complex adaptations. Realizing that we cannot be left in the dark about the nature of these hypothesized, quasi-directed, saltationary variations, Popper helpfully proposes a mechanism whereby these might be effected. First, supposedly, we will get mutations which cause a change in preferences, say from one food to another. These are purely accidental, but because of their nature, set up significant selection pressures. Without a response, the organism involved would starve. At this point, behavioural or skill-changing mutations are triggered. (Perhaps variations already existing are made functional.) Finally, backing up the behavioural changes, we get mutations causing anatomical changes, say allowing us to collect and digest the newly preferred food. All told, we get a rapid major change, which will seem in some way directed.

> I now suggest that only after the s-structure has been changed will certain changes in the a-structure be favoured; that is, those changes in the anatomical structure which favour the new skills. The internal selection pressure in these cases will be 'directed', and so lead to a kind of orthogenesis.
>
> My suggestion for this internal selection mechanism can be put schematically as follows:

$$p \to s \to a.$$

> That is, the preference structure and its variations control the selection of the skill structure and its variations; and this in turn controls the selection of the purely anatomical structure and its variations. (Popper, 1974, p. 174)

The Darwinian analogy is revived in all its glory, and note incidentally how one of the objections brought against Campbell is no longer pertinent. The essential action of selection in both the scientific and the organic worlds occurs at the same point, namely in the production of those quasi-directed variations on which all significant change relies. (At one point, Popper (1974) completed his case by arguing, negatively, that biological evolutionary theorizing had to have his directed variations, because selection, being tautological, is impotent. He has now withdrawn this charge (1978).)

Bold conjectures draw forth rigorous refutations. I trust that by now little argument is needed to explain why all of this simply will not do. You cannot play around with empirical theories in this way in order to preserve your metaphysics. There is no evidence whatsoever for Popper's additions to orthodox (biological) Darwinism. The supposed special quasi-directed organic variations are not needed. Popper is ignorant of modern evolutionary theory, especially of the way in which the balance hypothesis provides the variations necessary for adaptive responses. And if this were not enough, Popper's new kinds of variation would not be adequate anyway. Plants show intricate adaptations – just as great as those of animals – and yet they are virtually without behaviour. Obviously, they cannot evolve in the way supposed by Popper. So why suppose it for animals?

Nor should you harbour thoughts of bringing recent non-Darwinian hypotheses to Popper's rescue. *Prima facie*, the punctuated equilibria theory seems like the answer to a Popperian's prayer. Like Popper's supplemented Darwinism, it too (in some forms) argues that the big changes in organic evolution depend on significant one-shot (or near one-shot) variations. But, apart from punctuated equilibria theory's questionable truth-status, the nature of its supposed variations could not be farther from those proposed by Popper. The new saltationism wants to down-play adaptation, whereas Popper is so struck by adaptation he does not think natural selection adequate to account for it.

I might add, incidentally, that no one would be more embarrassed than Popper were he rescued by punctuated equilibria theory. This applies especially to that rather extreme form needed by Popper, where major new discrete variations are supposed to be the building blocks of evolution. Those who have pushed this position, especially Gould, have acknowledged that they see its postulated abrupt switches as symptomatic of a deeper reality. 'Changes such as those described by the dialectical laws do occur in nature. They describe what's important in the universe' (Gould, 1979, p. 12). Popper, as one who has fought long and hard against Marxism as theory and as political programme (1963), would never want to take this escape.[7]

The only conclusion we can draw is that Popper has been no more successful than others in making traditional evolutionary epistemology plausible. The growth of science is not genuinely Darwinian, and to pretend that it is ignores much that seems obviously true.

Conclusion

Do not think of this as a negative chapter. The comparison with organic change has taught us much. Most importantly, a picture of science and of its growth starts to emerge. Science seems to be cumulative, progressive, and directed towards an understanding of a real, objective world. No absolute proof that science is really like this has been offered. However, plausible points have been adduced in its favour, particularly the directed nature of the new elements in science, and the significance of consilience.

Cautiously, I have said nothing about whether this is progress with an actual humanly achievable end-point. Could the day come when we will have exhausted all of science's problems? The evolutionary analogy in

---

[7] I am *not* claiming that every version of punctuated equilibria theory is explicitly Marxist, especially not the more moderate position which sees changes taking up to 50,000 years. The fact does remain, however, that when he toyed with outright saltationism, Gould did start dropping hints about its extra-scientific virtues. Unfortunately, it is this extreme version that Popper needs.

its Darwinian form suggests that work will be forever ongoing – and this would seem to be the general opinion of today's evolutionary epistemologists, whether or not they believe that science attempts to map the real world. Less enthused with the analogy, I have no ready answer to the question, and am inclined to think it an empirical matter. However brilliant the scientist of the twenty-first century, he/she will never get to discover the double helix. On the other hand, perhaps there will always be smaller levels of existence waiting to be discovered and explained, not to mention connections to be drawn between already known phenomena. Practically, I do not think we need yet worry about running out of problems. (For an interesting discussion on this topic, see Rescher, 1978.)

Of more immediate concern here is the fact that we can see in our present discussion clues towards a more profitable approach to evolutionary epistemology – an approach which might tell us if the apparent nature of science is its real nature. Think for a moment of what made scientific change different from organic change. More than anything, we came up against the facts of variation. Scientific variants are directed. Organic variants are not. But what does this difference mean? It means that Nicholas Copernicus or Charles Darwin or James Watson had a goal in mind – understanding nature – and that this governed and regulated the science they produced. In other words, the *scientist* had an active role in the course of science.

Unfortunately, the traditional evolutionary epistemological approach relegates the scientist to the sideline. He or she appears only indirectly. The focus is on the product. We should therefore try bringing the scientist to the fore, making the human being the first object of our study. More particularly, if we are convinced that biology has to be crucially relevant to human understanding, we should revise our approach to epistemology by starting with humankind as a product of Darwinian evolution.

But this is to anticipate, somewhat. We have first to look at that other great philosophical problem: the nature and status of morality. What have evolutionists had to say about this?

3

Evolutionary Ethics

Hugh Miller, Scottish religious controversialist and popular science writer, characteristically put his finger right on the problem. The evolutionist is faced with a stark dilemma. He/she must embrace 'either the monstrous belief, that all the vitalities whether those of monads or of mites, of fishes or of reptiles, of birds or of beasts, are individually and inherently immortal and undying, or that human souls are *not* so' (Miller, 1847, p. 13). Obviously, thought Miller, no sane person would think that the brutes have souls. How could they possibly let Jesus into their hearts and thus be saved? Hence, given evolution, our own hopes for a future life crumble and fall. And with them go all reasons for the moral life today. The practical exhortations of Christianity are worthless. Why indeed should anyone 'square his conduct by the requirements of the moral code, farther than a law and convenient expedience may chance to demand' (p. 14).

Of course, not all felt this way. Religious people more sympathetic to science continued (ostensibly) to take seriously the dictates of the Sermon on the Mount, even as they embraced evolutionism (Moore, 1979). With John Paul the Second, they would have agreed that the Bible tells us where we are going to, not where we came from (Ruse, 1984c). However, as with epistemology, many of those who felt that biology had undercut religious belief, together with those whose religious faith had fallen away for other reasons, turned to evolution itself for guidance about actual moral precepts. Likewise, it was in evolution that they sought theoretical backing for the possibility of any justified moral theory whatsoever.

In this chapter, complementing the last chapter, I shall look at representative excursions into such 'evolutionary ethics'. I emphasize once again that my intent is not criticism for criticism's sake. I shall indeed have some harsh things to say about traditional attempts to link evolution with ethics. But, more importantly, I hope to use the discussion to clarify our thinking, and to see what exactly it is that a fully adequate evolutionary approach to ethics must do and explain.

As before, let us begin at a general level, spelling out some helpful conceptual points. Then we can turn to the claims of specific thinkers.

Moral issues

We should start with the most basic question of them all. We are using evolution to understand and perhaps justify morality, the subject which is at the heart of 'ethics'. What exactly is this morality which is the focus of our interest? At a rough level we know, of course. Morality is about guides to life: obligations. What you should do, and what you should not do. But, since we are going to be talking quite a lot about it, can we spell out the formal nature of morality a little more explicitly? I am asking now about meaning. What would be the criteria for classifying a sentence as a moral statement? In a moment, I shall move on to content and to evidence. (Non-philosophers might find Taylor, 1978, a combination of text and anthology, useful. Hudson, 1970, is a good introduction to recent technical moral philosophy. As you will learn, I have much sympathy with Mackie, 1977, although I doubt how good an introductory text he provides.)

Much has been written on the topic of how you separate off moral thought and language from non-moral thought and language. A good starting-point is the universality of morality, or rather, the universality of any claims you make in the name of morality (Hare, 1952). In a moral claim, we intend in some sense to go beyond the individual. Consider a statement which is considered unambiguously moral by everyone: 'You ought not to rape little girls.' Although, as in this case, I may be making reference to some particular individual, what makes the statement moral is that it is set against a universal prohibition: 'It is wrong for you, or me, or *anyone whatsoever*, to rape little girls.'

What is being said here is something which is above your particular desires, or my desires, or those of anyone else as such. If you told me (truthfully) that you wanted to rape some little girl, it would make no difference to the fact that rape would be wrong, that I would think it wrong, or (and this is important) that I think you should think it wrong. Morality, in other words, is not just a question of personal beliefs and inclinations. It is something which applies to all people – at least, to all responsible people who can be thought of as moral agents. (Later, I will dig a little more deeply into the question of being a moral agent. For the moment, think of him/her as a reasonably mature human.)

Of course, different circumstances call for different moral assessments

(Wellman, 1963). If I have medical training and you do not, then my obligations when faced with a sick person will differ from yours. But it is the same universal morality for us both, with appropriate *ceteris paribus* clauses built in. What all of this universality and generality means is that morality (as we understand it) crosses national boundaries. Morality is based on 'laws' applying to all people. We non-Germans think it was wrong of the Nazis to have killed the Jews, as was shown by our bringing them to trial at Nuremberg after the Second World War. It was not simply that we hated Goering and Streicher and the others – although that was certainly an overwhelming emotion – but rather that they had broken moral laws binding indifferently on all people. Thus, it is clear that although morality may coincide with the customs or legal laws of a country (rape is illegal in Canada, as well as immoral), morality transcends human-created permissions, obligations, and prohibitions. The Nazis created, and put into German law, their own rules. This did not make them morally right.

I have been stressing that an inherent aspect of morality – part of that which separates off moral claims from non-moral claims – is that it applies to all people. But, clearly, this is only part of what we mean when we speak morally. All people (more or less) have two legs, but human bipediality has little to do with morality. Morality is about behaviour, including perhaps mental behaviour. But more than this. I walk to school. I do not take a bus. This is not a moral issue, although it might have something to do with health. Morality is about what we *ought* or *should* or *may* do, and about what we ought or should or may not do. Morality, in other words, is about desired or permitted or required behaviour, or about unwanted or forbidden behaviour. Morality is about 'good' and 'bad', 'right' and 'wrong'.

Hence, there is a certain *prescriptive*, as opposed to merely descriptive, air to morality. Morality says that you *should* not rape little girls. It does not simply record that, as a matter of contingent fact, you *are* not in the habit of raping little girls. Another way of putting all of this, given the universality of morality, is to say that what distinguishes a moral claim is that it is set against some universal standard of required thought or behaviour. Which means that, in a way, a moral claim is intended to be imposed on us all (Mackie, 1977). In itself, it is not a matter for debate.

But, of course, this is all at the level of meaning. A moral claim is intended to be universally binding. This is hardly to say that people will in fact accept such a claim as universally binding. The followers of the mathematician Pythagoras used to think that you ought, morally, to abstain from beans. I doubt that they would find many today prepared to accept this as a binding moral prohibition, although as a matter of fact it is apparently the case that Mediterranean peoples find certain beans poisonous. Whence, one presumes, came the prohibition.

It is clear, therefore, that having talked about meaning – how you distinguish the moral from the non-moral – we must now go on to talk about content and justification. Taking these questions in turn, the discussion of the content of your moral claims is known as *substantive ethics*. Here, you are offering what you believe should be the actual standards or guides to the properly governed moral life. Thus, for instance, in the religious sphere we find such offerings as the Ten Commandments, or alternatively, a moral code based more or less closely on Jesus' dictates in the Sermon on the Mount.

Likewise, secular thinkers, particularly moral philosophers, have made suggestions about the proper content of substantive ethics. One of the most influential proposals in modern times stems from the writings of the great eighteenth-century German philosopher, Immanuel Kant (1949; 1959). His supreme moral rule, the 'Categorical Imperative', made the rights of the individual basic. You must treat human beings as 'ends in themselves', and not as mere tools or 'means' to the ends of others, especially not to the end of your own self-gratification. The chief rival with comparable influence to this Kantian philosophy is the substantive ethics of the 'utilitarians'. They argue that the binding principle of morality is the 'Greatest Happiness Principle'. You should act in order to maximize as much happiness as you can, and to minimize as much unhappiness as you can (Mill, 1910; Sen and Williams, 1982).

The existence of these various substantival ethical proposals – all of which have obvious merits – raises with some urgency the other big question in moral enquiry, namely that of justification. Here, we enter the domain of *meta-ethics*. Now we are asking about the ultimate basis of one's moral position. What stands behind one's substantival ethical claims? Again – in illustration and not in exhaustive cataloguing – we find various suggestions. In the religious sphere, many people (but by no means all) simply refer everything to the Will of God: 'That which is right is that which God wills. God wants us to love our neighbours; therefore, we should love our neighbours.' Secular thinkers are often 'intuitionists', believing that we have some special faculty enabling us to perceive eternal verities. Others take a more 'naturalistic' approach, arguing that the basis for morality is to be found in the physical world.

Or you could be a 'moral sceptic'. You do not deny the existence of morality at the substantival level, but you do deny that it has any ultimate justification whatsoever. Of course, those who take such a sceptical approach have the obligation to show just why, when we think morally, we believe we are dealing with something which has a universal prescriptive force, independent of individual whims and wishes. This could lead to a naturalistic enquiry, even though it is denied that ultimately nature justifies morality (Mackie, 1977).

Evolution and ethics

Enough of abstract talk about ethics. We have taken up the question of meaning. We have taken up the question of content. And we have taken up the question of justification. In the light of the points just raised, let us now look for a moment at how an evolutionary approach to ethics might be made. Or rather, not to pretend coyly that we do not know how thinkers have actually proceeded, let us lay out the general strategy which guides the classic evolutionary ethicist. How does one relate evolution to meaning, content, and justification? Then we can end these preliminary matters, and turn to specific arguments.

Evolution is being divided into three separate components: the fact of evolution, the course or paths of evolution, and the mechanisms or causes which push animals and plants along their paths down through time. To state the obvious, none of these three components – or, more precisely, no statements about any of these three components – looks very much like the kinds of things we have identified as moral claims. The statements of evolution do not, as they stand, fit the meaning-criteria for morality. There is nothing demanding or prescriptive about anything that the evolutionist says, even when he/she is making universal claims. Grant that it is indeed true that all organisms evolved. So what? What bearing does this have on the courses of action we *should* take? Or how does it affect us that the trilobites flourished but are now extinct, or that certain genes are held in populations by the action of natural selection? Talk of such facts as these is descriptive, not prescriptive.

But, although it is well to note that morality does not sit right on the surface of evolution, we must not give up on evolution and ethics before we start. It is often the case that unexpected consequences follow from premises which, prima facie, are quite irrelevant. On first sight, who would think that Euclid's axioms lead to Pythagoras' theorem, or that claims about little balls buzzing about in a container would lead to the ideal gas law? If we squeeze what we know about evolution, perhaps it will yield some moral insights.

For obvious reasons, given the nature of our search, neither the fact of evolution nor the path of evolution seem the right places to start. We are after moral-type statements, which can then be gathered to form our substantive ethics. Only when this has been done will meta-ethical questions of justification arise. But, since we are seeking moral claims, the fact of evolution seems excluded as a source, since it just tells of one unique event and does not have the desired universality. Indeed both the fact of evolution and the path of evolution seem excluded because they tell us of what has happened. Neither seems promising as a guide to present and future actions, which, after all, are what prescriptions are all about.

This then turns us to the third element of evolution, causes or mechanisms. Here, there is much more promise of those claims which, collectively, make a substantival evolutionary ethical system. Evolution is still going on, and may be expected to continue. Presumably, therefore, what we should do, as moral beings, is aid the process of evolution. It is our moral task to see that evolution does indeed continue. The standards of right action are set by the causal laws of evolution.

There are, I suppose, weak and strong versions of this moral thesis. You could endorse either, and properly consider yourself an evolutionary ethicist (*qua* substantival level). On the one hand, you could argue that your moral obligations extend only to seeing that evolution occurs without impediment. Your job, simply, is not to stand in the way of evolution, and to see that others do not stand in its way either. On the other hand, you could argue that you have an obligation, positively, to enforce the process of evolution. You should seek out the way in which evolution is proceeding, and use all means in your power to see that its ends are achieved.

This is substantival evolutionary ethics. But wherein lies the meta-ethical justification for such a morality as this? Here, we must surely circle back to the fact and course of evolution. Evolution in itself in general, and the paths of evolution in themselves in particular, are the sources of all that is right and good. It is they which stand behind and guarantee all that is morally worthwhile. Presumably, if you endorse such a meta-ethics as this, you believe that the fact of evolution confers moral value, and the paths of evolution help us to spell out exactly how this value is manifested, quite apart from confirming the truth of the mechanisms which inform your substantive ethics.

Therefore it can be seen that in our aiding evolution we are contributing to the morally worthwhile, which is the accomplished evolution itself. The rules of conduct do not exist in splendid isolation, but are rooted in the very essence of living beings, just as the dictates of the Sermon on the Mount are rooted in the very essence of the living God. As you must therefore now recognize, evolutionary ethics is thus a naturalistic philosophy *par excellence*.

So much for theoretical preliminaries. As with the evolutionary epistemologist, we now know the basic motivation and approach of the evolutionary ethicist. Indeed, as you might expect, there are significant parallels between traditional evolutionary epistemology and traditional evolutionary ethics. The epistemologist argues analogically from mechanisms of change in the organic world to supposed laws in the world of knowledge, setting this against a background of the fact and paths of change. The ethicist likewise argues analogically from mechanisms of change in the organic world to supposed laws in the world of morality, setting this against a background of the fact and paths of change. (In both cases, if you dislike analogies, you can recast the arguments in literal forms – in the moral argument, you can think of yourself as arguing from the laws of evolution, as they apply literally to humans.)

Let us turn now to actual exercises in evolutionary ethics, to see how the programme is worked out in detail. As in the last chapter, the place to start is in the decade before Darwin's *Origin* appeared, with the writings of Herbert Spencer.

Herbert Spencer and the moral value of progress

More than anyone, it was Spencer who proclaimed the putative links between evolution and ethics, and who thus became the symbol of the archetypal evolutionary ethicist. Indeed, not entirely fairly, Spencer tends even today to be identified with virtually all nineteenth-century fusions of evolution and morality. But, whilst it is true, given Spencer's huge, less-than-rigorous output, that there are few ideas he did not somewhere endorse, his main ethical position stands somewhat to the side of what it is often taken to be. Here, I shall concentrate on the core of Spencer's own views, leaving other speculations until later. As with epistemology, Spencer proves an excellent foil for getting right into the subject.

To dig right into Spencer's philosophizing on morality, we must go to his views on evolution (Spencer, 1852, 1855, 1857, 1864). Already, we know the main outlines of his thinking. Spencer believed in the fact of evolution, and that the path of evolution is inevitably one of simplicity developing into complexity, of homogeneity growing into hetero-geneity. Most crucially, life's history took a path up from the most simple of organisms, to the most heterogeneous organism of them all: *Homo sapiens*. Standing behind this evolutionary drive upwards was Spencer's chief evolutionary mechanism, a form of Lamarckism, the inheritance of acquired characters. He believed that in life's stresses, we get new features developed (thus the heterogeneity), and these are then passed on.

Recalling the outline sketched at the end of the last section, in order to see how Spencer got a moral code out of all of this, we must focus in on his thinking about mechanisms. This means that we must look at the background against which his Lamarckism was set. Here we should tread carefully, and avoid being misled by superficial similarities with other evolutionists, especially Darwin. It is true that, like Darwin, Spencer had read and been impressed by Malthus's claims about population explosions and consequent struggles for existence. It is true also that, like Darwin, Spencer even went so far as to say that this all could lead to a natural form of selection. However, very much unlike

Darwin, Spencer never thought of this selection as a really significant cause of change. Rather, concentrating on the struggle, Spencer saw in it the source of tension and strain which would bring about Lamarckian change! In other words, for Spencer the struggle was less something which wiped out the losers, and more something which spurred the winners to success (Freeman, 1974).

This puts within our grasp the chief elements of Spencer's thinking about the rules of morality. That is, we are at the point where Spencer extracted those moral claims which would make up his substantive ethics. Quite simply, Spencer (1892) felt that we have a positive moral obligation to foster a situation in which a struggle, as he conceived it, can do its work. It is true, indeed, that at times Spencer did note and approve the negative, selective aspects of the struggle.

> To aid the bad in multiplying, is, in effect, the same as maliciously providing for our descendants a multitude of enemies. Doubtless, individual altruism was all very well, but organized charity was intolerable: unquestionable injury is done by agencies which undertake in a wholesale way to foster good-for-nothings; putting a stop to that natural process of elimination by which society continually purifies itself. (Spencer, 1874, p. 346)

However, this was never the main thrust of Spencer's thinking. His emphasis was much more on the need to enable the biologically endowed actually to win in life's struggles. The competition had to be made fair.

One should add, incidentally, that it was primarily this aspect of his thinking which endeared Spencer to many of his most influential American supporters (Russett, 1976). After the carnage of the Civil War, people had had quite enough of the negative effects of the struggle. They preferred to stress the upbeat message in Spencer. Industrialists, particularly, liked to think that they had succeeded through their own strivings, rather than through the inadequacies of their competitors. It was for this reason that Andrew Carnegie, self-made steel magnate and Spencerian enthusiast, devoted much of his wealth to the endowing of public libraries. His philanthropy was Spencerian morality in action. Thanks to the libraries, the poor but worthy child could hope to compete successfully in life's trials.

This, then, was the truly innovative part of Spencer's ethics. But it would be a distortion were one to suggest that his morality (that is, his substantive ethics) said no more than that free competition should be allowed to thrive. In fact, thanks to some typically Victorian opinions on reproduction, Spencer felt able to flesh out his position with rather conventional views about the need to co-operate and help each other, and the like. This all comes about, apparently, because each organism has only a limited quantity of vital bodily fluid, which can be used either to further reproduction or to increase brain-power. Since the long-term effects of Lamarckism, down through the years, is to promote heterogeneity, which (in animals at least) is progressively manifested more and more as an improved brain, we find that the ultimate effect of evolution is to diminish reproductive potential. Humans have fewer offspring than herrings. The English have fewer offspring than the Irish (Spencer, 1852).

What this all adds up to is that, among the higher organisms – humans in particular – the potentials for population explosion and consequent struggle drop away significantly. What we get is their replacement by the activities proper to intelligent, thinking beings, namely harmonious working together, and so forth. This means then, thought Spencer, that if we are to further and confirm the natural process of evolution, we ought to help and co-operate. Only by so doing, can we behave as is proper for beings at our stage of evolution. Not to behave this way is to turn our backs on the natural process of evolution.

> I recur, to the main proposition set forth in these two chapters, which has, I think, been fully justified. Guided by the truth that as the conduct with which Ethics deals is part of conduct at large, conduct at large must be generally understood before this part can be specially understood; and guided by the further truth that to understand conduct at large we must understand the evolution of conduct; we have been led to see that Ethics has for its subject-matter, that form which universal conduct assumes during the last stages of its evolution. (Spencer, 1879, p. 20)

This is Spencer's substantive ethics. To complete our enquiry, we are entitled to ask about justification. What meta-ethical foundation does he give to support his moral dictates? At this point, we expect to see the evolutionary ethicist circle back, and pounce on the fact and path of evolution. And as the passage just quoted above hints at strongly, this is precisely what Spencer does do. He finds the ultimate source of value in the progressive upward climb of the course of evolution. As we go higher and higher, things get better and better. The ultimate culmination is humankind, the very apex of the evolutionary process. It is the existence of humans which makes all worthwhile. Thus it follows naturally that, at the substantive level, morality must be directed towards the production and cherishing of these, the 'highest' kind of beings. It is progress which makes all possible, and it is progress which confers all value.

Spencerian problems

In the epistemological discussion, to those staid readers who did not find exposure to Spencerian thought-processes reward in itself, I

defended our time with him on the grounds that (historical completeness apart) we would thus be better prepared to understand and
evaluate ideas which do have less-obvious failings. Here too, I would
offer the same defence. Spencer's views on evolution, more a function of
his own psycho-sexual development than of anything to do with real
organisms, render his ethics less than totally compelling. However, as
before, Spencer has value to us in showing the moves an evolutionist
tackling philosophical problems can, will and must take, and in helping
us sharpen our critical claws.

In the evaluation of a scientific system, the bottom line is surely
empirical experience. That is not everything there is to be said about
science – I myself have appealed to all sorts of other factors – but what
we sense is the final arbiter. Does the theory, or item of putative
knowledge, fit in with what we know through our senses, or does it not?
Analogously in ethics, the bottom line is surely moral experience, where
by this I mean that which we feel or intuit as right or wrong. (By
speaking of 'feeling' or 'intuition' I mean nothing formally about
whether or not there is an objective morality, or whatever.) If a moral
system simply comes out wrong, right down the line – asking you to
rape little girls, stamp on babies, and blackmail your friends – this is
surely the best of all possible reasons for rejecting it.

However, as in science, there is more to moral evaluation than this.
You want to be consistent, for instance; you want your moral beliefs to
mesh with your non-moral beliefs, like your scientific opinions; and,
very much analogously to science where you must harmonize upper-
level beliefs about ultimate factors (like genotypes), with lower-level
more empirical consequences (like phenotypes), you want your upper-
level meta-ethical foundations to be the sorts of things which lead
naturally to your lower-level substantival ethical norms. All of this
entails aiming at a state akin to what the contemporary moral
philosopher John Rawls (1971) has labelled 'reflective equilibrium'. The
various bits of moral experience must be fitted together into a coherent
whole.

Spencer's ethics yields a beautiful case study of how the evaluation of
a moral system should occur. The most natural starting-point is with his
substantive ethics. To begin at the bottom, is it really true that the sorts
of things he would have us do are the sorts of things we would naturally
think we should do? Does his substantive ethics fit in with our
common-sense intuitions about morality? In fact, in this respect,
Spencer fares quite well. As indeed he should, for he calmly identifies
the end-point of the evolutionary process with that state in which we all
behave in the most moral way conceivable.

Admittedly, some of Spencer's views on personal morality read as
though lifted straight from the Boy Scout manual; but even today there
are those who would defend his position. And, in what I have

suggested is the central, innovative part of Spencer's moralizing, his position is in respects not merely acceptable but positively inspirational. Who would gainsay the moral worth of allowing anyone, no matter how humble their origins, to exercise their talents to the highest possible degree? People of all political and moral persuasions come together and agree that everyone should have the chance to realize their potential. It is not only stupid of society to deny the bright child a place in the sun. It is positively immoral.

So far, we can go with Spencer. But a full assessment of a moral theory must also turn to the meta-ethical justification. It is here, obviously, that he comes to grief. There is no empirical evidence whatsoever that the path of evolution is as Spencer sees it. In fact, the evidence is much the other way. And Spencer's central mechanism of evolution, Lamarckism leading to a diminution of fertility, is just plain wrong. None of this destroys the credibility of Spencer's substantive ethics, but it does destroy his pretension to have provided an adequate naturalistic, evolutionary backing to morality.

However, we should not stop here, for more detailed examination shows that Spencer's plight is even worse than one of mistaken science. And the way in which it is worse is one, I suspect, that will come to haunt more than just his attempt to ground morality in evolution. Suppose Spencer were absolutely right in everything he said about evolution – its fact, its paths, and its causes. This would still not justify his substantival ethical claims. Quite simply, there is absolutely no reason why a heterogeneous state should be considered morally better than a homogeneous state, or a complex state morally preferable to a simple one. In fact, as we saw in the last chapter, scientists value and seek simplicity. This is what a consilience is all about, making unity and order out of the complex. Thus, at one level of value, a simple state is often preferred over a complex state, although admittedly this is more an aesthetical preference than any other.

Suppose, in defence of Spencer, you argue that it is not heterogeneity or complexity *per se* which matters, but the fact that these phenomena end with the human species. Chauvinist that I am, I myself would put a higher value on humans than on anything else. Thus, in a way, I would agree that this move does help you to get closer to deriving values from evolution. But, even if you could now get all the values you wanted, your success would be a Pyrrhic victory. You would derive your values, not from evolution, but from your prior decision to value humans above all else. You would have read the values in, and then read them right back out again. And this is not what we were supposed to be doing. The idea was to get values from evolution itself.

Spencer, incidentally, had a fair inkling of these and related troubles. No sooner had he argued that the unaided course of evolution yields values, than he turned round and supplemented his position by arguing that 'life is good or bad, according as it does, or does not, bring a surplus of agreeable feeling' (Spencer, 1879, p. 27). Unfortunately, although this claim may or may not be true – the utilitarians think that it is – it is certainly not part of any known evolutionary theory. In fact, today's evolutionists argue that aggression and consequent unhappiness can be highly adaptive (Wilson, 1975, p. 255). This tells us little about morality, but it shows that even if we understand 'good' as meaning 'good from a biological perspective', Spencer fails to get morality from evolution. (More, later, on such topics as aggression.)

We can now therefore turn our backs firmly on Spencer's own distinctive evolutionary ethicizing, although whether we shall rid ourselves quite so quickly of his legacy is perhaps another matter.

William Graham Sumner and Social Darwinism

We know what we must do. Forget heterogeneity. Forget Lamarckism. Forget progress. Concentrate instead on the true theory of evolution. Look for your moral guides in the central mechanisms of natural selection. And justify your position in terms of the organic world which results. Thus, the unfettered success of the successful is taken to be a morally good thing. Analogously, the disastrous consequences of life for its losers is considered, at worst, a necessary evil and, at best, a healthy cleansing of the human species. And all is made right in the name of evolution, especially its present state and future prospects.

This moral philosophy was known, naturally enough, as 'Social Darwinism'. In various forms, it enjoyed widespread popularity in the late nineteenth century. It was a sub-theme in Spencer's writings, and even Darwin himself tested the waters, in a somewhat cagey manner.

> With savages, the weak in body or mind are soon eliminated; and those that survive commonly exhibit a vigorous state of health. We civilised men, on the other hand, do our utmost to check the process of elimination; we build asylums for the imbecile, the maimed, and the sick; we institute poor-laws; and our medical men exert their utmost skill to save the life of every one to the last moment. There is reason to believe that vaccination has preserved thousands, who from a weak constitution would formerly have succumbed to small-pox. Thus the weak members of civilised societies propagate their kind. No one who has attended to the breeding of domestic animals will doubt that this must be highly injurious to the race of man. It is surprising how soon a want of care, or care wrongly directed, leads to the degeneration of a domestic race; but excepting in the case of man himself, hardly any one is so ignorant as to allow his worst animals to breed. (Darwin, 1871, 1, p. 168)

Darwin added, at once, that he was not advocating the untrammelled rule of selection. But not everyone has been as cautious as he.

Many people have been prepared to launch quite forthrightly into full-scale Social Darwinian theses. Indeed, as the twentieth century draws to its close, Social Darwinism (if not by that name) seems to be enjoying a renaissance, if that is the appropriate term for such a notion.

As predicted earlier, we find all degrees of such philosophizing. Some, basically, have wanted only to let natural selection run its course, without too much human interference. 'Thou shalt not kill, but needst not strive, officiously to keep alive.'[1] Others have felt that we should get right into the business of selection, actively promoting what they took to be its ends, either by preventing the (perceived) unfit to breed, or even by suggestions of judicial matings. A. N. Whitehead once said that the whole of philosophy is just a series of footnotes to Plato. This surely proves him right, for in the *Republic* Plato advocated just such a breeding programme for the Guardians of his ideal state. I should add quickly that not only was Plato not an evolutionist, but his ideas were one of the major obstacles to evolutionism for two millenia (Mayr, 1982).

A paradigmatic example of a middle-of-the-road but ardent Social Darwinian enthusiast was the early American sociologist, William Graham Sumner. He began with Darwinism, as he saw it, applying to our own species. Like Malthus (1963), he saw an inevitable struggle for existence. This has a two-pronged thrust: 'first the struggle of individuals to win the means of subsistence from nature, and secondly, the competition of man with man in the effort to win a limited supply' (Sumner, 1883) This then led Sumner straight to the conclusion that such a state of affairs is inevitable, and that it would be wrong of us to try to oppose it.

> Let it be understood that we cannot go outside of this alternative: liberty, inequality, survival of the fittest; not-liberty, equality, survival of the unfittest. The former carries society forward and favors all its best members; the latter carries society downwards and favors all its worst members. (Sumner, 1914, p. 25)

As far as morality is concerned, essentially at the individual level it amounts to little more than keeping out of the way of others. At the group level, the state should restrict itself to two rules. 'At bottom there are two chief things with which government has to deal. They are, the property of men and the honour of women. These it has to defend against crime' (Sumner, 1883, p. 101). All else is convention.

Completing a case which sounds eerily modern, Sumner introduced his nineteenth-century equivalent of the Silent Majority: the 'Forgotten

---

[1] Ironically, these words are usually solemnly quoted today in support of a mild social Darwinism. Their author, the poet Arthur Clough, meant them sarcastically and bitterly, as a reflection of what he saw to be the moral insensitivity of his age.

Man'. To go against the stern rules of Social Darwinism is not simply foolish but immoral. You pamper the drunkard, which does him or anyone else little good. At the same time, you put unfair pressures, social and financial, on the decent, hard-working member of the working and middle classes. 'He works, he votes, generally he prays – but he always pays – yes, above all, he pays' (Sumner, 1918, p. 491). (For a somewhat more sympathetic account of Sumner than I have given, see Bannister, 1973. Of course, I am using Sumner as an archetype, and no one would deny that such ideas as I have quoted were commonly held.)

Before turning to detailed critical discussion, I want to separate out a number of extraneous themes which I find running, not only through Sumner's work, but through the writings of most Social Darwinians, including those with like inclinations today. Some of these themes strike me as obviously false. Some are almost certainly true. But they need identifying and putting aside, so we can focus clearly on the main evolutionary argument of the Social Darwinian.

First, what you could be saying as you attempt to relate Darwinism to ethics is that there is absolutely nothing you can do about anything, particularly about the forces of evolution, and even more particularly about these forces as they pertain to the human existential state. There exists, hanging over the writing of much Social Darwinian writing, a gloomy pall of inevitability. As much as to say: 'Don't bother. You won't get anywhere. The cosmic processes of natural selection will go on, unimpeded, whatever we puny mortals try to do.'

Of course, if this be true, then what Social Darwinism is providing is not a new morality, an evolutionarily backed substantive ethics. Rather, it is arguing that no morality is possible at all! In order to have decisions between right and wrong, you must have freedom or choice at some level.[2] The man who is simply locked into a course of action is not free, and thus is not a moral agent. If indeed it be true that there is nothing whatsoever we can do about the inevitable process of selection, then there can be no morality. All we can do is stand on the metaphorical sidelines and watch.

I shall not stay to discuss this position in detail. There may well be some element of truth in it. Nature often proves a great deal more difficult to change than we think it will be. However, as a general thesis, the inevitability claim is clearly false. To give a simple example: certain forms of diabetes have a genetic basis (Levitan and Montagu, 1977). Without human intervention, there would be strong selective pressures against its carriers. Today, however, thanks to insulin and other drugs, such carriers can lead active, useful, reproductive lives. The forces of selection can be and are beaten back.

---

[2] Aristotle made this point, in the *Nicomachean Ethics* (Barnes, 1984). I shall be discussing the point, in more detail, later.

Moreover, even if there were no such ready examples as this to refute the inevitability thesis, note that its truth would hardly stem from our knowledge of evolution (which sets the outer limits for the evolutionary ethicist). It would stem from what, for want of a better term, I shall call a metaphysical thesis about the laws of nature and human choice. There is nothing about evolutionary theory *per se* which says that its mechanisms are uniquely impervious to human effort. (I ignore the trivializing claim which says that even as we humans counter selection, we are thereby following new evolutionary forces. The inevitability claim is cast in terms of selection.)

A second theme, even more depressing than the first, will also get only a glancing look by me. This allows that humans can do something about the forces of evolution, but concludes that human intervention will necessarily make things worse. If you will forgive the anachronism of referring to Malthus as a Social Darwinian, this seems to be basically his message, at least in his early writings. In one generation you avoid the struggle and consequent selection by massive welfare schemes, and all you do is make things far worse in the next generation. Instead of a few poor starving to death, you now have a multitude without food and shelter.

Again, as a general position, this is clearly false. It is regretfully true that even in the late twentieth century in North America there are those who succumb through inadequate nutrition. Nevertheless, no reasonable person could deny that life today is significantly improved over life yesterday, because of our success in shielding ourselves from the struggle and consequent selection. And in any case, the criterion of value in this argument has nothing to do with evolution *per se*. Right and wrong are being judged in terms of the happiness or unhappiness which follows on our tampering with nature. Do not misunderstand me. I am not now arguing against utilitarian criteria for making value judgements. It is just that they are not, in themselves, evolutionary criteria.

A third theme is much more reasonable. This is the one which says that you should not tamper with nature without being prepared to cope with all of the consequences. In fairness to Darwin, I think that this was basically what he had in mind in the passage quoted above, and it is hard to gainsay its truth. Consider an unambiguously good act which involved fighting the evolutionary forces of nature: the actions of the World Health Organization in eliminating smallpox. This whole species was forced into extinction, and thus much misery and terror was eliminated. And yet what we have now is many more mouths to feed. Or rather, given what is actually happening, what we have now is many more Africans starving to death.

I will not slip back to earlier themes, agreeing that this tragedy is an inevitable state of affairs; but, it does indeed show how difficult it is to keep the balance of our actions on the side of right, rather than wrong.

Note again, however, that it is not evolution *per se* which is the ultimate source of value. As before, it is the consequent happiness or unhappiness which is decisive. Thus, although this theme is sufficiently important to merit a book in its own right, as with the other themes, I shall rush past it since it is not strictly central to our main discussion.

This then leaves us with what I take to be the heart of Social Darwinism – a heart where it really is evolution which dictates and stands behind values. In life's struggles for existence, without active interference, some humans will succeed and others will fall by the wayside and probably die. The Social Darwinian claims that it is right and proper that this should happen. Furthermore, we ourselves should allow (perhaps aiding) such struggle to happen, because this is the way of nature. The end result justifies the means. All answers are to be found in the evolution of organisms, especially the evolution of humans.

I take it that the justificatory part of this argument is closely allied with (if not absolutely identical to) another argument which is very popular today. This is that there is some innate virtue in something being 'natural', whether it be a breakfast cereal, a laxative, or footwear. It is felt that All Bran has a merit of its own, simply because it has not been messed about with polluting artificial chemical additives. Although in the case of this contemporary argument there are related sub-suggestions akin to the themes sketched and dismissed just above (for instance, that the human body is better able to handle foodstuffs that have not been processed), essentially the very untampered being of food or clothing, or what have you, is felt to be an argument in itself. Whether indeed any enthusiast would really want to say that the virtue of one laxative over another is a moral virtue is perhaps a nice point; but, as with classical Social Darwinism, the quest for standards ends with the state of nature.

Thomas Henry Huxley and his stand against nature

Not all of the Victorians liked Social Darwinism, and there were those who were outspoken in their opposition. To aid our critical discussion, let us avail ourselves of a fiery polemic from the pen of Thomas Henry Huxley (1894), who sounds as modern in his way as does Sumner in his. Although Huxley favoured a Darwinian approach to epistemology, he would have none of it for ethics. Again and again, Huxley went after the substantival pretentions of Social Darwinism, flatly countering claims that true moral behaviour lies in the mimicking of a bloody struggle for existence. 'Whatever differences of opinion may exist among the experts, there is a general consensus that the ape and tiger methods of the struggle for existence are not reconcilable with sound ethical principles' (Huxley and Huxley, 1947, p. 64). Indeed, Huxley went further, arguing that morality usually consists in doing precisely the opposite to that suggested by biology. 'Let us understand, once for all, that the ethical progress of society depends, not on imitating the cosmic process, still less in running away from it, but in combating it' (p. 82).

Obviously, then, rejecting the substantival ethics, Huxley could not accept the second move of the Social Darwinian, namely a meta-ethical justification of the rules of morality in terms of the intrinsic value of the evolutionary product. And this he certainly did not. Humans, argued Huxley, escape the purely biological in important respects. They get into the cultural or intellectual dimension. Thus, there is absolutely nothing impossible or even improbable about their opposing the forces of evolutionary biology. Science does not state that humans must always be in harmony with that from which they evolved. 'Even in the state of nature itself, what is the struggle for existence but the antagonism of the results of the cosmic process in the region of life, one to another?' (p. 40).

This refuted the inevitability that Social Darwinians generally built into their systems: 'There's no point in trying to counter evolution, because you won't succeed anyway.' But what about the central Social Darwinian claim on which our interest focuses? What about the claim that you should cherish the evolutionary process, because the product is good? Huxley drew an analogy. Consider a cultivated garden, which the horticulturalist wrests out of the primitive state of nature. No one would want to say that this was wrong, or deny that the end product was far superior to the original wilderness. Obviously, therefore, one can oppose nature and produce something of higher value. The same holds of morality. You can oppose nature and produce something of higher value, namely that world of civilization and harmony recognized by all the right-thinking people. There is, in short, nothing in the fact of evolution which makes its realization a moral guide for us humans.

> The thief and the murderer follow nature just as much as the philanthropist. Cosmic evolution may teach us how the good and the evil tendencies of man may have come about; but, in itself, it is incompetent to furnish any better reason why what we call good is preferable to what we call evil than we had before. (Huxley and Huxley, 1947, p. 80)

I confess that I have not always found it easy to warm to Huxley as a person. Some of his attacks on opponents in the Darwinian controversies verge too far into the personal (Ruse, 1979a, chapter 6). However, you cannot deny that at his best, as he is in this attack on Social Darwinism, Huxley is truly splendid. But is he right? Is Social Darwinism the travesty of good thinking that he claims it to be? Let us concentrate here on substantival ethical questions, leaving for a moment matters of meta-ethics.

The pure Social Darwinian argues that life is a bloody struggle for existence, and this is as it should be. We must not stand in the way of the forces of nature, particularly the forces of natural selection. Like Huxley, I find these views taken to the extreme to be morally repellent. They are the epitome of all that is immoral, and anything but a guide to proper behaviour. However, we must not be unduly hasty. We have seen that the bottom line for moral evaluation has to be our personal feelings about right and wrong (not to be confused with our feelings about what we want or do not want). Nevertheless, pure feelings without reflection are dangerous guides. We must aim for a Rawlsian type of equilibrium.

The preliminary question is whether the Social Darwinian is properly drawing on the science, the evolutionary mechanisms, which he/she claims is the foundation of his/her moral theory. Following the discussion of chapter 1, the general truth of Darwinism can be taken as given. For this reason, we have no reason to condemn the Social Darwinian as we condemned Spencer, simply for having the science wrong. Conversely, we can dismiss the critic of Social Darwinism like the nineteenth-century anarchist, Prince Kropotkin (1902), who argued that all theories based on competition must be mistaken, because the true mechanism of evolutionary change starts with co-operation – 'mutual aid'. We now know it was Kropotkin who was mistaken, for he endorsed a group selection perspective on evolution, whereas (as the Social Darwinian correctly assumes) it is individual selection which counts.

More interesting is the question raised by a claim threaded through Huxley's discussion that, although evolution through selection may indeed be true, when we come to humans – especially humans as moral beings – selection is no longer effective, and really is no longer wanted.

> For his successful progress, throughout the savage state, man has been largely indebted to those qualities which he shares with the ape and the tiger; his exceptional physical organization; his cunning, his sociability, his curiosity, and his imitativeness; his ruthless and ferocious destructiveness when his anger is roused by opposition.
>
> But, in proportion as men have passed from anarchy to social organization, and in proportion as civilization has grown in worth, these deeply ingrained serviceable qualities have become defects. (Huxley and Huxley, 1947, pp. 63-4)

However, the Social Darwinian can surely complain that this all rather begs the question. If we do nothing about it, selection will take place among humans. That is a truth which cannot be gainsaid. We can oppose selection. This is perhaps denied by the Social Darwinian when he is in his inevitability mood; but (as we know), truly, such freedom of opposition is crucial to the central thrust of Social

Darwinism. The point is whether or not one should oppose selection. You cannot simply take humans out of the evolutionary process, as Huxley does. This is to trivialize the very matter at issue.

In fact, as you will learn later in this book, it is by no means certain that Darwinism implies a naked hand-to-hand bloody battle for supremacy among humans. But this will require argument (which Huxley does not give) which will reaffirm our place in nature (which Huxley does not do). For the moment, then, we can give the Social Darwinian his/her picture of science. However, in return we should demand a certain fidelity from him/her. Sumner may indeed desire the protection of the virtue of women. But, given that his morality supposedly centres on a scientific theory stressing the maximizing of reproduction, one would like some reassurance that his views are more than a mere projection of his own emotions. Again, I am not sure that all-out pillage and rape is the true message of Darwinism; but Sumner's thesis requires argument, not flat assumption.

Let us move on to the questions raised by the urgings of Social Darwinism in itself. As admitted, my gut reaction is to throw these urgings out without argument. Ignoring nature's unfortunates – or encouraging the state to ignore nature's unfortunates – strikes me as the immorality of the callous oaf, not the sensitive response of the person of goodwill. This philosophy I believe (generally) to be grossly immoral. No doubt also, it was this perceived immorality which was the main critical ground of Huxley's fiery polemic. But, for a number of reasons, we should not simply dismiss without discussion those prescriptions which the Social Darwinians would have us obey.

First, the mere fact that something strikes us as 'obviously' immoral is a dangerous guide to its true status, as history shows time and again. And this is so even though our own feelings are the bottom line in moral justification. Consider something which most of us initially sense as clearly wrong, for instance, permitting neo-Nazis to stand in a public square to spew forth filth and hatred against Jews. What could be more hurtful, particularly in the light of this century's history? And yet reflection shows that there are perhaps even more powerful reasons why we have an obligation to let the Nazis speak. Democracy and freedom mean letting people do what they like because they want to, even if you hate it. That is the very thing Hitler wanted to deny. I am not saying definitively that the Nazis should be allowed to speak. But the matter is at least arguable. Initial feelings of revulsion are dangerous guides. Ultimate judgements must wait on reflective enquiry.

Second, it cannot be denied that many people today (as yesterday) do not find Social Darwinism as obviously immoral as Huxley and I do. They think it right and proper that the state abstain from providing welfare safety nets, protecting the falls of the weakest and less successful (see, for instance, Friedman, 1975). Moreover, although I disagree strongly with people who think in this way, they are (as individuals) far from moral monsters. In fact, it may well be that they and I agree on many ultimate ideals. Our drastic disagreement rests primarily on methods of achievement. Hence, a certain caution is demanded of me, and my fellow thinkers. At least one part of rational moral enquiry has to be the consideration of others' views, and the allowing of the open possibility that you yourself may be wrong.

Third, most important of all is the fact that, despite opposition to the central claims, there are few of us today who would not want to go some way with the Social Darwinians. I do not want to let the poor and unlucky fall by the wayside. But consider some of the problems raised by genetic defects. Tay-Sachs disease is caused by having a certain sort of gene homozygously (i.e. you have two identical alleles). Children with the disease develop at first in a normal manner. Then at six months they start to collapse into zombies, and die by the age of four (Hilton *et al.*, 1973). I see nothing immoral about detecting and aborting such children. In fact, I believe we have a positively moral obligation to do so (Ruse, 1980b). What is this, but to hurry along evolution? And the number of cases could be greatly multiplied. Unfortunately, this all starts to make the unreasoned opponent of Social Darwinism as much a slave of his prejudices as someone like Sumner. In itself, is my allowing of the aborting of Tay-Sachs' fetuses any more supportable a counter-instance than Sumner's protection of the virtue of women?

I would argue, therefore, that we cannot just dismiss the substantive claims of Social Darwinism because we find them upsetting. We must dig deeper. And this, obviously, turns us towards meta-ethical questions. The Social Darwinian argues that we must take him/her seriously, because his/her dictates are rooted in the moral virtue of the natural. The processes of evolution yield moral guides, because the present state (and possibly future prospects) of the organic world are in themselves inherently valuable. It is this claim that we must now consider.

Hume's law and the naturalistic fallacy

Perhaps we can short-cut the discussion at this point. This will be the opinion of most of my fellow philosophers. They will argue that there is no need to delve into the details of Social Darwinism – or of any evolutionary ethics for that matter – since all such attempts to base morality on the natural state of the world are doomed to eventual failure. We can forget about the struggle for existence and natural selection. The world around us can tell nothing of values.

Those who feel this way will want first to invoke the name of David Hume. In a celebrated passage, in his *Treatise of Human Nature* (1978),

Hume wrote as follows:

> In every system of morality, which I have hitherto met with, I have always remark'd, that the author proceeds for some time in the ordinary way of reasoning, and establishes the being of a God, or makes observations concerning human affairs; when of a sudden I am surpriz'd to find, that instead of the usual copulations of propositions, *is*, and *is not*, I meet with no proposition that is not connected with an *ought*, or an *ought not*. This change is imperceptible; but is, however, of the last consequence. For as this *ought*, or *ought not*, expresses some new relation or affirmation, 'tis necessary that it shou'd be observ'd and explain'd; and at the same time that a reason should be given, for what seems altogether inconceivable, how this new relation can be a deduction from others, which are entirely different from it. (p. 469)

People have generally read this as a denial by Hume that you can go by a direct logical inference, from the language of facts ('is' language) to the language of morals ('ought' language). The two are logically distinct, and therefore any attempted linkage is necessarily fallacious. 'Is' does not deductively imply 'ought'. Applying this point to Social Darwinism, its inadequacy as a moral philosophy becomes at once obvious. We go from the language of facts, 'Natural selection occurs', to the language of morals 'It is right that natural selection occurs, and we humans ought to help it and value its products.' One could not have a more blatant violation of the is/ought barrier. Thus, Social Darwinism, and all such evolutionarily based ethics, collapse.

Without denying the undoubted force of some of what Hume is saying – there is a striking difference between 'is' language and 'ought' language – to dismiss Social Darwinism merely by mentioning 'Hume's law' is surely too quick. In the first place, it is not absolutely clear that Hume himself denies that the is/ought chasm can be bridged. Perhaps he is just remarking on the fact that people do tend to bridge it without noting that they do. Having drawn attention to the fact (which we noted earlier) that there does seem to be a difference in meaning between factual and moral claims, Hume is merely noting that many assume without argument that the latter follow from the former. He is not denying that such a connection (presumably deductive) is possible. (The literature on this topic is vast. Hudson (1970) has a good review.)

Second, even if Hume is denying that you can go from 'is' to 'ought' (and I rather suspect he is), some further argument is needed. It is true that most putative bridging attempts flop; but I can imagine an evolutionary ethicist agreeing that normally you cannot go from 'is' to 'ought', yet insisting that in one case you can. Evolution uniquely bridges the gap. At this point, and at this point alone, you can go from the way things are, to the way things ought to be.

The philosopher will return to the attack, and now it will be the name of G. E. Moore that is raised. In his influential *Principia Ethica*, first published in 1903, Moore argued that all efforts to justify claims about good and bad, right and wrong, by reference to a natural, physical foundation are bound to fail. Although Moore does not mention Hume by name, his thoughts clearly run on the same lines. However, Moore's treatment has the virtue of spelling out in some detail precisely why he believes you cannot go from facts to values. Also, he presents it in the context of a positive alternative theory of his own. And he explicitly includes evolutionary ethics within his critical fire. (In fact, Moore criticizes Spencerian ethics, for much the same reasons that I did earlier in this chapter.)

Moore argues that all attempts to ground morality, the good, in a natural, physical foundation commit what he labels the 'naturalistic fallacy'. He writes:

> It may be true that all things which are good are *also* something else, just as it is true that all things which are yellow produce a certain kind of vibration in the light. And it is a fact, that Ethics aims at discovering what are those other properties belonging to all things which are good. But far too many philosophers have thought that when they named those other properties they were actually defining good; that these properties, in fact, were simply not 'other', but absolutely and entirely the same with goodness. (Moore, 1903, p. 10)

But why, you may ask, is this fallacious? Here Moore brings up what is known as his 'open-question argument'. How do we know that yellow is a 'simple property', essentially indefinable in terms of anything else? Because any properties that go with yellow are contingently connected with it, rather than part of its essential meaning. Invoke a property, and it is an 'open question' as to whether yellowness is also present. Suppose that, as a matter of empirical fact, yellow is always associated with a certain wave-length, but that you do not know this. From your perspective, it is an 'open question' as to whether yellow is associated with that wave-length which it would not be were the wave-length part of the meaning of 'yellow'.

Put matters this way. You can ask, meaningfully: 'Is yellow associated with a wave-length of x Angstrom units?' You cannot ask meaningfully: 'Is a colour associated with x Angstrom units associated with a colour associated with x Angstrom units?' This shows yellow is a 'simple property', essentially indefinable in terms of anything else. It cannot be defined in terms of Angstrom units, otherwise the first meaningful question would collapse into the second (nonsensical) question.

The same line of argument holds true of the property of goodness. Good too is a simple property. It is always an open question as to whether some property, particularly some natural property, is associated with that which we would call 'good'. Thus, taking up our particular concern, it is an open question as to whether or not good is associated with evolution. You can ask meaningfully whether that which is good is that which has evolved. You cannot ask meaningfully whether that which is good is that which is good, or whether that which has evolved is that which has evolved. And yet, if the evolutionary ethicist's claims are well-taken, and the notion of good is contained in the notion of evolution, the first statement should be no more meaningful than the others.

As noted, complementing his critical thrust, Moore had his own positive position. He endorsed a version of the meta-ethical theory of intuitionism mentioned earlier. He argued that whereas yellow is a natural property, meaning that we know it through our senses, good is a 'non-natural property'. We come to know it through a non-sensory, intuitive faculty. But this intuition is not just a matter of gut feeling. If I say that moral goodness is inherent in something – like giving generously to the sick and poor – I am referring to an objective property of such a thing. I am not speaking merely of my own subjective inclinations or feelings. Goodness is 'external' to me, even though, as with mathematics, such externality does not refer to the physical world. In other words, Moore regarded 'all ethical propositions as defined by the fact that they predicate a single unique objective concept' (1903, p. xi).

Turning now to the reaction of the would-be evolutionary ethicist (Social Darwinian or other), I doubt that either Moore's defence of the naturalistic fallacy or his invocation of intuitionism would be much regarded. As far as the naturalistic fallacy is concerned, I can imagine the response going like this. 'It is indeed true that most people think it an open question whether that which is good is to be identified with the course and product of evolution. But this is a function of ignorance, not of logic. If you work at the problem and study evolution, then you too will come to see that the good emerges from evolution, and that claims about this fact are virtually trivial. Undoubtedly, this all adds up to a change in the meaning of "good" from pre-evolutionary times: but, you will excuse me if I rather welcome this change. After all, I am an evolutionist! Change is what happens to words and concepts. The point is that, in the light of our new-found scientific knowledge, the meaning of "good" can be no more and no less than something to do with the course and product of evolution.'

Moore's own intuitionist alternative would fare little better. The idea of non-natural properties which are intuited would be regarded as being on a par with angels dancing on the heads of pins, or pink rats running up the wall after you have been on a heavy drinking session. Moore's case for the 'non-naturalness' of good would be considered particularly inept, because all he does is argue for the simplicity of good, and the analogous example which he gives is of a *natural* property, namely yellow. Without further argument, there is little reason to take seriously this supposed intuited property that purportedly hovers around acts that we call good.

As you can imagine (I speak now to those readers who are not philosophers), a very great deal has been written both in defence of Moore, and against him. I have no intention of getting bogged down here with detailed discussion. Let me simply say, with the evolutionary ethicist, that as far as Moore's critical attack is concerned, I am not sure that the open question argument, taken just on its own, speaks definitively against the claim that the good is definable in evolutionary terms. The meanings of words do change as knowledge develops, particularly as scientific knowledge develops (Williams, 1980). Thus, if this is all the argument that you have, it is not enough to slap on the label 'naturalistic fallacy' and walk away. Something more is needed.

I wish to add at once, in Moore's defence, that my critical comments are directed more towards many of his followers than towards Moore himself. As mentioned, he went on to criticize Spencerian ethics itself, in some detail. All I argue is that, as with Hume's law, merely invoking a great authority and a clever label is no substitute for detailed criticism. Thus, it is going to be necessary to look at the meta-ethical backing of Social Darwinism in its own right. But as we turn to do so, let us glean from Moore what we learnt from Hume. Whatever else may be the case, there certainly seems to be a strong distinction between facts and values. I have argued that you cannot simply assume that there is a difference between facts and values. No less would I argue that you can assume that there is no such difference.

So great an apparent difference is there, that Moore was driven to intuitionism. I confess (while admitting that I give no full discussion), that I feel somewhat with the critic on this meta-theory. But a positive alternative is preferable to more negative criticism. Let me simply note that, whether or not intuitionism be true, Moore has surely put his finger on an important aspect of morality. This is an aspect to which any naturalistic approach must do justice. Morality, by its prescriptive nature, certainly seems to come from an objective source (Mackie, 1977). You cannot simply assert that morality is mere subjective feeling, for that is to deny that authority which is part of its very meaning. 'Rape is wrong' does not mean 'I hate rape' – the moral claim has an objective-seeming force which is lacking in reports of personal feelings. The non-objectivist may perhaps deny the ultimate reality of this force. He/she must not ignore it.

Is the natural innately good?

There is no quick answer to our problem. You cannot deny the traditional evolutionary ethicist simply by decreeing conceptual inadequacy. Thus, as forecast in the opening section, the question of justification brings us ultimately to the paths and products of evolution. Do we see something innately morally valuable in organisms, perhaps especially in humans? Is there something about nature which lifts it above itself, into the realm of values?

Huxley's counter-argument was based on the analogy of a cultivated garden, which he automatically took to be superior to the natural state. I suspect that today many would find this analogy singularly unconvincing. Apart from the fact that the garden deals with aesthetic, not moral values, there would be protestations on behalf of the wilderness.[3] Indeed, amusingly, no sooner had I finished the first draft of this chapter than I alighted on the following passage in the latest issue of the *New York Review of Books* (14 June, 1984, p. 15).

> Gertrude Jekyll was one of the most passionately inventive gardeners England has ever produced. Her revolutionary principles of subtle color blending and her naturalistic handling of flowers, wood, and water transformed the stiff, contained landscape of late Victorian England and have helped shape our American appreciation for natural landscaping and planting.

No comment is necessary.

Undoubtedly, much of today's obsession with the natural centres on the (already distinguished) separate argument that natural phenomena will in some way lead to better end results for humans. But what of the instrinsic moral worth of organic nature, as it is? What of the worth of going with things the way that they are? Variants of the argument in favour of a positive response go back long before the days of evolution. They were often employed in the realm of personal morality, and, for obvious reasons, you might think they could be brought directly to bear in support of Social Darwinism.

Take homosexuality (Ruse, 1984a). Both the Greeks and the Jews condemned homosexual activity on the grounds that it is unnatural. Plato (*Laws*, 804d-e) argued that birds and other animals do not indulge in such practices. No more should we. Likewise, St Paul regretted that 'men, leaving the natural use of the woman, burned in their lust one toward another' (Romans 1:26-7). And down through the passage of time, this argument kept resurfacing. Aquinas (*Summa Theologica*, 2a, 2ae, 154, 11–12) spoke of unnatural vices, with homosexuality figuring prominently. Five centuries later, Kant (1963) condemned homosexual

---

[3] Aesthetic values are about standards and qualities in the world of art (as in 'Beethoven's Fifth is a great symphony'). Without arguing the point, I assume that although there may well be connections, moral standards are not the same as aesthetic standards. Beethoven may have gone to heaven (I am sure that Mozart merely returned), but it would have been because of his dealings with his fellows and not directly because of his music.

acts as *crimina carnis contra naturam* (crimes of the flesh contrary to our animal nature).

Today, the argument still flourishes. Paradoxically, one even finds homosexuals eager to show that homosexuality is not biologically unnatural, and thus not immoral (Ruse, 1981a; Weinrich, 1982). Surely something can be extracted from the history of philosophy and applied to the product-of-evolution-as-good-because-natural cause? After all, homosexuality (to continue with this example) seems the epitome of opposition to true Darwinism. How can sexual relations with one's own sex lead to success in the struggle for reproduction?

I suspect, however, that the fact that the good-because-natural (or, wrong-because-unnatural) argument does have such a long history, eventually counts more against an evolutionarily based morality than for it. One presumes that whatever the argument's force, this has nothing to do with evolution. And indeed, as you dig into history, you find that this is the case. Aquinas explicitly linked the immorality of unnatural-ness, not with some innate fact in itself – and certainly not with something empirical – but with God's displeasure at seeing His creation misused. 'The developed plan of living according to reason comes from man; the plan of nature comes from God, and therefore a violation of this plan, as by unnatural sins, is an affront to God, the ordainer of nature' (*Summa Theologica*, 2a, 2ae, 154, 12). Likewise Kant made it very clear that his objection to unnaturalness lay not in the fact itself, but that it leads to the degradation of self and others, contrary to what he thought was the independent basis of all true morality.

It seems therefore that we have to look at the natural-is-good argument from our own perspective, irrespective of history. Specifically, is there something about the fact or course of evolution which enables the natural-is-good argument to stand unaided? And the answer is obvious. There is not. Here are some four reasons against accepting the argument.

First, Social Darwinians and others give no positive theoretical grounds for their case. Usually, all you get is a confusion between the natural-has-good-consequences argument and the natural-is-good-in-itself argument. This certainly does not prove definitively that the latter argument is wrong: but it does leave that yawning gap between 'is' and 'ought' noted by Hume, Moore, and other philosophers. The lack of positive argument, here and elsewhere, makes you start to suspect that perhaps there is a moral to be drawn, even if no morality is to be found.

Second, all the supposed examples where we follow (and should follow) the dictates of Social Darwinism turn out to be cases where it is other criteria which are morally decisive, not the fact of our having followed evolution. For instance, one aborts the mother carrying a Tay-Sachs foetus in order to prevent the incredible, otherwise inevit-able, consequent misery. One's standards are utilitarian, or some such thing (Hilton *et al.*, 1973). The aim is certainly not to beat evolution to the death-blow.

Third, if you were going to read values out of nature, you could as well read evil as good. Parasites, diseases, and the like are anything but morally valuable. (In fact, I would argue that in themselves they, like everything else, are morally neutral.) Were you to start picking and choosing – suggesting, for instance, that only humans, or human-aiding things, are morally valuable, then your reading of values into nature becomes even more brazenly obvious. You would be right back to the tricks for which we criticized Spencer (Ruse, 1979b).

Fourth, and most important of all, Darwinism turns its back on biological progressionism, which is surely the keystone of any attempt to find values in nature, especially evolutionary nature. Progression says that things are getting better – certainly morally better and perhaps better in other senses as well. How can you possibly get values from something which says that the building blocks of nature are blind, random variations? Darwinism says that you could as well have one organic state as another. The point about values is that you are dealing with standards. You are talking about things on an absolute scale. Forget your feelings. Forget my feelings. Find out the truth. Is it right? Is it wrong? Is it good? Is it bad? Without progress, the search for morality vanishes. And Darwinism denies progress.

Thus the meta-ethical basis for Social Darwinism crumbles and collapses. There is no reason to say that nature is good in itself, and strong reasons to deny the claim. And with this goes the support for the substantival ethics of the Social Darwinian. Lack of evidence does not mean that a position is wrong, but no longer can the Social Darwinian insist that his/her stern morality be accepted 'because it is the law of nature'. I shall not bother now to return to Social Darwinian substantive suggestions, for I shall have positive things of my own to say later. It is enough for me to assure you that, even as committed Darwinians, you will probably have no need to endorse a social philosophy somewhere to the right of Louis the Fourteenth.

Edward O. Wilson and the foundations of morality

This should be the end of traditional evolutionary ethicizing, in fact and for us. The approach simply does not work. And yet, although all of the arguments discussed in this chapter were aired, if not by the end of the nineteenth century then by the end of the first decade of this century, such an approach to morality flourishes even unto today. We have noted the current popularity of some very old-fashioned views about social welfare. It is true that others have tried to soften the harshness of classical Social Darwinism. Indeed, many recent writers draw very different conclusions from Sumner, and like thinkers.[4] But whatever your particular brand of substantival ethics, underlying twentieth-century excursions into evolutionary ethicizing remain the same old ways of doing moral philosophy. Causes give substantive ethics. Products and paths give meta-ethical justification.

Moreover, you should not think that only fringe figures would derive values from the process and product of evolution. Some of the most eminent of twentieth-century evolutionary biologists have – and still do – incline this way. For instance, Julian Huxley (1942) and Theodosius Dobzhansky (1937; 1951) were key persons in the synthesizing of Darwinian insights about selection with the by-then-developed theory of heredity. Yet both of these men were ardent evolutionary ethicizers, arguing that in the process of evolution we see the way of morality, and in the path of evolution we see the foundation of our knowledge of good and evil, right and wrong (Huxley and Huxley, 1947; Dobzhansky, 1962). Sensitive as they were to all of the arguments of the past, they nevertheless felt that one can derive an uplifting ethic from the way of evolution. This shared vision transcended the fact that Dobzhansky always showed the influence of his Russian Orthodox childhood beliefs, whereas Huxley always showed the influence of his non-religious childhood. Julian may have broken from his grandfather in linking evolution and ethics; but he never wavered from the Huxley credo that life's meaning must be found in this present world and not postponed for some future, yet-to-be-realized state.

My aims are analytic rather than historical. Hence I see little point in an extended survey of those twentieth-century thinkers, like Huxley and Dobzhansky, who have continued to argue, in a relatively traditional way, for an evolutionary basis to ethics. For all of the effort to clothe the subject in modern dress, the moves and the mistakes are those of yesterday. However, recently the case for evolutionary ethics has been opened up yet again by a new generation of evolutionary biologists. They argue that they know of the mistakes of the past, that they fully intend not to commit similar follies, and yet that they can say much which is important about the nature and basis of moral thinking.

Most prominent amongst these new evolutionary ethicists is the Harvard biologist Edward O. Wilson. He argues flatly that in evolution, in one or all of its various senses, lies the key to our full understanding of morality.

> Camus said that the only serious philosophical question is suicide. That is wrong even in the strict sense intended. The biologist, who is concerned

[4] Opponents of biotechnology like Jeremy Rifkin invariably appeal to the innate immorality of drastic tampering with nature, for instance in the formation of hybrids between species. See, for instance, the report in the *New York Times* ('Clerics urge U.S. curb on gene engineering'), 9 June, 1983.

with questions of physiology and evolutionary history, realizes that self-knowledge is constrained and shaped by the emotional control centers in the hypothalamus and limbic system of the brain. These centers flood our consciousness with all the emotions – hate, love, guilt, fear, and others – that are consulted by ethical philosophers who wish to intuit the standards of good and evil. What, we are then compelled to ask, made the hypothalamus and limbic system? They evolved by natural selection. That simple biological statement must be pursued to explain ethics and ethical philosophers, if not epistemology and epistemologists, at all depths. (Wilson, 1975, p. 1)

In fact, I am not convinced that Wilson is always quite so forward thinking as he himself supposes. Nevertheless, as a kind of epilogue to our main discussion, it will be well worth spending a moment or two on Wilson's work. First, I can show that even the most recent of thinking about evolutionary biology does not save the traditional approach. Second, and far more important, by looking at Wilson I can help turn our gaze from the past to the future. Although never fully and properly articulated, hints of a way out of our impasse may be discerned in his work: how to take seriously our animal nature and yet to avoid the conceptual and other errors discussed in this chapter. For all of my criticism of the evolutionary ethicists, I do most fervently agree that we must not turn our backs on biology. The question is not whether we are to fuse morality with biology, but how.

Taking all of his various pertinent writings, there are three arguments in particular which underlie Wilson's naturalistic thinking. I shall consider them in order, leaving what I believe to be his most suggestive until last.

First, running through much of Wilson's writing one senses almost a denial, not merely of any kind of objective or non-naturalistic basis for ethics, but even of the reality of ethical beliefs or claims themselves. He denies the need to offer a meta-ethical foundation for substantive ethics, because he denies the reality of substantive ethics! As an evolutionist, Wilson claims that he can see that all of our moral claims, hopes, desires, wishes, aspirations, are no more than selfish yearnings predicated on our evolutionary self-interest. 'Only by interpreting the activity of the emotive centres as a biological adaptation can the meaning of the [deontological canons of morality] be deciphered' (Wilson, 1975, p. 563).

By this Wilson means more than that Darwinian theory is going to explain the evolution of ethics. Rather, as Darwinians we see that, considered as a body of moral norms which by their very meaning logically transcend the factual, substantive ethics does not exist. There is no such thing as genuine morality. Thus, for instance, having drawn attention to the various biological mechanisms leading to intra-populational variation, Wilson argues that we should expect intra-populational differences in human desires. These, he equates at once with morality, writing thus:

> If there is any truth to this theory of innate moral pluralism, the requirement for an evolutionary approach to ethics is self-evident. It should also be clear that no single set of moral standards can be applied to all human populations, let alone all sex-age classes within each population. To impose a uniform code is therefore to create complex, intractable moral dilemmas – these, of course, are the current condition of mankind. (Wilson, 1975, p. 564)

In response, let me grant that Wilson may be putting his finger on a very important point in noting that modern evolutionary biology stresses intra-population variation, and that this could well have significant implications for morality, at some level. We shall have to touch on this possibility more fully, later. However, considered as an argument for an adequate evolutionary analysis of ethics, Wilson's case is altogether too quick and slick. If substantive ethics were no more than desires, hopes, and so forth, then the identification of it with evolutionary-fuelled beliefs and behaviours might make sense. But the trouble, of course, is that substantive ethics is much more than this. Moral desires and wishes take us to the level of obligations and duties. That is what we saw in our initial section, and that is what is underlined by the abject failure of evolutionary ethicists to smash their way through Hume's law. At the very least, there is a difference is meaning, an important difference in meaning, between: 'I don't much care for sex with children and it upsets me when you do it,' and 'Sex with children is wrong, and neither you nor I should get into it however we may feel.'

Even if you can prove (what has not yet been proved) that the only foundational backing for ethics (that is, the only meta-ethical justification for substantive ethics) is evolution – or nothing – this does not touch the point about the meaning of moral statements. When we use 'ought' statements, we mean something different from when we use 'is' statements. Wilson achieved his success only by ignoring, denying, or belittling this important fact.

Wilson's second argument is his most pervasive and yet, to us here now, it is probably his least innovative and interesting. It is, in effect, a rerun, in modern clothing, of nineteenth-century evolutionary ethicizing, with perhaps more of a flavour of Social Spencerianism than Social Darwinism. Wilson is certainly no Spencerian in his beliefs about mechanisms. He is an ultra-hard line Darwinian, believing in the randomness of mutation and the primacy of selection-caused adaptation. However, even the sympathetic reader (especially the sympathetic reader?) senses a Spencerian progressive aura to Wilson's view of life, and this infects his beliefs about facts and values.

Perhaps I exaggerate a little. But not that much. Wilson is not usually an explicit, old-fashioned, monad-to-man, chain-of-being theorizer.

Nevertheless, expectedly as one whose deservedly great claim to evolutionary fame is based on seminal studies of the social insects, especially ants, Wilson feels that the development of tight sociality is something special in the course of evolution.

> We should first note that social systems have originated repeatedly in one major group of organisms after another, achieving widely different degrees of specialization and complexity. Four groups occupy pinnacles high above the others: the colonial invertebrates, the social insects, the nonhuman mammals, and man. (Wilson, 1975, p. 379)

In itself, talk of 'high pinnacles' has a decidedly Victorian tone to it. But further than this, Wilson sees something distinctively special about the denizens of the fourth of these pinnacles, namely our own species. We learn that there is a paradox about sociality.

> Although the sequence just given proceeds from unquestionably more primitive and older forms of life to more advanced and recent ones, the key properties of social existence, including cohesiveness, altruism, and cooperativeness, decline. It seems as though social evolution has slowed as the body plan of the individual organism became more elaborate. (Wilson, 1975, p. 379)

However, we humans have reversed all of this. Indeed, we have carried our social structure 'to a level of complexity so high as to constitute a distinct, fourth pinnacle of social evolution' (p. 380). And what makes Wilson so excited about this is that human success has been a cumulative phenomenon. We have not reversed the trend of vertebrate evolution, going in the direction of ants, or some such thing. Rather:

> Man has intensified these vertebrate traits while adding unique qualities of his own. In so doing he has achieved an extraordinary degree of cooperation with little or no sacrifice of personal survival and reproduction. Exactly how he alone has been able to cross to this fourth pinnacle, reversing the downward trend of social evolution in general, is the culminating mystery of all biology. (p. 382)

If this is not to present Spencerianism in modern dress, I do not know what is. Even the order of chapters in Wilson's *magnum opus*, *Sociobiology: The New Synthesis*, confirms progressionism, with micro-organisms coming first and man last (just after the apes). Moreover, given this background Wilson, like Spencer (who is, incidentally, one of his heroes), is then all set to hymn the moral virtues of the preservation of the human species. This he does in detail in his full-length treatment of our species, *On Human Nature*. 'In the beginning the new [i.e. evolutionary-informed] ethicists will want to ponder the cardinal value of the survival of human genes in the form of a common pool over generations' (Wilson, 1978, p. 196). Note how the human genes do not simply exist. They are in themselves of 'value'. And this point is brought out more clearly as Wilson continues.

> Because natural selection has acted on the behavior of individuals who benefit themselves and their immediate relatives, human nature bends us to the imperatives of selfishness and tribalism. But a more detached view of the long-range course of evolution should allow us to see beyond the blind decision-making process of natural selection and to envision the history and future of our own genes against the background of the entire human species. A word already in use intuitively defines this view: nobility. Had dinosaurs grasped the concept they might have survived. They might have been us. (p. 197)

Similar themes emerge in other of Wilson's writings, most strongly in his recent remarkable personal testament, *Biophilia* (1984). Explicitly, in the Preface, he tells us: 'I have written a book about values' (p. 5). And the value that Wilson cherishes above all centres on life: human life, and our love of and need for living things of all kinds. But does this value come from the study of nature itself? Wilson believes it does. Moreover, he makes it clear that it is not life in itself that he values, but life as it relates to us humans, and as it satisfies our needs for the living. It is our species, now and as it continues on into the future, which counts.

> For if the whole process of our life is directed toward preserving our species and personal genes, preparing for future generations is an expression of the highest morality of which human beings are capable. It follows that the destruction of the natural world in which the brain was assembled over millions of years is a risky step. (p. 121).

Wilson is quite explicit that we probably do not feel any great sense of obligation to future generations, but he is adamant that our highest duty is to the future of the human species. And the ultimate reason lies in the neo-Spencerian grounds of our unique uplifting achievements in the process of evolution. We humans are innately valuable.

I need hardly say by now that this will not do. Wilson is certainly not pushing crude Social Darwinism. Indeed, I suspect that there is little to disagree with in his substantive ethics. However, there is no more value to be read out of the course and products of evolution in the late twentieth century than there was in the late nineteenth century. We humans value sociality and co-operation, and that is right and proper. It might be (as Wilson claims and as most nineteenth-century thinkers denied or ignored) that human sociality and co-operation are a consequence, not an escape from, Darwinism. This we shall have to see later.

The point is whether evolution – fact, path, or mechanism – teaches us that sociality and co-operation are morally worthwhile, or that beings that manifest these properties to the greatest extent are intrinsically of greater value than any others. The answer, obviously, is that it does not. Suppose that cooperation is a worthwhile evolutionary strategy for some organisms. Evolution through natural selection makes no judgements as to the moral virtues of such a strategy. Most especially, even if humans more than most pursue the strategy, the science does not tell us to cherish humans above all others.

The evolution of the moral sense

Wilson's third argument is incomplete. However, I believe that here at last we come to something which will help us to break from traditional moulds. I say this despite the fact that the argument will probably be dismissed as irrelevant by most philosophers. Consider, for a moment, the following passage, an attack on intuitionism which (curiously) Wilson takes as always having substantival consequences about being just through being fair.

> The Achilles heel of the intuitionist position is that it relies on the emotive judgment of the brain as though that organ must be treated as a black box. While few will disagree that justice as fairness is an ideal state for disembodied spirits, the conception is in no way explanatory or predictive with reference to human beings. Consequently, it does not consider the ultimate ecological or genetic consequences of the rigorous prosecution of its conclusions. Perhaps explanation and prediction will not be needed for the millennium. But this is unlikely – the human genotype and the ecosystem in which it evolved were fashioned out of extreme unfairness. In either case the full exploration of the neural machinery of ethical judgment is desirable and already in progress. (Wilson, 1975, p. 562)

Ignore Wilson's comments about justice as fairness. This is certainly not necessarily the key ethical principle of the intuitionist; nor, as I shall try to show later, is it necessarily so very alien or irrelevant to the would-be evolutionary ethicizer. Concentrate for the moment on the central thrust of the passage, namely the flat assertion that because the ethical capacity evolved, evolution must reach through to the very core of the claims that we make in its name. Here I think Wilson is striving to say something interesting and important.

You may think his claim true but trite. The moral capacity evolved. So what? If you argue next that morality is a function of this evolution, you violate Hume's law, and if you deny that morality is a function of this evolution, then you make the evolution irrelevant. However, I suspect that Wilson is trying to say something else, avoiding this dilemma, and that his 'something else' has more merit. He is trying to show that something of a moral nature can be a function of evolution, without violating Hume's law. He is not now saying that moral claims are *identical* with factual evolutionary claims (his first argument, and rightly dismissed). He is not now saying that moral claims can be *derived* from factual evolutionary claims (his second argument, and rightly dismissed). He is now saying that moral claims must be *explained* by factual evolutionary claims. This is the third argument, and will not be so easily dismissed.

Am I not splitting hairs? This you will have to judge for yourself, when all of the arguments are in. Just for the moment, I want to concede that, whatever else, the argument is incomplete as it stands starkly expressed in the passage above. At the empirical level, the biologist has got to make good the claim that he can show, through natural selection, how the moral capacity or sense could have evolved. Moreover, when this has been done, there has got to be an exploration of the implications of all of this for substantive ethics. Are revisions in our understanding required? Are some principles seen as more basic than others? And so forth.

But there is more needed than this. At the meta-ethical level, a defence must be mounted against the classic objections which will come pouring in. It will be argued that there is confusion between the origins of morality and its present status. This objection will be expressed in terms of the distinction between *causes* and *reasons* (Raphael, 1958; Flew, 1967). It will be claimed that it is one thing to give a causal analysis of how ethical thinking came about, and another to give a reasoned justification of why it should be believed.

Causally, for instance, I might believe that one should not hurt small children, because I was thus trained when a child myself. But this is not to say that it is a reasoned justified belief that I should not hurt small children. It is not to say that it is *true* that I should not hurt small children. After all, I was taught that you ought to eat everything on your plate, and I still feel ire when my children leave food behind. But is it true that one ought to clean one's plate? Perhaps that which held for a small child in war-time England does not hold for an overweight, middle-aged professor in Canada today.

Because Wilson thus supposedly confuses reasons and causes, it will be concluded that nothing has yet been shown about the ultimate status of ethics. Indeed, even granting all that we know about evolution – granting the wildest dreams of the Wilsonian that all of our moral capacities and abilities are shown, beyond doubt, to be a direct function of evolution through natural selection – it could still be that intuitionism is true. Perhaps there is an objective ethics existing apart from us humans. Evolution gave us the powers; but what these powers are good for is the reaching out to eternal verities, which exist independently of biological scaffolding. The ultimate end of natural selection is its own irrelevance.

I doubt this argument is as powerful as most philosophers (including my former self) take it to be (Ruse, 1979b; Nozick, 1981). But it must be answered. At this point, I shall merely note it for future discussion. All I want to do now is point you towards the shift in emphasis in Wilson's third argument. No longer are we using evolutionary theory as a guide to life. Rather we are turning to the evolution of the moral capacity itself. This seems to me an important move, and one worth exploring. Whether it will lead us to an adequate evolutionary approach to morality remains to be seen.

Conclusion

Let us sum up. Ethics deals with morality, both with its nature and with its justification: respectively, substantive ethics and meta-ethics. What distinguishes moral claims is that they lay upon us – they prescribe – obligations, which seem as if objectively, universally binding. They are not matters of personal whim, and indeed apparently are not factual claims at all. Herein lies the downfall of traditional evolutionary ethicizing, which tries simply to derive moral claims ('ought' claims), from the process and product of evolution (which yield only 'is' claims). Thus Hume's law is violated in an unacceptable way. (More precisely: I admit that I have given no ultimate theoretical proof that Hume's law cannot be broken. However, I have agreed with Hume that 'is' and 'ought' statements do seem very different, and I have argued further that the evolutionary ethicist improperly rides roughshod over the difference.) My presumption from now on is that Hume's law has real bite.

If we are to take Darwin seriously, believing that somewhere evolution through natural selection impinges fruitfully on ethics, then we must start again. I have just suggested that perhaps instead of taking evolution as a guide to life, we should begin with the evolution of our moral capacity. Here, you will see an interesting parallel with the conclusion reached in the last chapter. There, the suggestion was that instead of taking evolution as a guide to the growth of knowledge, we should begin with the evolution of our intellectual capacity.

Such a consilience cannot be ignored. And this is particularly so since at root the same problem seems to infect both traditional evolutionary epistemology and traditional evolutionary ethics. There, in order to accommodate *truth*, and our striving after it, we had to bring in an illegitimate sense of progress, something quite alien to Darwinism. Here, in order to accommodate *value*, and our striving after it, we had to bring in an illegitimate sense of progress, something quite alien to Darwinism. In both cases we have been Spencerians, still thinking essentially in pre-Darwinian ways.

A break must be made with the past. Knowledge and morality belong to humans, and we humans are the products of Darwinian evolution. Thus, we have got to look at *human* evolution, in a quite literal sense. In particular, we must look at human evolution as moulded and forced by natural selection. Only then will we be able to judge human abilities, intellectual and moral, and say how far their evolved nature is crucial in what they do and produce. Hence, at this point we must turn again to empirical enquiry. We know about the Darwinian theory of evolution. Now we must learn what Darwinians have to tell us about our own species, *Homo sapiens*.

4

Human Evolution

René Descartes thought that everything which God created reduces to one or other of two different basic world stuffs: thinking substance and material or extended substance. Angels are pure thought. They have no physical properties. They are *res cogitans*. Chairs and tables are completely material. They cannot think. Nor can animals, argued Descartes, claiming (in a move that still astounds and appals all English-born dog lovers) that they are but non-conscious robots. They are *res extensa*. Humans are unique, for they alone straddle the two substances. Their bodies belong to the world of material substance. Their minds belong to the world of thinking substance. The two parts meet and interact in the pineal gland (Williams, 1978).

For all its debts to the new mechanical science of the seventeenth century, Descartes's 'dualist' picture has obvious roots in much earlier, traditional philosophy and theology. Yet, even today, I suspect that dualism is essentially the common-sense view of most people who think about these matters, despite its limitations having been discussed endlessly for the past 350 years (Churchland, 1984). But, whether you are for Descartes or whether you are against him, subscribing perhaps to some sort of 'identity thesis', believing that mind and brain are different aspects of the same thing, the chances are that you are at one with Descartes on his crucial starting-point. Humans are in some sense special or different.

Of course, everyone concedes that, in some respects, humans are like animals. With cats and dogs, we breathe, sleep, eat, defecate, copulate – and die, in the physical sense at least. Nevertheless, you probably agree with Descartes that, qualitatively, humans are not mere animals. We have some special essence, which gives us a favoured place in this world and (perhaps) the next. This distinctive part of human nature is our rational faculty, or some such thing – that which enables us to see the truth about the world and about the proper courses of action binding upon us humans.

It is this picture of humankind that the Darwinian Revolution shatters. If you take Darwin seriously – accepting evolution through natural selection and not merely some Spencerian bastard version of evolution – then the special status of *Homo sapiens* is gone for ever. Any powers we have are no more than those brought through the crucible of the evolutionary struggle and consequent reproductive success. It is true that, as a species, we are unique, with our own special combination of powers and abilities. But then, so also is *Drosophila melanogaster* (a species of fruit-fly).

In this chapter, I present the empirical case for human evolution. Then, we can go on to explore the philosophical implications. Thus, we now pick up the exposition as it was left at the end of the first chapter. Since it has served us well, let us continue to employ the tripartite division of evolution into *fact*, *path*, and *mechanism*. Again, I emphasize that this is a somewhat artificial distinction and that there are points of overlap.

The fact of human evolution

Even as Descartes wrote, cracks were beginning to appear in the dyke. World travellers were bringing back reports and (then) actual specimens of pongos and jockos and other fabulous monsters, half-men and half-brutes (Greene, 1959, and figure 4.1). Hence, although it was significant, it was perhaps not all that revolutionary when the great Swedish taxonomist Linnaeus, in the eighteenth century, classified humans in the same family as the higher apes. But do not be deceived, Linnaeus intended to imply nothing about our origins. Humans are special: a fact proclaimed by religion, and (supposedly) confirmed by reason and the senses (Mayr, 1982)

It was Lamarck (1809) who first firmly linked humans with animals. We are the step above the orang-utan brought about by an evolutionary process which began with spontaneously generated worms. But, for all his daring, Lamarck continued to stress our human uniqueness. The chain of development is progressive, and all of the time it points upwards towards *Homo sapiens* (Burkhardt, 1977). And this was the position of those much influenced by Lamarck, including (as we know) Spencer.

Darwin made the decisive break (Herbert, 1974, 1977). Even from the first, he firmly admonished himself: 'It is absurd to talk of one animal being higher than another – we consider those where the cerebral structure/intellectual faculties most developed, as highest. – A bee

Figure 4.1 This is a picture of a young chimpanzee which appeared in a volume on apes, published in 1766. Notice how human it is made to seem.

doubtless would where the instincts were' (de Beer *et al.*, 1960-7, B, p. 74). Having had first-hand experience of the most primitive of humans (the denizens of the southernmost tip of South America), Darwin had no doubt of our animal nature. 'Compare the Fuegian and the ourang-outang, and dare to say differences so great' (Gruber and Barrett, 1974, M, p. 153; and figures 4.2 and 4.3).

In the *Origin*, however, Darwin wisely played things very cautiously. He knew full well that the monkey question would be foremost in people's minds. Thus, he neither could nor would pretend that his views had no bearing on the matter. But Darwin did not want everything swamped in controversy over our simian origins. It was important, first, that the general case for evolution and selection be presented. Hence, Darwin restricted himself to the greatest understatement of the nineteenth century, casually remarking, virtually at the end of the book, that: 'Light will be thrown on the origin of man and his history' (Darwin, 1859, p. 488).

Figure 4.2 Darwin's first sketch (in 1837) of what he then termed the 'coral of life', showing how he repudiated unilineal progression. (From de Beer *et al.*, 1960–7, Notebook B.)

Because Darwin was so reticent in public, it fell to T. H. Huxley to make the first comprehensive case for the fact of human evolution. This he did with enthusiasm, most notoriously in his clash with the Bishop of Oxford, Soapy Sam Wilberforce, at the British Association for the Advancement of Science meeting in the summer of 1860. ('Let me ask the learned professor. Is he more closely related to monkeys on his grandfather's side or his grandmother's side?' 'Let me tell my distinguished episcopal opponent: I had rather be descended from a monkey than from a bishop of the Church of England.')[1] Then, Huxley took to the pen, most notably in his classic, *Evidence as to Man's Place in Nature* (1863).

Huxley's argument for the fact of human evolution – an argument augmented later by Darwin himself in his *Descent of Man* – is, in outline, precisely that advanced by today's evolutionists. You start with the general background fact of evolution, pointing out that, in dealing with humans, you are not working in isolation. You are arguing from your general knowledge of evolution. Then you show that, judged by all of the usual criteria, humans are likewise a product of evolution.

But, what are the usual criteria? Here, Huxley and all other evolutionists work by drawing comparisons. When you look at humans up against the animals, particularly against the higher apes, you find great similarities. And these are just the kinds of similarities that you know, from the fossil record and elsewhere (increasingly today from experimental evidence), are associated with and indicative of organisms which share a common heritage. Furthermore, there are no unique features of humankind which put this matter into doubt. In other words, if you accept the fact of evolution at all, the fact of human

Figure 4.3 A Tierra del Fuegan, drawn by the artist on *HMS Beagle*.

evolution is a compelling corollary.

Filling in the line of argument as thus stated, evolutionists have little trouble in showing that the fact of human evolution is quite beyond reasonable doubt. The skeletal and other bodily similarities between humans and apes are there for all to see (figure 4.4). Huxley's conclusion of 1863 stands yet today.

Thus, whatever system of organs be studied, the comparison of their modifications in the ape series leads to one and the same result – that the structural differences which separate Man from the Gorilla and the Chimpanzee are not so great as those which separate the Gorilla from the lower apes. (p. 144)

Furthermore, our affinities with the brutes are underlined when you turn to embryology and development. In their early stages, humans and

[1] Like all good stories, there is much fiction mixed in with the truth, as even Huxley admitted (L. Huxley, 1900, 1, 192-204). A more accurate, albeit less entertaining, account is given by Lucas (1979).

GIBBON.   ORANG.   *Skeletons of the*   GORILLA.   MAN.
                            CHIMPANZEE.

Figure 4.4 Huxley's picture of man and the apes, underlining our similarity. (Taken from *Evidence as to Man's Place in Nature*, written by Huxley in 1863.)

other mammals are indistinguishable. Only those who are blind to scientific argument (like the Creationists) can refuse to draw the inevitable conclusion. Humans are animals, and like other animals they evolved.

Nor are there physical features standing in the way of this conclusion. Indubitably, as with other species, there are few characteristics in humans which do not speak to our distinctive nature. Bones are pulled and pushed, twisted, distorted, and modified. As also are other bodily parts. But the basic units are all shared by other species. Opponents of evolution searched long and hard for features uniquely possessed by humans. For a very short while after Darwin, they thought it had been found in the brain, with *hippocampus minor*. But, as Huxley showed with devastating force, this part's supposed absence in apes was more a function of wishful thinking and poor-quality preservation, than anything in objective reality (Ruse, 1979a, chapter 9).

A secure scientific claim leads to predictions. If humans are at one with the apes, then this should have been reconfirmed with the coming of microbiology, most particularly with the advent of molecular studies. And such is the case. The similarities between humans and apes at the chromosomal, genetic, and molecular levels are truly astounding. Genetically speaking, we humans have a more than 99 per cent overlap with the chimpanzees. If you are prepared to accept a natural explanation of human origins, you just cannot deny that we are animals, and that we share a common origin with the rest of the organic world (Yunis *et al.*, 1980; King and Wilson, 1975; and figure 4.5).

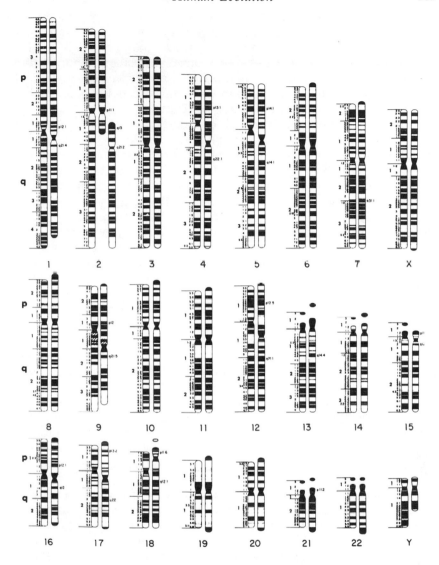

Figure 4.5 The very similar chromosomes of humans (on the left) and chimpanzees (on the right) point to a recent common ancestry. (Reproduced with permission from King and Wilson, 1975.)

The path of human evolution

From the time of Darwin and before, the cry of critics and doubters, especially those who subscribed to the traditional Judaeo-Christian story of human creation some 6,000 years ago, was for signs of the missing link. If indeed we are children of the primates (no Darwinian has ever claimed that we are descended from extant monkeys or apes), then we should expect some tangible evidence of this transition. And, the only definitive evidence would be unambiguous fossil remains of ape/men. Until such are forthcoming, human evolution can never be more than unsubstantiated fantasy. Or so said the sceptics.

As usually happens when this kind of objection is levelled, evidence for the fact of evolution was jumbled with evidence for the path of evolution. To repeat a point made often before: the fact of evolution can be established with virtually no knowledge of the fossil record. That this holds true of our own species was explained patiently, time and again, by Huxley, Darwin, and others. The comparative argument given above is entire and good in itself. But if we would trace the path of human evolution – our phylogeny – then the critics are surely right in crying that the successful search for fossil remains becomes pressing. Bone fragments are far from the sole source of information about the actual course of evolution, human or otherwise. This we shall ourselves learn very clearly in a moment. But such remains are very important.

The quest for relevant fossils is, inevitably, slow and uncertain. There is no guarantee of success. Nevertheless, after a century and a half of persistent effort, although dogged by man-made handicaps from nationalistic sensitivities to outright fraud, we do now have a solid palaeontological record on which to base our reconstruction of human phylogeny. There are still frustrating gaps; but they are no longer as daunting as they used to be, even recently (Johanson and Edey, 1981; Johanson and White, 1979; Pilbeam, 1984).

In fact, the story of human fossil discoveries goes back to before the *Origin* was published (Oakley, 1964). In the first half of the nineteenth century, a French customs keeper, Boucher de Perthes, uncovered strong evidence that humans had lived and thrived at least long enough ago to be contemporaneous with animals now extinct. If nothing else, these discoveries put in some doubt the supposedly recent origin of humankind, as inferrable from Genesis. Yet, as critics insisted, no one could deny the completely human status of these remains. And the same level of development had to be granted to the remains from the Neander valley, (in Germany), discovered almost exactly when Darwin published. It is true that the features of Neanderthal man were rather more massive than ours, but brain size and the like convinced authorities like Huxley (1901) that he was at most an early sub-species of *Homo sapiens*. This is a judgement that persists today.

As the nineteenth century drew to a close, the first real (and enduring) candidate for missing-link status came through the persistent efforts of the Dutch army doctor Eugene Dubois in Java (Oakley, 1964). He unearthed a skull-cap and thigh bone like those of humans, but significantly less advanced (from a human perspective). Today, Java man, originally given its own genus, *Pithecanthropus*, is placed more closely to us, in the same genus but with a different species: *Homo erectus*. Not until this century was a quarter over were strikingly different specimens of proto-man uncovered. These were so far distant that they could properly be put into a separate genus: *Australopithecus*.

Since then, in Africa, which appears to have been the birthplace of humankind, many more specimens of *Australopithecus* and of early *Homo* have been discovered. Thanks to radiometric and other techniques of calculating absolute time, we can say with some confidence that *Homo* evolved from *Australopithecus* about three million years ago. However, the earlier genus did not at once because extinct. Indeed, for some two million years (i.e. until 1,000,000 BC) we had two extant lines of hominids, that is of organisms descended from our earliest non-ape ancestors.

The earliest directly known hominid fossils, about four million years old (or somewhat less), are put in the species *Australopithecus afarensis* (Johanson and White, 1979; and figure 4.6). They come from Ethiopia, and through remarkable finds of near-complete specimens, we have been able to answer a major question which has long intrigued students of human evolution: which of the two distinctively human features came first, upright stance or large brain? There now can be no doubt that it was the former. Although it was possibly more suited for arboreal life than we, *A. afarensis* stood fully upright and walked. It was genuinely bipedal, unlike today's chimps, which are knuckle walkers. And yet, *A. afarensis* had an ape-size brain. It had a cranial capacity of some 500 cc, like gorillas. (I am *not* saying that it had a gorilla brain. To argue in such a manner is to slip back into Spencerian progressionism.)

Starting with *A. afarensis*, the fossils show a connected sequence through to ourselves. As the years went by, our ancestors got larger, and their brains just exploded upwards in size. From the small *A. afarensis* (rather more than one metre in height), we grew to the much taller *H. sapiens*. In the same span, the size of brain increased nearly three-fold, from 500 cc to about 1,400 cc. There is, of course, more to intelligence than brain size (or whales would be more intelligent than we); but, the implication is that there was an associated evolution of mental ability (Konigsson, 1980; Ciochon and Corruccini, 1983; and figure 4.7).

I shall have much more to say shortly about this crucial aspect of human evolution, and about related changes. Somewhat later, I shall discuss explicitly the evolution of those various things we would most distinctively call 'human'. It is enough to note here that once our ancestors got up on their back legs, there was parallel evolution to the physical form we have now. But what about the time before any of this?

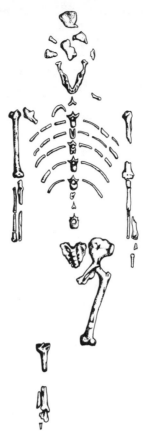

Figure 4.6 *Australopithecus afarensis:* the specimen known as 'Lucy'. (Reproduced with permission of the Cleveland Museum of Natural History.)

Where did *Australopithecus afarensis* come from? Unfortunately, here we do start to enter unknown, dangerous waters. We have little fossil evidence at all for the four or five million years before *A. afarensis*, and the same holds for the whole of recent ape evolution. Around ten million years ago, we find an ape-like creature in Africa, *Ramapithecus*. Much further back, some twenty million years ago, we find *Dryopithecus* which had a brain the size of that of a modern ape, was a tree-dweller and a fruit-eater.

Making bricks with very little straw (more literally, making phylogenies with very few bones), until recently the general consensus was that *Dryopithecus* was the last common ancestor between humans and apes, or at least was the last being for which we have fossil evidence when there were commmon ancestors. Supposedly, the human–ape split occurred around fifteen million years ago (Johanson and Edey,

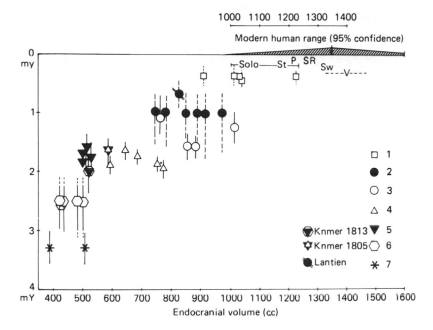

Figure 4.7 Endocranial volumes of hominid fossil skulls plotted against a time scale. The degree of uncertainty about age is indicated by the vertical bars. 7 shows two members of *Australopithecus afarensis*; 6 and 5 show later Australopithecines; 4 shows members of the earliest species within our genus *(Homo habilis)*, and 3, 2 and 1 are early, middle and late members of *H. erectus*. Finally, we get early members of our own species, *H. sapiens* (St, P, SR, SW, V). (Reproduced with permission from Isaac, 1983.)

1981). *Ramapithecus* is somewhere down the human line, either on the main track or on a side branch (figure 4.8). Note that, even with this scenario, humans and apes are very close – for at least three-quarters of the age of mammals, humans, chimpanzees, and gorillas evolved as one. If you go back to the first appearance of life, we humans have been apart from the brutes less than 0.5 per cent of the time (figure 4.8).

In the past five years, however, opinion has swung to even more drastic conclusions. Making use of those molecular and other microscopic similarities noted earlier, the probable point of human–ape divergence has been very significantly shortened. Direct examination of the chromosomes and of the biochemical cellular products of the genes suggests that humans are more like chimpanzees than chimpanzees are like gorillas. Biologically, we ought to rearrange the present classification of humans – one which puts us in our own subfamily – assigning

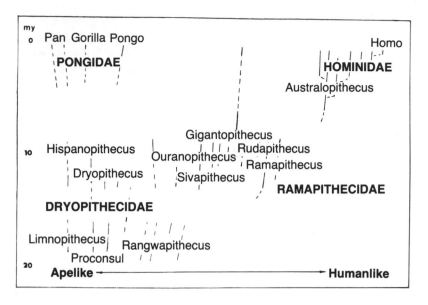

Figure 4.8 The view of human evolution in 1980. (Reproduced with permission of David Pilbeam.)

ourselves to the same genus as the higher apes. Were we fruit-flies, we would have done so long ago (Ayala and Valentine, 1979).

But how are we to interpret these similarities? Here, it seems safe to use the idea of a molecular clock, arguing that biochemical relationship is roughly proportional to (absolute) time since evolutionary divergence occurred. This is an argument with broad independent support from the fossil record. Thus, we arrive at the amazing conclusion that humans and chimpanzees split only five million years ago! Even if one stretches this a little, the opinion of molecular biologists (now generally accepted by students of the fossil record) is that the split simply cannot have been more than about seven million years ago. Gorillas apparently broke off from our joint human/chimpanzee ancestors a million or two years before that (Sibley and Ahlquist, 1984; and figure 4.9).

This is a truly astounding conclusion, with implications rivalling any of this century's discoveries in the physical sciences. Much work yet remains to be done, in theory, in experiment, and (very obviously) in the field. We simply must cross-check the implications of theory with solid fossil discoveries. But the main picture is now coming well into focus. The path of independent human evolution is much shorter than anyone has previously dreamed, even ten years ago. Any full picture of human nature must make this fact its starting-point.

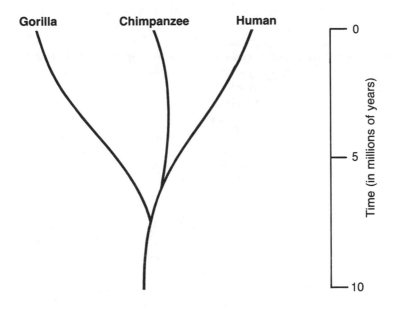

Gorilla   **Chimpanzee**   **Human**

Figure 4.9 The most recent picture of human evolution.

The cause of human evolution

We come now to the third and most crucial question of all. What causal process drove the evolution of *Homo sapiens*, and (relatedly) what does this tell us of our present state? For the moment, I will look at matters positively, ignoring some of the obvious queries, promising to address them later.

As with the fact and path of human evolution, it must be emphasized that in dealing with the cause of such evolution, we do not start in a vacuum. There is no need to feign ignorance of evolution in general, or of its causes. It is legitimate, and indeed surely proper, to start with the secure knowledge that natural selection is the chief causal force behind organic evolution. The presumption, therefore, must be that selection played a significant causal role in human evolution. And this presumption is undoubtedly well taken if we think of humans at a general physical level, taking features common to them and other animals. Hands, eyes, teeth, and more, all have obvious adaptive value, and clearly were put in place by natural selection.

This is not to say that every human physical feature relates directly to some past or present selective force. Male nipples, for instance, may simply be a side product of other forces and factors. But this is to allow no more than one always allows when looking at the whole organism.

Considered at the physical level, the importance of selection in creating and moulding the human frame cannot be denied.

Nor should you assume that selection working at this level is always a thing of the past. When most of the world goes to bed hungry, the assumption that the human struggle for existence has relaxed its hold on our species is the conceit of a few favoured peoples of the West. In fact, there is good evidence that natural selection has been actively impinging on human physiology in recent history, and there are similarly strong traces of such selection at work today. The interactions between humans and their diseases is a particularly rich lode of illustrative examples.

One striking instance of natural selection bringing about changes in the human genotype, in the past two centuries, comes by courtesy of the rapid urbanization associated with the Industrial Revolution. When large numbers of people moved into the fetid squalor of city slums, the incidence of tuberculosis shot sky high. Many died, having coughed their rotten lungs into tattered shreds. Today, all of this is mainly memory, and without doubt this is due in great part to human effort – drugs, improved sanitation, and the like.

However, there is much to suggest that even before humans themselves launched counter-measures, selection was increasing the natural immunity of our species to the tubercular bacillus. People with a susceptibility to TB – often readily identified as a 'type', with ethereal delicate features – tended to die young. That is, they tended to die before they could reproduce. Health records show that TB rates peaked and then went into significant decline well before we ourselves were able effectively to combat the disease. One can, in fact, plot the peak of TB incidence, as it moved out from Europe, to the East Coast of the USA, and then across that continent to California. This is precisely in accord with the workings of selection (Dobzhansky, 1962).

A paradigmatic example of selection in humans today comes through a kind of mechanism discussed in the first chapter of this book, when I touched on the potential balancing effects of selection. In Africa and other tropical parts of the world, people who get malaria have significantly reduced reproductive chances. However, heterozygous possession of a certain allele confers innate protection against the disease (i.e. when you have one copy of a certain gene-form you are safe). Unfortunately, homozygosity with respect to the malaria-protecting allele (i.e. a double possession of this gene-form) causes a particularly vicious form of anaemia – so-called 'sickle cell' anaemia – because of its distorting effects on the blood cells. This side-effect of malaria protection is invariably fatal in early childhood. Consequently, the sickle-cell allele does not spread through the entire population. Rather, it is held in a balanced state, with the advantage from malarial resistance exactly measuring the disadvantage from childhood anaemia. As unambiguous a case of natural selection as one could want (Allison,

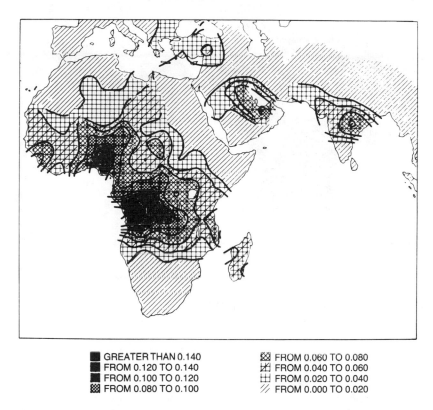

■ GREATER THAN 0.140	▨ FROM 0.060 TO 0.080
■ FROM 0.120 TO 0.140	⊞ FROM 0.040 TO 0.060
■ FROM 0.100 TO 0.120	⊞ FROM 0.020 TO 0.040
▩ FROM 0.080 TO 0.100	∕∕ FROM 0.000 TO 0.020

Figure 4.10 Distribution of haemoglobin-S gene in the Old World: this computer-generated map shows the frequency of the sickle-cell gene *S*. (Courtesy of D. E. Schreiber, IBM Research Laboratory, San Jose.)

1964; Raper, 1960; Livingstone, 1967, 1971; and figures 4.10 and 4.11).

More generally, the indirect effects of balancing and analogous forms of selection working on the human species (at least, until very recently) is confirmed by molecular studies on intra-group variation. *Homo sapiens* is an entirely typical mammalian species. At this level of discussion, if we ourselves did not have a vested interest, there would be no reason to pick out *Homo sapiens* for special attention (Ayala and Valentine, 1979).

So much for our present state. Let us now swing back into the past. The presumption is that natural selection was the significant cause of human evolution. The questions therefore are whether this presumption is consistent with what we know independently of human evolution, and whether we can make plausible hypotheses about the exact nature of the pertinent selective forces – hypotheses which are open to confirmation and extension in the usual ways.

Our independent knowledge of human evolution comes from the

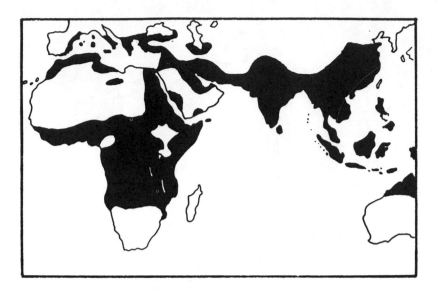

Figure 4.11 Distribution of malaria in the Old World. Note how the spread of the sickle-cell gene matches the malarial-infested parts of the world.

fossil record (as discussed in the last section). Nothing to be learnt in that direction conflicts with a presumption of the key importance of natural selection. I have shown earlier (in chapter 1) how the fossil record cannot really tell us directly about the mechanisms of evolution; but all agree that if selection were a significant force, there should be continuity rather than abrupt change (this being contingent upon a reasonably complete fossil record). In the case of humans, as can be seen from figure 4.7, the record of the past four million years is more than consistent with a path where selection was the leading causal force. It is true that the punctuated equilibria supporters have counter-claimed the record for their position; but, apart from any other difficulties with their view, such an interpretation of the human record is forced, to say the least. *Australopithecus* blends into *Homo*, *Homo erectus* blends into *Homo sapiens*, and so forth.

But if we grant this much, what then caused the evolution of *Homo sapiens*? How could selection have produced such a creature as the human? Until recently, the tendency was to propose an over-reaching hypothesis which would, at one stroke, explain both of those most significant of human features, bipedalism and the large brain (Isaac, 1983). Darwin (1871), for instance, argued that the key causal factor in our past was the use of weapons and tools, and the adaptive advantages thereby conferred. Proto-humans supposedly got up on their back legs to carry things in their hands. At the same time, brains (and consequent intelligence) started to grow, as those who most successfully used their artificial aids out-reproduced those who failed to exploit their new advantages.

However, opinion now has swung away from such a reconstruction, primarily because of the fossil evidence: upright walking occurred at least one or two million years before the brain started to grow. Even though the fossil evidence cannot unaidedly tell us if natural selection of the genes is the primary evolutionary mechanism, given the presumption of selection the record is clearly crucial in testing and inspiring particular causal hypotheses. Today's tendency, therefore, is to divorce the causes of bipedalism from those of brain growth. Unfortunately, this means that the putative causes behind the move to bipedalism must be highly speculative, because direct information is so slight. Perhaps the move was linked to environmental changes, most particularly droughts. These (for which there is independent, geological evidence) would cause a reduction of the aboreal jungle habit of pre-hominids. Consequently, there would be selective advantages to moving from one clump of trees to another, aided by bipedal adaptations like raised eyesight to spot predators and so forth.

The evidence for causal hypotheses explaining our evolution from *Australopithecus afarensis* to *Homo sapiens* is much stronger. The key question centres on the noted great increase in brain-size, and this was presumably linked to ever greater intelligence. But why should there have been such an adaptive premium on intelligence? Unlike the progressionist, the Darwinian has no guarantee that a high IQ is, in itself, an innately good thing. Two related, parallel changes in this period of human pre-history seem to hold the clue.

First, together with the increase in brain power there was a beginning to, and subsequent great development in, the manufacture and use of tools. From primitive chipped stones to sophisticated axes, as we evolved so also did our technological abilities and the artefacts which we produced (Clark, 1977; and figure 4.12). No doubt, there was a feed-back process, as the more intelligent hominid better controlled its environment through its new-found powers, and as such control led to ever greater reproductive success.

Why then was the use of tools so important? Most animals do perfectly well without it. Here, the second change was important. As the brain grew, as tool use improved, proto-human teeth changed from being apelike to the smaller, more 'refined' teeth that we have today. Fortunately, teeth are highly revealing (Wood, 1981). Microscopic examinations of their scratches tell much about diet. It appears from such studies that meat grew ever more important in the proto-human diet. That this should be so is readily understandable, since animal flesh is a valuable source of protein (Bunn, 1981; Potts and Shipman, 1981; and figure 4.13).

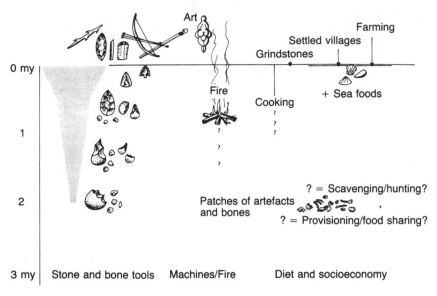

Figure 4.12 The archaeological record. Note how artefacts become more sophisticated as we approach the present. (Reproduced with permission from Isaac, 1983.)

But why was meat not used earlier by other primates? In fact, the chimpanzees are omnivorous, eating smaller animals when they can get them. There has probably long been a willingness to eat meat. Vegetarians who proclaim the unnaturalness of meat-eating may be morally elevated, but they are scientifically (not to mention philosophically) wrong. However, generally, we primates are really not that suited for the life of carnivores. Have you ever tried eating a whole, raw elephant? Unlike lions, for instance, we just do not have the needed weapons of destruction and the ready-made means of devouring our prey. Tools make the regular consumption of meat an immediate possibility. At once, even the weakest of us has a means to rip apart animal flesh into manageable portions, on which we can feast.

It seems likely, therefore, that the growth of brain was linked to diet. The more intelligent hominids were much better able to avail themselves of the large quantities of protein represented by the other animals of the savannah. Most probably, particularly in the early years of our evolution, there was little attempt at systematic hunting. Like jackals and vultures, we were scavengers, living off the kill of others, or eating the carcasses of animals which had died from natural or accidental causes. This is a somewhat less elevating picture than the noble, heroic scenarios that are usually painted for our evolution; but it is a more realistic assessment of the limited skills which our ancestors would have possessed (Isaac, 1978, 1980, 1981).

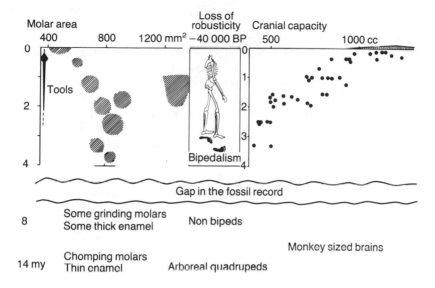

Figure 4.13 Changes in pre-human anatomy over the past 4 million years. Left: teeth and jaws; centre: body and walking patterns (essentially unchanged); right: cranial capacity. (Reproduced with permission from Isaac, 1983.)

Given the move towards meat scavenging and consumption, there would be related selective pressures on hominid social structure. Animal food comes where you find it. Yet there are obvious disadvantages to whole troops of hominids traipsing around, trailing pregnant or nursing women, not to mention small children. More reasonable is a central depot, with men going out for supplies and returning with booty. Thus we get the evolution of co-operation, as men work together to find and fetch meat. Also, there is a premium on strong human sexual bonds, promoting the desire of men to return to mates and children. From a biological perspective, an isolated male is worthless, however full his belly (Lovejoy, 1981).

Why should not females have adopted the male strategy, going off scavenging in their own right? Here, we must remember the long-term childcare demanded by a large-brained primate. This ties females down, who cannot just look to their own interests. However, do not think that selection works in a sexist fashion, making drudges out of mothers, and liberating fathers to a blissful fulfilled lifetime of searching and scavenging. Co-operation and intelligence would be no less important to women. Also, males have an interest in offspring care. At the most basic level, the male proto-human who helped raise his children was more likely to be a successful reproducer than otherwise. In this respect, we humans are like the birds, where males likewise are involved in childcare. We are quite unlike most mammals, where unaided females do virtually everything.

A causal picture of human evolution starts to emerge. No one pretends that it is anything like complete or final. Yet, do not swing to the other extreme, supposing it to be merely the latest fantasy of light-headed palaeoanthropologists, pandering to a gullible public. A story like the one just presented has a great deal of empirical backing, and leads to all kinds of testable predictions. For instance, some of the most important recent fossil discoveries are of distinctive sites which, apparently, were used for long periods of time to cut up and consume meat (Bunn *et al.*, 1980). By studying bone and tool fragments, we can infer much about early hominid diet – what was eaten, how it was eaten, and more. The hypothesis of a home base, where food was brought, grows stronger with every study (figure 4.14). And once this is firmly established, many other parts of the picture start to fall firmly into place. This is especially true, given that today's workers are sensitively aware that their work must be governed by factual discoveries, rather than by an idealized image of a progressive past that we think exhalted beings like ourselves ought to have had (Landau, 1984).

The preliminary conclusion, therefore, is that there is no good reason to deny the importance of natural selection in the evolution of *Homo sapiens*, or to think that our abilities are not biologically advantageous in some broad – but absolutely literal – sense.

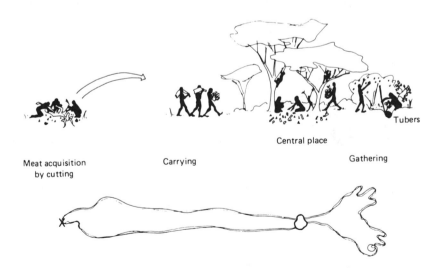

Figure 4.14 A model for the formation of a central site to which food would be brought. We know that stones and meat were brought to such sites, as were probably plant foods. The amount of sharing is hard to judge. (Reproduced with permission from Isaac, 1983.)

The problem of culture

At this point, we can no longer ignore the obvious objection. For the sake of argument, let us suppose that everything that has thus far been said is completely well taken. Let us suppose that the vital role of natural selection in human origins is secure beyond doubt. Nevertheless (runs the objection), virtually all of this is totally irrelevant to the real matter at issue. *Homo sapiens* has been on this earth about 500,000 years – given the gradualness of evolution, the exact point is somewhat arbitrary. Some 100,000 years ago, when the Neanderthals flourished, there were perhaps some very primitive ceremonial practices – possibly a recognition of mortality and deliberate rites associated with it. But there was hardly more. There was little that one would think of as distinctively 'human' (Trinkaus and Howells, 1979). The coming of this had to wait until about 30,000 years ago, when Neanderthal man was abruptly replaced by modern man. Then, virtually overnight, we get much more complex tools, ornaments, cave paintings, and other signs of a being recognizably like ourselves. At last we have a real human – one which has escaped the realm of biology and entered that of *culture*.

Expanding on this point, the critic will probably note that the arrival of culture is clearly bound up with the development of recognizably human language. Also, no doubt, as we entered this new realm, the conscious self-awareness that is the unique possession of our species came into full being – at least, consciousness was probably either cause or consequence of such entry. But surely this all has very great implications for our understanding of ourselves – implications which render otiose virtually all of the biological discussion thus far in this chapter.

Do not misunderstand. No one today wants to pretend that the appearances of culture and related phenomena were uncaused, or to deny that the causes were perfectly natural. There is no supposition that God intervened miraculously or anything like that. If we have immortal souls, then this is beyond the ken of science. Nevertheless, with modern man biology has outgrown itself, and brought about its own irrelevance. Culture clearly has no one-on-one relation with biological advantage, as we expect and find in the non-human world – not to mention the physical world of humans. No one could pretend, for instance, that subscription to a particular scientific or philosophical system makes a ha'porth of difference to adaptive advantage. It is ludicrous to suppose that being a Darwinian rather than a Creationist, a Kantian rather than a utilitarian, has much to do with survival and reproduction.

Moreover, the independence of culture from biology is shown dramatically in the fact that cultural change is very much more rapid than would ever be possible were biology a key causal factor in human nature. To take a much-invoked example, in status as the dominant religion and source of innovation in the West, the rise and fall of Islam took but a handful of generations. In the millenium that the cycle lasted, the genes would have changed barely at all. Natural selection could not have been effective (Allen *et al.*, 1977).

What all of this means is that, in understanding humans today, biology is quite unimportant. Of course, we go to the lavatory because of our biological nature. But when it comes to understanding science or morality, not to mention religion or music or anything else which makes humans truly human, natural selection and the genes tell us nothing. Few want to return to classical Cartesian dualism, but humans as humans – as rational cultural beings – are autonomous. Thus, in the assessment of truth – whether it be in the scientific realm or in the moral realm or wherever – we can and must work, as cultural beings, by the standards of reason and evidence. Biological advantage has nothing to tell us about '2 + 2 = 4', Mendel's laws, or the Greatest Happiness Principle.

This is a powerful argument. However, in the light of what we now know about human evolution, it can no longer be sustained. It is infected with the disease of Spencerian progressionism. In concluding this chapter, I shall show that the humans-are-purely-cultural argument has simply been overtaken by the march of science. This will prepare the way for the philosophical discussions of subsequent chapters. But before turning to detailed scientific analysis, let me make two general comments. These will define the Darwinian's case for the importance for an evolutionary perspective in our understanding of human nature. With clear limits articulated, perhaps we can avoid those dreary misunderstandings which frequently drag out discussions of the biology–culture relationship.

First, as is so often the case with powerful, misleading arguments, there is an important kernel of truth in the culture-as-all-important argument. This holds particularly if you understand 'culture' not so much as denying biology as transcending it. Not even the greatest enthusiast for Darwinian biology could pretend that every last element of culture is tied to biology, as tightly as are (for instance) hands and eyes. I would hope that my own arguments concerning the nature of science (in chapter 2) have established this much. We saw (in the case of science) that the new elements of culture are hardly 'random' in any biological sense. Equally, it is clear that the transmission of cultural elements is not straightforwardly biological. New mutations in biology have to be transmitted through generation, which means that all information has to go, via the gametes (sex cells), into the zygote (that fertilized egg which is the beginning of each new individual). Cultural variants can be passed from one adult phenotype to another (Cavalli-Sforza and Feldman, 1981).

These two differences are clearly major reasons why cultural change is so very much more rapid than biological change. They are why culture is, as it is often said, 'Lamarckian' or (as I would say, in the terms of this book) 'Spencerian'. You get a direction to change, towards the best or right solution to a problem, rather than a random change which may or may not do. And, in a funny sort of way, you get an inheritance of acquired characters. I learn from you a good idea that you thought up, even though this idea did not come to you until you were fully grown. (Remember: in speaking harshly of Spencerianism, I do not deny that science is progressive, even if not in quite his sense. That is the whole point. To all appearances science is progressive. Thus its change cannot be reduced to Darwinism. I am now arguing for a Darwinian approach to humans – one which will, at some point, obviously have to account for the Spencerian nature of cultural change.)

The second general point about biology and culture is as important as the first. Notwithstanding the obvious new elements introduced by culture, nothing as yet denies the importance of biology in a full understanding of culture. On the one hand, let us not dismiss too readily the fact that culture, taken as a whole, does indubitably have a broad adaptive value. Without culture – our ideas, our theories, our technology, our medicine – humans would be a lot less successful as a species than we are now. As one who lives in Canada, I am strongly reminded of this fact from November to April every year. Moreover, the distinctive mechanisms of culture are clearly tied to adaptive advantage. Being able to come up with good ideas as needed, and then to pass them straight on, requires no defence to a Darwinian. This is so, irrespective of whether the critic is right in thinking that biology can say nothing about the choice between (say) Creationism and Darwinism. (Problems like these will be discussed in the next chapter. Here, I simply make the obvious point that a thoughtful attempt at a solution has biological merits over a blind stab. On this point, see Sober, 1981.)

On the other hand, in defending the importance of biology for a full understanding of culture, as always, we should not pretend that we come to the evolution of a new organ or capacity – including even culture – with no background knowledge. Everything we know of evolution suggests continuity and improvisation. Major new organs or capacities simply do not come out of nowhere. They involve modification, expansion, constriction, distortion, and more, of organs and capacities already existing. I emphasize what has been emphasized before. Darwinian evolution is a string and sealing-wax process. You cannot go back to the drawing board and start again. You must work with what you have. The human upper limb – one of the most wonderful adaptations possible – is no more than a transformed fin. As also are all of the other magnificent forelimbs of the vertebrate members of the animal world (look back to figure 1.2).

This does not prove logically that culture cannot be something totally new, with absolutely no roots in the biological past. However, it does surely mean that the onus is upon the person who denies the relevance of Darwinism to culture to prove his or her point. We do not – and should not – address this question with an open mind, meaning a mind with no predispositions. Until proven otherwise, the expectation is that the legacy of our animal past will still be a potent factor in the understanding of our human present.

So much for general points. I admit that culture soars beyond biology, but I suspect its roots are firmly within biology. Can we now be a little more specific? In response to the culture-as-distinctive critic, can we go on to spell out, a little more concretely, exactly how our special human cultural dimension might have evolved through normal biological forces, specifically through the actions of natural selection? And most importantly – particularly, most importantly given our philosophical interests – can we give some fairly specific indications of how our biological heritage actually affects and moulds our thinking and actions in the cultural realm? It is to these two crucially important questions that we must turn, to complete the Darwinian picture of humankind.

The biology of language

For fairly obvious reasons, a full analysis of the evolution of culture – taking this concept in the broadest sense, from thought, through action, custom, and artefact, to beyond – raises horrendous theoretical and methodological questions. We know that *Australopithecus afarensis* walked on its hind two legs; but who knows what it would mean to say that it had already developed a significant component of human culture, for instance a belief in God. And how would we test for such a belief anyway? Restricting and clarifying the problem somewhat, I shall concentrate here on language, and on its physical manifestation, speech.

Some might feel that this choice is to dodge the really crucial issue, namely human consciousness. Unless we explain how this came through natural selection, nothing important has been said. Human culture only takes on meaning in so far as we have a conscious being exploring and understanding its environment. Perhaps this is so. I will take no stand on the matter here, refusing to get side-tracked into a lengthy digression on the full nature of such a slippery notion as consciousness. I suspect, however, that whatever you think is the real essence of being human, whether it be consciousness or something else, you will come fairly shortly to proclaim the importance of language. Presumably, the growth of brain power has at least some link to the growth of consciousness. If the one does not translate directly into the other, what is the extra, needed ingredient? Could it be language?

Many, including many philosophers, certainly think or imply that this is so. Max Black (1968), for instance, asks: 'What, if anything, most clearly distinguishes men from all other animals? What makes men truly human?' (p. 3). His answer:

Man is the only animal that can talk (*homo loquens*). More generally, he is the only animal that can use *symbols* (words, pictures, graphs, numbers, etc.). He alone can bridge the gap between one person and another, conveying thoughts, feelings, desires, attitudes, and sharing in the traditions, conventions, the knowledge and the superstition of his culture: the only animal that can truly *understand* and *misunderstand*. On this essential skill depends everything that we call civilization. Without it, imagination, thought – even self-knowledge – are impossible. (p. 4)

Hence, without necessarily agreeing with those who maintain that language is either a necessary or sufficient condition for consciousness, I will simply rest my choice on the fact that language is undoubtedly a vital factor in human culture as we see it today. If we can link its origins and present nature to biological factors, we have surely made good on one of our major promissory notes. In this claim, we have the support of Descartes, since he saw language-ability as lying right at the heart of our distinctively human nature. (Griffin, 1981, especially chapter 5, has a good discussion of this point. See also Griffin, 1984.)

Are our language abilities a product of natural selection? And, if so, does knowledge of this causal process significantly aid our understanding of our modern selves? Before moving back into our past, let us take a quick look at the way we are today, beginning with the human brain, the centre of thought and action. Since the middle of the nineteenth century, it has been known that there are certain specific areas of the brain directly involved in human linguistic functioning (Geschwind, 1974; 1979). Thanks to various natural experiments – the debilitating effects of tumors and the like – together with the consequences of human surgical interventions, we know that there are two areas of the left half of the cerebral cortex which are primarily responsible for language and speech, their production and their comprehension. Broca's area is crucial in the act of speaking. Defects lead to laborious, inarticulate noises. Wernicke's area is active in the reception of external information, and the production of thoughts. Defects break up the meaning of the language produced (figure 4.15).

Surrounding and connecting these parts of the brain are various other delimitable units, likewise identifiable through natural and other disruptions. Much more remains to be learnt than is yet known; but, already, we can with confidence state that language ability has as firm (and typical) a base in the brain as any other human activity like walking or copulating (Lieberman 1975; 1984). There is nothing disembodied

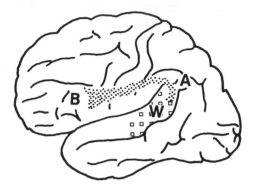

Figure 4.15 Lateral surface of the (left hemisphere) of the human brain. B, Broca's area; W, Wernicke's area; A, arcuate fasciculus, connecting Wernicke's to Broca's area.

about language, in the sense of existing in some purely cultural world with no links to our physical bodies.

Nor, apparently, is a capacity for language something which could (as it were) simply be extracted from the rest of the completed human frame – a capacity for which we were not designed but which, fortuitously, it so happens that we can derive in a secondary manner. In fact, as is the case with many other abilities, it appears that other parts of the brain can often substitute when specific language areas are damaged. However, the language areas are well localized, and by analogy from all we know, this strongly suggests that they were produced by natural selection for today's purpose.

Language has been defined as 'a communications system that is capable of transmitting new information' (Lieberman, 1975, p. 6). This draws attention to its public nature, particularly as it pertains to culture. Language is far more than a lot of private thoughts, produced by the workings of an isolated individual's brain. It involves the ability to speak, transferring information from one being to another. Here, more than anywhere else, we see how strong are the biological roots of our linguistic nature. Speech requires sounds, and at once we are plunged into a classic Darwinian collage of adaptation, modification, and compromise. It has long been known that human speech sounds are produced initially by breath from the lungs, as it passes through and vibrates the larynx. This is anything but a distinctively human organ, for it is a device which evolved initially in fish, for keeping water out of lungs. More recently, it has been used by mammals to prevent food from inadvertently entering the lungs. Only lately has it taken up the new career of sound production. In other words, no less than our forelimbs, our larynx has had a typically varied path down through the years (Negus, 1949 and figure 4.16).

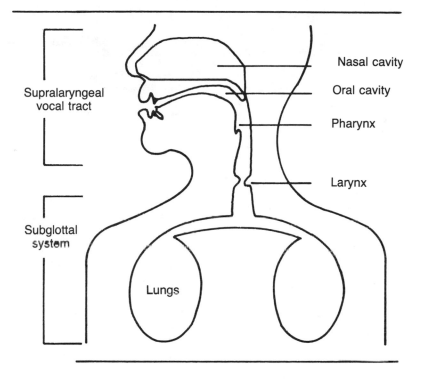

Figure 4.16 The human respiratory system. (Reproduced with permission from Lieberman, 1984.)

This is not all. Anatomical and other studies show clearly that human speech requires more than noise from a vibrating larynx. Of equal importance is the filtering effect on the noise as it comes up the throat, across the tongue, and through the lips (figure 4.17). This produces sounds which we recognize as human. Most crucially, this produces sounds which are extremely stable – they are recognizable by us all, despite the variations in the anatomies and abilities of the individual producers. The adaptive significance of all of this needs no defence. Speech would be useless if we all produced our own distinctive sounds, and if no one else could recognize them.

The human supralaryngeal vocal tract is a perfect instance of natural selection working, in its usual make-do fashion, and arriving at a certain end – in this case, stable, usable speech. If you compare us with the apes, you can see at once that, although they have a larynx which can (and indeed does) function to produce sounds, the elongated pharynx is entirely missing. They simply cannot speak in the way that we can (compare figures 4.18 and 4.19). Our speech abilities require special

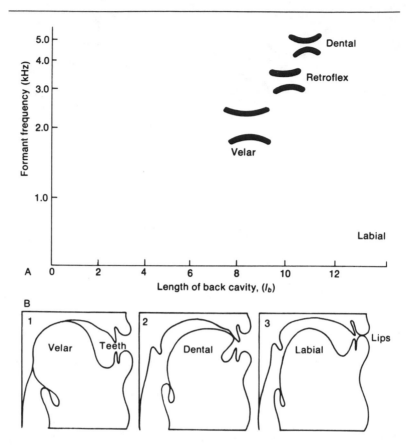

Figure 4.17 'Quantal' spectral energy concentrations that occur as the constriction shifts to various points along the supralaryngeal vocal tract. Sketches for the velar, dental, and labial consonantal articulations that occur in English are also shown. (Reproduced with permission from Lieberman, 1984.)

organs, which we alone have. However, anatomy also shows that there are very good reasons to think that the human vocal tract does not just exist accidentally, perhaps as the by-product of other selective forces. In respects, it is highly maladaptive, and thus there must be strong biological forces keeping it in place. With the kind of throat that we humans have, it is all too easy for food to 'go down the wrong way', that is, into the lungs, and to choke us. Even today, selection keeps up a fairly vigorous campaign against this aspect of our anatomy, as every steak-house-restaurant owner knows, only too well. We have just the kind of trade-off which the Darwinian expects, as an organ produced for one end is turned, not altogether efficiently, to other purposes.

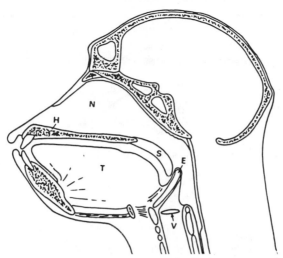

Figure 4.18 Cross-section of the head of an adult chimpanzee: *N*, nasal cavity; *H*, hard palate; *S*, soft palate, *E*, epiglottis; *T*, tongue; *V*, vocal cords of larynx. (Adapted with permission from Laitman and Heimbuch, 1982.)

Physically, therefore, the evidence is strong that biology is important in the production and communication of language. This point is confirmed by numerous other pieces of evidence, for instance about how we learn language, how we hear speech, and so forth (Brown, 1973). Every adolescent who has sat through the grinding boredom of foreign-language classes fully appreciates how quickly the natural ability to learn language fades. Like geese, we seem to have an early-childhood period of imprinting receptivity, when we can soak up a language. Obviously, such a talent is highly adaptive. Then, when the value fades, so does the ability. Even educators are now realizing that language training cannot be postponed until high school.

Switching now from our physical states to specific languages in themselves, already there is the strong presumption that not any old kind of language will do for humans. Imagine if we all tried to speak in sentences as German philosophers write them. We would die of asphixiation before we ever got to the verbs. The primary purpose of the lungs is breathing, not speaking (Negus, 1949). Sentences must be reasonably short and crisp. But this starts to push us beyond semantics (the reference of words) to syntax (the structure of sentences). It is necessary to combine several ideas into one sentence, otherwise language would become incredibly prolix, as every thought had to be spelled out separately. Analogously, the limited number of stable sounds puts constraints on the possible ranges and natures of language. Subtle syntax is required to avoid ambiguity.

Fortunately, there is no need to labour this point. Thanks to the work

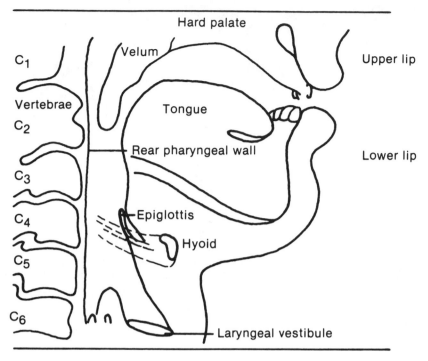

Figure 4.19 Midsagittal view of the adult human supralaryngeal vocal tract. (Reproduced with permission from Lieberman, 1984.)

of Noam Chomsky (1957, 1965, 1966) and other linguists, there is growing recognition that languages, and the way they are learnt, are far from random or arbitrary. Chomsky himself argues that all human languages possess basic underlying ground plans – 'deep phrase structures' (figure 4.20). These are then brought to the surface, into the actual words and sentences which we use, by a restructuring device – a 'transformational grammar or syntax'. What attracts the attention of the biologist is the suggestion that the deep structures of quite distinct human languages are strikingly similar (Wilson, 1975). This supports the implications of the physical evidence, namely that the very form of human language is bound by shared biological constraints. If biology plays no role, then as with transient cultural epiphenomena, one looks for variation and change.

Chomsky's work is controversial. I refer to it, not as definitive support in itself, but in illustration of a growing tendency among linguists to propose theories which invite a biological underpinning. It must be admitted that, in Chomsky's own case, although he posits an innate biological component to language, he himself is far from an enthused Darwinian. Rather, he subscribes more to a saltationist view of change, believing language to have come uniquely to humans, through special

RULES OF PHRASE STRUCTURE GRAMMAR

1. SENTENCE ⟶ NOUN PHRASE + VERB PHRASE
2. NOUN PHRASE ⟶ ARTICLE + NOUN
3. VERB PHRASE ⟶ VERB + NOUN PHRASE
4. ARTICLE ⟶ <u>the</u>, <u>a</u>
5. NOUN ⟶ <u>man</u>, <u>dog</u>, <u>leash</u>
6. VERB ⟶ <u>walked</u>

TREE OF PHRASE STRUCTURES

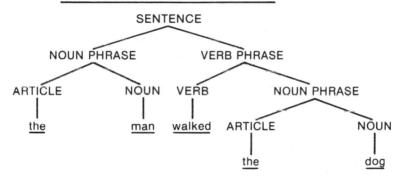

Figure 4.20 An example of the working of the rules of phrase structure grammar in English. The simple sentence 'The man walked the dog' consists of a hierarchy of phrases. Substitution of phrases is allowed but the phrases cannot be split, nor can their elements be interchanged.

organs, more or less entire (Chomsky, 1980a, 1980b). In the light of the physical evidence already introduced, such a stance is implausible. But in arguing as he does, Chomsky directs us to ask if there is support for a Darwinian picture of language-ability evolution. If natural selection was crucially involved in the evolution of language, then change would have been gradual rather than abrupt. Is there evidence which favours such a conclusion?

This sends us back to the fossil record (Laitman, 1983; Laitman *et al.*, 1979; Lieberman, 1984). Unfortunately, language *per se* leaves little trace. Thus, we need to focus more on its physical expression, namely speech. Happily, when we do this, we find strong indications that evolution occurred very much in the way one would suppose if natural selection were the prime evolutionary factor. Reconstructing the shape of the vocal passage from skulls, we find that, up to *Homo sapiens*, the passage was much as one encounters in today's apes. Then, we get a gradual lengthening of the supralaryngeal tract, until some 30,000 years ago the modern human form was fully developed. This coincides with the beginning of the explosive growth of human culture. Most significantly, the newly born human does not have such a lengthened passage (Laitman, 1983). Obviously, the infant does not need the passage, and given its selective liabilities one would not have expected it to have evolved.

Actually, the story of human-speech-capacity evolution is more complex and interesting than one of straight unilinear development to the present. It appears now that *Homo sapiens* tried alternative strategies. One group, the Neanderthals, kept their apelike vocal system and evolved stronger and more efficient teeth and jaws (Lieberman and Crelin, 1971). Thus these were well adapted for the consumption of tough, fibrous vegetables, as well as of other foods. The other group, our ancestors, went the way of articulate speech. With the full development of the supralaryngeal tract, communication and acquired information started to build. Eventually, the speaking-humans quite out-reproduced the Neanderthals, who thus went extinct (figure 4.21).

But there was nothing magical about what occurred. Neanderthals succeeded very well for a long time, and were certainly a lot less prone to choking than we. It was just that our ancestors reached the point where they were incredibly more efficient than any other human form (Laitman and Heimbuch, 1982; Lieberman, 1984). Then, they were all-conquering. This is how Darwinian evolution works. Competition is always strongest between those most alike. They want to occupy the same ecological niche.

Ape language

The case for the Darwinian evolution of language is nearly complete. There is one final step back that we must take. Suppose some stubborn critic objected that, by switching from language to speech (as we just did), we lay ourselves open to fatal objection. Perhaps early *Homo sapiens*, or some other hominid, jumped suddenly (from nowhere) to the point of human-language ability, which then took years of selection to bring to fruition in speech and subsequent culture. Hence, all of the fossil evidence for the evolution of speech, although most interesting, is irrelevant. (Given the maladaptive nature of human-speech ability, I take it that no one would claim that speech ability predated language ability.)

I would hope that, by now, this kind of counter-hypothesis is looking increasingly implausible and *ad hoc*. How are we supposed to believe that the relevant parts of the brain appeared? Why should language-ability have a non-selective origin, when its full exploitation as human speech was tightly controlled by selection? But, taking the objection seriously as a foil to our own exposition, let us complete the evidential picture of the evolution of language.

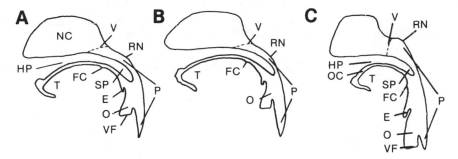

Figure 4.21 Outlines of supralaryngeal vocal tracts of today's humans and reconstructed Neanderthal drawn to same size: A, Newborn human; B, La Chapelle-aux-Saints fossil; C, adult human. NC, Nasal cavity; V, vomer bone; RN, roof of nasopharynx; P, pharynx; HP, hard palate; SP, soft palate; OC, oral cavity; T, tip of tongue; E, epiglottis; O, opening of larynx into pharynx; VF, level of vocal cords; FC, foramen cecum. (Adapted with permission from Lieberman and Crelin, 1971.)

The Darwinian expects that language would have its roots well back in our pre-cultural, pre-human-speech, early hominid (or pre-hominid) existence; that, in its early stage, language would be very much more primitive than it is now; but that such language would nevertheless have obvious adaptive value, pointing towards yet greater value as it grew stronger. Even without proper speech, cruder methods of communication could serve the ends of survival and reproduction. Presumably, this occurred right up to *Homo sapiens*, when the rapid evolution of the supralaryngeal system unlocked a vast, hitherto unsuspected, potential. (Perhaps one should rather say that the rapid evolution made possible far more efficient use of a faculty which already was proving its selective worth.)

Since we cannot test *Australopithecus* or *Ramapithecus*, we have to do the next best thing and turn to our nearest cousins, the living great apes. Their brain size is more or less what it was when the hominid split occurred. Brain size is not the sole determining factor of intellectual ability. But if the apes do show genuine, albeit primitive signs of language ability, the case for a similar early hominid ability is made stronger. To deny this is to presume that our joint ancestors had no such abilities, and that apes and humans independently developed them. If nothing else, extant rudimentary linguistic ability shows it to be a possible stage in human evolution.

As is only too well known, there have been few more controversial areas of study in recent years than that of ape language. Wild and enthusiastic claims for its possibility and actuality have been staked, and equally wild and ferocious objections have been lodged. (See, for example, for some positive assessments Gardner and Gardner, 1969; Savage-Rumbaugh, Rumbaugh and Boysen 1978, 1980; Premack, 1972; and Premack and Woodruff, 1978; and for the other viewpoint Terrace, 1979, 1983; Terrace *et al.*, 1979; Gardner, 1980; and Sebeok and Umiker-Sebeok, 1980. de Luce and Widder, 1983, is a balanced overview collection.)

What cannot be denied is that a great deal of time and effort has been wasted in trying to teach apes that which they cannot do (such as speaking like us). Also, much trouble has been caused by undetected artefacts of experiments. Notorious is the distortion of the 'Clever Hans' effect, where a human unsuspectingly cues his/her animal subject (Rosenthal, 1965; Sebeok and Umiker-Sebeok, 1979). Fortunately, work in the last decade has been much more cautious and sophisticated than previously. Great pains are taken to avoid the troubles which marred earlier attempts to teach apes language, and just as much effort is directed towards assessment of apes' innate capacities for a linguistic mode of thought. Hence, given our own interests, we can today turn more confidently to the work of primatologists.

Most noteworthy and impressive are the efforts and results of workers at the Yerkes Regional Primate Research Center, who have tried to teach their chimpanzees an artificial language, 'Yerkish' (Rumbaugh, Savage-Rumbaugh and Scanlon, 1982). This system uses geometric symbols, 'lexigrams', to stand for particular items, and effort has been directed towards seeing if and how far chimpanzees can grasp the meaning of such symbols or 'words'. Thus, the emphasis has been on semantics rather than syntax although, in early stages of the study, it became clear that chimpanzees could combine their symbols to make sentences (or if you prefer, 'sentences'). Look after semantics, and the syntax will look after itself.

The key issue in the study of ape semantic capacity, became that of 'symbolic representation'. Apes can easily learn to associate symbols with objects. (As of course can many other animals. My dog associates his lead with walks.) The question is whether the apes can, as it were, use the symbols to think abstractly. Can they use the symbols when the objects are not around? Can they pass information to others? Can they check back that others have got the information? And so forth.

It appears that any given instance of true linguistic representation involves, at a minimum, four components.

1 An arbitrary symbol that stands for, and can serve in lieu of, a real object, event, person, action, or relationship.
2 A common or shared knowledge among animals regarding the action, objects, and relationships relating to that symbol (though this stored knowledge may not be completely identical for all users).
3 The use of that symbol to convey knowledge or information from one

animal to another who has similar real-world experiences and who has related them to the same symbol system.

4 The appropriate decoding of, and response to, the symbol by the recipient. (Rumbaugh *et al.*, 1982, p. 373)

A number of subtle tests were therefore devised to see if chimpanzees really are capable of mastering true linguistic representation, in the terms just given. And the answer strongly suggests that they are.

For instance, in one experiment, having been taught the different generic symbols for food and tool, the chimpanzees were asked to categorize symbols for specific foods and tools, even though they had never previously been taught to associate these specific items with the general terms. Thus, having been taught that 'food' goes with bread and potatoes, and that 'tool' goes with hammer and wrench, they were asked to categorize banana and ruler. The chimpanzees performed surprisingly well in this and related experiments, thereby showing that they really were working at a general abstract level. They were not using lexigrams as associated tags, but as representational labels. In some sense, they knew the meanings of the terms with which they were working (figure 4.22).

The Yerkes researchers write:

[W]e believe that the chimpanzees' behaviors are compelling us to reintroduce such words as *intention* and *imagination*. Chimpanzees give evidence of symbolic intentionality, we believe, when the following behaviors are observed:

1 When they linguistically announce what it is that they are about to do and then do it.
2 When they quite obviously time the appropriateness of their requests to enhance the prospects of others complying with them.
3 When they express their requests in a wide variety of ways to 'make their point'.
4 When, in communication, they stop and check to determine whether the animals about them have taken note of their communication and have altered their behavior to reflect compliance or harmony with them.
5 When one chimpanzee literally intervenes in the behavioral pattern of another and declares its termination. (Rumbaugh *et al.*, 1982, p. 382).

But, enthusiasm aside, what do findings and results like this really mean? What they certainly do not mean is that chimpanzees can have a full language, if only one presses the right buttons. However impressive the achievements, they are limited. No chimpanzee is yet writing a poem, even about food and tools! Nevertheless, the findings do surely bring comfort to the Darwinian evolutionist. Language apparently is not an all-or-nothing phenomenon. It is something which can come in degrees, existing in lesser degree in today's apes than in today's

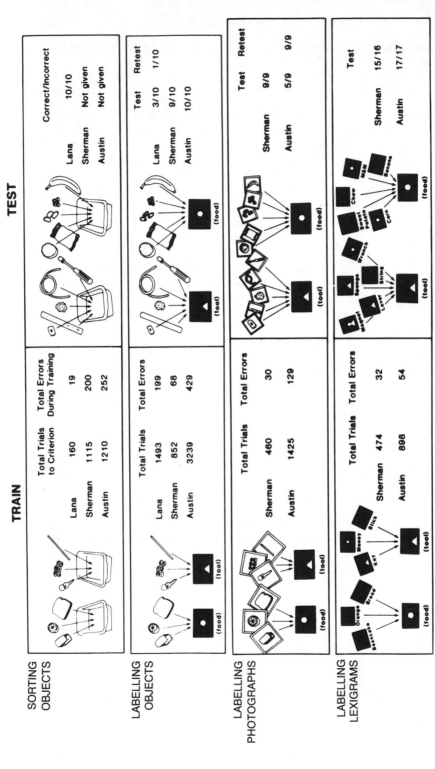

Figure 4.22 Animals were trained with items on the left and then tested with items on the right. Special care was taken not to cue the animals inadvertently. (Reproduced with permission from Rumbaugh *et al.*, 1982.)

humans, with clear implications for the putative linguistic abilities of our early hominid ancestors.

> The range of ape capacities is not completely known at present. It is clear, however, that it is a much closer approximation of human beings' than we have held it to be in the past. It now appears certain that the ape (not necessarily to the exclusion of other life forms) has carried through its own evolutionary history many of the behavioral processes and potentials in which lay the very foundation for the linguistic competence of modern human beings. (Rumbaugh *et al.*, 1982, p. 383)

Given their obvious relevance to our enquiry, I shall later be looking at other studies into ape capacities for thought and behaviour. Here, with this discussion of chimpanzees and their linguistic abilities, the case for the Darwinian evolution of human language is now complete. Let me sum up, putting together the elements of our story, filling gaps and weaving a whole.

If language (including speech) is produced by Darwinian factors, that is by natural selection, one looks for a gradual growth brought about by such selection. That language does seem to have a primitive origin is supported by studies of the linguistic abilities and capacities of apes, particularly chimpanzees. That even such crude abilities and capacities nevertheless have adaptive value needs no argument: the beast who could think conceptually, grasping universals, outreproduced its cousin who could not. Nor is argument needed for the claim that language-abilities improvement would be favoured by selection.

The evidence from brain growth and tool use and the like is that more complex and sophisticated language abilities were probably part of a package deal, as our ancestors increased the general power of their intellectual capacities. This increase was gradual, not saltationary. *Australopithecus* and early *Homo* would communicate by making sounds, as well as through body gestures. But, although adaptively important, by our standards such means of communication would be crude. Speech as we know it required special modifications, and these are recent – within the span of our being *Homo sapiens*. Again the evidence is that selection was involved, as it was in the alternative evolution and ultimate demise of our fellow species' mates, the Neanderthals.

Culture was contingent on the development of modern speech. Although it obviously goes beyond biology, it grows from it and (*qua* language) is embedded in it. Our thought today, and its physical expression, is constrained and shaped by the biological engineering which goes into the making of a functioning human being. Everything points to the conclusion that the designer of this being was not a master planner, but natural selection.[2]

[2] See Walker, 1983, for an excellent, comprehensive discussion of animal thought which stresses the continuities so important to the Darwinian thesis.

Is culture independent of biology?

This completes the first part of the response to the humans-are-unique-because-of-their-culture critic. By anyone's standards, language is surely a major factor in what makes humans distinctive. Yet the scientific evidence is strong for its Darwinian origins and underpinning. I speak English rather than French because my parents spoke English rather than French. I use Americanisms which make my father want to disown me because I have lived in North America for over twenty years. My vocabulary includes new technical terms, like 'sociobiology', or new slang terms, like 'Yuppie', because I can pick them up, despite my advancing years. But underlying and informing all of this is the idiosyncratic biology of my species: *Homo sapiens*.

The time has come to move on to the second promised part of the response. Resisting the temptation merely to dig more and more deeply into language, I aim more broadly. I look now for an overall Darwinian perspective on thought and action, seeking clues to general biological influences on our thinking about the nature of the physical world and about the rules of proper conduct. The evolution of language, therefore, serves as a model, a guide, and a starting-point, rather than as an end in itself. Countering the critic, I argue that Darwinian factors inform and infuse the whole of human experience, most particularly our cultural dimension.

What sort of model is language? What does it suggest as the overall nature of culture, and how does it imply that this will relate back to our biology? Fairly obviously, in line with the general points made earlier, it guides us towards a central position, between the extremes where biology is all-important and where biology plays no role at all. We are not genetically programmed to speak English, rather as some birds innately sing their own species' songs. But neither is biology irrelevant, as it undoubtedly is for an electronic synthesizer. We modern humans are as we are, and not as Neanderthals, because of the adaptive virtues of our sophisticated language and speech.

What is the nature of the middle-line position emerging here? In theory, there are two broad possibilities. On the one hand, there is the

---

And this, despite the fact that Walker is somewhat less enthused by work on ape language than I. Like Walker, I argue that our knowledge of the brain and its development should be stressed rather more than has been the case in the discussions of many Darwinians (for instance, Dawkins, 1976, and Wilson, 1978; although Lumsden and Wilson, 1983, make more of the brain and its significance). Griffin (1981, 1984) also stresses the natural origins of thought and language, although (agreeing with Walker) I feel somewhat uncomfortable with the ease with which he switches to us from animals very different.

view endorsed by many, including (in his later, more philosophical writings) the great American pragmatist William James. Here, we recognize the general biological significance of culture, but as far as possible divorce the actual content of culture from the control of the genes. Basically, the human mind is taken as a *tabula rasa*. Humans can learn (and act upon) virtually anything, irrespective of its adaptive value. Selection comes into play after ideas have been adopted, wiping out those unfortunates who have endorsed maladaptive notions. To take an example: we can as well learn and believe that snakes are man's best friend, as that snakes are dangerous for human well-being. However, herpetophiles unlike herpetophobes would tend not to survive and reproduce. Analogously with other beliefs. Thus, as time has gone by, our culture has been infused with a number of adaptive premises (see Campbell, 1974, for references to this kind of position).

On the other hand, we have the view where the genes play a stronger role in human affairs. Here, it is supposed that the genes make you believe certain things (or act on certain beliefs), because it is biologically advantageous for you so to believe. The environment, in the guise of parents and educators and other impinging factors, can fill in various of the details: but the genes set firm limits on your thought patterns. You may perhaps learn to distinguish between very dangerous snakes, and those which are less poisonous: but you are born with an innate fear of all creepy-crawly beasties. (As we shall learn, this position is akin to that endorsed by the early William James.)

Deciding between these middle-ground alternatives is not easy. And indeed, do note that they are not really stark disjunct options. You could certainly believe that the influence of the genes is indirect, working through contingent environmental factors. Suppose, for instance, one foodstuff is far better for you than another, say milk rather than Coca-Cola. Genetically, we might be equally receptive to either. However, it might be the case that, in childhood, we are susceptible to imprinting for desirable/undesirable tastes. Also, it so happens, for various obvious reasons, that in our early years we are more likely to drink milk rather than Coke. Thus, as adults we have a fixed adaptive preference for milk rather than Coke. This has been caused by the genes, although there are no 'milk-preferring' and 'Coke-preferring' alleles. (This is obviously a pretend example, given that many people cannot digest milk, and that many adults love Coke.)

Positive argument, backed by examples, is more impressive than mere criticism. But there are general evolutionary reasons, not to mention the specific case of language, which point away from the purely environmentalist option. Even if culture takes us beyond biological Darwinism, it must be consistent with it. And yet, from a general Darwinian perspective, to suppose that culture sits in isolation on top of the genes makes for both inefficiency and danger. A *tabula rasa* mind demands a brain with a great deal of useless capacity (Lumsden and Wilson, 1983;

Ruse and Wilson, 1986). We would need the ability to believe all sorts of things which are, biologically speaking, completely crazy, and which one would hope we never would believe. Such total receptivity probably requires a cranial capacity several times larger than the one we now possess. This requirement makes the hypothesis highly improbable. Natural selection is inefficient, but it tends not to be this profligate.

The environmentalist option would be inefficient also in our having to learn all sorts of things in each generation which could as readily be passed along encoded within the genotype. And it would be dangerous, in that one or two wild thoughts could steer you straight into maladaptive oblivion. This, more than anything, should make you wary of the environmentalist position. One of the most striking things about natural selection is the extent to which it prizes a certain innate conservativism. It is well known that you often get substantial genetic change, with little corresponding effect on the phenotype (Dobzhansky, 1970). If a particular form is working well, there is a strong adaptive advantage in not being disturbed by every stray mutation. A balance has to be struck between the advantages and dangers of change.

Such caution is no less important for culture, granting (what we are now granting) an adaptive connection. Potential for rapid, innovative change may be highly adaptive. To have no safeguards is biologically stupid. And yet, this would be the case, if culture were perched on the backs of the genes. Of course, I am not denying that sometimes people do have crazy thoughts, ending their biological fitness. The Shakers, who were totally celibate, spring at once to mind. Selection never guarantees that everything works all of the time. Rather, that we can usually muddle through. The power of culture compensates for its dangers.

These general points about the implausibility of the culture-on-top-of-the-genes option are backed by the specific example of language. It is not divorced from the genes. Rather, it is deeply embedded in, and moulded by, biology. The ape evidence points this way. There seem to be innate capacities for using universals, and so forth. The physiological evidence points this way. The mechanics of breathing and of making appropriate sounds put all kinds of constraints on language. Real, living languages point this way. The very structures of English and French suggest unlearned basic patterns. And more. Only by turning your back on a massive amount of empirical research can you deny the direct imput of biological causal factors.

Everything, therefore, directs us towards the other middle-road option on the relationship between biology and culture: that that which we think and do is structured by our biology, meaning our genes, as fashioned by natural selection. But there are others who have reached this point before us. Most particularly, in recent years such a vision of human nature has been ardently championed by one of the evolutionists whose ideas we have already encountered. Edward O. Wilson concedes that 'the genes have given away much of their sovereignty'. Yet he insists that 'the genes hold culture on a leash' (1978, p. 176). Hence, concluding my discussion of human evolution, completing the case against the culture-is-distinctive critic, I shall turn briefly to his most recent and detailed thinking on the subject.

Epigenetic rules

Central to Wilson's perspective on human nature, and the culture to which it gives rise and within which it is embedded, is the notion of an 'epigenetic rule'. This is a constraint which obtains on some facet of human development, having its origin in evolutionary needs, and channelling the way in which the growing or grown human thinks and acts. In *Genes, Mind and Culture*, a work co-authored with a young physicist, Charles Lumsden, Wilson characterizes epigenetic rules in the following formal manner:

> Any regularity during epigenesis that channels the development of an anatomical, physiological, cognitive, or behavioral trait in a particular direction. Epigenetic rules are ultimately genetic in basis, in the sense that their particular nature depends on the DNA developmental blueprint . . . In cognitive development, the epigenetic rules are expressed in any one of the many processes of perception and cognition to influence the form of learning and the transmission of [units of culture]. (Lumsden and Wilson, 1981, p. 370)[3]

Elaborating, a division is made between so-called 'primary rules' and so-called 'secondary rules'. The former are at the receiving end, as raw information comes into the human organism. The latter then go on to process this information, in ways that are adaptively useful to us as biological beings. Examples will show the scope and power of these rules.

An important primary epigenetic rule is at work when we humans classify colours. Although the wave-length of light varies continuously, we tend not to perceive it continuously. And this, despite the fact that luminance is perceived continuously, reflecting what science tells us is its true nature. Apparently, unconsciously, we break colours up into four basic categories – blue, green, yellow, and red (Bornstein, Kessen and Weiskopf, 1976; Bornstein, 1979). We do this even as infants, and carry the practice through to adulthood. Thus we are led to have precise names for the categories. Our terms are not arbitrarily chosen, nor is the

---

[3] There does seem some ambiguity here between process and product: the development of the organism and the end result. I will emphasize the product – the constraints on thought and action.

fact that we consider these categories to be our major colours (unlike, say, indigo). The words and feelings reflect our perceptual divisions.

The primary epigenetic rule at work here, one transforming our perception of colour, is the common heritage of all humans. People of radically different cultures, thinking quite unrelated languages, use much the same classificatory schema.

> The epigenetic constraints in colour perception are reflected in the verbal color classifications employed in the languages of all cultures thus far studied . . . [Native] speakers of twenty languages around the world (which included Arabic, Bulgarian, Cantonese, Catalan, Hebrew, Ibidio, Japanese, Thai, Tzeltal, Urdu, and others) were shown arrays of chips classified by color and brightness in the Munsell system. They were asked to place each of the principal color terms of their language within this two-dimensional array. The results . . . show clearly that the languages have evolved in a way that conforms closely to the epigenetic rules of color discrimination. The terms fall into largely discrete clusters that correspond, at least in an approximate manner, to the principal colors that appear to be innately distinguished by infants. This central result has been subsequently confirmed by many investigators . . . (Lumsden and Wilson, 1981, pp. 45–6)

Obviously, this underlines the way in which all humans process visual information, received according to channelling constraints. (See also Berlin and Kay, 1969; Rosch, 1973; and figure 4.23.)

What evidence is there that the genes play a role in the perception of colour just described? The species-wide nature of the phenomenon hints at genetic control. Purely environmental factors tend to vary from culture to culture. More concretely, there is growing evidence that colour perception is rooted in the actual physiology of the eye – the various colour cones of the retina mirror the basic colour types (Wald, 1969). Additionally, there are pertinent differences in the nerve cells responsible for the transmission of colour information to the visual cortex of the brain. Also, experiments on animals show that colour sensitivity is strongly controlled by the genes. This is backed by 'natural experiments' on humans, particularly those resting on various kinds of colour blindness caused by genetic defects (Stern, 1973).

What is the adaptive significance of such innate colour discrimination? In the case of most of the as yet explored primary rules, the significance is fairly obvious. For instance, parallel to colour perception is a striking categorizing of tastes, with humans discriminating and much preferring sweet over sour tastes (Maller and Desor, 1974). Those of our would-be ancestors who had such taste discrimination had a clear adaptive advantage. Ripe fruits, honey, and the like are more nutritious than unripe fruits, acids, and so forth. The last thing you want is a being which is quite indifferent as to what enters its mouth.

The case of colour is harder to explain. However, perhaps guidance

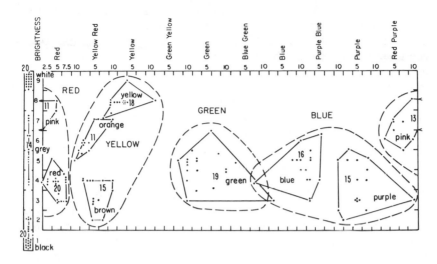

Figure 4.23 How our language reflects the primary epigenetic rules of colour classification. The points mark the positions of colour terms of various cultures as estimated by native speakers. The discrete clusters that result suggest that all people interpret the visual world in a distinctive shared fashion. (Reproduced with permission from Lumsden and Wilson, 1981.)

here can be sought from our fellow primates. As a rule, mammals are not that sensitive to colour. In this, they stand strikingly opposed to birds, whose bright plumages used for sexual display rival the gaudiest of artist's canvasses. The mammalian insensitivity probably reflects the fact that, for most of their existence, mammals were nocturnal beings, with little need for colour discrimination. Primates are much above the mammalian-average in such discrimination (Fobes and King, 1982).

One therefore suspects that our shared capacity with the birds points to our shared history and needs. Most primates, like most birds, spend much of their time among the trees, and are most active in the daytime. Consequently, they have adaptations for such aboreal life, including abilities to estimate distances, and so forth (Riesen, 1982). Colour perception is probably part of this adaptive complex, although the precise details and uses have not yet been fully established. Whatever is the complete truth, the human perception of colour may well be primarily a legacy of our primate past, rather than something of immediate adaptive value.

The much-discussed phenomenon of human incest barriers, particularly those between siblings, provides us with a good instance of a secondary epigenetic rule (Alexander, 1979; Fox, 1980; Shepher, 1979; van den Berghe, 1979, 1983). Human beings, with rare exceptions, put up barriers between those who have the greatest opportunities to copulate and reproduce: close relatives. Sometimes (although not invariably) these barriers are backed by formal taboos. But whatever the nature of the gap, explicit or implicit, close family relationships spell the decline of sexual desire. Moreover, in the case where sexual opportunities most readily present themselves, namely between siblings, the decline is greatest. Even in those rare instances where sibling unions are permitted (or obligatory), nature takes a hand. For special economic or political reasons it may be advantageous to keep marriage within the family; but the respective proportions of illegitimate to legitimate births show that people simply do not care to have sex with siblings. Human nature just does not work that way.

Why? Building on an insight of the nineteenth century anthropologist Edward Westermarck (1891), Wilson and Lumsden suggest that a secondary epigenetic rule keeps relatives, especially brothers and sisters, from each other's beds. There are very good evolutionary reasons why close inbreeding is a very bad thing. Progeny from close unions tend to be horrendously physically handicapped (Seemanova, 1971). This is because most deleterious alleles are recessive (i.e. show no effects unless they are paired homozygously) – in major part, because a maladaptive mutant usually involves the blocking of manufacture of some substance, and because one functioning allele in a pair can unaided create enough of the desired substance for successful living. Hence, there has been massive selection against close inbreeding. Thus, we now have a secondary epigenetic rule against incestuous links with close relatives, especially siblings.

The incest example shows beautifully how the biology/culture relationship being sketched here does not necessarily suppose 'hard wiring' throughout by the genes. Reality mimics the pretend-example I gave earlier of milk/Coke preferences. There is no automatic genetic mechanism which makes us repulse on sight the sexual advances of siblings, simply because they are siblings. Indeed, it is hard to see exactly how such a mechanism might work, except perhaps with some fairly complex system of chemical signals ('pheromones'). And the trouble here is that humans have become relatively insensitive to chemical modes of perception.

The action of the genes is indirect. In childhood, humans seem to go through a kind of negative imprinting phase. If you are brought up with another person in a sibling relationship – 'share the same potty' – then, psychologically, you are turned off them sexually when you reach adulthood. This is shown most clearly by human 'experiments', where nature is fooled. For instance, on the kibbutzim, biologically unrelated children are raised as if they were all part of one family. Although there are no barriers to sex and to intermarriage between children thus raised, such couplings and unions never occur. There is simply no heterosexual activity of any kind. And this is despite the fact that the children of kibbutzim families feel strong emotional bonds – just as is felt by normal siblings (Shepher, 1979).

In short, when it comes to sexual relations with others, humans seem to be channelled by their biology into certain fixed paths of thinking and behaving. The genes work indirectly on us as we mature. Normally, social siblings are biological siblings. Hence, the desired adaptive epigenetic rule is put into place: 'Stay away from the family!' (Strictly speaking, what is put into place is a special kind of inclination to avoid incest. How this is articulated takes us into culture. I shall speak more on this point later.)

These two examples of epigenetic rules backed by an evergrowing list of like rules – many of which will be presented in the following chapters – bring my case to an end. In the light of Darwinian evolutionary theory, the humans-as-beyond-biology thesis was never that plausible. Now, I suggest, is the time to leave it entirely. Human culture, meaning human thought and action, is informed and structured by biological factors. Natural selection and adaptive advantage reach through to the very core of our being. And the link between our genes and our culture is the epigenetic rule.

Conclusion

We have pushed right up to the frontier of our subject. We stand at the boundary of the evolutionary understanding of humankind. In fact, based on their thinking about epigenetic rules, Wilson and Lumsden have formulated highly mathematical models of how human cultures might change, and what effect such changes could have on human genotypes (Lumsden and Wilson, 1981). However, it is not necessary for us now to comment on the worth of such gene/culture 'coevolutionary' speculations. The bare notion of an epigenetic rule will let us make a good start on the epistemological and ethical questions which are at the core of our enquiry.

Let us therefore turn back from science to philosophy, taking with us the message of this chapter. A Darwinian approach to humankind demands recognition that our culture is not some special disembodied phenomenon – a Cartesian-like substance – isolated from our animal bodies. Culture is the flesh on a biological skeleton, and the bones are epigenetic rules, controlled by the genes and fashioned by selection. The question now is whether we can carry the argument forward, showing that Darwinism is relevant to life's most fundamental questions. As a naturalist, I believe that success in our enquiry will rebound to the credit and support of the scientific picture of humankind presented in this chapter. But now, my attention turns again to philosophy.

5

Darwinian Epistemology

The Darwinian theory of evolution through natural selection, taken literally, throws important light on the status of knowledge. By this I mean that it can advance us in the kinds of concerns about knowledge that have traditionally absorbed philosophers. As before, I take scientific knowledge as my paradigm; but I expect my conclusions to have consequences for knowledge of all kinds.

At one level, given the general implications of the last chapter, the programme which I contemplate seems almost trivially true. At another level, it seems even more trivially false. As noted, virtually no one will deny that human culture is biologically adaptive in some broad sense, and this applies particularly to science and technology. Think of the coming of fertilizers, or of efficient transportation, or of new drugs, and of how these phenomena were rooted in science. The case for the adaptive value of science and technology is made at once. Nor is the fact that we shall probably soon destroy ourselves, thanks to science, a counter-argument. Darwinian adaptive advantage is directed towards the immediate present, not the long-term future.

Yet, as also noted, it would be just plain silly to try to tie in specific scientific ideas with direct biological advantage. No one seriously thinks that evolutionists are going to have a quantifiable reproductive edge over Creationists. Indeed, for fairly obvious reasons, it would not surprise me to learn that in North America today Creationists have larger families than evolutionists. And, as we cast our minds back through the history of science, there is little reason to conclude that great scientific prowess has led inexorably to biological success. To name but three giants – Copernicus, Newton and Mendel all died childless.

Moreover, any attempt to give a (literal) Darwinian analysis of science runs straight into the problem identified earlier (in chapter 2). Science is progressive or very apparently so. Despite diversions, there is a passage towards the goal of complete understanding, or (not to mince words) of truth. However, Darwinism is the epitome of non-progressionism. Evolving organisms are simply not going anywhere. There is no higher or lower, better or worse, truer or falser. For this reason, if for no other, it would seem that you simply must divorce science from any biological origins.

To resolve this paradox – science as adaptive and science as beyond biology – I argue that the methods of science are rooted in selective necessity, but that the product soars up gloriously into the highest reaches of culture, quite transcending its organic origins. And it is the epigenetic rules which play the key mediating role. The nature and development of science is constrained and informed by the biologically channelled modes of thinking imposed on us by evolution – a consequence of the reproductive struggles faced by humans today, and even more a consequence of those struggles faced by humans in the past.

To make the case, I begin with a thumb-nail sketch of the nature of science. For brevity, I ignore interesting side-problems, such as those posed by historical sciences like geology. Next, I unpack the methodology which leads to this science, and try to convince you that such methodology grows out of the biological needs of humans in the ongoing struggle for survival and reproduction. With the main position laid out, I can then go on to explore some of the more metaphysical consequences of my Darwinian epistemology, and to see if and how it can be fitted into the historical mainstream of philosophical inquiry.

The nature of science

The chief distinguishing mark of science is the attempt to understand through *law*, that is through unbroken empirical regularity (Ruse, 1982a, 1982b, 1984c). Science shows that things fall into place, because of laws. Thus, building on the work of Kepler and Galileo, Newton persuaded us that the motions of moving bodies follow certain fixed rules – things do not fly about randomly, without rhyme or reason. Furthermore, he showed that things down here on Earth follow laws – the same laws – as do the heavenly bodies (Westfall, 1981). Analogically, Darwin's great achievement was to show that organisms are no less subject to law than is the inanimate world, and that the consequence of such laws is evolution (Ruse, 1979a).

It is important to note that the laws of science are not just happenstance contingencies. It is thought that the regularities *must* hold (Braithwaite, 1953; Nagel, 1961; Hempel, 1966). It is not purely chance that any two bodies are attracting with a force inversely proportional to the square of the distance between them. Because of Newton's law of gravity, this is something which had to be. Thus laws support counter-factuals – 'I know that the pressure on this gas isn't 2 lb. per square inch, because if it were its volume would be 5 cubic feet.' More on this 'nomic' necessity in a moment.

In all of the emphasis on law, we have the starkest contrast with non-science. Creationists openly appeal to events outside of law, that is to say to miracles. The first appearance of matter itself, the arrival of man, the start of Noah's flood – all of these things supposedly stand without and beyond law.

> The simple fact of the matter is that one cannot have *any* kind of a Genesis Flood without acknowledging the presence of supernatural elements . . .
> That God intervened in a supernatural way to gather the animals into the Ark and to keep them under control during the year of the Flood is explicitly stated in the text of Scripture. Furthermore, it is obvious that the opening of the 'windows of heaven' in order to allow 'the waters which were above the firmament' to fall upon the earth, and the breaking up of 'all the fountains of the great deep' were supernatural acts of God. (Whitcomb and Morris, 1961, p. 76)

This may be good theology. (As it happens, I do not think it is.) It is certainly not science.

Laws do not exist in splendid isolation. Science aims to bind them together, into theories. There is much debate about the nature of this binding, but generally (and to a first approximation) it involves showing that some laws follow deductively from other laws. Kepler's laws of planetary motion and Galileo's laws of terrestrial motion follow from Newton's three fundamental laws of motion, together with his law of gravitational attraction. Arguably, the ultimate ideal is a full-blooded axiom system, with everything following rigorously from just a few premises. But, obviously, most scientists most of the time (i.e. in their everyday work) are not aiming for massive overarching theories, deducing one fundamental law from another, producing systems readily applicable wherever and whenever. Rather, against a known background, scientists specify certain peculiar conditions, which they feel (or hope) obtain at certain times and places, and then try to build limited law-networks around them (Giere, 1979). Often these 'models' include simplifications of reality, in order to avoid unmanageable complexity. You get many examples of models in population genetics (Lewontin, 1974).

How are theories or models brought into contact with empirical reality? Through prediction, explanation, and testing. You use science to try to predict and explain particular phenomena, like the motions of individual planets, or the peculiar distribution of a certain set of organisms, or the presence of volcanoes in one part of the earth and not another. This involves showing how the phenomena under study follow from your science. They are proven to be consequences of the laws of your theory or models. In other words, from the science you aim to infer specified empirical phenomena. At least, you aim usually to make such inferences from the science as seen in conjunction with other specified empirical phenomena, so-called 'initial conditions'.

The difference between explanation and prediction is essentially formal.[1] In explanation, you probably know full well just what you are inferring. In fact, that being explained is often the stimulus for the whole enquiry. In prediction, you are going on to infer new things. In common talk, 'prediction' usually means inference of expected future phenomena. Scientific usage is somewhat broader – from the known to the unknown. A palaeontologist might predict that a newly-discovered fossil should have certain as yet undescribed features.

These inferences all give us a way of checking our ideas, and of correcting as needed. If our science leads us to predict conclusions which simply are not true, then there must be something wrong with the science. It needs scrapping or at least revising. This process of testing scientific ideas against the evidence is at the heart of Karl Popper's well-known criterion of demarcation between science and non-science. According to Popper (1959, 1962) and his school, a genuinely scientific theory must expose itself to the real world. It must be *falsifiable*. But, although this property is obviously fundamental to the essence of science, it is clear that there is more to what we usually think of as *good* science. Amongst other things, in good science you look for a certain elegance or simplicity. In other words, good science cuts through the surface complexities of the world, showing that all can be explained by a few powerful laws.

And closely connected to this (indeed, some have argued, the other side of the same coin), the best science tries to bind together different areas of investigation into one unified whole (Kitcher, 1981). It shows how the same idea can explain different things, and conversely how the different things point to the genuineness of the thing explaining. Newton's genius was to subsume so much – the world of our earthly experience and the mysterious domain of the heavenly bodies – beneath but a few powerful laws. As we have seen, this mark of good science, what the Victorian man of science William Whewell (1840) called a 'consilience of inductions', was also at the heart of Darwinian evolutionary theory (Ruse, 1975a, 1975d). And, as we have also seen, this was not

---

[1] I must emphasize that I am only giving a rough characterization of science – a *very* rough characterization, my fellow philosophers of science would say. The literature on the explanation/prediction connection is as long as it is boring. Suppe (1974) is a good introduction to many of the issues which have engaged recent philosophers writing about science.

fortuitous. Darwin modelled his thinking on Whewell's vision of Newtonian mechanics. Today, the selfsame criterion of excellence continues to function powerfully. Plate tectonics is a contemporary theory which succeeds because, beyond all else, it is consilient (Ruse, 1981c).

Whewell argued that what lies at the centre of a consilience is a *vera causa*, or true cause. This is the power or force or some such thing which makes other things (effects) occur. Given the cause, then the effect simply must follow. The force of gravity is the cause of the ball's falling down to the ground, and of the moon's spinning around the Earth, rather than flying off into space. I am not sure if Whewell was right in elevating some causes (*verae causae*) above others. As you will learn in a moment, I tend to see the essence of a consilience in the *vera* rather than the *causa*. Nevertheless, without yet trying to say exactly what characterizes a cause – is it really something like a power? – we must certainly agree that the notion of cause is very important in science.

This notion is obviously tightly bound with the aim of explanation – to explain something is frequently to pick out underlying causes – and naturally, therefore, talk of causes tends to predominate more in the upper reaches of theories. Newton's major law, about the force of gravity, is a premise casting light on all that follows. It is probably no exaggeration to say that the (nomic) necessity of laws is intimately connected with causation. Laws are necessary by virtue of the fact that they refer directly to causes – bodies *must* attract each other – or because they are consequences of laws about causes. The necessity of Kepler's laws follows from their place within the Newtonian causal law-network.

Talk of causation leads straight to a related aspect of science. Observation of any kind, even the crudest, tends to occur in the context of various ideas or thoughts or enquiries, of one sort or another. Nevertheless, much of the content of science refers to the world of relatively raw experience, the world of sensation. It is about colours and shapes and sounds, about prisms and pendulums and plants. However, as science develops and produces more and more subtle theories, as you go up through the framework which the scientist has created, to the highest-level claims – finally, unto the very premises themselves – the talk tends to become increasingly abstract, theoretical, divorced from immediate experience. One hears mention of forces, and electrons, and genes, and the like. Often, indeed, one is dealing with microentities, invisible to the unaided human eye – things which are never (nor very soon likely to be) experienced (Nagel, 1961).

I doubt that anyone today would claim that there is an absolute sharp distinction in science between reference to observables and unobservables (or however else you label them); but there does seem to be a difference nevertheless. Picking up on what was said just previously about causes, there is an obvious conclusion which many draw, namely that real causal understanding necessarily requires reference to the unseen ultimates, occurring in the highest level of science. For instance, to understand what is going on in chemistry, say when you mix an acid and an alkali and get a salt, you simply have to know about the underlying protons and electrons and so forth.

Some commentators on science push this approach to the limit, arguing not only that science progresses, but that such progress consists simply in elucidating the unseen entities lying behind the phenomena. This requires that one makes reference to smaller and smaller things – from molecules to atoms to protons and electrons to . . .? Combining what is known with what is hoped, it is argued that the ultimate end for science is one grand unified theory, which talks about a mere handful of sub-atomic particles. If one mixes this argument with a parallel case supporting the fallibility of perception (the so-called argument from illusion), the ready conclusion is that the familiar world of experience is but a chimera. True reality resides only at the unseen micro-level, referred to in the premises of the most high-powered of theories. The physicist Arthur Eddington (1929) was one of the most famous proponents of this thesis. He claimed to sit before two desks – the familiar brown, solid desk, and the desk of the physicist, a mass of buzzing molecules. Supposedly, only the latter was truly real (see Graham, 1981, for more details).

Sorting out the sense from exaggeration in this line of argument, it has already been agreed that science does seem to be progressive. This point was argued in detail in chapter 2. Moreover, much that convinces us of progress has indeed involved the invocation of smaller and smaller unseen particles, of one sort or another – be they atoms in physics, genes in biology, or neurons in the study of the brain. Nevertheless, the drive for smallness, taking science beyond the possibility of direct observation, does not seem to be the essence of progress. Darwin's theory progressed beyond the views of his non-evolutionary predecessors, even though the theory of the *Origin* made no direct reference to microentities. (It is true that neo-Darwinism, incorporating Mendelian genetics, makes such reference; but, this was a later development.) The geological theory of plate tectonics signifies great progress in the earth sciences, but again there is no reference to the very small. (This is not quite true, because geologists certainly use microphenomena in their work. But the basic claim is about moving continents – the ultimate in macroephenomena.)

Reverting again to previous argument (of chapter 2), I prefer to stay with a characterization of progress which finds it within the building of bigger and better consiliences. Coincidentally, these have often required a drive towards the small and unobservable; but the essence of forward-moving change lies in the fact that we just cannot imagine that a strong consilience would let us down. In other words, the key to progress in science is getting closer to the truth, and consiliences are taken to be a mark of this truth. Outrageous coincidences just do not happen.

'Closer to the truth' about what? Showing their fondness for extremes, there are those philosophers who argue that scientific theories are mere tools for predicting the future, and that we have no right to assert that any of the theoreticals/unobservables really exist. These are the 'instrumentalists', as opposed to the 'realists', who include in their numbers the above-mentioned extremists (like Eddington) who go so far as to argue that only the unseen is truly real!

Taking the common-sense approach (which will be scrutinized before the chapter is over), I assume here that science presupposes and justifies a fairly robust sense of reality (Hacking, 1983). If something is at the focus of a consilience, say a sub-atomic particle, it really is strained to pretend that we might not be talking about anything at all, or that our talk says nothing about the true nature of that about which we talk (Smart, 1963). After all, to recall a favourite analogy of mine, we use consiliences constantly in courts of law, when we convict on circumstantial evidence. Does anyone truly believe that we always hang people for fictions? In short, progress in science consists in ever increasing knowledge of what the world is really like. The only people who seem to have genuine doubts about this are those impressed by modern physics, and by its assertions about such funny entities as electrons, which (apparently) have contradictory properties (van Fraassen, 1980). I shall speak later to these concerns.

As a corollary to the common-sense approach just endorsed, I would argue that even though we believe the key unseen entities of science to be truly real, this is no good reason to claim that the world of phenomena is totally unreal. After all, granting the solidity of the marbles in the bag is not to downgrade the reality of the bag, or of the bag-of-marbles taken as a whole. Thanks to science, we have different ways of looking at things. Of course, this is not to deny that, at the phenomenal level, claims are more prone to the vagaries of individual perception.

There is much, much more that can be said about the nature of science. Many points will occur in the course of this chapter. But concluding this introductory discussion, let me disavow one possible misunderstanding. If you follow me in unpacking the progress of science in terms of an approach to a full understanding of reality, and if you take consilience as the mark of such an approach, you might nevertheless still think that the ultimate end of science has to be one great unified theory. A theory where everything – inorganic and organic, non-human and human – follows from one or a few key premises. However, while one does expect to see ever greater binding together, I doubt that the goal must necessarily be one grand theory.

Perhaps it is just empirically the case that different subjects require different premises, or even different modes of understanding (Ruse, 1977). This strikes me as an open question.

We have enough to go on now. Virtually every statement which I have made could be elaborated and qualified. But too much information can be as dangerous as too little. Let me move straight on to try to relate the exposition of this section to Darwinian factors, that is to the epigenetic rules.

Scientific reasoning

Our enquiry is about the true nature and status of science. Starting with the sketch given above – one which is intended to be blandly uncontroversial – we can at once say that, whatever else science may be, it is a human product. It may be the aim of the scientist to mirror reality – an aim which may or may not be realizable – but the science itself is a product of human intentions and powers and thought processes. The science results from human reasoning ability. The ways in which we think and argue and infer are those things which constrain and mould the product. This is so whether you think that reason is some peculiarly human phenomenon, or something ultimately with a distinctively extra-human status and validity.

In other words, in order to understand why science is as it is – why laws, why predictions, why falsifiability, why consiliences – we need to look at the principles of scientific reasoning or methodology. And as I am sure you now realize, what I argue is that these principles have their being and only justification in their Darwinian value, that is in their adaptive worth to us humans – or, at least, to our proto-human ancestors. In short, I argue that the principles which guide and mould science are rooted in our biology, as mediated by our epigenetic rules.

More particularly, since we are now really dealing with the processing of information, the methodological principles are a direct function of our secondary epigenetic rules. I certainly do not want to deny the pertinence of primary epigenetic rules of science. I take it that their existence fits in with much that commentators on science (including working scientists) have concluded about the way in which one rarely (if ever) simply acquires and uses raw sensations – uninterpreted chunks of experience (Hanson, 1958; Marr, 1984). Everything that human beings take in is filtered and transformed in some way. To argue that our evolutionary heritage also takes a hand is a natural extension of this thesis about the theory-ladenness of experience. However, at the level of enquiry now under discussion – that of the foundations of scientific methodology – it is the secondary epigenetic rules which come to the fore.

What then are the crucial epigenetic rules lying beneath the principles of scientific reasoning? Ideally, one would turn to the Darwinians, particularly those working on human thought and behaviour, and find already elaborated and well justified those very rules which science most obviously requires. This is hardly yet possible. The work we discussed at the end of the last chapter is right at the edge of evolutionary enquiry, and here in this chapter (and the next) we are moving over into unexplored land. Indeed, I would like to think that we are beating a path for empirical scientists, showing human evolutionists the sorts of things for which they need to find support, in order to make their case complete. Philosophers' hands reaching down, as it were, to grasp the hands of scientists reaching up.

However, this is not to say that we move now into a never-never world of philosophical fantasy, with any wild speculation allowed, so long as you offer a promissory note that future scientific investigation will support it. Given the sketch of science offered just above – a sketch articulated by philosophers, without any regard for evolution – the place to find plausible putative rules is obvious. We must continue to look at the work of philosophers (working in a non-evolutionary mode), and search out those principles of reasoning they think yield the now elaborated science. The principles will mirror or support or show the appropriate epigentic rules.

This is in no way to concede implicitly that success in our (non-biological) enquiry will thereby prove the irrelevance of evolution for science. Rather, it is to presume that a full Darwinian epistemology will (like all good philosophy) help us to understand more deeply what we already dimly grasp, rather than force upon us the pretence that we must destroy and begin completely anew. As Darwinians, we are not trying to deny human nature. We are trying to explain that nature which biology gives to us intuitively. We are not trying to persuade that science is other than it is. We are trying to put evolution behind science.

Taking our cue, therefore, from the work of others, it is generally agreed that science is the product of roughly two kinds of reasoning: deductive and inductive (Salmon, 1973; Hempel, 1966). Beginning with deduction, we find the scientist constrained and guided by inference of a formal kind, where conclusions follow necessarily from premises. An important branch of such formal reasoning is (deductive) *logic*, where the scientist is bound, or (if you like) *qua* scientist agrees to be bound, by certain basic logical principles, together with fixed laws or rules of inference. What I have in mind here are general principles, like the law of excluded middle ('Either it is raining outside, or it is not raining outside'), and the law of non-contradiction ('It cannot both rain and not rain, at the same time'). Rules include *modus ponens* ('If it is raining, we shall go to church. It is raining. Therefore, we shall go to church'), and alternation ('Either we shall go picnicking or to church. We shall not go picnicking. Therefore, we shall go to church').

More generally and symbolically, the law of excluded middle says 'Either p or not-p must be true' (or, completely symbolically, '$pv \sim p'$); the law of non-contradiction says 'p and not-p cannot both be true' (or '$\sim (p. \sim p)'$), *modus ponens* says 'Given "if p, then q" and "p" as both true, then "q" is true' (or '$p \supset q, p \vdash q'$). In setting up an argument or a full system, you must have statements and at least one rule of inference. A purely logical system, something not usually encountered within empirical science, has only logical statements, like the law of excluded middle (Braithwaite, 1953). Obviously, there is interplay between statements and inferences of logic. Instead of a statement about the law of excluded middle, you could have a rule commanding: 'Reject any claim of the form "neither p nor not-p"' (Copi, 1973).

Logic alone is not enough for the scientist. His/her concern is with the world around us. The very essence of a scientific system is to bind together empirical claims about this world. But, logic constrains and informs the scientist's work. Logic sets up boundary conditions within which the scientist must work. He/she cannot afford to be illogical. Thus, for instance, the law of non-contradiction is crucially important. You must not permit contradictory claims within your system. Anything which seems to be leading to contradiction has to be side-tracked and eliminated in some way. If the evidence is that a species went extinct, then you cannot permit it to be still living. If an area of the globe is not volcanic, then you cannot have volcanoes in that spot.

This is all somewhat trite, but very important for all that. Occasionally, the law can be seen to have real bite. A classic instance occurred in quantum mechanics. You have electrons, with apparently contradictory features – wave characteristics and particle characteristics simultaneously. Hence, Heisenberg's Uncertainty Principle was needed. This bars the asking of awkward (i.e. contradiction implying) questions. If you get close to asking about wave-like features, then you cannot ask about particle-like features, and vice-versa. Contradictions are therefore avoided (Hanson, 1958).

A similar use of logic is made in scientific inference, often with very far-reaching implications. Consider falsifiability. Stripped to its bare essentials, it is no more than the rule of *modus tollens*: 'Given "If p then q" as true, and "q" as false, then "p" is false' ($p \supset q, \sim q \vdash \sim p$). Falsifiability dictates that, if you have an inference – an empirical prediction – and it leads to a false result, then you must turn back to your theory or model and revise or reject it. It cannot be true as it stands. This follows logically from the rule of denying the consequent (*modus tollens*). And, clearly, similar rules of inference are used again and again as you try to refine and extend your scientific ideas.

Logic is vitally important to the scientist. Its only rival in this respect is *mathematics*. Arithmetic, algebra, geometry, calculus, and much more – all are absolutely crucial to science, particularly the well-articulated, sophisticated parts of modern science. You need the premises of mathematics, and you need the inferences of mathematics. One is tempted, indeed, to say that progress is a direct function of mathematization. Certainly, the two go hand in hand. We see this very clearly in the development of evolutionary theory itself. Darwin used little mathematics, although that which he did use was crucial. (The struggle for existence follows from the Malthusian fact that food supplies have a potential arithmetic rate of increase, and population numbers have a potential geometric rate of increase, and the latter is greater than the former.) Today, population genetics – the very heart of the modern evolutionary enterprise – relies very heavily on algebra, calculus, statistics, and other tools of the mathematician's kit-bag. There can be no doubt that, without such a form of reasoning, little could be done in science.

Moving now from the more formal aspects of science to its more empirical side, it is here that we encounter the results of what we might think of as inductive argumentation in its broadest sense. One important kind of inductive argument is *analogy*, where we compare two similar (although different) things, trying to draw conclusions about one on the basis of the other. We saw in earlier chapters (especially chapter 2) that analogical thinking is very important to the scientist, despite debate about how far analogy persists in a fully mature science. What cannot be queried is that analogy is vital in scientific discovery, and, whatever its problems, remains for long periods in the actual theories of working scientists. Darwin's analogy between artificial and natural selection proves this (Ruse, 1980c).

Even more crucial than analogy is the mode of thought whereby we pick up particular instances and mould them together into general statements – statements which we do not just think happen to be true, but rather which in some important sense have to be true. I refer, of course, to the scientist's penchant for binding his/her particulars into *laws*, the very key to the scientific enterprise. There is much debate about how this is done, and I do not very much want to get side-tracked into a discussion of the psychology of the scientist (although as a Darwinian, I obviously have thoughts on the matter). My point is only that an important part of scientific methodology is the creation of a general or universal way of thought, out of specific instances (Nickles, 1980a, 1980b).

This, as we have seen, is all very much bound up with our tendency to think in terms of *causes* – indeed, perhaps (as noted) all laws are themselves causal laws, or the consequences of causal laws. The scientist believes that things do not just follow on from each other in a random fashion, but are connected because some things – causes – make other things – effects – occur. Obviously, much of the scientific enterprise consists of distinguishing genuine cases of causation from pseudo-instances. As you can imagine, a great deal has been written on this topic, most famously by John Stuart Mill, who proposed four methods for identifying genuine causes. For instance, the first method, the method of agreement, states: 'If two or more instances of the phenomenon under investigation have only one circumstance in common, the circumstance in which alone all the instances agree, is the cause (or effect) of the given phenomenon.' (Mill, 1884, p. 255).

Laws and causal thinking are at the heart of science. But we know now that, at the non-formal level, there is more to scientific methodology. Most importantly, questions of *simplicity* or elegance govern the work of the scientist. For instance, in the Copernican revolution, there is little doubt that the earliest supporters of the heliocentric world view were swayed less by an appeal to brute fact (knowledge of which was notoriously inaccurate) and more by aesthetic factors. Take the inferior/superior planet distinction, something already briefly mentioned (in chapter 2). The inferior planets, Mercury and Venus, never move far from the Sun. The superior planets, Mars, Saturn and Jupiter, wander right through the heavens, sometimes being far from the Sun. Copernicus explained the difference as a simple consequence of the fact that the inferior planets are closer to, and the superior planets farther from, the Sun than the Earth. That this inferior/superior planet distinction stemmed at once from the heliocentric theory (as it did not do from the geocentric theory) was a decisive factor in many astronomers' minds. Copernicanism was simpler (Kuhn, 1957).

And also, bound up with causality and with simplicity, we have the urge towards *consilience*. Scientists aim to gather their ideas beneath one or two sweeping, all-powerful hypotheses. When they can do this, they feel happy. And when they can do this between widely disparate areas, perhaps even using the new theory to push into new and surprising areas – making predictions which might have been thought false, but which prove to be true – they feel satisfied that they have captured some important facet of reality. Even though that of which they talk may be unseen, scientists think they are describing an objective world in the way that it really is. In short, they have made progress.

> No false supposition could, after being adjusted to one class of phenomena, exactly represent a different class, when the agreement was unforeseen and uncontemplated. That rules springing from remote and unconnected quarters should thus leap to the same point, can only arise from *that* being the point where truth resides. (Whewell, 1840, 2, 230)[2]

These then are some of the main features of scientific reasoning,

[2] Note that I am not yet saying that there really is an objective world, towards knowledge of which science progresses. That is the topic of this chapter. My point is that made earlier, that this is what scientists think.

deductive and inductive. Because people – scientists – think in these sorts of ways, and only because they think in these ways, they produce bodies of claims of the type described in the last section. I trust that all of my readers will feel fairly comfortable with this conclusion, even those who may hesitate before the full Darwinian programme. As noted, my hope thus far has been to draw on the standard work of others. If I have produced a picture of scientific methodology which is not broadly recognizable by, and acceptable to, most commentators on science, I have failed in my aim.

Of course, I do not pretend that everyone who has written on science will accept everything exactly as I have stated it. For instance, Popperians deny the validity of all forms of inductive argument. Others have attacked Mill's methods (e.g.. Whewell, 1860; Cohen and Nagel, 1934). Some have tried to set simplicity in a deductive context (Hempel, 1966; Sober, 1975). And so forth. Nevertheless, important though these differences are, they are details. All commentators agree on a certain broad methodology which creates science, and which certainly gives the sensation of progress towards genuine understanding of the real world. If there are parts of what I have said which are truly anathema to you, then I am sure your own version of scientific methodology can be substituted for mine, without much affecting subsequent discussion.

Indeed, I rather take comfort in the fact that there will be some alternative analyses and disagreements about the nature of science and its methodology. If, thanks to divine inspiration, the rules of science were written on tablets of stone, or if they were intuited objective realities (or some such thing), then and only then would I expect them to be unambiguously discernible. My claim is that the epigenetic rules lie behind the methodology. Even if my wildest dreams are realized, I very much doubt that our brains will prove to be compartmentalized, in an old-fashioned phrenological way, so that one part deals with the first of Mill's methods, and another part deals with the second, and so forth. Reasoning abilities will be like other adaptations, for instance hands. We can subdivide reasoning abilities, as we can break down hands and talk of fingers and thumbs. But division, although conceptually useful, is somewhat artificial (Ghiselin, 1966). We expect different people to cut up the pie in different ways. Fortunately, nature is indifferent to our efforts. For it, what counts is the functioning whole.

The case for a biological backing

As a philosopher, I am pushing biology out from its established boundaries, trying to understand the nature of knowledge. I argue that the methodology presented in the last section, leading to the science sketched in the first section, is produced by Darwinian-selected epigenetic rules. There are rules for approval of *modus ponens* and consiliences, no less than there is a rule setting up incest barriers. This is the hypothesis.

Nevertheless, despite all the talk of incompleteness, you are surely entitled to a little more than a flat assertion that the principles of scientific reason have their being in human Darwinian needs, that their foundation is no more (and no less) than a bed of epigenetic rules. Supposing now that you accept the description of scientific method-ology just given, why should you go on to take the crucial step which I urge? Why should you accept that *modus ponens* and the drive to consilience are produced by epigenetic rules? The following points are pertinent.

First, we are not now operating in a vacuum. We know a great deal about humans, which can properly be regarded as relevant background. In particular, we know from the discussion of the last chapter that humans are the product of evolution through natural selection, and that this mechanism reaches right up into the distinctively human area of culture. We saw that this is true of language, which infuses and influences everything else. It is true, moreover, of other aspects of culture, for instance those governing human sexual conduct – a major area, if anything is, since it enters into our morality, our social customs, our religion, our art and literature, and virtually all that we think of as cultural. Feminists and others argue, with some success, that sexuality reaches right into science (Harding and Hintikka, 1983; Ruse, 1981b).

In other words, in dealing with supposed epigenetic rules, specifically those pertaining to the creation of science, it is not necessary to go right back to the beginning, pretending that the very idea that something like science might have a biological substratum is novel to the point of absurdity. We are now working from a background knowledge of human biological nature. This does not, in itself, prove that the epigenetic rules required for the methodological principles given just above are in fact correct; but we do expect to find influential epigenetic rules – either these, or others.

To put the point another way: already we can go beyond the vague concessions about the adaptive advantage of science allowed at the beginning of this chapter. We may now reasonably presume that Darwinian advantage reaches through science like bones through a vertebrate. And this, despite the other concession, that utimately in its highest reaches, science pushes to the limits of culture where direct adaptive advantage sits lightly.

Second, following straight on the first point, the requirements of methodology given above certainly presuppose highly plausible candi-dates for full epigenetic-rule status. They demand just the sorts of directives one would expect to find valuable in the ongoing struggle for survival and reproduction. Consider two would-be human ancestors, one with elementary logical and mathematical skills, and the other without very much in that direction. One can think of countless situations, many of which must have happened in real life, where the former proto-human would have been at great selective advantage over the other. A tiger is seen entering a cave that you and your family usually use for sleeping. No one has seen the tiger emerge. Should you seek alternative accommodation for this night at least? How else does one achieve a happy end to this story, other than by an application of those laws of logic that we try to uncover for our students in elementary logic classes (Michalos, 1969)?

Analogously for mathematics. Two tigers were seen going into the cave. Only one came out. Is the cave now safe? Again: you have to travel across a plain to get to your hunting grounds. You can only walk a limited distance in this heat. Should you set off now? Should you wait until tomorrow? Should you plan to camp out for the night? And so forth. The proto-human who had an innate disposition to take seriously the law of excluded middle, and who avoided contradictions, survived and reproduced better than he/she who did not. The proto-human who innately preferred '2 + 2 = 4' to '2 + 2 = 5' was at a selective advantage over his/her less discriminating cousin.

Much the same holds when we turn to the inductive side of reasoning. Why should we think causally, or in terms of laws? W.V. Quine puts his finger precisely on the problem and the solution.

> One part of the problem of induction, the part that asks why there should be regularities in nature at all, can, I think, be dismissed. *That* there are or have been regularities, for whatever reason, is an established fact of science; and we cannot ask better than that. *Why* there have been regularities is an obscure question, for it is hard to see what would count as an answer. What does make clear sense is this other part of the problem of induction: why does our innate subjective spacing of qualities accord so well with the functionally relevant groupings in nature as to make our inductions tend to come out right? Why should our subjective spacing of qualities have a special purchase on nature and a lien on the future?
>
> There is some encouragement in Darwin. If people's innate spacing of qualities is a gene-linked trait, then the spacing that has made for the most successful inductions will have tended to predominate through natural selection. Creatures inveterately wrong in their inductions have a pathetic but praise-worthy tendency to die before reproducing their kind. (1969b, p. 126)

Again, we can see good biological reasons for favouring simplicity. The whole point about simplicity is that formally there is nothing to choose between two options (Foster and Martin, 1966). Either alternative fits the evidence. Nevertheless, the primate who innately favoured the simpler option would be ahead of his/her fellow with a taste for the complex. The former would be spending a lot less time and effort on his/her decision-making and execution. Of course, sometimes it turns out that the more complex solution is the correct one. But evolution never guarantees perfection. It aims rather to maximize the benefits, given limited options. And, as the Popperians never tire of telling us, you can always learn from your mistakes.

Incidentally, here we surely have the answer to certain inane paradoxes which have much absorbed post-war philosophers of science. Formally, on known evidence, you cannot decide between the statements, 'All emeralds are green' and 'All emeralds are grue', where 'grue' is defined as 'green before time t and blue after time t', and t is some point in the future. Any emerald studied confirms its grueness, no less than its greenness. Obviously, the caveman who filled his head with grue-type predicates rather heroically sacrificed the needs of day-to-day life for the joys of philosophical discourse. By the time he had puzzled out that what stands before him is a 'tigamb', namely a 'tiger before time t and a lamb after time t', and that t is not yet in the past, he would have been eaten.

I should add that Nelson Goodman (1955), who gave rise to this industry, immediately pointed his finger towards the solution. He argued that 'grue' is to be rejected, because it is not 'well-entrenched', where this latter property has to do with the already-established virtues of using predicates of certain kinds. The point is that, up to now, in respect of emeralds and things like them, no one has needed to cover themselves about what will happen after some future point t. This pragmatic solution meshes nicely with the Darwinian approach. (Scheffler, 1963, has a good discussion of Goodman's and other paradoxes. Sober, 1981, argues for the kind of biological perspective which I urge, neatly defusing the problems.)

Finally, pointing to the plausibility of the epigenetic-rule status of the sorts of things my position demands, let me make brief mention of the biological value of consilience. One hominid arrives at the water-hole, finding tiger-like footprints at the edge, blood-stains on the ground, growls and snarls and shrieks in the nearby undergrowth, and no other animals in sight. She reasons: 'Tigers! Beware!' And she flees. The second hominid arrives at the water, notices all of the signs, but concludes that since all of the evidence is circumstantial nothing can be proven. 'Tigers are just a theory, not a fact.' He settles down for a good long drink. Which of these two hominids was your ancestor?

The pointers, therefore, are that those rules which I have identified as lying behind science are precisely the inclinations which would prove to be of maximum selective value. If we wanted the best possible candidates for epigenetic-rule status, we could not do better than turn to these rules. The proto-human who ignored such rules underlying science would be in a real mess. Conversely, if selection is going to make anything innate, it would do well to start here.

The case for (continued)

And this is a conclusion supported by my third and final point, namely that there is already uncovered empirical evidence, expectedly of different kinds, backing the epigenetic-rule status of the formal and informal aspects of scientific methodology.

First, there is the evidence from comparative studies of different societies, with very different surface cultures – advanced and primitive, East and West, old and new. There is growing realization that, for all of the variations, beneath such cultures lie similar senses of logic and mathematics, not to mention inductive reasoning. It is true that many societies do not have the sophisticated systems possessed by us in the Western industrial world; but the underlying patterns are there, all of the same. Indian logics and Chinese logics, for instance, are remarkably isomorphic to our logic. 'Although it remains uninfluenced by Western logic and stems from an entirely different tradition, Indian logic offers striking parallels to Western logic' (Staal, 1967, p. 523; see also Bochenski, 1961). The same holds for mathematics, and for much reasoning about causality.

Of course, different societies believe different things, and we all know that some of the things believed in some societies sound pretty weird to alien ears. In fact, some of the things believed by our own ancestors have a distinctively odd sound to us today. I doubt that many people in the late twentieth century believe that women really can ride on broomsticks. But the important point is that, beneath differences, the same kind of generalizing ability seems to be at work, with people of all kinds drawing similar-type connections – necessary connections – between diverse phenomena. Socrates knew that hemlock would kill him, and so do we. And all humans share other recognizable (to us) standards, like the refusal to take coincidences as coincidences, preferring rather to look for underlying unifying causes – the mark and aim of a consilience.

As admitted in the last chapter, consistency across societies is not in itself definitive proof that something is rooted in the genes. It could be that in scientific methodology we are looking at something sitting on top of biology, that could in theory be changed by environmental manipulation – rather as some feminists argue that universal sexual attitudes could be changed. However, such uniformity does press for an explanation. It is too much of a coincidence. If nothing else, one begins to suspect shared adaptive needs. Combine this suspicion with the fact that, if the needs are pressing, it is unlikely that nature would have left them open to random environmental disturbance, and the Darwinian case starts to look ever more plausible.

A second piece of evidence pointing towards the reality of the supposed epigenetic rules of science comes from studies of childhood development. As with language, it is becoming more and more evident that children do not simply learn the crucial elements of their cultures, as though their brains were *tabulae rasae*, soaking up any piece of information offered, in the order it is offered. Learning occurs in highly stylized ways, with certain things being learned before other things; with learning only being possible after certain critical periods (and often only before later developments), and with the learning of some things much easier than the learning of other things (Keil, 1979, 1981).

Much study, for instance, has been put into childrens' acquisition of number skills: numerosity. It has been found by many investigators that virtually all children learn to count in the same way, grasping most of the essential notions with little in the way of formal instruction. They pick up simple, but vital, concepts like 'greater than' and 'less than', almost by osmosis, as it were. They hardly need to be taught (Gelman, 1980; Gelman and Gallistel, 1978). This all rather suggests that teaching – formal and informal – is but one part of the overall story. The other part is that humans have an innate disposition to think along certain basic mathematical lines.

Similar findings about learning pertain to other aspects of scientific methodology. We show untaught appreciations of similarity and difference, as are needed in order to think analogically. Likewise in the case of causality and other modes of thinking. Interestingly, not only do we have innate predispositions to think causally, but, reflecting our primate nature, some of the very content seems built into our biological thought patterns (Seligman, 1972). Humans, like other primates, automatically associate heights with falling, snakes with danger, closets with suffocation (Marks, 1969). In these cases, we do not simply look for effects. We know innately what the effects are likely to be.

The adaptive significance of such unlearned knowledge hardly needs stressing. 'Better to crawl away from a cliff, nauseated with fear than to casually walk its edge' (Lumsden and Wilson, 1981, p. 85). Nothing more dramatically points to our biological nature than that most of us at once associated snakes with danger, even though snakes are a very minor part of our daily existence. At the same time, we have much difficulty in linking light bulbs and electric sockets with trouble. Snakes were of much greater concern to our Australopithecine foreparents than were light bulbs and sockets.

Third, in support of the epigenetic rules of science, we have an already large and steadily growing body of reliable, relevant studies of animals. As noted earlier, no one claims that we are the descendents of animals living today – extant primates have their own distinctive adaptive needs, as we have ours – but properly designed studies can be and are highly suggestive. As far as formal reasoning is concerned, there is much evidence that the higher primates have rudimentary notions of logic and of mathematics, and that these are not simply things forced upon them by over enthusiastic human experimenters (King and Fobes, 1982). It is true that these notions are rudimentary – chimpanzees, for instance, seem to run out of conceptual steam around the number seven, whereas human children of the same age can go much higher with comparative ease. But this is to be expected. No one is claiming that chimpanzees are human. The point is that non-human and human animals show the kinds of overlap of formal reasoning ability which one would expect were natural selection at work, leaving its mark.

A good example of chimpanzees showing human-type (formal) reasoning powers concerns the concept of conservation. This centres on the ability to discriminate between cases where quantity changes, and cases where there is no change, despite superficial appearances to the contrary. An appreciation of conservation is obviously crucial to any kind of formal reasoning. (Especially geometry. How could you have Pythagoras' theorem, if it were impossible for the area of one square to equal the sum of the areas of two other squares?) In a carefully controlled experiment, researchers showed that a chimpanzee which had been trained to understand the concepts of 'same' and 'different' (Premack, 1976) had little difficulty in distinguishing cases where quantities of water or solid matter were altered in shape but not in size, from those cases where there were differences not only in shape but also in size. (Much care was taken not to cue the animal inadvertently.) What makes the experiment particularly interesting to the evolutionist is that when the problem of conservation was moved towards a more abstract level, using beads and requiring counting, the ape's abilities started to fall away significantly – just what one would expect of a being with far less brain power than we (Woodruff, Premack and Kennel, 1978 and figure 5.1).

In the case of non-formal reasoning, we have much evidence that the apes (particularly chimpanzees) have a significant innate grasp of inductive logic. The experimenters just mentioned (from the University of Pennsylvania Primate Facility) carried out an extensive series of tests with their sixteen-year-old chimpanzee, Sarah, to see if she could think analogically (Gillan, Premack and Woodruff, 1981). The tests were varied in order to discover if she did really reason properly. On one test, for example, the chimpanzee was asked to complete an analogy, given two alternatives (one correct and one incorrect). On another test, she was asked whether one did in fact have an analogy on display, or not. She was not trained to think analogically, so the question was not whether one can learn to think analogically, but whether the chimpanzee had an innate power. Great care was taken to exclude distorting experimental artefacts. At all times, for instance, Sarah was left alone to do her work, so that she was not improperly fed pertinent information (figure 5.2).

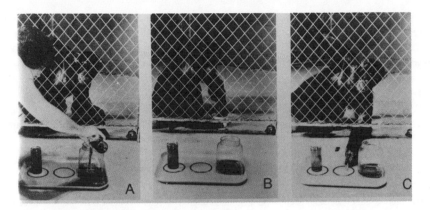

Figure 5.1 Conservation test for liquid quantity. A: While Sarah watches, the trainer pours liquid from one container into another of different proportions. The trainer then gives 'same' and 'different' symbols to Sarah and leaves the room. B: Sarah opens the dish and removes a symbol. C: Sarah places the 'same' symbol in the circle between the two containers. She then calls the trainer back into room by ringing a bell. (Reproduced with permission from Woodruff, Premack and Kennel, 1978.)

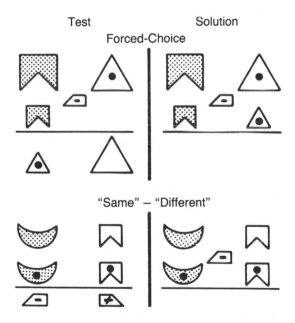

Figure 5.2 Forced choice and same–different analogy problems. The arrangement of stimuli presented to the subject is shown on the left; the correct solution is shown on the right. (Reproduced with permission from Gillan *et al.*, 1981. © American Psychological Association.)

Suffice it to say that the chimpanzee performed extremely strongly on the tests, even those asking fairly subtle questions. (Is orange to orange peel the same as to apple to apple peel or apple to knife?) The most reasonable conclusion to be drawn was that Sarah did indeed have a sense of analogy. And this was despite the fact that she knew no language nor had she been trained in any artificial facsimile or substitute. 'The data, taken as a whole, strongly support the hypothesis that Sarah can reason analogically in a variety of circumstances' (Gillan, *et al.*, 1981, p. 10). See also Gillan (1981) for more on ape reasoning.

The case is made – as much as it is possible to do so at this point. We are pushing beyond the bounds of proven knowledge; but there is positive evidence favouring the claim that scientific methodology is grounded in epigenetic rules, brought into existence by natural selection.

The case against

We cannot leave matters here, for there will be many detractors. Ideally, the full brief for the Darwinian would offer a complete critical examination of all rival positions. I shall not offer such an examination here, for my aim (as throughout this book) is positive rather than negative. Much has been said about the nature of logic and mathematics, as well as about the non-deductive side to science. Were I to get side-tracked into a critical discussion, I could never do the issues full justice. Hence, I shall touch upon other positions only tangentially, and then only in so far as such mention can help me to enhance the positive case I am making for a Darwinian perspective.

No doubt some readers will object to the whole naturalistic approach of the Darwinian, especially as it applies (more accurately, purports to apply) to logic. Even if naturalism worked for induction – even if naturalism worked for mathematics – logic is above and beyond the world of natural selection. It deals with relations between ideas or some such thing – it is 'empty' or purely formal, and thus simply not the sort of thing which can be a guide to life, in quite the way that the Darwinian supposes (Salmon, 1968). There is, to use a term made popular by Gilbert Ryle (1949), a 'category mistake' in supposing that logic yields claims and connections that could be encoded in epigenetic rules.

In reply to this objection – one which I confess rather haunted me when I first became a naturalist in philosophy – I shall make three points. First, supposing that the objection is well-taken, then the Darwinian programme can still apply to those parts of thought and action which really matter to us as humans. And conversely, logic suddenly seems rather less important, since it preserves its integrity (if that be the right term) only by emphasizing its irrelevance to real life.

Second, the objection ignores the various findings and arguments of this century which point away from the distinctive, almost holy status that some would claim for logic. I think here, for instance, of the worries that many have expressed about the necessity of the law of excluded middle ('either p is true or the negation of p is true'),[3] and by the arguments of such philosophers as Quine (1953) about the impossibility of drawing sharp distinctions between knowledge claims of various types.

Third, as shown in the last section, it is just plain wrong to pretend that logic and its inferences stand above the struggle for survival and reproduction. We need the law of non-contradiction and *modus ponens* to get through life (Michalos, 1969), so why should they not be part of our biologically informed, innate conceptual apparatus? My suspicion is that, far from being useless, logic is so necessary and is so deeply ingrained in our nature that we cannot imagine that we ourselves thus structure and inform our experiences.

Allow that logic is not necessarily a subject apart (Quine, 1970). A more dangerous objection to the Darwinian case concedes that it may well be true that an awareness of the law of excluded middle or '$2 + 2 = 4$' has adaptive value. Perhaps, therefore, these parts of logic and mathematics are even encoded in the epigenetic rules as produced by selection. But it is pointed out that logic and mathematics are a great deal more than the law of excluded middle, '$2 + 2 = 4$', or other such elementary propositions. Consider: '$1,000,000 = 999,999 + 1 = 10^6$'. There is hardly an epigenetic rule for these equalities.

Nor is it likely that there is a rule for the theorem that there is no greatest prime number. It is doubtful, indeed, that there is an epigenetic rule for Pythagoras' theorem. What then is the status of most of logic and mathematics – that vast bulk on which modern science rests? Supposedly it is grounded in biology; but now it seems that much which occupies logicians and mathematicians most of their time has little to do with evolution and natural selection.

Responding to this objection, all would agree that there is no epigenetic rule for each and every one of the claims of logic and mathematics. I doubt that knowledge of the properties of prime numbers aided Australopithecines in their journey along the path of evolution. But the Darwinian has a direct and unforced way out of this dilemma. The statements of logic and mathematics, particularly the

---

[3] These worries are of many kinds, especially including those of mathematicians (Körner, 1960, 1966). This is not to mention the problems that quantum mechanics causes for the law. If the naturalist is not right, then just what is going on? Interestingly, William James who, at one point, argued for a Darwinian backing to logic and mathematics much like that being proposed in this chapter, attacked the supposed distinction between the formally necessary ('analytic') and empirical ('synthetic') in the very ways taken by modern philosophers. (See James, 1890, especially the last chapter.)

complex ones, do not exist in splendid isolation. They are built up from
simpler statements, by fixed rules. That is what axiomatic systems are all
about. Thus, even though Pythagoras' theorem may not have an
epigenetic rule to itself, the fairly basic ideas expressed in Euclid's
axioms seem relatively close to nature. Grasping ideas about going in
straight lines, and so forth, could certainly be of use in life's struggles. In
other words, you can readily argue that more advanced mathematics is
an epiphenomenon on a biologically based set of simple statements and
rules.

Remember also that no one claims that the whole of science – referring
here specifically to advanced logic and mathematics – has (or ever had)
direct and immediate adaptive advantage. The claim is that such science
is rooted in adaptive advantage – it is built around principles informed
and constrained by the epigenetic rules. It is these latter which are the
legacy of the Darwinian process. But nothing says that science cannot
take off from there, going beyond instant biological needs – for in the
cases of logic and mathematics it clearly does.[4]

Yet you might rephrase your critical point as follows: two centuries
ago one could plausibly claim that logic and mathematics were
grounded in biologically produced foundations, as described just above.
However, such a claim is now ruled out by developments in logic and
mathematics themselves. We have now alternative logics and non-
Euclidean geometries, and the like. No one could root these in biology,
and yet we know that in some respects they are more representative of
the world than are the traditional ways of thinking. Thus Darwinism still
fails.

There are two issues here. On the one hand, there is the very
existence of alternative systems in themselves. The Darwinian can
handle these relatively comfortably. So long as no one pretends that
they mean very much, there is nothing to stop logicians and mathematicians spinning whatever fantasies they like. Most of us do not think in
sonnet form. But that never stopped poets. Similarly, I see no reason
why logicians and mathematicians should not abstract (or deviate) from
present systems (which are grounded in epigenetic rules), and play all
sorts of fantastic games. The principle seems no different from many
other games, which are frequently based on real-life situations, with
certain artificial contraints and the like introduced.

On the other hand, there is the problem that some areas of modern

---

[4] The most shocking mathematical discovery of this century was Gödel's
theorem, which shows that there will always be parts of mathematics that
you cannot prove. Why is this shocking? To the naturalist, the surprise is that
mathematics gets as far as it does. Worries about failures in completeness are
vestiges of Platonic/theistic thinking. See Newman and Nagel (1958) for
discussion of Gödel's theorem.

science actually reject traditional logic and mathematics, relying instead on new alternatives. The use of non-Euclidean geometry by relativity theory springs at once to mind. At this point, you can hardly argue that unorthodox logics and mathematics are merely game playing. But, while this is true, the Darwinian still has no cause for fear. Most crucially, whatever modern science may say, as far as our everyday life is concerned, nothing is changed. No one walks in a curve to get across a room as quickly as possible.

The fact that the development of modern science takes us into all kinds of non-intuitive realms should be no cause for surprise. The epigenetic rules were developed to help with day-to-day living, not for mapping the intricacies of the universe in the pursuit of Nobel Prizes. Yet, in any case in the development of modern science, the influence of epigenetic rules is hardly stilled. Consider why one might use a non-Euclidean geometry. It is no mere fancy. Questions of simplicity and elegance aside (factors which apparently much influenced Einstein), the basic fact is that traditional systems, using traditional logics and mathematics, just will not work (Pais, 1982). They yield false predictions (Grünbaum, 1973).

In other words, in going with alternative logics and mathematics, the very last thing you are doing is throwing over the epigenetic rules. You are trying to keep as many of them afloat as possible. The use of alternative systems does not show the irrelevance of epigenetic rules. Rather, it shows that we recognize an ordering among them. We would rather stick with *modus tollens* than with Euclidean geometry, if the choice be forced upon us. That such an ordering would exist seems virtually predicted by Darwinism. The epigenetic rules are guides to thought and action. There is no guarantee of a perfect fit all of the time. You expect some rules to be more powerful than others. You use both your sight and your hearing, but I expect most of us would go by what we saw even if our hearing suggested otherwise. An analogous situation obtains in science.

Parenthetically, it is interesting to note that the non-Euclidean geometry demanded by relativity theory required the rejection of the Fifth Postulate. This axiom had always been suspect, long before Lobachevsky and others tried to work without it (Nagel, 1961). Could this suspicion be a direct result of the fact that the other postulates lie much closer to direct adaptive needs? I can well imagine an Australopithecine needing to know that a straight line is the quickest way from *A* to *B*. But who cares about whether or not parallel lines ever meet? In short, the deeper you dig into modern science, the more Darwinian it becomes.

So far, I have dealt with direct attacks on the Darwinian position. Another possible objection concerns less a sin of commission and more one of omission, which is brought strongly to the fore by the above characterization of pure mathematics as 'game playing'. My experience is that most formal thinkers, particularly mathematicians, are Platonists. By this I mean that they feel most strongly that their subject is not merely a game – marks on paper which can be changed at the whim of the player – but a reflection of true reality (Russell, 1937, p. xv). Moreover, this is a reality which is not just contingently true of this world, but something which had to be. Gottfried Wilhelm Leibniz (1890), as great a mathematician as he was a philosopher, spoke of things being true in all possible worlds.

More generally, whatever the philosophical case may be – whether logic and mathematics are about real things, or about abstract relations of ideas, or whatever – many find there to be something psychologically dissatisfying about Darwinism. Somehow, putting everything back on natural selection does not seem to account for the necessity we feel about logic and mathematics – a necessity which, in science, we transfer into our dealings with the physical world. The law of excluded middle, '2 + 2 = 4', and Pythagoras' theorem seem to have a force and reality beyond the contingencies of the struggle for existence.

This is a natural emotion, the power of which we all feel. It is one to which the Darwinian must speak, given that he/she is claiming to be explaining our common-sense feelings, not denying them. Do note however, that the objection is more a report on human psychology than a definitive refutation of a Darwinian approach to formal thinking. And, considered in this light, the Darwinian has a ready answer. He/she agrees that we 'objectify' the truths of logic and mathematics, believing them to be above the whims of individual humans. But there are very good biological reasons why we would do precisely this. The human who believes that '2 + 2' *really* equals '4' is going to act upon it without question, as are his/her fellows. And this will give them a selective advantage over those who question the basic premises of logic and mathematics, sometimes disobeying them.

I shall have much more to say on the biological backing of this kind of psychological conviction of certainty when we come to morality; but the central truth should be apparent. Natural selection simply does not care about giving us a meticulously true and comprehensive insight into the nature of things. There is much that we find out, as in a philosophical enquiry which now engages us, despite selection (although through its tools). Selection cares only about keeping us alive and our passing on of our genes. Less anthropomorphically, biological fitness is a function of reproductive advantage rather than of philosophical insight. Thus, if we benefit biologically by being deluded about the true nature of formal thought, then so be it. A tendency to objectify is the price of reproductive success.

I will have much more to say shortly about reality and about our knowledge of it. For the moment, do not understand me as simply saying that formal thought is an illusion, where anything goes. Of course, we can distinguish between true and false statements in logic and mathematics. The point is that formal thought is not quite all we think it is. What is illusory is the objectivity – that beautiful world of eternal verities – not the subject itself.

I have now answered some of the more obvious objections to the naturalistic approach to logic and mathematics. Even the criticisms can be turned to the advantage of Darwinism. I admit that I have hardly offered a fully developed philosophy of logic or mathematics. But my sketch will have to suffice for now. Nevertheless, as regards mathematics I draw your attention to the recent empiricist approach to mathematics endorsed by Philip Kitcher (1983b): 'arithmetic describes those structural features of the world in virtue of which we are able to segregate and recombine objects: the operations of segregation and recombination bring about the manifestation of underlying dispositional traits' (p. 108). Kitcher does not link his position to Darwinism, starting rather with elementary notions learned at the beginning of civilization; but I suspect his thesis lends itself readily to an interpretation in terms of epigenetic rules, thus showing how the naturalistic programme can be carried forward.

What about objections to the Darwinian approach stemming from its treatment of inductive inference? I doubt that there will be quite so many objections to the Darwinian excursions in this realm. I am sure that many who would object most strongly to a naturalistic approach to human thought themselves tend to feel uncomfortable about inductive inferences. If an inference is not deductive, then they wonder why one should take it seriously at all. This worry about induction by lovers of formal reasoning has been intense since the time of David Hume (1978), who showed in a devastating critique that the necessary connections we 'see' between events or phenomena in the physical world are really figments of our imaginations. There are no necessities or separate causes out there – at least, not such as we can sense in the way we sense objects. (More on Hume shortly.)

Obviously, the Darwinian does not join the wallow in metaphysical angst over the dubious status of inductive inference. Indeed, he/she rather welcomes Hume's problem. It is the sort of situation his/her approach leads him/her to expect, and for which he/she has a ready answer. Not for him/her are the moves of someone (like Popper, 1959) who would deny that we reason inductively or that we even need to reason inductively. Of course we reason inductively. But, contrariwise, neither does the Darwinian favour the moves of those (like Rudolf Carnap, 1950) who would convert all inductive inference into a form of deduction. The Darwinian argues that there is no ultimate deductive validity of this kind to our informal reasoning. It exists purely because it has proven its worth in the struggle for existence. We should not look for some deep meaning beyond this.

Note, incidentally, that the Darwinian is not denying causality *per se*, or claiming that it is irrational for humans to depend on it. Far from it. Certainly there are causal connections, and only a fool would ignore them. The point is that causes are not *things* (over and above the physical world), like powers or invisible fluids or such phenomena – although we have a tendency to think they are. Nor are there metaphysical hooks, or any such things, binding causes and effects. The world works in a regular way. It is in our biological interests to take note of this, and so as an adaptive response we tend to make something of the regularities. But, as philosophers, we should not try to make more of the regularities than they are. Causes are projected into the world by us, through our epigenetic rules. The human who believes in real connections has the biological edge over the human who sees only contingency.

My claim, therefore, is that the Darwinian really goes on the offensive when we turn to non-formal-type inferences, making a virtue out of those very things which so many find troublesome. Furthermore, any possible objections to his/her programme in this respect are probably of a kind that have been encountered already. For instance, if it be objected that modern notions of causality seem to have little to do with anything which our ancestors might have found useful in the struggle for existence, it can be replied (as with non-Euclidean geometries) that there is no reason to expect such parts of modern science to fit smoothly with our immediate adaptive needs. And in any case, as before, new non-orthodox notions of causality are introduced to preserve more basic rules, like those of logic.

As noted, those philosophers who sometimes toy with denials of the reality of unseen entities, opting rather for some sort of operationalist view of science, tend to be those looking at quantum mechanics and like portions of modern physics (van Fraasen, 1980). It is these thinkers who are most aware of the need to suspend some of our basic beliefs, in order to preserve others yet more basic. I suspect that there is an innate feeling that true nature 'wouldn't let us down in this way'. Hence, they pull back. My own attitude is that it is silly to expect nature to show such moral integrity. So long as we get consilience, I am happy to forge ahead. If, at some point, consilience starts to break down, then that is the end of the scientific endeavour.

Concluding this part of the discussion, therefore, I suggest that we have seen no fatal objections to our Darwinian epistemology, and much to commend it. I emphasize again that the empirical case is not definitively proven. But it is well above the level of wild speculation. Its philosophical implications must be taken seriously.

The rivals to science

Stop and take stock. The picture of science which has emerged is one of dynamic interaction between the enquiring human and the world around us. We have powers of understanding, forged in the evolutionary crucible of struggle for survival and reproduction. These powers stood our ancestors in good stead, and now we have inherited them. Driven by our sense of curiosity, itself surely a product of biological needs, we transcend our simian origins as we peer deeper and deeper into the mysteries of nature. That our common-sense notions are stretched and at times even broken should come as no surprise. Indeed, we might even have expected this to happen.

Science, therefore, is a human interpretation of the physical universe. We cannot escape our own mind-injected element. This element comes through selection, and thus in this sense science is attached to biology. It has its feet in Darwinian forces. But its head reaches up into non-adaptive clouds, as we push our enquiries further and further. And because our push gets a favourable response back from nature – our predictions are fulfilled and get ever more accurate, and our consiliences get yet more powerful – we feel convinced that we drive in a successful direction.

I doubt if there is any guaranteed necessity to scientific progress. Even given the existence of a real world – in any of the various meanings (to be discussed shortly) – I am not sure that our powers must be such that we can forever penetrate further and further into its nature (Rescher, 1978). As always when using evolutionarily evolved powers, we have a boot-strap operation, doing the best with what we have got – which works, for now (Glymour, 1980). However, as it happens our efforts do seem to be remarkably fruitful. Thus, we have little doubt that we are getting more and more insight into the true nature of reality. In this sense, the Darwinian acknowledges and understands the progressive nature of science, even though the Darwinian mechanism itself is totally non-progressive. The tools of the scientist do not have some special ontological status, but given these tools we produce direction within our created system.

At once a question intrudes. If science is indeed successful, and if (for all of its flights upwards) science is grounded in selection-produced epigenetic rules, and if evolutionary biology is as vital to humans as I say it is, then why is it that so many people embrace so enthusiastically a pot-pouri of non-scientific doctrines, from catholicism to scientology? Consider, for instance, the success today of so-called 'Creation-science' (Morris, 1974). As noted in the preface, this is crude biblical literalism, tarted up to look respectable, in order to get around the US constitution's separation of Church and State. It is a total sham, misquoting authorities, mangling calculations, ignoring evidence, and blatantly breaking with law and invoking miracles (Futuyma, 1983; Kitcher, 1983a). It is the touchstone of anti-science. Yet it persuades countless people, including President Ronald Reagan (Ruse, 1982c, p. 292).

Creation-science is an extreme case of irrationality, but the more conventional and respectable forms of religious belief also strain credulity, to put the matter mildly. Take, for example, the central claim of all non-heretical versions of Christianity, namely that God is all-powerful and all-loving. People have been sent to the stake for denying one or other of these predicates. Yet an application of elementary logic to overwhelming factual evidence shows that such a conception of God is downright inconsistent. An all-powerful, all-loving God simply would not allow small children to die in screaming agony – and that is that (Mackie, 1955; McCloskey, 1960). But, incessantly, excuses are made on His behalf. We are told, for instance, that God allows evil in order to make room for man's free will. And this, despite the fact that detailed scrutiny shows that no such response stands up. On the one hand, much of the pain and evil in this world comes from natural causes. On the other hand, does anyone seriously think that Hitler's free will outweighs the death of six million Jews – not to mention twenty million Russians?

I am not now trying to convert Christians to atheism. They have heard all of the counter-arguments, and more. Indeed, they are often willing to tell you of such arguments, proudly aware that their religious beliefs will not stand scrutiny judged by the methods of science. However, they go on believing in God on the basis of faith or some such thing, telling us that science is not all that there is to life. Some, like Kierkegaard (1936), go so far as to argue that unless you defy the methods of science your religious commitment cannot be genuine and fully worthwhile!

Religion is perhaps the most extreme form of non-science, but as you know only too well, there are many other areas where the epigenetic rules of reason sit somewhat lightly. Think, for instance, how flimsy, yet how effective, is the politician's rhetoric. Or dwell on people's irrationality in the realm of health care. Any quack will find a market for his nostrums. Cancer-ridden patients gobble down laotrile, despite solid evidence as to its worthlessness. At the same time, these very people and their relatives continue to smoke heavily and to gorge on red meat and additive-packed convenience foods.

All of this and more apparently denies what I claim about the nature of science. If the epigenetic rules are so powerful, then surely we should be governed by them all of the time. We should all be good old-fashioned scientific rationalists. Even though we may grant that science reaches up and beyond immediate adaptive advantage, we should surely not ignore the basic premises of logic, as so many religious people are wont to do. We should not play fast and loose with causality, supposing that people can walk on water and raise others from the dead, abilities claimed for a certain well-known Nazarene. We should not blatantly ignore threats to our health from unwise living, as some of us do all of the time and all of us do some of the time.

Prima facie worrisome as these all too frequent instances of human irrationality seem to be, in fact they threaten the Darwinian approach to science not a whit. Indeed, I would argue that irrationality (judged by the standards of science) is more of a problem for the person who argues that logic, mathematics, and the methods of science are eternal, objective verities, or some such thing. This person must argue that many (most) people much of the time simply ignore the disinterested truth, thinking erroneously.

The fact of the matter is that humans, like other organisms, are complex beings, balancing diverse interests and needs. Evolution has not produced computers, indifferent to relationships and social constraints, uncaring about inevitable ill consequences, and so forth. On the contrary, we are social beings, with needs to mesh with fellow humans, and with awareness of crushing experiences like illness and (eventually) death – an awareness which could paralyse our effective present functioning, had we no counter-resources. Quite clearly, therefore, success in the struggle for survival and reproduction needs more than epigenetic rules about logic and science. It needs dispositions for the other aspects of the human experience. I shall talk much of some of these in the next chapter, but here already you can see why science cannot (and must not) claim total control of the human psyche. It has to take its place along with other products of human needs.

Thus, for instance, one need look no further than the story of Job to see how powerful a psychological crutch the belief in a supreme being can be. A happy and successful businessman is tormented by one misfortune after another, and none of it is of his own making. Why did not Job curse God, which would certainly have been the rational thing to do? Because, as the astute author of the Book knew full well, when things go wrong you need something to help you go on living (literally). And if that something is belief in a supreme being, then so be it, even though such belief may be blatantly anti-scientific.

More generally about religion, Wilson points out its value for group cohesion, social status, and the like.

> The highest forms of religious practice, when examined more closely, can be seen to confer biological advantage. Above all, they congeal identity. In the midst of the chaotic and potentially disorienting experiences each person undergoes daily, religion classifies him, provides him with unquestioned membership in a group claiming great powers, and by this means gives him a driving purpose in life compatible with his self-interest. (Wilson, 1978, p. 188)

Similar sorts of defences can readily be given for other irrational human beliefs and practices, whether they be in the realm of politics or medicine or whatever. I am not, of course, arguing that the urge to take laotrile has an immediate Darwinian advantage, not possessed by more conventional treatments of cancer. All of the evidence is that it does not. But the general urge to take quack medicines is readily explicable in terms of the desperate human urge to maintain life, almost at any cost.

No one ever said that this urge would never prove counter-productive.

The point should be clear. Non-science needs no special explaining away. It stems from our biological nature as much as does science. You may now start to complain that this reduces my overall case to a virtual tautology. Apparently any belief is compatible with my version of Darwinism, be the belief rational or irrational. However, this is not quite so. All beliefs have to have their roots in adaptive advantage. For instance, in their times religions have had some funny ideas about sex, with all sorts of restrictions. But, by and large, they have been pretty careful to promote reproduction – often, lots of it. The great recent exception is the Shakers, and look how many of them there are today (Reynolds and Tanner, 1983).

Moreover, note that, even though taken as claims about truth, you may get tensions, in fact science and non-science usually sit reasonably comfortably together within the same individual. If is one thing to believe in the miraculous nature of Noah's Flood. It is quite another to think that a miracle caused the water in your basement. People know when to use the appropriate epigenetic rules. Furthermore, where religion (and the like) do come right down into people's lives, there is rarely a direct clash with science. Take food taboos, for instance. Regarding the cow as sacred has little warrant in zoology, but such a belief does not in itself violate basic principles of physiology and the like. Actually, it is interesting to note just how often an irrational religious belief later turns out to have a good scientific basis. There are, for instance, very good economic and agricultural reasons why Indians should have (religious) prohibitions against wholesale slaughter and consumption of their cattle (Harris, 1971). Would that we had like prohibitions against turning our fields into shopping plazas, and our lakes into pools of acid.

Note also, incidentally, how frequently devotees of non-science defend their beliefs and practices by reference to supposed principles of science, real and apparent. Astrologers claim to be more scientific than astronomers, chiropractors more scientific than doctors, and Creationists more scientific than evolutionists (Gish, 1972). Rationality is important to us all, no matter how strong may be the call of other forces. (Although Creation-science was developed as a political ploy, I am sure its devotees think that it is genuinely scientific).

Philosophical precursor: Kant?

To develop more fully the philosophical implications of the Darwinian picture of science which I have been sketching and endorsing in this chapter, I shall turn now from conceptual analysis to the great thinkers of the past. It is indeed true that a plausible theory of evolution has been with us only 5 per cent of the time since the Western philosophical tradition sprang into life. Nevertheless, it would be most odd had not one of the great pre-evolutionary thinkers glimpsed the picture of knowledge which I have presented thus far in this chapter. This would be even odder, given that Darwin and his fellow evolutionists had their own intellectual roots deep in the past (Greene, 1959; Mayr, 1982). Let us therefore ask: were there great pre-Darwinian philosophers who pointed the way to the analysis of science which I am unfolding and endorsing? If there were, then perhaps by looking briefly at them, we can learn something about our own position.

One name springs at once to mind, namely that of the greatest of all modern philosophers: Immanuel Kant. I have argued that scientific knowledge of the external world is not just something 'read off' from experience, much as a police pathologist's photograph is supposed to give us an unemotional, uninterpreted picture of the corpse. Rather, any scientific knowledge is forced out of experience, virtually by the sweat of our hands – at least, by the sweat of our senses. We mould and interpret according to our epigenetic rules, rather as a painting of a nude by Picasso twists and distorts in order to get at some vital facet of the human soul. (Note that the Picasso painting tells us no less, and probably much more, than does the police photograph.)

This view of science seems to be precisely that of Kant, who argues that knowledge is made and informed by the mind, acting on the raw material provided by the senses. Our empirical 'synthetic' knowledge is infused by non-empirical elements, which are therefore 'a priori'.

> Hitherto it has been assumed that all our knowledge must conform to objects. But all attempts to extend our knowledge of objects by establishing something in regard to them *a priori*, by means of concepts, have, on this assumption, ended in failure. We must therefore make trial whether we may not have more success in the tasks of metaphysics, if we suppose that objects must conform to our knowledge. (Kant, 1929, p. 22)

This was the nub of Kant's so-called 'Copernican revolution' in philosophy. The mind does not passively receive knowledge. It actively participates in its creation.

Obviously, we should not expect an exact isomorphism between my evolutionary position and that of Kant, and indeed there are clear differences. Kant is less radical than I about the status of logic. He does not link it with experience, as I would. But, as we move down to other claims, there is a strong parallelism between Kant's philosophy and my Darwinian epistemology. As is well known, Kant (breaking from predecessors like Leibniz) believes that the claims of mathematics are 'synthetic a priori' – they are constructions in space and time, which are thus not simply read out of nature, but which are rather preconditions for thinking about nature. A statement like '5 + 7 = 12' is no mere empirical generalization; but neither is it something which could be thought up in isolation, as if nothing existed. When we add five apples to seven apples, inferring that there will be twelve apples, we are interpreting experience.

Similarly, Kant argues that our claims about causality, as in 'the lead ball falling on the cushion caused the depression', are mind-structured. 'We can extract clear concepts of them [i.e. causes] from experience, only because we have put them into experience, and because experience is thus itself brought about only by their means' (1929, p. 223).

In the cases of both mathematics and causality, what Kant says seems to fit well with a position which affords the epigenetic rules a vital role in thinking. The Darwinian agrees that the human who thinks that '5 + 7 = 12' is (biologically) fitter than the human who thinks that '5 + 7 = 13'. The Darwinian agrees that the human who is aware of the tendency of lead balls to cause depression – in cushions, heads, or what have you – is (biologically) fitter than the human who is blithely unaware of any such connections. The point about claims of mathematics and causality, for both Darwinian and Kantian, is that we do not simply believe in them, but that we believe claims made in their names to be *necessary*. It is not just that '5 + 7' so happens to equal '12', and falling balls coincidentally cause depressions in cushions. We think in terms of compulsion or inevitability.

Nevertheless, although both Darwinian and Kantian acknowledge (and emphasize) this mind-contributed necessity in certain key aspects of our thought, I sense at core radically different attitudes underlying these acknowledgements. Or rather, I see our old split between the Darwinian and the Spencerian, with the position being promoted in this chapter on the side of Darwin and the Kantian position essentially on the side of Spencer. Despite surface similarities, because of the evolutionary factor – specifically because of the non-progressive evolutionary factor – there is a fundamental difference between Darwinian and Kantian on the nature of the necessity which enters into scientific thinking. And this puts them far apart.

Consider the Darwinian case. We believe that the ball causes a depression, and that (all other things being equal) it *must* do so. Why? Because that is the way we think the world is, and was. But this is all very much a contingent psychological matter. You shove your hand in the fire. You feel the pain. You say the fire causes pain, and so you withdraw your own hand and warn others against fire-play. There are good adaptive reasons for all of this, and for why you think in terms of necessity. But if the physical world had been otherwise, then the sense of necessity would not have been required (and presumably would not have appeared). And particularly, if you had been otherwise, you might not have had the sense of necessity, even though the physical world is as it is. Remember, adaptations, including human thought processes, are just a way of handling the world. They have no special ontological status – you cannot (should not) say that one adaptation is inherently superior to another, and must always come into place. If this were so, why is everyone not intelligent like humans?

What all of this means in the case of beliefs about causality (not to mention mathematics and the other elements of science) is that, although it so happens for us members of *Homo sapiens* that casual thinking carries implications of necessity, such implications begin and end with our contingent nature. The non-progressiveness of all evolution – including human evolution – means that we could have thought about the fire and the burning, in an adaptive way, without necessarily thinking in terms of (necessary) causal connection.

I realize that, thanks to our biology, which is working flat out against me at this point, this contingency of our belief is highly counter-intuitive. But, anticipating the discussion of the next chapter, think for an instant of our feelings about morality. The notions of 'right' and 'wrong' make little sense unless a person has a capacity for choosing between them. Yet, for all the enthusiasm we have for causal necessity, when it comes to making individual choices, there are few doubts perturbing us about being locked into our actions. We have a strong sense of personal freedom. And this sense persists, despite the fact that there is much evidence pointing to humans being part of the causal nexus. It persists despite the fact that we ourselves rely constantly on the causally bound nature of humans. Why bother with the punishment of small children, if you do not think it will evoke warning memories, somewhere down the line?

I am not denying that some meaning can be given to free will. As you will learn, I am sure it can. What I am saying is that our moral capacities clearly demand some sort of phenomenological awareness of freedom – which, to say the least, puts pressure on the notion of causal necessity. Since, apparently, morality does have adaptive value (a point to be proven later), selection calmly gives us a sense of freedom. At which point, I confess that my conviction that we *must* interpret the world in the causal way that we do, starts to crumble. Perhaps there was some other way of avoiding the fire. For instance, we might have worshipped flames, and felt ourselves too unclean to draw near to them. Then we would not have associated the pain of burning with causal necessity, but with punishment by the Deity.

What of the Kantian? I have accused him/her of being akin to the Spencerian. Remember, this is the person who sees progress in the course of evolution, and the end-product (namely us) as being better or in some way superior to that which has gone before. We humans are the culmination (or near-culmination) of evolution, and therefore our thought processes really do have a validity unto themselves. Now, stripping away the evolutionary paraphernalia, this feeling of something special about human thought processes is a crucial element of Kant's stand on the synthetic a priori. For Kant, there is nothing accidental about his necessity. Even though it starts in the mind, it has its own special validity. Thinking mathematically and causally and so forth are preconditions of the possibility of any rational thought whatsoever. Having conceded the importance of sensation, Kant then goes on to ask rhetorically:

> The question now arises whether *a priori* concepts [like causality] do not also serve as antecedent conditions under which alone anything can be, if not intuited, yet thought as object in general. In that case all empirical knowledge of objects would necessarily conform to such concepts, because only as thus presupposing them is anything possible as *object of experience*. (Kant, 1929, p. 126, his italics)

And Kant's resounding answer is that such necessary conformation is a feature of all empirical knowledge. This takes Kant away from the spirit of Darwinism. Although Kant, like the Darwinian epistemologist, invokes a mind-structuring element in knowledge, the 'a priori' intended to have a hold on knowledge which is lacking from that of the epigenetic rules. For the Darwinian, had things been otherwise, one could well have had different rules and thus would have structured knowledge quite differently. Hence, for all his brilliance, Kant looks backwards, rather than forwards. His thought is alien to the radical naturalism forced upon us by Darwinism.

Philosophical precursor: Hume?

We must not stop here. If Darwinism is not truly in the spirit of Kant, is there any other great figure of the past with which it might be more happily allied? For a number of obvious reasons, one possible precursor stands out above all others: David Hume.

First, Kant himself was responding to problems set by Hume, particularly those about the total lack of direct sensory evidence for such notions as causality (Kemp Smith, 1923). Thus, similarities between Kantianism and Darwinian epistemology could well be primarily similar responses to shared problems. I have already myself noted that the Darwinian analysis of causality neatly explains the dilemma raised by Hume – why do we believe in necessary connections when there is no tangible evidence? Second, historically, looking back to Hume (rather than Kant) makes much sense, because Darwin himself owed much to British empiricism, the greatest representative of which was Hume. We know that Darwin studied Hume's own writings and was much impressed. The historical expectation is that Darwinian epistemology will stand more in the British than the continental tradition (Manier, 1978; Huntley, 1972).

Third, unlike Kant, Hume was always stressing links between human thought and action and animal thought and action. Such links are the very essence of the Darwinian programme. Kant, in the tradition of continental rationalism, had a low opinion of the status of animals, denying them consciousness or any capability of reasoned thought. They are merely complex machines: *'apprehensio bruta* without consciousness' (Kemp Smith, pp. x-ix, quoting a letter from Kant to Furst von Beloselsky, 1792). Hume, on the contrary, wrote: '[N]o truth appears to me more evident, than that beasts are endowed with thought and reason as well as men' (1978, p. 176). Fourth, finally, and most importantly of all, the Darwinian approach to morality stands directly in line to Hume's moral thinking. It is very different from Kant's approach. This is a matter that will be explored in detail in the next chapter. But, it can properly be noted here that Hume's moral philosophy was probably that which led to his epistemology, rather than conversely (Kemp Smith, 1941).

The signs are all that the Darwinian epistemology sketched in this chapter will be a twentieth-century counterpart to Hume's eighteenth-century thinking. And, indeed, expectations are fulfilled. It is true that Hume (like Kant) regards logic as something different ('relations of ideas') – indeed he (unlike Kant) drops mathematics into the same bucket also – but when we get to the non-deductive side of reasoning, particularly when we get to such topics as causality, we have a very close connection between Hume's analysis and that of the Darwinian. To prove the point, let us run quickly though Hume's celebrated discussion. (A good general introduction is Stroud, 1977).

We humans believe nature is a highly structured system, ordered by countless binding regularities. Therefore, we pick out phenomena which we identify as 'causes', and think they must be followed by phenomena which we identify as 'effects'. We say that fire causes pain and burning, and that the effects of pain and burning necessarily follow the fire. Moreover, we distinguish such causes from mere accidental successions, where there are reasons to think the successions might not always hold.

But where is the source of our convictions of causal necessity? Hume argues that we read necessity into nature. There is no necessity, no set of binding causal 'powers', to be found there, prior to our perception. Rather, we see that things which we call 'causes' are constantly followed by those things we call 'effects'. This sets up a feeling of necessity in the mind, which then in turn imparts this necessity to nature, as though it were an external power. 'Tis the constant conjunction of objects, along with the determination of the mind, which constitutes a physical necessity' (Hume, 1978, p. 171). But wherein lies our conviction of the objectivity of necessity? 'Tis a common observation, that the mind has a great propensity to spread itself on external objects, and to conjoin with them any internal impressions, which they occasion, and which always make their appearance at the same time that these objects discover themselves to the senses' (Hume, 1978, p. 167).

Let us go over this argument slowly. Events follow each other with regularity in nature. Fire – 'Ouch!' Fire – 'Ouch!' Fire – 'Ouch!' Humans notice these successions, and they trigger in the mind expectations and feelings of necessity. 'Beware! Fire causes burning and pain.' But why is there such a triggering? Because of the way the mind is made. The mind has a *propensity* to see necessity in successions, which propensity is activated by the successions themselves (Wolff, 1960). The content of the successions, however, is given by nature. Finally the mind (unconscious to itself) reads this necessity into nature, thinking nevertheless that it has found it as an objective fact of nature. If I tell you to beware the fire, I think I am doing more than simply reporting on my own psychology. It is not my intention to convey to you that I personally have a phobia about fires. My aim is to persuade you that fires are objectively dangerous.

This is all about as close to the Darwinian position as you can be without being an explicit evolutionist. Hume's propensities correspond precisely to Wilson's epigenetic rules. For Hume and Wilson, the mind thinks about nature in a causal fashion, believing that it is finding powers rather than creating them. This is not to say that Wilson, or any other modern thinker, would (or must) necessarily accept the details of Hume's psychological speculations about how the mind is triggered into action. But, for Hume and modern thinkers, the reason for such propensities seem the same, namely their value to us as functioning beings. Hume explicitly relates the utility of animal reason with 'their own preservation and the propagation of their species' (1978, p. 177). You will remember how Hume declines to draw a sharp line between animals and us humans.

The advance of the Darwinian on Hume is the giving of an evolutionary interpretation to the propensities, thus converting them into epigenetic rules. However, the propensities do seem to have the contingency which I have earlier identified as an essential mark of epigenetic rules (or the products of such rules), and which distinguish the Darwinian from the Kantian. For Kant, causal thinking stems from the way we must be. This is to introduce a factor alien to Darwinian non-progressionism. For Hume causal thinking stems from the way we are, and that is that. This is the position of the Darwinian. I claim Darwinian epistemology as a natural growth from British empiricism.

Common-sense realism

We cannot stop here. Grant that a firm bond has been forged between Hume and Darwinian epistemology. Is this not a matter for regret, rather than celebration? Hume, notoriously, was a sceptic. His analysis of causal connection led to his related discussion of the nature and existence of material objects.

> Objects have a certain coherence even as they appear to our senses; but this coherence is much greater and more uniform, if we suppose the objects to have a continu'd existence; and as the mind is once in the train of observing an uniformity among objects, it naturally continues, till it renders the uniformity as compleat as possible. The simple supposition of their continu'd existence suffices for this purpose, and gives us a notion of a much greater regularity among objects, than what they have when we look no farther than our senses. (Hume, 1978, p. 198)

Here we have at work another propensity, constancy of objects. We believe that tables and chairs and trees go on existing, whether or not anyone is around. We think that there is a real, objective world. Yet, as with causation, this belief is something we impose upon experience, rather than draw from it.

Given the Hume–Darwin connection just established, we must presumably allow a related epigenetic rule, which leads us to believe in that real world, towards a fuller knowledge of which science is supposedly progressing. One supposes that this rule is closely allied with the rule that tells us consiliences are not mere coincidences, but reflect the true nature of reality. However, since such a rule (or rules) is that which makes us believe in reality, we must concede with the Humean that our belief has no objective foundation. The aim of science is based on a fiction of human psychology, rather than on the true nature of an objectively existing universe.

And so the story continues, laying you open to doubt about virtually anything you might want to claim. Why take the propensities seriously in any way?

> 'Tis impossible upon any system to defend either our understanding or our senses; and we but expose them farther when we endeavour to justify them in that manner. As the sceptical doubt arises naturally from a profound and intense reflection on those subjects, it always increases, the farther we carry our reflections, whether in opposition or conformity to it. (Hume, 1978, p. 218)

And:

> I have already shown, that the understanding, when it acts alone, and according to its most general principles, entirely subverts itself, and leaves not the lowest degree of evidence in any proposition, either in philosophy or common life. (Hume, 1978, pp. 267-8)

Sauce for the goose is sauce for the gander. Problems for the Humean are problems for the Darwinian. It may be true that we are governed by the epigenetic rules, but what does this tell us about real truth? What is to counter the sceptic who agrees that we use epigenetic rules, but who denies that we know anything about truth or reality or whatever? Does not Darwinian epistemology wither before the doubter? We believe that science is progressing towards knowledge of a real world, because our consiliences get better and better, and our predictions are more and more accurate. But who is to say that any of this truly means a thing?

Quite apart from the existence of things when no one is perceiving them, why should we take seriously the conviction of the power and importance of consilience (Laudan, 1971)? By the Darwinian's own admission, the conviction is no more than an adaptive tool. Thus, there is no defence against the claim that everything collapses into a morass of opinion and prejudice, from which only an entirely different philosophical approach can rescue us. Perhaps we were a little too quick and glib in our dismissal of Kant. He may have seen the virtues of the Humean analysis; but he at least knew of the pitfalls to be avoided.

This is a very serious problem for Darwinian epistemology – *the* most serious problem. Turning to Kant or some other Spencerian-type solution will not help. We must extract ourselves as best we can with what we have, not with what we would like to have. Let us see what we can do. I do emphasize that, although I feel the Darwinian is working in the spirit of Hume, my present interest is not in historical discussion *per se*, but in defending the epistemology of this chapter against sceptical attacks. (Stroud, 1984, contains a good discussion of these issues, although I doubt he would accept my answers.)

Let me begin with the critique of the most basic common-sense notions of truth and reality. What should one say to the critic who would have us doubt everything, even chairs and tables as they are to us in everyday life? Probably, not much needs to be said. It is certainly true that the Darwinian sees the knowing subject actively involved in our common-sense understanding of reality. Epigenetic rules enter into our awareness of ordinary objects. But the pretence that nothing exists strikes me as self-refuting. Whether existence is quite what we think it is will be considered shortly. (Could life be a dream or totally a fiction of some sort?) However, the basic starting-point is that there is a common-sense existence, and that 'truth' and 'knowledge' purport (in a correspondence fashion) to be about it. To be honest, I do not quite know what it would mean to say that 'nothing exists' or 'at the common-sense level, nothing exists or has the nature that we think it has'. At this level, appearance and reality do surely merge, because this is the level of appearance.

Of course, as we have just been shown by Hume, there is more to common-sense reality than the world of immediate perceptions – the chair as perceived by me, here and now. The world of common-sense is the world where objects persist. To this we can add that it is the world in which science progresses apparently to knowledge of deeper and deeper levels of these persistent objects. What then of sceptical worries about the use of epigenetic rules leading to object-persistence and progress? In response, note that, even if there is some sort of effective scepticism at the deepest root, the Darwinian epistemologist no less than the Humean can (and does) run his life in an ordinary common-sense sort of way, distinguishing 'true' from 'false', 'reality' from 'illusion', and asserting the existence of an external world. Through coherence, consistency, and the like, we can distinguish fictions like Macbeth's dagger from the real thing, like the daggers which killed Caesar. The epigenetic rules, no less than the Humean propensities, justify our ordinary ways of doing things. That is the whole point. *The ordinary way is the way of propensities or rules.*

For this reason, the last thing one intends to do in identifying the propensities or rules is to make ordinary life dissolve into paradox. Hume was explicit in his commitment to a common-sense realism. 'As to what may be said, that the operations of nature are independent of our thought and reasoning, I allow it . . . .'(1978, p. 168). I confess that the notion that there is not something solidly real to this world sounds somewhat ludicrous to a person whose basic thesis is that we all got here in an ongoing clash between rival organisms. Are we really supposed to doubt the continuous existence of tigers and wolves, antelopes and lambs?

In the same vein, the Darwinian endorses our knowledge of the objects of science, like electrons and genes. Subject to the proviso that we get to know them gradually (which is true also of everyday objects), the Darwinian asserts their existence in a likewise 'common-sense' way. Again, epigenetic rules (like consilience) are involved, but again this is what 'common sense' is all about. (Earlier in this chapter, I spoke of the tensions which some perceive between existence at the everyday level and at the sophisticated scientific level. At the end of this section, I will speak more to this problem, showing how the Darwinian handles it, but showing also why there is an air of paradox.)

But, what about the question of progress, a problem which has been nagging at us throughout this book? Even at the 'common-sense' level, can we truly speak of it? Progress has been tied to consilience, and this centres on coincidence. Unfortunately, however improbable, a coincidence could be no more than that – a coincidence. This sceptical worry probably does not deny some sort of reality, or even that consiliences can work. But it does suggest that we have no right to feel confident that we are actually making progress in science.

Let me make the following three points. First, do note that, even if our worst fears are realized and we end up in scepticism of some sort, we should not thereby conclude that we have a decisive philosophical criticism of Darwinian epistemology. We must not assume that the best possible analysis of the foundations of science must show us on the road to the certainty that Descartes thought his good God should provide, and for which philosophers ever since have hankered. We are animals, using our evolutionarily aquired powers to delve into questions for which such powers were certainly not intended. For the Darwinian, there is no hot line to total truth. If it turns out that the belief in progress is illusory, this will be philosophically disquieting. It will not be a *reductio* of Darwinism.

Second, complementing this first point, the Darwinian recognizes that philosophical failure to avoid scepticism is quite irrelevant when it comes to the questions which truly count – getting on with survival and reproduction (or even doing science). Epigenetic rules, like Humean propensities, not only let us do these really important things, but help us to do them rather well. The burnt child fears the fire, and avoids it the next time. The caveman looking for his club turns confidently to the corner where he left it, knowing that things do not pop in and out of existence. And his mate carries away the children when there are tiger signs about. Relatedly, the human mind is such that, even if abstract philosophy leads to scepticism, unreasoned optimism keeps us afloat. As human beings, we all believe in the reality of causality and of the external world and of the worth of consiliences, whatever philosophy might prove. And that is what counts.

Here, incidentally, we have another very strong reason for setting Darwinian epistemology in the Humean tradition. Hume saw with crystal clarity the irrelevance to everyday life of the scepticism towards which his philosophy might be thought to point.

> Most fortunately it happens, that since reason is incapable of dispelling these clouds, nature herself suffices to that purpose, and cures me of this philosophical melancholy and delirium, either by relaxing this bent of mind, or by some avocation, and lively impression of my senses, which obliterate all these chimeras. I dine, I play a game of back-gammon, I converse, and am merry with my friends; and when after three or four hour's amusement, I wou'd return to these speculations, they appear so cold, and strain'd, and ridiculous, that I cannot find in my heart to enter into them any farther. (1978, p. 269)

The Darwinian's important contribution is to pick up on Hume's astute psychological observations, showing just why such scepticism fails. We are animals, and have adaptations to protect us from the worries of our reason. If we got overly depressed about the conclusions of our thinking, we would simply stop functioning properly. Specifically, what counts in the case of science is the scientist's happy and confident belief that he/she is on the road to success. I do not mean to be cynical, but at a certain level philosophy does not matter. Do you think a new Nobel prize-winner will be perturbed at the news that consiliences do not guarantee absolute truth? Or that, whatever the arguments of the philosophers, he/she will think that he/she truly does not know about reality?

Third, when looking at consiliences and at the legitimacy of making claims about progress and true understanding of reality, it is surely proper to distinguish between what is logically possible and what it is reasonable or rational to believe. P. F. Strawson (1952) has argued that the question of whether induction is justified really does not make much sense, because the proper use of induction is precisely that which marks a sound justification. This is precisely the Darwinian's point at this common-sense level (which might, of course, lead to some very non-common-sense scientific results). The proper use of consiliences defines what we mean by 'truth' and 'rationality' – and the only justification given or needed is that they do not let us down. In real life, the logical possibilities of the philosopher (or the writer of outlandish detective fiction) simply do not occur. When people like Kuhn (1962) and Laudan (1981) question whether science is truly progressing towards knowledge of reality, we do not reject their position because they alone properly use terms like 'progress' and 'truth' – which usage the rest of us illegitimately refuse to acknowledge. Rather, their case fails through an inadequate or incomplete analysis of the nature of science and its change. They ignore or deny the cumulative, ever more consilient nature of science and its theories (see chapter 2, and Boyd, 1981).

The upshot of this discussion is that there is no more reason to be genuinely sceptical about the existence and reptilian nature of dino-saurs, than there is to be sceptical about the existence and mammalian nature of cows and horses. Note, moreover, that although the Darwinian's approach even to common-sense reality necessarily is a function of the contingent workings of the individual human mind, he/she quite escapes any epistemological relativism which you might fear is lying in wait. Why is my world also your world? Why do we not get a fragmentation of realities? For the Darwinian, the required universality follows on the unity of humankind. Those humans who believed that $2 + 2 = 5$, or that fire causes orgasms rather than pain, or ignored the virtues of consiliences, got wiped out in the struggle for existence. Remember how Quine (1969b) made this point.

Of course, since scientific methodology reaches right up into the ethereal levels of culture (somewhat far from immediate adaptive necessity), one does expect to find (as one does in fact find) disputes about proper principles of scientific reasoning. For instance, much of the debate about Darwin's *Origin* was less about facts and more about method (Hull, 1973). But this does not deny the underlying, genetically caused, stable uniformity of human thought.

Indeed, when it comes to handling the world, the Darwinian notes a sharing of response patterns across species, including those species very different from *Homo sapiens*. Some organisms like insects have very different senses from us, using chemicals ('pheromones') for much of their contact with the outside world (Wilson, 1971). Obviously, the information of the insect is not the information of the human. Nevertheless, there is a stability and correspondence in how the information is used, which supports the Darwinian in his/her belief about the non-relativistic nature of his/her thought about an objective world, shared by all living things. Insects do not fly through things like trees, objects that humans regard as solid and thus impenetrable. On the contrary, all organisms seem as if they are adapted to the same objective world as we. It certainly makes more sense to argue for a shared world with different (non-relativistic) ways of responding, than for completely different existences for different organisms.

One final point. You might object that, earlier, I claimed (or implied) that notions like God and cause are mere illusions, pushed upon us by our biology for their reproductive virtues. And yet now, apparently, I turn round and speak of a realism, which requires the backing of epigenetic rules no less than does (say) theology. Is this not grossly inconsistent? If it is acceptable to rely on a rule for the continued existence of objects, why can we not rely on a rule for the reality of God or causes?

This objection misses the nub of the Darwinian's case. First, no one is denying causality. Rather, the claim is that it is not quite all we think it is, and that we do ourselves create causal necessity. Second, regarding notions like God, the crucial point is that we are involved in an ongoing process of trying to make sense of our experiences, our beliefs, and so forth. Through our scientific and other enquiries, we find that some of our ideas simply do not hold up as true reflections of reality (although we also learn why we might think these ideas are about reality). Trying to make consistent coherent sense of life, some things are explained (or explained away) in terms of other things – the belief in God, in terms of its adaptive value, for instance. But what we also find is that the whole of life does not collapse into a morass of shifting, transient paradox. Consiliences do work. We do, historically, get a sense of real progress, as we push towards an understanding in terms of laws, predictions, testability, and, above all, the unification at the heart of great science. Here, at least nature does not let us down. Thus in this sense we get (and are justified in believing in) what I am characterizing as common-sense realism. Ultimately, it works.

Of course, this is not to deny that in esoteric science we are not being very common-sensical, in the usual meaning of the term (although see below). It is also to stress again that our enquiry is empirical. There was no *a priori* reason why causes should not have been found to correspond to (say) fluids. Nor is there that within Darwinism itself which makes the notion of God logically incoherent, or even something denying that theism is so basic a belief that it is necessarily presupposed by the rest of knowledge. The Darwinian did not capriciously invent the problem of evil as a barrier to religious commitment. (This is an important point. Darwinism *per se* is not atheistic.)

To sum up. We sense material objects. The apple is round, shiny, green flecked with red, crisp, sweet yet with underlying tartness. Is it really this way? Yes, of course it is. It is not pink and gooey, like candy-floss. But we know there is more to the story than this. Our investigations show that the apple is made from cells, which in turn are made from molecules, and so on. The (causal) reason why we sense the apple as we do, is because of features down at these levels, together with our own evolved natures. Because we are primates, the colour and taste are important and appear to us as they do. The primary epigenetic rules are crucial here. (See Goldman, 1967, and especially Shimony, 1971, for philosophical discussions pertinent to the claims of this paragraph.)

The underlying particles are removed from immediate sensation, and given to us in consiliences. Because of this, and because of their causal role, such entities do not strike us as being so dependent upon the peculiarities of our nature. Indeed, they appear to us as part of a deeper, more profound side to reality. And so they are – DNA really is the key to the code of life (and, in another context going to the macroscopic, continents really did move). Science, as we know it, aided in its work by our skill with mathematics and the like, successfully progresses towards an ever stronger grasp of this reality. Nevertheless, this grasp is still one in which the enquiring mind plays its crucial part, as we use the secondary epigenetic rules to dig into and construct our experiences. Unfortunately for philosophy (but fortunately for real life), this work of the mind is normally concealed from us, for the success of the epigenetic rules lies in our taking them at face value. We think that mathematics talks of some world of eternal truths and that molecules exist quite independently of the observer.

Part of the paradox of common-sense realism, looked at scientifically or philosophically as we do now, is that we turn it back on itself to examine its own nature. Causes really are necessary and yet we can see that the necessity results from constant conjunction combined with a propensity. Apples really are red, and yet we can see that the redness is a result of light, molecules, neurons, and so forth. This self-examination is not a viciously circular process, if we realize that reality rests ultimately on a sense of coherence and success – consiliences, and the like, really do work. If they did not, all would fall apart.

Should we talk of surface or naïve realism for the redness of apples, and (perhaps) scientific realism for the deeper understanding? I confess to feeling little sympathy for the scholastic (and Popperian) practice of making ever more minute divisions. And, in principle, such a dichotomy seems misleading, for the epigenetic rules are active throughout. Let us simply remember with Quine (1964) that ultimately (despite reservations expressed above) 'science is self-conscious common sense' (p. 3).

Enough has been said. At the common-sense level, the Darwinian epistemologist is no more of a sceptic or a relativist than is Hume. Like everyone else, he/she believes in a shared real world, towards a knowledge of which science progresses.

Metaphysical scepticism

Unfortunately, having raised the name of David Hume, we cannot halt here. We must go on to what many take to be the centre of Hume's scepticism, and to the Darwinian's potential for such scepticism. At this centre is Hume's philosophical or metaphysical scepticism (Wright, 1983). Here we have the problem which many critics would say should have been tackled first, and which makes suspect any naturalistic approach to knowledge – be it Humean or be it Darwinian.

Hume locates our belief in the existence of an objective external world in a sense of coherence, bound up with a propensity to give objects a continued existence. But, as Hume himself says, for all of our common-sense realism, this supposition is all truly a kind of story, and 'that fiction [of a continued existence], as well as the identity, is really false' (1978, p. 209). At root, we cannot claim an ultimate stable reality, which we know.

The point being made here is that, of course, at one (everyday) level we believe in the reality of chairs and tables and trees. They are not chimeras like Macbeth's dagger. This is common-sense realism, which the propensities inform and support. Chairs and tables and trees have a solid, ongoing existence. Today, we can include electrons, genes, and dinosaurs. But at another philosophical level – the ultimate level if you will – we have to admit that there is simply a justificatory void. We believe what our propensities direct us to believe, because it is they which provide us with our criteria of truth and reason. If you doubt these, there is no secure base on which to fall back. Objects pop in and out of existence, which is hardly the mark of the truly real.

I am sure many critical readers will think that this concession is to give away virtually all of the gains. Since the Darwinian stands with Hume on the propensities, the inescapable conclusion seems to be that he/she – likewise – has to be a sceptic of this fundamental, metaphysical kind.

Indeed, if anything, the problems seem even greater than Hume acknowledges. The metaphysical sceptic pounces at the point where we humans simply cannot peer or enter. When there is no one around in the forest, you cannot look at the tree and confirm its existence. You rely on your propensities/rules for belief in continued existence; but, by definition, you have had no experience or confirmation of that which your beliefs carry you across.

Matching these temporal gaps (now you see it, now you don't, now you do), there is the spacial void, as science approaches the domain of the ever smaller. We can see ants. We can see chromosomes. Perhaps we can even see genes, in some way. We just cannot see electrons – nor will we ever see them. But, at this point, belief in electrons – their nature and their very reality – becomes a matter of faith, on a par with unseen trees. It is no good saying that, if electrons do not exist, then we are stuck with a miracle – that the indirect effects call either for real entities or for supernatural forces beyond our ken (Smart, 1968). This kind of argument works only when you have analogous situations, which point to the reality of objects, causing effects.

Let us be reasonable. Perhaps it would be a miracle if dinosaurs did not exist. Why? First, because we have all of the dinosaur effects. *And*, secondly, because we have analogous cases where effects do point to real entities. Dinosaur droppings are proof of dinosaurs, because cow droppings are proof of cows – and we have experienced cows. But, again by definition (as in the temporal case), we have never experienced anything too small to be experienced. Nor have we ever experienced anything analogous to something too small to be experienced. Thus, there has to be a radical scepticism about the nature and existence of the ultimate microentities of science.

Apparently, you have two options. Either you leave knowledge, including scientific knowledge, caught in this unhappy half-world. Or (as most will think) this uncertainty must be countered. Perhaps, therefore, yet one more time we should turn to Kant, hoping to grasp the security towards which he strained. Furthermore, the philosophically knowledgeable objector will point out, it is at this point that we get one of the most significant differences between Hume and Kant. In part to avoid Humean scepticism, Kant argues that there is a reality behind all of our perceptions – the thing-in-itself (*der Ding-an-sich*): 'Though we cannot *know* these objects as things in themselves, we must yet be in position at least to *think* them as things in themselves; otherwise we should be landed in the absurd conclusion that there can be appearance without anything that appears' (1929, p. 27).

Without conceding that his/her position is anything like as bad as the critic charges, I am sure you can see at once why the Darwinian is highly sceptical of a Kantian thing-in-itself: something lying behind perceptions and guaranteeing an ongoing existence to the world. Indeed, I would go so far as to say that for the Darwinian the thing-in-itself seems to be, not so much a false notion, as an incoherent one. To speak of something which really exists, independent and beyond human awareness (direct or indirect), immune to the limitations of human sensory and intellectual powers, does not make too much sense. One should not think of objects being hollow, as it were, waiting for reality to fill them up. Or of the tree in the forest, when no one is around, as having a new kind of being which takes over until we can get back.

This kind of reality – something outside the sensing, interpreting subject – is meaningless. The Darwinian can have no more truck with it than with the super-sensible reality of the Platonist – the supposed home of the truths of mathematics. Like the Christian God, it is difficult to know, in human terms, precisely what nature a thing-in-itself would possess. It cannot be a shadowy version of what we perceive, for this is to make it subject to all of the problems of normal objects. But then, what is it?

You cannot evade the unknowableness of the thing-in-itself by identifying it with the unseen entities of science, like electrons. You cannot satisfy Kant by arguing that electrons always exist, even though our perceptual world may be open to doubt of some sort. On the one hand, the Darwinian denies that electrons are quite as unknowable as the Kantian thing-in-itself. On the other hand, the supposition that electrons always exist surely requires invocation of an epigenetic rule. The Darwinian believes that electrons do go on existing, but this is part of his/her common-sense realism. The thing-in-itself was supposed to salvage the reality of electrons, not conversely. For reasons like this, which show that the thing-in-itself raises more problems than it solves, the Darwinian is still not attracted to Kantianism.

This seems to plunge us back to the nether-world of torment by the metaphysical sceptic. Hume's predecessor, Bishop Berkeley, when faced with scepticism about ultimate truth and reality, saved the absolutist day by invoking God. 'To be is to be perceived'; but it just so fortunately happens that God is always on Perception Duty.

> There was a young man who said: God
> Must think it exceedingly odd,
> When He finds that this tree
> Still continues to be
> When there's no one about in the Quad.
>
> Young man your astonishment's odd,
> Since I'm always about in the Quad.
> And that's why this tree
> Still continues to be
> Since observed by, Yours Faithfully,
>   God!

Since a belief in the existence of God is, to say the least, hardly more secure than a belief in the continued existence of external objects, such an avenue of epistemological belief is as closed to the Darwinian as is the Kantian route.

However, by this stage one begins to wonder if perhaps the strength of metaphysical scepticism might not also be its downfall. Is it that much of a threat to anyone, including the Darwinian? If metaphysical scepticism is something which can be avoided only by invoking such problematic notions as the thing-in-itself or the Christian God, can it really be quite the devastating critique it appears to be? My hunch is that, for all its prima-facie reasonableness, there is something radically flawed about the sceptic's attack. One is raising the ante until no answer is possible, and then demanding an answer – an answer which went with the old rationalist ways of thinking.

Suppose it be pointed out, for instance, that many microentities previously hidden (like chromosomes) are now visible. Suppose it then be argued that this is surely analogical reason for taking seriously the existence even of electrons. At once the sceptic lowers the barriers, claiming that he/she is referring to that part of putative existence which lies beyond our reach – including a reach augmented by television and microscopes. Clearly, the sceptic is trying to wrench from the naturalist (like the Darwinian) an answer to a problem to which, by definition, no answer can be given. Since, under these conditions, it is difficult to see what response would satisfy, the suspicion is that there is no genuine assault on the Darwinian.

Put matters this way. I am sceptical about my lover's professed intentions. My beloved vows undying love, but combines this with mysterious absences and so forth. I know what the options are. Either my suspicions are well founded, and my lover is seeing someone else on the side. Or my suspicions are false, and my lover is true and is secretly preparing some treat for me. In the case of metaphysical scepticism, I really cannot imagine what truth or falsity would be. Thus, I am inclined to think that neither the Humean nor the Darwinian need be as flummoxed as Hume himself professes to be. Without in any sense pitchforking the Darwinian into the logical positivist camp, Carnap was surely right when he wrote:

> neither the thesis of realism that the external world is real, nor that of idealism that the external world is not real can be considered scientifically meaningful. This does not mean that the two theses are false; rather, they have no meaning at all so that the question of their truth and falsity cannot even be posed. (Carnap, 1967, p. 334, quoted by Stroud, 1984, p. 172, italics in original)

We all have a feeling of wonder about the unseen and unseeable. Such a feeling clearly has its own adaptive value. Unfortunately, this sense persists, even when the problems are not genuine.

Putting the matter yet another way, what is happening is that we have projected our common-sense reality into a commitment to metaphysical reality – that is what our epigenetic rules make us do. Because of our biology, we think that the reality which we have helped to create has to be a person-independent reality. We should not be surprised when this latter reality collapses into paradox and non-being.[5]

But, in any case, as we know already, Hume brilliantly put his finger right on the only solution that a naturalist like the Darwinian cares about anyway. What philosophy opens up, psychology closes. Once we leave the classroom or the study, we have a total inability to remain worried by any kind of scepticism. We have an innate tendency to believe in the continued and continuous reality of objects, and this is backed up by our experience. We do not have things popping in and out of existence. They exist only in so far as they are perceived; but when they are perceived (which is what matters to us), they do exist. If you persist in finding metaphysical scepticism upsetting – hankering after a thing-in-itself or some such thing – all I can do is remind you that natural selection is not in the business of satisfying philosophers. Natural selection has seen to it that we flesh out experience, assuming that objects continue to be, all of the time, and in all dimensions. That is enough for its purposes. If Socrates is not satisfied, he will simply have to go away puzzled.

Konrad Lorenz and the biological a priori

Having made these remarks on metaphysical scepticism, I shall leave critics of naturalistic approaches to philosophy to tell you how happy they now feel. However, candour does force me to admit that, not even all of those basically sympathetic to my position will feel I have done the topic of Darwinian defences against scepticism full justice.

I deny that the Darwinian can establish and elaborate on the Kantian

---

[5] Putnam (1981) argues that it makes no sense to claim that we are all brains in vat, manipulated to think that our thoughts (about trees and so on) are real. Clearly, this is a position with which the Darwinian empathizes, accepting Putnam's 'internal' (i.e. common-sense) realism and with him rejecting 'external' (i.e. metaphysical) realism. Perceptively, Putnam writes: 'Today the notion of a noumenal world (i.e. world of the thing-in-itself) is perceived to be an unnecessary metaphysical element in Kant's thought. (But perhaps Kant is right: perhaps we can't help thinking that there is *somehow* a mind-independent "ground" for our experience even if attempts to talk about it lead at once to nonsense.)' (pp. 61–2).

In Putnam (1982) there is a short, sharp critique of all evolutionary epistemologists, faulting them for being metaphysical realists. I agree with Putnam's criticisms, but deny that his is the final word.

thing-in-itself. This is hardly that stern a line, for I deny also that the notion makes much sense or that our 'ignorance' is very troublesome. But even in arguing this, my line is sterner than that of the distinguished ethnologist, Konrad Lorenz, who argued (nearly 50 years ago) for a Darwinian approach to epistemology.

Like me, Lorenz (1941) endorses an approach which makes the mind's interpretative contribution an essential element in knowledge. Like me also, Lorenz thinks that natural selection is the key causal factor in the nature and operation of this interpreting mind. However, not only is Lorenz not a metaphysical sceptic, he does not take the approach (which I favour) of denying such scepticism on grounds of its essential incoherence and psychological irrelevance. He is prepared to grant the merit of the sceptic's attack, arguing instead that the Darwinian can mount a positive defence against it. Seeing Darwinism as an extension of the philosophy of Kant, Lorenz claims that the coming of an adequate theory of evolution confirms the existence of the thing-in-itself. Moreover, because of this theory, we can now do that which Kant thought impossible. Thanks to Darwinism, Lorenz believes, we can comment meaningfully on the true nature of ultimate reality.

How can this be so? Lorenz argues (truly) that, in Darwinian evolution, we have the organism adapting to its environment. Thus, for instance, the horse's hooves adapt to the grassy steppes. Lorenz thinks of this process as a kind of mirroring or corresponding of the organism to reality. Somehow, the equine feet mesh with the steppes, in a way (for example) that webbed feet would not. Pushing the argument, Lorenz suggests that we can properly think of our own view of the external world, not as an exact copy of the thing-in-itself, but as a kind of adaptive correspondence – one which got better as the human line evolved more sophisticated organs of sense. Furthermore:

> What we witness as experience is always a coping of the real in us with the real outside of us. Therefore the relationship between the events in and outside of us is not alogical and does not basically prohibit drawing conclusions about the lawfulness of the external world from the lawfulness of the internal events. Rather, this relationship is one which exists between image and object, between a simplified model and the real thing. It is the relationship of an analogy of greater or less remoteness. The degree of this analogy is fundamentally open to comparative investigation. That is, it is possible to make statements as to whether agreement between appearance and actuality is more exact in comparing one human being to another, or one living organism to another. (Lorenz, 1941, p. 126)

Moreover:

> Many aspects of the thing-in-itself which completely escape being experienced by our present-day apparatus of thought and perception may

lie within the boundaries of possible experience in the near future, geologically speaking. (p. 123)

What can we say of this attempt to pour new scientific wine into old philosophical bottles? Putting to one side the question of the Darwinian's true intellectual ancestor, my feeling is that Lorenz has quite misunderstood the philosophies of both Hume and Kant, not to mention the proper import of Darwinism. No one here wants to deny that organs are adapted to reality; although whether we would really want to say that the hoof 'mirrors' the steppe is perhaps another question. But, this point of terminology apart, notice that what we have at issue in the biological example is a triadic relationship: the horse, the steppe, and the observers (us).

In other words, transferring the example to the case of human perception, we have the kind of common-sense awareness of reality that all admit. However, here (in the case of perception), we also do not simply have a diadic relationship, with a person observing the world and seeing ('mirroring') its true nature. The human perception case must likewise be seen as triadic. We have the observer (hoof) looking at (fitting to) a world (the steppe), the nature of which we have already determined independently, though our own senses (us). I see you looking at the chair. How do I know you see what the chair is really like? Because you tell me that it is brown, leathery, shiny – all of the things I know about, through my own efforts.

Hence, at best, Lorenz protects against the sceptic of common-sense realism. The problem of Humean metaphysical scepticism arises (the problem which the thing-in-itself is supposed to answer) when all we have is the observer and what he/she takes for reality. I see the chair. The question to me, as a Humean/Darwinian, is whether I can assert anything about 'real' existence, other than that based on what I get through my organs of sense, and the filtering effect of my epigenetic rules. And the answer is that I cannot. I may see the chair in finer and finer detail. Based on the evidence of the senses, I may spin theories incorporating ever more powerful consiliences, leading me to suppose that the chair is composed of sub-sensory particles like electrons. Additionally, I may have no reason to doubt my senses or my consiliences, because everything else meshes smoothly with my chair-awareness state. Other beings walk around the chair, rather than through it. But, at the bottom line, there is no perceiving of ultimate reality. What you see is what you get.

Reverting to Lorenz's own example: how do I know that the steppe is really as it is? This question must be answered before I can go on to say that the hoof really 'mirrors' it. If the steppe is not really hard, but porridge-like, no mirroring of ultimate reality occurs. Thus the Darwinian denies that his/her theory gives him/her an easy way out of metaphysical scepticism, and an insight into true reality, in the way supposed by Lorenz. However, as you now know, as a human and as a philosopher I remain untroubled. Common-sense reality is all we have. This is quite enough. (Neo-Lorenzian discussions include Riedl, 1980; Wuketits, 1978, 1981, 1983; Schilcher and Tennant, 1984.)

The ultimate foundations

There remains yet one more question. What about the circularity which haunts every discussion of the kind we have just been having? The findings of Darwinian evolutionary theory, including the extensions to human thought processes, have been taken as basic. From these, we have argued to a neo-Humean epistemology, claiming that our grasp of such notions as causality is very much dependent upon human nature. But, can we not – should we not – turn the argument back on itself? Are not the very claims about Darwinian evolution themselves infected with the same subjectivity? (See Quine, 1969a, and Stroud, 1984, especially chapter 6, for discussions of this problem.)

If our understanding of the world is a function of our evolution, have we any answer to the person who refuses to take us seriously? Are we not now caught in the paradox of the person who says that everything is relative? What can be said to the critic who simply insists that, in order to command attention, we must find some extra-evolutionary 'objective' claims ot serve as our initial premises? Just as Descartes found his *cogito ergo sum*, which was immune to metaphysical doubt, so we likewise need claims which are beyond the human evolved faculties. We need to establish the independent truth of Darwinism, so that we can then turn it on ourselves. (Of course, this then creates the paradox that we have some non-'subjective' knowledge, which Darwinism denies; but that can be a matter for later concern.)

Note incidentally that this objection is philosophical, not scientific. No one is now denying the arguments of chapters 1 and 4. No one is claiming that Darwinism, including its applications to humankind, is not a genuine, well-established theory, in the usual sense. The objection goes to the very methods used to establish and confirm Darwinism. If these have no ultimate foundation other than their biological utility, what is to stop the critic who simply refuses to take any of them seriously? You cannot simply say: 'Because otherwise you will die.' Apart from the fact that this response is hardly about truth, it presupposes the very understanding which is in question.

Perhaps the critic's worry can be put into concrete form by focusing in on natural selection, the concept right at the heart of Darwinism. How does an epistemologist like myself counter the following line of argument? 'We know that natural selection can "deceive" organisms for their own (biological) good. The belief of primitive people in spirits and the like is a clear case in point. Obviously, the sun does not have a mind of its own. Yet people believe precisely this, and the reason why they believe it is because such beliefs have adaptive value. Clearly, therefore, such beliefs are illusions, fostered upon us for reproductive purposes.

'Now, we all have a tendency to think that the fallacies of the "poor benighted heathen" could never extend up to us "civilized" Western folk. But if history and anthropology have taught us anything, it is of the need to be a little more modest on this score. Rationality hardly has an exclusive franchise in a society where leaders embrace Creationism and supply-side economics. Perhaps, therefore, the deceit of natural selection extends much further than we dream. Perhaps many of our basic principles of methodology are illusory. Possibly the illusion extends right to natural selection itself, the very basis of your case! If it sounds somewhat crazy to suggest that natural selection might be deceiving us about the true nature of natural selection, for our own good, remember it was you who undermined the principles of logic, by lumping them in with your general naturalistic approach.'

Versions of this argument are commonly made against any naturalistic approach to philosophy. Indeed, even Darwinians are sometimes given to self-doubts along these lines. '[T]he conventional view that natural selection favours nervous systems which produce ever more accurate images of the world must be a very naïve view of mental evolution' (Trivers, 1976, vi). And, who could deny that, at one level, the criticism has considerable force. I can certainly imagine humanoids more intelligent and more sensitive than we, and that they would learn many things about the world of which we are ignorant (Ruse, 1985). I can even imagine that they would learn things that (for biological reasons) we understand in quite different ways. This is an easy enough thought experiment, since we humans tower intellectually over other beings, and (as the critic notes) the average human in the twentieth century takes as commonplace that which would quite flabbergast the most sophisticated denizen of fifth-century BC Athens. Only extreme arrogance would pretend that, at last, as the twentieth century draws to a close, all is revealed to humankind.

Nevertheless, the possibility of super-beings poses no threat to the essential validity of the basic principles of biological science, as we now understand them. The evidence we have – evidence which only grows stronger as time goes by – is that advance in science is essentially a process of revision and refinement, rather than a succession of total revolutions. Moreover, such human-like beings would presumably be basing their thinking on principles of logic and causality. These principles might be modified somewhat from forms we hold, as we ourselves have modified older ideas. Yet, in recognizable ways, the beings would think from premises, using methods we also accept.

History (and anthropology) is the friend, not the foe, of the Darwinian at this point.

I suspect that the critic will respond that the force of his/her objection has been missed entirely. We are not talking about beings, who are like us, only more so – whether these be our evolved descendants, or extra-terrestrials (from the planet Krypton?), or even the traditional Christian God. Of course, these do not pose a radical threat to our knowledge, because virtually by definition they think in the same way that we do. The real point, the critic will say, is that the very thought processes themselves are at issue – particularly those leading to Darwinian theory. At the least, the Darwinian approach – with its fundamental commitment to non–progressionism – has to lay itself open to radically different interpretations of the world, where nothing we hold as intuitively true or obvious holds.

At the extreme, the Darwinian approach has to admit that everything we believe may simply be false, even unto the very principles of Darwinian evolutionary theory. Remember how Descartes (1951) introduced the idea of an Evil Demon, who undermined all of our knowledge, even logic and mathematics. Natural selection does exactly the same to the naturalistic philosopher. And there is no escape. It is true that Descartes thought that his *cogito ergo sum* was immune, even to the doubts brought on by the Demon. But there is much hesitancy about how much more Descartes could ever really protect from the Demon (Williams, 1978). And, in any case, both Descartes and the Darwinian want to do more than simply feel their own existence.

In response, I suspect that in a way this argument proves rather too much. Suppose that much (perhaps all) we believe is false. Presumably, this means that some possible Being could know the truth – otherwise you are hardly using the word 'false' in the usual way. But if you grant the possibility of this Being, then although it is much wiser than we, between it and us there has to be some meeting – some overlap – of minds. I think God exists. You know It does not. There have to be some common thought patterns here for us to have a genuine disagreement. And if this be so, we have a Being of the kind discussed just above: like us, only brighter. Which means that the above-given argument comes into play. Although we may now know much that the ancient Greeks did not, and although others will presumably know much that we do not, the development of knowledge is not purely random, with any old belief following on any other old belief. We have evidence of progress, with earlier views having elements of truth but being refined down through the ages.

Moreover, we have shared views (with this Being) about logic and the rest of reasoning. In other words, although we may not yet be absolutely correct about natural selection – I would be the first to be surprised if everything said in this chapter about epigenetic rules were to persist unchanged – we need not worry that we are heading completely in the wrong direction. The common-sense approach defended earlier saves us from total collapse into paradox. Put matters this way: if everything we believe is false, then there are no standards of right and wrong, and thus the universal claim is meaningless. If natural selection in particular is false, then we are allowing usual criteria of scientific evaluation, and the progress argument comes into play, defending selection.

Suppose now the critic pulls back and claims only that the Darwinian argument allows the possibility of a Being which thinks in a radically different way from us. This Being does not think our beliefs are false. Rather, to use a trendy term of the philosophers of science, its thoughts are quite 'incommensurable' with ours (Kuhn, 1962). Does this not still subvert the Darwinian approach, because it would have to be admitted that our naturalistic position is only one amongst who-knows-how-many alternatives – perhaps an infinite number? To say the least, the possibility of such a Being should undermine the confidence of the Darwinian epistemologist.

This point certainly brings forward an important conclusion which has emerged from the discussion of the last few sections, namely that, in some ultimate sense, the Darwinian rejects a correspondence theory of truth. That is to say, he/she rejects the idea that his/her thought corresponds to true reality, where 'reality' in this context is some sort of absolute entity, like the thing-in-itself. Obviously, working within the common-sense level, the Darwinian is just as much of a correspondence thinker as anyone else. ('Does the Freudian libido truly correspond to fluids in the human body?') But at the final level, defending common-sense reality, as we have had to accept, the Darwinian subscribes to a coherence theory of truth, believing that the best you can do is to get everything to hang together. (See Putnam, 1981, for a similar point and Rorty, 1980, for a powerful attack on the correspondence theory.)

However, within these coherence terms the Darwinian really is untroubled by the critic's objection. As far as we are concerned, different ways of thinking are (literally) unimaginable. and the unimaginable is no threat to what we do believe. Within our world, we see that scientific knowledge does progress towards greater insight; that Darwinism seems to be well down this path; and that, thus, we can legitimately form loose natural selection to provide a sound basis for epistemology. Within our frame of reference, this is the best we can do. Fortunately, it is enough. As Quine is wont to say: 'I see philosophy and science as in the same boat – a boat which, to revert to [Otto] Neurath's figure as I so often do, we can rebuild only at sea while staying afloat in it. There is no external vantage point, no first philosophy' (Quine, 1969b, pp. 126-7).

Have I saved Darwinian epistemology only by cutting it off from its Humean roots? Perhaps you will object that the tenor of my argument now becomes rather less Humean and rather more Kantian – rather less

Darwinian and rather more Spencerian. Have I not given human reason a privileged place, inasmuch as I claim that living without it is unimaginable? Hume argues that, contingently, we believe what we believe to be necessary. Kant argues that, necessarily, we believe what we believe to be necessary – no rational being could think and reason in any way, other than that way which we do think and reason. Has not the Darwinian turned to Kant in order to be saved from Hume?[6]

Let me say at once that, if this be so, I shall certainly not be shocked or unduly perturbed. After all, Kant himself was responding to Hume. The fact that he did not work truly in the spirit of Darwin does not as such preclude his anticipating conclusions of Darwinians. Yet, while conceding a Kantian flavour to this point of the discussion, I am loathe to concede all to Kant. As always, there hovers the non-progressive nature of Darwinian evolution. And, because of this, I hesitate to say (what Kant would insist) that any successful life-form, with a fair claim to rationality, must think in the way that we do. As Darwinians, we must leave open the possibility of a being interpreting and coping with the world in a way radically different from anything we can or could comprehend. You might object that such a being would not qualify for that which Kant would call 'rational'; but that would be cheating. At the least, if we have life-forms which, by human criteria, do the sorts of things we would call rational, but which do not share our thought-patterns, the Kantian position is a lot less exciting. (I take it that these beings, as viewed by us, would seem rational – avoiding obstacles, and so forth. The question is whether they must think as we do. The Kantian insists that they must, and the Darwinian denies that this need be so.)

Before you dismiss as neurotic fantasy my hestitancy about the privileged status of human thought processes, just one more time look the non-progressionism of evolution squarely in the face. We are what we are because of three and a half billion years of random mutation. There was no inevitability about our coming to the stage where we are now. People who think otherwise read into evolution all of those seductive but mistaken ideas about progress, and about the intrinsically special nature of the human species. Evolution is going nowhere – and rather slowly at that. For this reason, there is just no warrant to

---

[6] Somewhat diffidently relating this discussion to modal logic, the idea that necessities reside in things – are objective facts of nature – corresponds to Leibniz's view of necessity as 'true in all possible worlds.' This is captured in the modal *System S5*, which includes the axiom $Mp \supset LMp$, ($\lozenge p \supset \square \lozenge p$, or 'if p is possible, then necessarily p is possible'). The Kantian makes the rather weaker claim that a necessary statement simply has to be necessary ($Lp \supset LLp$). This axiom is included in the *System S4*. I take it that both Hume and Darwinians would deny $Lp \supset LLp$. Their necessity would therefore be that of the weakest of modal systems, *System T*. (The only modal axioms in this system are $Lp \supset p$, and $L(p \supset q) \supset (Lp \supset Lq)$.) For more on this point, see Hughes and Cresswell, 1968, especially pp. 75–80.

suppose, and every warrant to deny, that all thought or conciousness (or, if you like, 'thought' or 'consciousness') would have had to have been shaped by precisely those epigenetic constraints shaping us. To get from *A* to *B*, humans walk, monkeys swing through trees, horses run, birds fly, snakes slither, fish swim. No one, apparently, invented the wheel (Gould, 1980b). Why should thought processes be any different? Ignorance and arrogance alone deny the possibility of living beings which are subject to epigenetic thought processes foreign to us. Somewhere in the universe, such beings may well exist.

Of this much I am certain. Such strange beings are far more in tune with Darwinian theory than the extra-terrestrials of the average Hollywood science-fiction movie. Only a Spencerian would give ET large appealing eyes, a fondness for candy, and an inability to hold his liquor. Do not misunderstand me. I am not saying that were we to take a space ship out to look at these beings, and were our search successful, after a week in their company we would come back doubting logic and mathematics and causal thinking. Of course we would not, because we would be looking at such beings through our own eyes. I am simply saying that it is naïve to expect a neat meshing of minds.

If nothing else, I see no reason why such beings should have our understanding of space and time. If we were dealing with, what was by human standards, a very large entity, such as the intelligence in Fred Hoyle's story *The Black Cloud* (1957), I would expect it to have (at least) a non-Euclidean perceptual space. Of course, a super-large, non-Euclidean thinking being could be much like us in most respects – and we would be able to understand and perhaps communicate with it. I suspect that Darwinism points to beings far more different than this even. Yet if you grant the possibility of totally weird beings (or 'organisms'), the truths yielded by our epigenetic rules have more of a Humean than a Kantian status. They have a contingency, conferred on them by the evolutionary process, that denies them the status of the Kantian synthetic a priori. We are back at the level of Humean propensities.

But in arguing that radically different beings might have evolved, is not the Darwinian letting in the thing-in-itself by the back door? We have humans and we have aliens, responding to ultimate reality in their different ways. I admit that this is virtually the only way we can think of things – the propensities are highly effective – but this is not quite a fair charge against the Darwinian. The natural metaphor of people speaking in different languages about the same thing (bread, *Brot*, *pain*) is misleading. As far as we are concerned, there is only one reality. If we encountered aliens, from our perspective they would be evolving by natural selection and so forth. They might, perhaps, by doing some odd, non-adaptive things, but biologically they would be understandable in our terms (i.e. in human biological terms). The point is that we have no right to assume that their way of thinking is our way of thinking, for instance that they would have an alien biology by which they could understand us, or that there is an alien Kant who proposes a thing-in-itself.

This may strike you as all rather unsatisfactory – highly impausible in fact – but that is what incommesurability is all about. We cannot understand it. We must not be like many mystics, who characterize their experiences as ineffable, and then promptly proceed to talk about them. Again, I can only point out that we are probing into mysteries for which our biology has not fitted us – nor is there reason to think that it ever could fit us.[7]

The only way around this conclusion is a last-ditch defence of progressionism. But what are you going to throw into the barriers? As we have seen, only too clearly, arguments for progression have a nasty way of assuming that which you want to prove. You set up human-like qualities as your ideal, and then profess amazement when we turn out to possess them (Midgley, 1978). It is true that as different ecological niches get used up, organisms come up with new solutions. But these are not better or higher. Most importantly, they are not truer. To be honest, I have qualms about treating consciousness as another eco-logical niche to be filled, like land, sea and air. But even if some extraterrestrials have gone the route of consciousness in some way, there is no reason to think that our rules prevail.

What about the suggestion that parallel evolution gives cause for comfort? When faced with an ecological challenge, organisms of quite different types frequently respond (i.e. evolve) in much the same way. The analogy between the fins of whales and of sharks is a good example (Lewontin, 1978). Mammals and fish developed similar adaptations to swim through the water. Perhaps, therefore, we should expect separate instances of thinking beings to be governed by similar epigenetic rules. After all, I myself have made the similarities between chimpanzees and humans a major part of my case.

Unfortunately, there are (at least) two problems with this prima facie plausible suggestion. First, not all evolution is parallel. Some organisms responded to the water by getting out of it! We have no right to assume that all extra-terrestrial evolution will (or must) parallel ours. Second, we should not forget that many cases of parallel evolution occur between organisms which evolved together for a long time. This is especially true for humans and chimpanzees. If we are not dealing with homologies

[7] No doubt religious folk will be encouraged here, for in arguing thus the Darwinian seems to be conceding that very paradox and mystery at the heart of so much worship. Perhaps. I can only say that I can see absolutely no connection between what is being argued here and the content of major world religions. Why should strange aliens make it plausible to accept Jesus as the son of God?

(i.e. features which have been passed down from common ancestors), then at least we are dealing with organisms possessing essentially the same genotypes and whose possibilities of response are thus subject to similar constraints. Even sharks and whales have much in common, quite apart from facing similar selective pressures (as from predators). Suppose, however, that we were dealing with organisms which had never evolved together, and which never faced similar sorts of conditions. Then the possibility of evolution in the two cases ending at exactly the same point seems increasingly remote.

In short, because Darwinian epistemology takes seriously the non-directed nature of evolution, our beliefs are Humean rather than Kantian.

Conclusion

To sum up. Human thought is moulded and constrained by the epigenetic rules. In the case of science, we use deductive and inductive methodologies because these have proven their adaptive worth in the struggle for existence. Through them, we progress towards a greater understanding of the real world – the world that no person of common sense would ever dream of denying. There is no conflict between the non-progressionism of evolution, and the progressionism of the development of science, for organic change and scientific change are different things. We get the tools through organic evolution. What we produce has a meaning of its own, transcending biology, as we push our tools of understanding to produce ever better pictures of the world.

The philosopher whose programme is thus being carried forward by neo-Darwinian epistemology is David Hume. Like the Darwinian, Hume emphasized that our knowledge of the world is based on propensities of the mind. This means that, with Hume, the Darwinian has to wrestle with the problem of scepticism. There is no guarantee that a philosophically satisfying answer will emerge. Fortunately, in real life this does not matter, for we have the world of common-sense reality. Moreover, natural selection has seen to it that we are psychologically inured against the torments of metaphysical doubt. In any case, the Darwinian epistemologist need not really fear even the deepest barbs of scepticism. Total deception of the kind that the metaphysical sceptic threatens is a far-from-plausible notion. So long as one recognizes that, ultimately, truth rests in coherence, not correspondence, all is well.

Yet we must never forget that human knowledge is *human* know-ledge. Vanity and ignorance alone support the claim that human reason has a privileged status. Because we are the product of a long, directionless, evolutionary process, we are forced to accept that there is something essentially contingent about our most profound claims. In this, the Darwinian is a true naturalist.

6

Darwinian Ethics

We come to the second of the great problems of philosophy. What is right? What is wrong? What should I do? What should you do? What, if anything, should I tell you to do? What can I expect of you, and what can you expect of me? In short, we come to the problem of morality; the question of ethics.

We must tread carefully here. A philosopher *qua* philosopher is not a preacher, nor yet even a moralist in the usual sense of the term. Whatever the value of moral exhortations may be, it is not in any straightforward way the job of the philosopher to spout forth as a font of moral wisdom: 'Love your neighbour!' 'Abstain from sex!' 'Return your library books!' This is not to say that philosophers have never taken on such a moralistic role, or that they were wrong to do so. John Stuart Mill's campaign for women's rights was a good thing, as was Bertrand Russell's opposition to nuclear weapons.

But the philosopher's intrinsic interests lie elsewhere. He/she is trying to understand the nature of morality, and the grounds which support it. As we know, the first of these tasks is known as 'substantive' or 'normative ethics'. Here, we try to find the basic premises of moral thought and action. To what, precisely, are people subscribing when they talk of 'right' and 'wrong'? What are their first principles? The second task is known as 'meta-ethics'. Here, we look to meaning and support. What is it about the moral way of thought that makes it distinctively moral? What, at the ultimate level, makes morality plausible or reasonable?

In order to press our Darwinian investigation into both of these tasks of moral philosophy, it will be helpful if first we review some of the basic points which should guide and inform any student today. In this review, as with epistemology, we can draw on and incorporate our own earlier findings about ethics.

Substantive ethics

We all know what morality is about. It is about helping other folk. It is about giving to the poor and to the sick. It is about loving your neighbour as yourself. It is about being decent and kind and truthful and honest and reliable, and a host of other things. It is about being a good person rather than a bad one. But how do we tie together all of these different feelings and insights? Obviously, if you believe that honesty is the best policy, you should not cheat on your income tax returns. Yet does this mean that you should scrupulously tell the truth to a dying child? Does honesty have anything to do with not swearing in front of maiden aunts (or uncles)? Can we spell all of this out without making reference to God, in some way?

To pick up first on the last point, there is little doubt that many (most?) people would indeed spell out their moral beliefs within some sort of religious context. They would refer you to the Ten Command-ments, or to the Sermon on the Mount, or (if they were against sex) to the Epistles of St Paul. However, this only takes you so far. Grant that one ought not to kill and that one ought not to commit adultery. Are these moral absolutes, or do they derive from more powerful premises? Jesus reduced the Ten Commandments down to two – but why stop there? And what of those of us who do not subscribe to the Judaeo-Christian religion? Are we beyond the moral pale? Obviously not!

In modern times (as mentioned in chapter 3), there have been two great attempts to weld together all moral sentiments into a single overriding theory, with all particular matter of moral judgement derived from shared ultimate premises. These are *utilitarianism* and *Kantianism*. In some version or another, they form the background of nearly all contemporary discussions of substantive ethics. Since there is general agreement (to which I myself subscribe) that, taken singly or together, these attempts capture the major elements of moral experience, I shall concentrate on them here, in this brief introductory review.

Advocates of utilitarianism argue that pleasure or, in more refined versions, happiness, is the supreme and indeed only good. One's actions should be directed towards the promotion of happiness, for oneself and others and, conversely, towards the diminution of unhappi-ness, for oneself and others. The classic statement comes in John Stuart Mill's celebrated essay on the topic:

> The creed which accepts as the foundation of morals, Utility, or the Greatest Happiness Principle, holds that actions are right in proportion as they tend to promote happiness, wrong as they tend to produce the reverse of happiness. By happiness is intended pleasure, and the absence of pain; by unhappiness, pain, and the privation of pleasure. (1910, p. 6)

Thus, morally, all you have to do is ask: 'Does my thought or act make for an increase in happiness?' If it does, it is right. If it does not, it is wrong. Helping the sick increases happiness. Therefore, such actions are right. Robbing widows decreases general happiness. Therefore, such actions are wrong.

Today, there are enthusiasts for two major variants of utilitarianism (Lyons, 1965). So-called 'act utilitarians' argue that it is the happiness/unhappiness of each individual act that counts. 'Rule utilitarians', on the other hand, argue that it is the general policy that counts. Does the policy normally increase happiness/decrease unhappiness, or not? Thus, an act utilitarian might decide that a particular situation calls for a lie, whereas the rule utilitarian might feel that the general policy rules out any untruth. Even though a certain deception might indeed reduce unhappiness, the general end of maximizing happiness is better served by sticking to the rule of honesty and plain speaking. (Both positions are discussed in Mackie, 1977, chapter 6.)

Utilitarians include all humans within the moral sphere, and apply their supreme maxim indifferently. I have an equal obligation to myself, to you, or to a stranger. Some supporters of the theory treat all pleasures as the same ('Pushpin is as good as poetry' said Bentham), but others (the usual?) would distinguish between varieties or pleasure. For instance, the animal gratification felt in a brief sexual encounter would probably not be put on a par with the joy of sustained intellectual achievement.

> It is better to be a human being dissatisfied than a pig satisfied; better to be Socrates dissatisfied than a fool satisfied. And if the fool, or the pig, are of a different opinion, it is because they only know their own side of the question. The other party to the comparison knows both sides. (Mill, 1910, p. 9)

Ideally, utilitarianism would have it that pleasures/happinesses are quantifiable, and that one can do a relatively simple sum to work out the morally right course of action. Whether this is even remotely possible in real life is a nice point. What is true is that utilitarianism puts an emphasis on consequences. What really counts is how things turn out. Sophisticated utilitarians certainly take seriously motives and intentions.[1] However, ultimately, the emphasis is on ends and results.

---

[1] In a footnote to a later edition of his essay, Mill distinguishes the motive of a man saving a drowning person, and his bad intention, intending to save in order to inflict more pain. 'The morality of the action depends entirely upon the intention – that is, upon what the agent *wills to do*. But the motive, that is, the feeling which makes him will so to do, when it makes no difference in the act, makes none in the morality: though it makes a great difference in our moral estimation of the agent, especially if it indicates a good or bad habitual *disposition* – a bent of character from which useful, or from which hurtful actions are likely to arise' (reprinted in Taylor, 1978, p. 171).

Is happiness maximized, or not? Hence, utilitarianism is a consequentialist or teleological theory. Rule utilitarianism is, undoubtedly, a move to soften somewhat this aspect of the theory. An action would be judged right, even though the consequences increased unhappiness, if the general rule led to increased happiness.

Along with the emphasis on results goes a predisposition towards group effects. If, theoretically, you can quantify units of happiness, then maximizing the total is what counts. If everybody benefits at the expense of a few, and if this is the only way of achieving such benefits, then so be it. Those old high-school debating topics about whom to jettison first from a sinking balloon over a shark-infested sea are meat and drink to the utilitarian. No neurotic worries about the loser, or the fact that there must be a loser. At least, this is the case in theory. More on this point later. (A good introduction to utilitarianism and its problems is Smart and Williams, 1973. A well-rounded modern collection is Sen and Williams, 1982.)

The major substantive ethical alternative to utilitarianism was most brilliantly articulated in the eighteenth century by Immanuel Kant (1949, 1959). He argued that, in the moral world, as rational beings we are subject to what he called the 'Categorical Imperative'. This supreme norm was presented in a number of different ways. In one version, Kant picked up on the notion of universality, which (as we learnt earlier) is central to the very meaning of a moral claim: 'Act only according to that maxim by which you can at the same time will that it should become a universal law' (1959, p. 39). Thus, for instance, borrowing money with no intention of repaying is wrong, because if everybody did that society would collapse. There would be 'contradictions'.

I shall have more to say later about this version of the Categorical Imperative. We shall see how it links us straight to meta-ethics. But, the version of the Imperative which I will stress for the moment is that which most strongly brings out the dissatisfaction that many feel with utilitarianism.[2] Whereas the philosophy of happiness makes the collective well-being of people the supreme moral criterion, Kant (and fellow thinkers) puts the emphasis on the rights of the individual. The ultimate Kantian principle of morality is that which stresses the need to be just to everyone. 'Act so that you treat humanity, whether in your own person or in that of another, always as an end and never as a means only' (Kant, 1959, p. 47).

Note that, connected with his emphasis on human-as-ends, thus highlighting the worth of the individual, Kant differs from the utilitarian in another important way. He locates morality in the act, in

---

[2] Kant gave a third version: '[A]ct only so that the will through its maxims could regard itself at the same time as universally lawgiving' (Kant, 1959, p. 52). I shall later have things to say about the human will.

the response to the call of duty, rather than in consequences. What count morally are your intentions, even if they go awry. If you look merely to consequences, you are liable to ride roughshod over people, thus treating them as means and not as ends in themselves. In this emphasis on the will behind an act, Kant's is a 'deontological', rather than a teleological theory. (Solid introductions to Kant's moral thought include Paton, 1946; and Beck, 1960.)

Varieties of Kantianism, as with varieties of utilitarianism, abound. An incredibly influential modern-day version is that of the Harvard philosopher John Rawls (1971). Building on Kant's concern for the individual, Rawls argues that any just society must be one that is *fair*, that in some sense gives everyone the best possible chance at life's starting-gate. He writes:

> The guiding idea is that the principles of justice for the basic structure of society are . . . the principles that free and rational persons concerned to further their own interests would accept in an initial position of equality as defining the fundamental terms of their association. These principles are to regulate all further agreements; they specify the kinds of social cooperation that can be entered into and the forms of government that can be established. This way of regarding the principles of justice I shall call justice as fairness. (p. 11)

Translating this into concrete terms, Rawls argues that we must, as it were, put ourselves behind a 'veil of ignorance'. If we knew we were going to be born talented, then probably, out of self-interest, we would opt for a system that maximally rewards achievements. But we do not know this. We might, in fact, be born handicapped. What then are the principles that a rational being would opt for, assuming that he/she does not know his/her starting-point in life? (Note that here we get more than a hint of the meta-ethical theory lying behind Rawls's Kantianism. Morality in some way is being related to what we humans most want, especially for ourselves. Keep this point in mind later in the chapter, when we return to Rawls in the light of our Darwinian discussions.)

Rawls suggests there are two such principles attractive to a rational being. First, one would demand that society provide as much liberty as possible, compatible that is with the liberty of others. Second, we would want a distribution of goods and rewards done in such a way that essentially everybody benefits. *Contra* to some misunderstandings, Rawls is not here preaching a type of Utopian communism, with everybody getting exactly the same rewards. This would hardly be compatible with the liberty principle, which takes precedence. Rather the idea is that inequalities in rewards are permissible, but only if they benefit all. For instance, you might agree to pay doctors large sums. But, to do this, you must show that money is the chief attraction to medicine, and that only through such large payments can you thereby attract the most talented students, whose expertise will in turn rebound in far-superior medical care for us all.

Rawls develops his theory at length, with much subtlety. I shall have occasion to return to it later (see Barry, 1973; and Wolff, 1977). For the moment, before concluding this preliminary sketch of substantive ethics, I want to stress one important general point about ethics, which, all-too-often, gets missed in the heat of debate. You might by now be thinking that there is a significant difference between science and ethics. With science, there is (more-or-less) general agreement on what criteria yield good science. Simplicity, causal regularity, consilience, and so forth – these are acknowledged by all to be the rules of the game. However, in ethics we seem to have a split between utilitarians and Kantians about what is even to count as a good action, let alone agreement on specific cases. In the discussion of epistemology, the nub of the Darwinian case was the finding of shared epigenetic rules. Extension of any similar line of thought to ethics seems doomed before we start, if only because there are no shared sentiments from which the Darwinian can theorize.

This is a natural worry, but probably not as troublesome as it appears at first. Leave on one side the question of how uncontentious the rules of science really are, and whether an evolutionary position prohibits any flexibility in interpretations. What you must not forget is that it is the philosopher's job to push difficult cases, emphasizing differences. In real life, whatever substantival theory you take, most of the time you will have agreement about specific instances of right and wrong. The utilitarian is not indifferent to the joys of liberty. John Stuart Mill (1910) wrote its classic defence! The utilitarian can and will argue that real happiness is much diminished when liberty and individual rights are reduced. Would there be true happiness aboard your formerly sinking balloon, if you had ganged up on your weakest member and heaved him overboard? Conversely, the Kantian can and does appreciate happiness, for all the pietistic talk about duty. 'To secure one's own happiness is at least indirectly a duty, for discontent with one's condition under pressure from many cares and amid unsatisfied wants could easily become a great temptation to transgress duties' (Kant, 1959, p. 15).

Hence, when we come to actual situations demanding moral evaluation, people of all ethical persuasions generally come together. For instance, no one would say that it is morally acceptable for grown men to have sexual intercourse with little girls. Under any conception of utilitarianism, happiness is being diminished. Many utilitarians would deny that even the act of sexual gratification in this case gives genuine happiness. And, obviously, the Kantian sees the child being used as the means to the adult's ends. Conversely, no one denies the value of time spent visiting and aiding the sick. Happiness is increased, and ends are being respected and served.

Do not overlook the fact that many – most – moral disputes are not about principles, but about facts, empirical or otherwise. Take the abortion debate. We all agree that wanton killing of a human being is wrong. The real question at issue is whether the foetus is a human being, and it is becoming increasingly clear that this is a matter beyond morality. Your answer will be a function of your religious imperatives, and other such internal commands. The ethics of the situation is clear to all. What divides people is how the ethics should be applied. (The literature on the morality of abortion is huge. Good introductory essays, with a large bibliography, are included in Baker and Elliston, 1984.)

This is not to deny that sometimes we do finally get real clashes in moral insight. Consider the paradigm case of the British soldier trying to escape from his Nazi prison camp, so that he may return to the fray. Should he bribe the guard in order to do so? Ultimately, the utilitarian has to accept and urge that this is permissible. The ends justify the means. Conquering Hitler increases the net sum of human happiness. However, the Kantian surely has to argue that it is immoral to corrupt the guard in this way, no matter what the consequences. If the Categorical Imperative has any bite, it bites here.

Both the general agreement between holders of alternative substantival ethical positions and their points of conflict are highly suggestive. We shall return to them. But now, we must turn to a quick review of the other task of the moral philosopher.

Meta-ethics

We have just learned something of the claims which people make in the name of morality; but what is it truly? What is the nature of a moral claim, and where should I turn for support of moral values? I know that I should not harm small children, but why should I not harm them? If you appeal to the Greatest Happiness Principle or to the Categorical Imperative, the question is just put back one stage. Why should I heed the call of these supreme principles? Thanks to our earlier discussion (in chapter 3), we can already go some way towards answering these questions, albeit in a somewhat negative fashion.

Most crucially: you just cannot read off values from facts about the world, and certainly not from evolutionary facts about the world. It is a fact that, as part of their biology, men tend to be physically bigger than women. Moreover, there is evidence suggesting that such a size-difference reflects alternative evolutionary pressures (Symons, 1979). Apart from anything else, for men (as with many other mammals) there was probably a sexually based selective pressure towards being big. But, in itself, this tells you nothing about morality. If, for instance, you believe that it is morally wrong for women to participate in armed combat (but not men), you can get at this conclusion only by adding additional premises, which talk explicitly about moral issues. You must back up your evolutionary findings with a claim like: 'War is a necessary evil, and to prosecute it most successfully, thus minimizing suffering, we must use our strongest and biggest citizens.'

This gap between the moral and the purely factual is what we have seen labelled as 'Hume's Law' (Hare, 1963; Hudson, 1970). At heart, it points to a fundamental difference in meaning. A moral claim and a factual claim are things of different types, like chalk and cheese. Factual claims tell you how things are. 'I am happy. I want you to be happy. Sick people are unhappy.' Moral claims tell you how things *ought* to be, or *should* be. They *prescribe* courses of action, and tell of *obligations*. 'I should make you happy. We all have an obligation to reduce the unhappiness of the sick.' The contrast is between 'Men are stronger and more aggressive than women' and 'Women ought not be soldiers'.

The difference in meaning between the moral and the factual underlies the failure of all traditional attempts at evolutionary ethicizing. This, at least, was the conclusion towards which we were driven by our arguments in chapter 3, which suggests that there is something wrong, even in principle, in trying to deduce moral cheese claims from factual chalk claims. We are therefore plunged straight into the biggest dilemma of meta-ethics. What is the ultimate justification of morality? If the sources of right and wrong are not just out there, part of the physical world, for the asking or grabbing, where then are they? And if we do not see or otherwise physically sense morality, how do we become aware of it? Extending the all too brief remarks of earlier discussion, although still speaking very crudely (I shall remove some of these crudities later, but by no means all), there have been two main answers. I take them in turn.

First, there is the answer which replies that, in some sense, the ultimate basis of ethics is *objective*. By this is meant that moral norms exist independently of humans – at least, independent of human emotions – in some non-physical way. It is usually also claimed that we humans intuit or otherwise rationally grasp morality. Although it is true that moral norms could be changing, in analogy with mathematics the 'objectivist' tends to think of such norms as fixed and eternal. This is not to deny that, in the cases of both mathematics and ethics, you need humans to activate crucial principles and give rise to knowledge. The point is that moral norms, like mathematical truths, are (at a minimum) conditions laid upon us, independent of our contingent nature.

Wherein lies the ground of this supposedly objective ethics? There are a number of options. As noted, some people (it would not surprise me to learn that *most* people) think morality is simply the will of God. God says that killing is wrong and that homosexuals ought not to indulge their vile practices, and that is it. Aquinas said that homosexuality is worse than rape, because the latter only sins against humans whereas the former sins against God. 'The developed plan of living, according to reason, comes from man; the plan of nature comes from God, and therefore a violation of this plan, as by our natural sins, is an affront to God, the Ordainer of nature' (1968, 2a, 2ae, 154, 12).

Some people think that morality exists in a kind of disembodied way, as it were in a supersensible world. Plato (1941) argued that the ultimate Good exists after this fashion. Some argue that morality is a more down-to-earth phenomenon, but not part of the physical world. We know that G.E. Moore (1903) argued that the good is not a regular natural property, like red. It is a 'non-natural' property, which therefore requires our faculty of intuition. Yet others, like Kant, argue that morality is a condition which holds necessarily on the interactions of rational beings. This supposedly comes directly from the first version of the Imperative.

> For the universality of a law which says that anyone who believes himself to be in need could promise what he pleased with the intention of not fulfilling it would make the promise itself and the end to be accomplished by it impossible; no one would believe what was promised to him but would only laugh at any such assertion as vain pretense. (Kant, 1959, p. 40)[3]

There is an obvious plausibility, if not to each of these various views equally, at least to the general approach. Objectivism captures our strong conviction (uncovered in the discussion of evolutionary ethics) that morality is just not a personal matter. It is not merely a question of your choice or my choice. It is bigger than the both of us. Hence, I am not being presumptuous when I instruct you morally. Nor were the Allies simply wallowing in blood lust at Nuremberg. Hitler's cronies and followers merited stern punishment, because of their evil deeds. Killing Jews because they are Jews is absolutely, objectively wrong. Period.

Nevertheless, although objectivism highlights the fact that the very use of terms like 'ought' or 'should' seems to take us beyond personal whim – morality involves universal, binding prescriptions – it harbours serious problems. And these soon become apparent when you dig into the various forms which objectivism takes. For instance, if morality is merely God's will, does this mean that God could have made it morally obligatory to rape little girls? I suspect that most of us would say 'no'. But, then it starts to seem that God's will is right, not merely because it is God's will, but because God always wills what happens to be (independently) right. In other words, reference to God's will simply

---

[3] Although Kant (and Kantians) are surely truly put in the objectivist camp, I fully agree that their view of morality's foundations differs from that of most objectivists. I will acknowledge and discuss this point later.

puts off the problem of justification. It does not solve it. This is the so-called Euthyphro problem, since Plato raised it first in the dialogue of that name.

Other attempts to make plausible an objectivist approach to morality likewise run into problems. For instance, it is all very well talking of intuiting non-natural properties (whether they be of this world or the next). Intuition is notoriously fickle. Who is to say that such a foundation is not personal prejudice by another name (Hudson, 1970)? I do not raise these questions as definitively refuting objectivism. Presumably, for instance, the author of the story of Abraham and Isaac did not share my qualms about having to construe all of God's idle fancies as morally binding. However, with an eye to future discussion, I do raise them as problems for objectivism, best avoided if possible. Certainly, they have been enough to sway many to the other major meta-ethical option: *subjectivism*.

Here, you quite openly argue that morality is a function of human nature, and that without humans there is no right and wrong. There is no independent source of morality. It all depends on human feelings, thoughts, and inclinations. Probably the most popular version of subjectivism, in this century, has been so-called 'emotivism' (Ayer, 1946; Stevenson, 1944). According to this doctrine, morality is a function of likes and dislikes, backed up by gut emotions. Thus, if I say 'Killing is wrong', basically what I am saying is: 'I don't like killing – Boo to those that do!' I am reinforcing my feelings with emotions, which of course (as morality is supposed to) may well affect you. If I say simply 'I don't like spinach', why should you care less? On the other hand, if I show strong disgust at murder, you as a fellow human may well be likewise negatively aroused.

An off-branch of emotivism is 'prescriptivism', which explicitly brings in the sense of command underlying moral claims. 'Killing is wrong' translates into 'I don't like killing – don't you or anybody else do it'. The key here is the already noted sense of universality which goes into a moral claim. Somehow, you do not intend or mean morality to be merely a personal thing. If something is wrong for me, then by its very nature, all other things being equal, it is also wrong for you (Hare, 1952; 1963).

The subjectivist steers away from the Scylla of a disembodied objective morality. But can he/she ever avoid the Charybdis of reducing ethics to mere likes, dislikes, and feelings? Can he/she escape the relativism which goes with all of this? For the subjectivist, is morality ever really any more than irrational hot air, lacking the binding and reasonable nature which we think is the essence of a moral claim? I like spinach. You do not like spinach. So, who cares? I do not hate you because of your tastes in vegetables, nor do you excoriate me because of my catholic palate.

I think sex with young boys and girls is wrong. You think sex with children is morally acceptable. Here the difference is serious. The clash between us seems to be more than mere whim. There is the apparently, objective, external reference noted above, and a feeling that a reasonable person ought to be able to find the true, unique answer. With no external criteria by which to judge and be judged in moral matters, there seems no way of escaping from the relativity of individual inclinations. I can make all sorts of claims and demands, but ultimately ethics seems to have lost its crucial essence and *raison d'être*.

Again, as with the objectivist position, I do not raise queries like these in definitive refutation of subjectivism. After all, it would be odd indeed if human nature and inclinations were totally irrelevant to the foundations of morality. But the queries do suggest that traditional subjectivism, unreformed, will not do – any more than will traditional objectivism, unreformed.

Enough by way of preliminary. The thesis of this chapter is that a full knowledge of our own Darwinian origins will carry us forward, both in our understanding of substantive ethics and in our meta-ethical enquiries into the true foundations of moral claims. In order to prepare the way for the attack, with our background sketches now complete, let us turn again to science.

The evolution of morality

For the moment, I would have you shelve any purely philosophical worries you might harbour about the very futility of embarking on an empirical enquiry. Obvious queries will be tackled later. But even with the immediate task thus restricted, you may still be feeling great unease. Think back to the discussion of chapter 3 ('Evolutionary Ethics'). Agreeing that there is no ready identity between factual claims, specifically factual claims about the Darwinian process of evolution, and the dictates of true morality, nevertheless much of the kind of 'morality' which Darwinism seems to inspire is (by and large) not that edifying. At the substantival level, endorsements or facilitations of the process of natural selection seems so often to be so immoral. If morality means anything, it means being prepared to hold out a helping hand to others. Christians, utilitarians, Kantians, and everyone else come together on this. (Duties to oneself are a different, more complex matter; but they need not detain us here.)

The problem, raised by Huxley and a host of others, is that natural selection and its products are prima facie the very antithesis of help and cooperation. We start with a struggle for existence, and go on to find that winning alone counts from an evolutionary perspective. Because of this, virtually all of our features, physical and mental, are directed to personal success. Selfishness personified! No wonder that Huxley wrote: 'Let us understand, once for all, that the ethical progress of society depends not on imitating the cosmic process, still less in running away from it, but in combating it' (Huxley and Huxley, 1947, p. 82). There is nothing moral in the process of evolution, and there is no morality in its effects.

However, as Charles Darwin (1871) himself and many followers down to and (especially) including Edward O. Wilson (1975, 1978) have pointed out, to assume that matters rest here is naïvety personified. Supporters of evolutionary ethics, like Sumner, and opponents like Huxley, have been sharing false empirical premises.[4] Natural selection does indeed promote features that rebound to self-benefit, but to conclude that we all spend our days like characters in a Spaghetti Western, forever grinding opponents into the dust, is to show a farcically incomplete grasp of the evolutionary process. You can frequently further your own ends much more successfully by subtle alternative strategies. In particular, you can often get a lot more for yourself by aiding and working with others. In other words, selection can be expected to promote what biologists call *altruism*. (For the moment, let us understand this as a technical, metaphorically derived term of Darwinian science, meaning no more than co-operation which furthers the individual participant's reproductive interests. Whether it ever is or can lead to genuine altruism will be discussed shortly.)

It is necessary to tread carefully here. A good number of evolutionists, thinking they were working in the true spirit of Darwinism, have argued that humans (and other animals) help each other as a natural consequence of that inevitable spirit of friendship which binds members of the same species. This friendship supposedly evolves because it is of benefit to the whole group. Zebras working together against predators thus keep up the species. This was the refrain of natural selection's co-discoverer, Alfred Russel Wallace (Marchant, 1916), and (as noted earlier) was stressed in most detail by the late nineteenth-century Russian anarchist, Prince Peter Kropotkin (1902). However, as we know, this approach was explicitly rejected by Darwin, as well as by his modern-day supporters. Any 'group selection' analysis of behaviour, including human behaviour, falls before strong counter-evidence (see chapter 1).

The Darwinian insists that we stay with the individual. All help given must rebound ultimately to the individual's benefit. Any benefits which others receive should be seen as incidental, and might well be selected against. Nevertheless, even within these constraints, help and co-operation can evolve. We all know of the principle of enlightened

---

[4] I hasten to say that getting the facts right will only be part of my argument Once this is done, I shall not blithely ignore Hume's law.

self-interest, where I help others because I thereby get help in return. And we all know that frequently I am much better off because of the help received (or potential of such help being received), despite any payments in help that I might have to make. Buying insurance is a classic case in point. Most of the time my premiums go to pay other people's debts. But, against this, I have the security of knowing that should I ever be faced with a large bill, I need not bankrupt myself to pay it. I speak with some feeling as the owner of a parked car that was recently smashed up, by a drunken lout driving without insurance.

How might selection work through such a business or bargaining process, thus promoting features and behaviours of help or altruism? Remember that evolution is not interested in mere survival for survival's sake. It is reproduction that counts. Or, more accurately, success in evolution lies in increasing the percentage of one's own genes in future generations, at the expense of others. Hence, any co-operative or helpful behaviour promoted by selection must be such that one's own genes' reproductive chances are improved. Behaviour without such a pay-off is going to be at a selective disadvantage.

Against this background, Darwinians who study social behaviour ('sociobiologists') strongly favour two primary mechanisms supposedly capable of producing help and co-operation between humans (Wilson, 1978; Alexander, 1979; Trivers, 1971; Ruse, 1979b). The first is the relatively obvious process whereby humans develop innate tendencies to work together, because the cost of co-operation is (on average) significantly less than the hope of return. Suppose we all stand in risk of drowning. I help you from drowning, because of my biological urges to do so. Although this puts me at a 1 in 20 risk of drowning myself, I in turn avoid the 1 in 2 risk of drowning were you never to respond to my sometime cry for help. I may not need such help now, but we were all young once, we will all grow old someday, we all fall sick on occasion. We all have a share of bad luck during our lives, and the same goes for our children, the most immediate bearers of our genes.

This mechanism for promoting co-operative interactions between humans is called a 'reciprocal altruism' (Trivers, 1971). It can occur between genetic strangers, although in real life these could and may well be good friends. In theory, it can even occur between humans and members of other species (the shepherd and his dog). The important distinguishing feature is that, although help is given, returns are in some way anticipated. Pushing the insurance model, one does not necessarily expect immediate repayment for every kind act. Rather, one throws one's help into the general pool, as it were, and expects to be able to draw on the pool as needed. (Why not cheat? Why not take without giving? Because, if everyone behaved this way, the system would collapse. Nevertheless, because evolution is always looking for ways to get ahead, you expect a certain amount of cheating. Also, you expect the evolution of techniques for spotting and preventing cheating.)

Darwin himself proposed reciprocal altruism as a possible causal factor behind the help that we humans give to each other: 'as the reasoning powers and foresight of the members became improved, each man would soon learn from experience that if he aided his fellow-men, he would commonly receive aid in return' (Darwin, 1871, 1, p. 163). Note, however, that Darwin did not (and, because of his ignorance, could not) relate his insight to our underlying genetic nature.

The second supposed mechanism of (biological) altruism is much more recent, and indeed could not have been developed without a proper knowledge of the principles of heredity. The key to evolutionary success lies in improving your gene ratios. This means passing on your genes at a higher rate than do others. But note that, literally, you do not pass on your genes. If successful, you leave behind *copies* of your genes. My children do not have my actual genes. They each have a half-set, which are exact replicas of mine. But this possession of genes exactly like mine holds true of people other than my children – parents, siblings, nephews, nieces, grandchildren, and more. All of one's blood relatives have, to greater or lesser extent, copies of the same genes as oneself. Therefore, inasmuch as relatives reproduce, copies of one's own genes are being passed on. Reproduction by proxy, as it were.

What this all means is that help given to relatives in itself rebounds to the favour of one's own reproductive interests, even though these relatives may themselves reciprocate with little or no help. As a consequence, what you expect through this process, known as 'kin selection', is the evolution of help-giving attributes, without necessarily having the parallel evolution of attributes, expecting or enforcing tangible returns. Any return comes indirectly, via the genes (Wilson, 1978; Alexander, 1979).

As I am sure you can see, this simple conclusion readily lends itself to higher levels of refinement. You are more closely related to some relatives than to others. To children, siblings, and parents, first. Then to half-siblings, grandchildren, uncles and aunts. Eventually, to cousins, at various degrees of remove. The Darwinian, therefore, expects stronger acts and sentiments of altruism towards one's own children, rather than (say) to one's siblings' children. And likewise, as the circle of relatedness widens. There will be some help given toward lesser relatives, but not as much as towards greater relatives.

Also, one expects evolution to have taken time and age into consideration. For fairly obvious reasons, there are diminishingly small returns on promoting the well-being of grandparents. In general, there will be a predisposition towards youth. Most obviously, your own children will be the focus of attention. Then, in lesser degrees, siblings and their children, grandchildren, and so forth. You are more closely related to your siblings than to your grandchildren. But your siblings normally will be past need of help by the time you can offer it, and when your own children are launched, your grandchildren will be next in need of help.

Summing up, Wilson labels the results of the mechanisms of help as 'hard-core' and 'soft-core' altruism. The former is the result of kin selection. It occurs between relatives, and there is no expectation of direct return. The latter is the result of reciprocal altruism. It occurs between non-relatives, and there is expectation of return, or at least of the potential for such return:

> Individual behaviour, including seemingly altruistic acts bestowed on tribe and nation, are directed, sometimes very circuitously, toward the Darwinian advantage of the solitary human being and his closest relatives. The most elaborate forms of social organization, despite their outward appearance, serve ultimately as the vehicles of individual welfare. Human altruism appears to be substantially hard-core when directed at closest relatives, although still to a much lesser degree than in the case of the social insects and the colonial invertebrates. The remainder of our altruism is essentially soft. The predicted result is a melange of ambivalence, deceit, and guilt that continuously troubles the individual mind. (Wilson, 1978, pp. 158-9)

All that remains is an interpretation of these ideas in the language of epigenetic rules, those intermediaries between the genes and human thought and action. And, in theory, this is readily done (Ruse and Wilson, 1986). The Darwinian's claim is that we have genetically based dispositions to approve of certain courses of action and to disapprove of other courses of action. But they are more than mere likes and dislikes. Here we start to move towards genuine morality and its evolution – from 'altruism' (in the biological sense of working harmoniously together, thus promoting reproductive ends), to altruism (in the literal sense, demanding genuine sentiments about right and wrong).

Logically, there is no demand by Darwinism that we be moral. 'Altruism' could have been effected, as with the ants, by firm genetic control. But then we would have had to waste the virtues of our brain power, and the flexibility which it gives us. Conversely, 'altruism' could have been effected by purely rational, consciously self-directed decisions. But this would have required massive brain power to calculate probabilities and the like. And pure rationality might not have been sufficiently rapid for real life. (Even computers have not the time to explore every option, when playing chess.) Thus selection has taken a middle-road option, setting within us epigenetic rules that will incline us towards actions that are (unbeknownst to us) 'altruistic' in the biological sense.

The key move in this middle-road option is morality. It is absolutely fundamental to the Darwinian case that, in order to spur us into action – perhaps indeed to go against other self-directed emotions – we have rules incorporating that prescriptive force which is distinctly characteristic of morality. As in the case of sibling incest, our feelings are backed by a (likewise innate) sense that approved actions are 'right' and that disapproved actions are 'wrong'.

It is not just that we do not want to go to bed with our siblings. We feel that we *ought* not have to intercourse with them. We have such a strong drive to copulate, particularly with any member of the opposite sex who is almost literally thrown at us, that (biologically) we need something really strong to steer us away. Morality does the trick. Similarly, in the face of our general inclination to serve ourselves, because it is biologically advantageous to us to help and co-operate, morality (as mediated through the epigenetic rules) has evolved to guide and stiffen our will. We are moved by genuine, non-metaphorical altruism. To get 'altruism', we humans are altruistic.

Thus, in the light of our current biological understanding, we expect the epigenetic rules to influence our thought and behaviour towards relatives. We will feel that we *should* love and care for our children and others (biologically) close to us. Moreover, our obligations will be particularly strong towards these people – if someone is carrying (copies of) your genes, that surely measures well against any possible help from others. 'Blood is thicker than water.' And we will feel that our obligations to these people persist, even though no returns come or are expected. 'All I ask of my children is that they do for their children what I did for them.' Then we expect the rules to influence our thought and behaviour towards other people, especially those with whom we come into close and/or ongoing contact. Here we look for a sense of the need to help and work together with our fellow humans. But again, note, we are talking of more than a mere feeling that we want to help others. It will be an innately based sense of obligation towards others. We have a duty to help. However, in this case it will be a balanced sense of obligation. Because we are helpers, we expect help in return. If no such help is forthcoming, then the reciprocity breaks down and tensions arise.

I must add at once, however, that this expectation (of which, more later) has, within its content, nothing to do with the biological facts of the case. Neither regarding human sentiments caused by kin selection, nor regarding human sentiments caused by reciprocal altruism, is the Darwinian claim that we humans know wherein lie our biological ends. The person who helped another, consciously intending to promote his own biological advantage, would not be moral. He would be crazy. The Darwinian's point is that our moral sense is a biological adaptation, just like hands and feet. We think in terms of right and wrong. It so happens that the overall effects are biological.

This is the (empirical) Darwinian case for morality, and for its biological underpinnings. Epigenetic rules giving us a sense of obligation have been put in place by selection, because of their adaptive value. Of course, as with scientific knowledge, no one is claiming that every last moral twitch is tightly controlled by the genes. In science, the claim was that human reason has certain rough or broad constraints, as manifested through the epigenetic rules. The application of these leads to the finished product, which in many respects soars into the cultural realm, transcending its biological origin. In the case of ethics, the Darwinian urges a similar position. Human moral thought has constraints, as manifested through the epigenetic rules, and the application of these leads to moral codes, soaring from biology into culture.

Obviously, a great many questions demand answers. I expect the bile will be surging up the throats of most of my fellow philosophers, particularly after some of the comments of the last two paragraphs. A short while back, I asked you to shelve some of your worries about the use of the term 'altruism' in the biological context. But why should you keep such worries on the shelf? How can one slide from 'altruism' (in the biological sense) to altruism (in the human sense)? Furthermore, how can one link morality and returns in the same sentence? And how, most importantly of all, can one suppose that an empirical thesis about the evolution of morality has any bearing on philosophical questions about the nature and justification of morality? How can one suppose that Hume's law is not being either broken or ignored? (For just such negative philosophical responses, see Hampshire, 1978; Nagel, 1980; Flanagan, 1981; Singer, 1981; Trigg, 1982.)

Let me simply say that I am as eager as the critics to get to the queries, for I shall argue that many of the apparent problems prove, on closer examination, to be a source of strength for the Darwinian case. But, first, we must pause. Ours is a *naturalistic* approach. The claim is that modern Darwinian evolutionary theory is pertinent to the problems of morality. I have allowed that we are pushing empirical science to the limit and beyond. Yet, as in the case of epistemology, you are entitled to some support for the basic thesis that epigenetic rules influence human thought and behaviour – this time, in the social, moral realm. It is to the completion of this empirical case that I turn next.

The empirical evidence: social animals

As we begin this too brief review of the underlying empirical support for the Darwinian account of the evolution of morality, I must first restress an important point made earlier. By this stage in our enquiry, we are not starting out in total ignorance, as though the very idea that evolution might have some connection with *Homo sapiens* requires a totally fresh, comprehensive, supporting brief. We know that evolution occurred, that it was Darwinian in nature, and that humans are part of the natural order. Therefore, in something as important to us as our morality, there is a strong presumption that natural selection will have had a causal influence. Such a presumption may ultimately prove wrong. I doubt anyone expects a definitive case. Nevertheless, we go into our enquiry with a great deal of positive background knowledge.

Turning to the task at hand, let us begin with the animal world considered as a whole. At the most general level, the past two decades have seen the accumulation of a simply colossal body of data attesting to the tight control exercised on animal behaviour by the genes (Wilson, 1975; Dawkins, 1976; Barash, 1982; Maynard Smith, 1982). Furthermore, every sign is that such behaviour is directed to the betterment of the individual's reproductive chances. I emphasize that in speaking of 'behaviour' here, I refer not simply to those actions where the individual obviously benefits – as when the predator chases the prey and the prey runs to escape. I am speaking of social behaviour, within the same species, where individuals interact in such ways as will improve their own biological fitness.

To illustrate, I will mention but one elegant study, drawn from literally hundreds. A group of researchers from Cambridge University has recently shown, with much detail and subtlety, that the behaviour of red deer (living on an island off Scotland) is just as much a function of natural selection as are the animals' various body-sizes and shapes (Clutton-Brock, Guinness and Albon, 1982). Males, for instance, gather the females into harems. Females, conversely, let themselves be so gathered. The actions of both sexes can and must be seen in the light of selection for individual success, and strong quantitative evidence supports the conclusion that to the victor goes the prize. More prosaically, those animals which do most successfully and efficiently precisely what everybody seems to be trying to do – gathering and being gathered – are those very animals which leave the highest representation of genes in the next generation. Red deer behaviour is not random, or a function of causes beyond biology. It is as much a result of natural selection, working at the individual level, as is any other feature of the animals (figure 6.1).

What of co-operation and (biological) 'altruism'? In particular, does the animal world taken as a whole support the case for the effective operation of kin selection and reciprocal altruism? Few workers today, within the field of animal social behaviour, would doubt the importance of either mechanism. Kin selection, in particular, is one of the great triumphs of twentieth-century biology. From before the time of Darwin, naturalists were troubled by the self-sacrificing behaviour shown by workers in the social insects, particularly the Hymenoptera (the ants, the bees and the wasps). Why does one find females, who are themselves sterile,

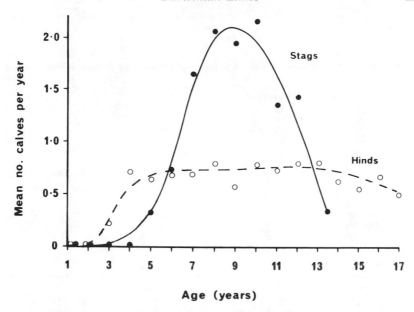

Figure 6.1 Mean number of calves sired/born per year by red deer stags and hinds of different ages. Note that females keep reproducing steadily whereas males who get through youth (and only such males) really hit the reproductive jackpot. The options are akin to buying government bonds (female strategy: safe but low yielding), and buying stock in a computer software firm (male strategy: very risky but with potential for colossal gains). (Reproduced with permission from Clutton-Brock, 1983.)

spending all of their lives in toil, raising the offspring of their fertile mothers? Such 'nobility' seems the very antithesis of a life of Darwinian struggle for reproduction.

Thanks to the brilliant insight of William Hamilton (1964a, 1964b), we now know that the family lives of social insects owe much to kin selection. Because of a rather odd reproductive system, females are more closely related to sisters than they are to daughters. Thus, biologically, they are better occupied raising fertile sisters than fertile daughters. In other words, ultimately, there is nothing paradoxical about the behaviour of workers. They are simply reproducing vicariously, as one expects when kin selection is at work. Males have no such unusual relationships with siblings and offspring. Significantly, there are no worker males. Kin selection did not operate. (See also Wilson, 1971; Maynard Smith, 1978; and figure 6.2.)

Reciprocal altruism likewise finds confirming instances throughout the animal world. Some of the most interesting cases involve animals from different species. For instance, members of some species of fish are cleaned by members of other species – the former being thereby freed of

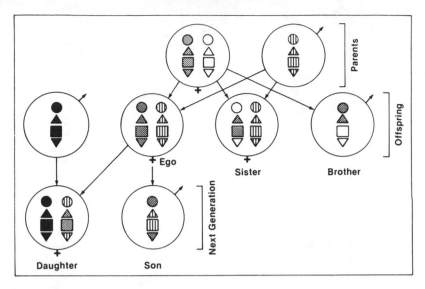

Figure 6.2 A diagrammatic representation of the genetic relationships in the *Hymenoptera*. Females are diploid (i.e. have two half sets of chromosomes); males are haploid (i.e. have one half set of chromosomes). Only females have fathers. It can be seen that sisters have a 75 per cent shared genetic relationship, whereas mothers and daughters have only a 50 per cent shared genetic relationship. Kin selection therefore favours the raising of fertile sisters rather than fertile daughters. Males have no such special relationships, and therefore do not form sterile worker castes. (Adapted with permission from Maynard Smith, 1978 © Scientific American Inc.)

parasites and the latter gaining a nutritious lunch (Trivers, 1971). That such behaviour is not accidental, but tightly controlled by selection, is shown by a number of factors. Most pertinently, the cleaning fish are often of a type that would normally at once be eaten by the other (larger) fish. They have, however, developed behavioural signals that simply shut down the aggressive impulses of the cleaned fish. Interestingly, one now gets mimics which take advantage of the situation. Members of yet a third species show the aggression-reducing behaviours, but fail to reciprocate with cleaning. Rather, they are liable to bite big chunks out of the now passive, unsuspecting monsters.

In many branches of the animal world, reciprocation has been found to operate within the same species – in birds, in fish, and in mammals, to name but three such branches. For instance, in one bird species from Africa, the white-fronted bee-eater, there is much help given and received in nest-building, food-gathering, and nesting care. This is most probably a direct function of the fact that the birds' nests are extremely vulnerable to flash-flooding. A high level of reciprocity is an effective way of dealing with irregular yet ongoing calamities. (These, and many other instances, are surveyed in Barash, 1982.)

Let us be quite clear what all of this means. Humans are not white-fronted bee-eaters. Even less are they the bee-eaters' prey. No one would pretend that the way in which humans work together is the exact way in which ants work together, any more than does the fact that humans and ants have each developed organs of sight prove that their principles of perceptual functioning are identical. Nevertheless, reference to social behaviour in the animal world taken as a whole does show that such behaviour – including co-operation and 'altruism' – can be produced and promoted by natural selection, working at the level of the individual. It can be done, and is in fact done time and again through the animal world. If humans are part of this world, possibilities and expectations are obviously raised.

The empirical evidence: chimpanzees

How can expectations be raised beyond the point of intriguing prospect to that of plausible hypothesis? What, in the study of the animal world, would lead us to suspect that there really is something in the Darwinian case for the nature and foundations of morality? Going again down a path taken earlier, what we must do is move closer to our own species. If indeed we have an innate predisposition to work with and help our fellow humans, and if this was truly brought about by selective demands, then we might reasonably expect to find something akin to moral behaviour in our closest relatives, the higher primates. They cannot tell us whether they heed the urgings of the Categorical Imperative; nor is there reason to think that they do this in any explicit fashion. However, if the Darwinian is right in claiming that morality is rooted in epigenetic rules, then, as in the case of logical and mathematical reasoning, we may properly look for suggestive behaviour in chimpanzees and gorillas. (The 'higher' primates are closer to us. Neither they nor we are higher in some biologically absolute sense.)

Darwinism insists that features evolve gradually, and something as important as morality should have been present in our (very recent) shared ancestors. Furthermore, if morality is as important biologically to humans as is being claimed, it would be odd indeed had all traces now been eliminated from the social interactions of other high-level primates. Conversely, if human morality does not have a biological base, and is for instance a cultural invention of humans some few thousand years ago then there would be no reason to find it present in our ape relatives.

Recent, extended studies of the apes, particularly of chimpanzees, must shake all but the most dogmatic defender of the uniqueness of the human moral capacity (Hrdy, 1981). I emphasize that these studies are recent. Anecdotal reports of apes showing friendliness and concern are obviously of limited worth. Apart from anything else, if an ape is reared close to humans, you expect it to learn human-like behaviours, including those simulating morality (Goodall, 1971). The question is whether the brutes show moral-type behaviour innately, without human intervention, in situations which are clearly directly or indirectly of biological value. And to answer such a question, you need long-term studies of apes in natural (or virtually natural) situations, seeing whether or not such behaviour appears. At last, such studies are being performed, and the answer is strong and clear. Apes interact in remarkably human-like fashions, including fashions which, were we to believe them true of humans (rather than apes), we would unhesitatingly label 'moral'.

I draw your attention to perhaps the most remarkable of all the studies, that of the Utrecht primate ethology group (de Waal, 1982). For over a decade, its members have been observing the dynamics of some fifty semi-wild chimpanzees at the nearby Arnhem Zoo, recording almost every move. Time and again, the primatologists have seen behaviour which differs not at all from human moral behaviour. This is particularly true of the older females. Although it is the mature males who are the physically dominant members of the group, the older females have great authority. For instance, the males seek their aid in forming alliances, younger females look to them for protection, youngsters are wary of them and set them up as models. In a human group, these females would have an important stabilizing effect, helping to mediate disputes and to avoid quarrels. The same is precisely true of the Arnhem chimpanzees.

Consider the following vignette:

> On a hot day two mothers, Jimmie and Tepel, are sitting in the shadow of an oak tree while their two children play in the sand at their feet (playfaces, wrestling, throwing sand). Between the two mothers the oldest female, Mama, lies asleep. Suddenly the children start screaming, hitting and pulling each other's hair. Jimmie admonishes them with a soft, threatening grunt and Tepel anxiously shifts her position. The children go on quarrelling and eventually Tepel wakes Mama by poking her in the ribs several times. As Mama gets up Tepel points to the two quarrelling children. As soon as Mama takes one threatening step forward, waves her arm in the air and barks loudly the children stop quarrelling. Mama then lies down again and continues her siesta. (de Waal, 1982, p. 47)

One should not underestimate the importance of Mama's role here. Conflicts between children regularly escalate into conflicts between adults, leading to fighting and physical damage. In acting as a quietening influence, Mama has brought benefits to all. If this is not to act as a moral force – or, let me say cautiously, a proto-moral force – I do not know what is. 'Blessed are the Peace-makers: for they shall be called the Children of God' (Matthew, 5, 9).

It must be stressed that behaviour like Mama's is not isolated or aberrant. Again and again, you see one ape aiding another, materially or (even more impressively), as in the above instance, in resolving conflict or promoting harmony. Chimpanzee groups are forever on the edge of exploding into conflict, primarily because of tensions between alpha males. Group members are, accordingly, forever smoothing over differences, reconciling rivals, and binding psychic wounds. It is, therefore, hard to deny the conclusion of the Boswell of the Arnhem chimpanzees.

> The extra faculty which makes chimpanzee behaviour so flexible is their ability to *combine* separate bits of knowledge. Because their knowledge is not limited to familiar situations, they do not have to feel their way blindly when confronted with new problems. Chimpanzees use all their past experience in ever-changing practical applications.
>
> The terms we use to describe the ability to make new combinations of past experiences in order to achieve a goal are 'reason' and 'thought'. No other words exist. The result is considered, rational behaviour. In their *social* application of reason and thought, chimpanzees are truly remarkable. Technically their inventiveness is clearly inferior to that of human beings, but socially I would hesitate to make such a claim. (de Waal, 1982, p. 51)

We are still at an early stage of detailed primate studies, and much work remains to be done on sorting out the various aspects of help and co-operation. In particular, great effort will have to be expended in seeing how far behaviours correspond to proposed causal models. That blood relationships are important determinants in primate social interactions is beyond doubt. In particular, females will frequently assist in the care of the offspring of close relatives. The primatologist Sarah Hrdy (1977) has demonstrated this fact impressively among the langurs. Also, there is already strong and still growing evidence of co-operation between non-relatives – co-operation of a kind one would expect were reciprocal altruism a significant causal factor. Again and again, apes (in particular) work helpfully together, in ways which give all the appearance of being deliberate or intentional (see, for instance, Menzel, 1972).

Thus, although we cannot yet bolster our empirical case with a vast well-confirmed body of primate (especially higher ape) evidence, unequivocally establishing the Darwinian evolution of moral capacities, we can say that there is a growing body of data pointing to precisely that conclusion. What we have learned thus far, especially in the past ten or fifteen years, is precisely what we would expect were human moral feelings the product of the Darwinian process of natural selection (see figure 6.3).

Figure 6.3 Collaboration among chimpanzees in order to climb a tree while avoiding electrified wires. (Reproduced with permission from Menzel, 1972.)

The empirical evidence: humans

We come now to our own species. The claim is that human moral thought has constraints, as manifested through the epigenetic rules, and the application of these leads to moral codes, soaring from biology into culture. The question is not whether every last act of Western man or woman is governed by kin selection or reciprocal altruism or some such thing. I am quite sure it is not. Rather, the question is whether we have innate tendencies or dispositions inclining us to social thoughts and actions, which latter would improve our reproductive chances. And, if there be such tendencies, is there reason to think that the proposed causal models for promoting social interactions had any significant input?

Of one thing we can be fairly certain. In the quest for such tendencies, our own society is not the best place to start. Who can doubt that Western technology has distorted and otherwise changed traditional social and moral patterns, making more difficult the discerning of any possible underlying biological factors. Think of the coming of cheap, efficient contraception, and of the changes in sexual mores in the past two decades. We need to focus our attention on societies where science and its after-effects have not yet been fully felt. (I am *not* implying that pre-industrial societies show only the forces of biology. Nor am I implying that biology is now irrelevant to the interactions of the Western human. The Pill may have changed sexual practices. It has hardly eliminated the biology from sex.)

With the scene thus set, we have first the general question about whether (pre-industrial) human societies function in a way suggesting that a prime formative factor is reproductive success, regardless of whether this be explicitly acknowledged. Were one to look at our own species as one might look at a species of ant or monkey, would the reasonable conclusion be that social behaviour is a product of the genes as selected in the struggle for reproduction? And is the corollary that particular behavioural adaptations are directed towards the increase of one's future genetic representation?

These are queries which have sparked much controversy in the past decade. Debate continues almost unabated (for instance, Lumsden and Wilson, 1983; Lewontin, Rose and Kamin, 1984). In this book, true to my policy of stressing the positive – I have myself discussed the whole issue, in its own right, at length elsewhere (Ruse, 1979b; 1982c) – I shall here state simply that there is growing evidence that Darwinian factors are important in a full causal understanding of human society. The explicit goals sought by humans tend to be power and status and material riches and the like. Also actively pursued are peace and security, freedom from war and want, and from other humanly caused disasters and disturbances. Virtually all of these things translate readily into reproductive success, and their absence spells reproductive failure. Powerful and rich men and women in societies do not simply contemplate their power and riches. They cash them, in terms of bigger families or, relatedly, in aid to their kin.

A dramatic illustration of this is proved by Napoleon Chagnon's (1980) studies on the Yanomamo Indians from Venezuela and Brazil. These people are almost always at war with each other, with the victors gaining power, land and, ultimately, breeding opportunities. Within the groups, as can be seen in table 6.1, the effects of success – becoming the leaders – is shown in the extent to which headmen out reproduce the others. Note also that this is not a one-sided affair, with males alone striving to pursue the best reproductive strategies. The wives of headmen have significantly more children than do other women.

Table 6.1 Marital and Reproductive Performance of Headmen Compared to Other Males 35 Years Old or Older

Status of male	No.	Wives	Average no. of wives	Offspring per wife	Mean number of offspring
Headmen	20	71	3.6 ± 2.9	2.4 ± 2.5	8.6 ± 4.6
Non-headmen	108	258	2.4 ± 1.4	1.7 ± 2.0	4.2 ± 3.4
			$P = 0.007$	$P = 0.238$	$P > 0.001$

(Adapted by permission of Westview Press from Chagnon, 1980, p. 553 © American Association for the Advancement of Science.)

Many more examples could be given showing that 'success' in human societies bears strongly on the number of offspring, and that attitudes and behaviours are directed to reproductive ends. But then, what of the second, more specific question? Is there evidence of kin selection and reciprocal altruism? Is it reasonable to invoke these Darwinian models in explanation of the help which people give to each other, and the co-operation which exists between individuals and groups?

A convincing example of the importance of kin selection has been stressed by Richard D. Alexander (1977, 1979). Theoretically, one would expect parents to show most concern of all to their own children. After all, there is a 50 per cent genetic relationship binding parent and child. This compares (say) with the 25 per cent relationship you have with the children of your siblings. (Note that strictly, in making evaluations of comparative relatedness, one is speaking only of those genes that vary within the overall group.) In fact, however, in many societies the adult male responsible for childcare is not the father, but the mother's brother. Maternal uncles have the duty and obligation to provide sustenance, education, and other care needed to achieve full adulthood. How can this be? Alexander points out that the independent evidence is that, in societies where mother's brother's care is common (and only in such societies), there is considerable doubt as to paternity. Because of the looseness of sexual bonds between married couples, biological father-hood frequently does not equal social fatherhood. However, the mother–child connection is securely known, as is the identity of siblings.

In other words, in such societies where this kind of care occurs, although the mother's brother substitutes a 25 per cent relationship for a 50 per cent relationship, he also substitutes a genuine blood tie for a dubious blood tie – just what one would expect were kin selection at work. Interestingly and surely significantly, we do not have an exactly analogous mother's sister's phenomenon. We do, however, get some expected-according-to-kin-selection interactions where sisters marry the same man. (Of course, if paternity is is doubt, mother and brother may not be full siblings. Figure 6.4 addresses this point.)

Note that what the Darwinian would extract from a case like this is more than that we simply do things, or even merely that we want to do things – whether this be for biological or other reasons. The claim is that we want to do things because they are right. Mother's brother's care involves a sense of duty and obligation. Why otherwise should one care about someone else's brats? In short, the Darwinian's claim is that here kin selection achieves its (biological) 'altruistic' ends by filling adult males full of (moral) altruistic sentiments.

There is also much evidence in human societies of the kinds of interactions one would expect were non-relatives influenced by recip-rocal altruistic causal mechanisms. What is significant is the extent to which these social encounters can be distinguished from those between

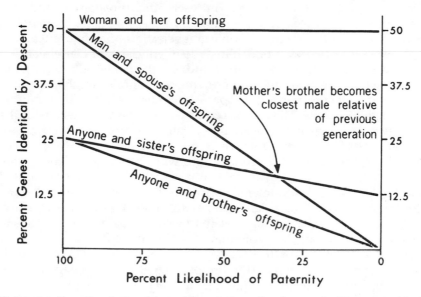

Figure 6.4 Genetic relationships with putative offspring, and with various kinds of nephews and nieces, with variations in confidence of paternity. (Reproduced with permission from Alexander, 1979.)

kin. The outsider notes at once that social intercourse between non-relatives is balanced. Help and co-operation is given; but, equally, help and co-operation is reciprocated and expected. People form social relationships and alliances for their mutual benefits; but, when one side fails in a relationship, things tend to break down and partners pull out from the pact.

That we do relate differently towards relatives and acquaintances (and yet differently again towards strangers and enemies) is a fact long noted by anthropologists, including those who have been most hostile towards suggestions that biology might play a significant causal role in human thought and behaviour. Marshall Sahlins (1965), no friend of Darwinism, has identified three levels of social interaction between peoples in pre-literate societies. Between relatives, we get what he calls 'generalized reciprocity', which involves giving without hope of return. Between non-relatives who have day-to-day social intercourse, we get 'balanced reciprocity', which involves giving with expectations of return in some form. And with strangers, especially with threatening strangers, we get 'negative reciprocity', where there is tension, suspicion, and the ever present possibility of violent conflict.

This analysis is precisely that forecast by the Darwinian. Generalized reciprocity is what we expect from kin selection. Balanced reciprocity is what we expect from reciprocal altruism. And negative reciprocity is what we expect from people who find each other threatening, and who have not yet found reason to co-operate. In these matters, humans are paradigmatically the products of natural selection. (See figure 6.5, and Ruse 1979b for discussion of Sahlins's 1976 criticisms of Darwinism.)

These are but a few straws in the wind; yet they must suffice for now. Summing up: there is strong, and growing, evidence through the animal world that members of the same species interact socially to their mutual reproductive benefits. The nature of these interactions fits well with the claim that kin selection and reciprocal altruism are important causal mechanisms. Our closest relatives, the chimpanzees, have complex social lives, and behave in precisely the ways one would expect were morality a legacy of our simian past, and were that legacy also inherited by other primates. We humans, especially in our pre-industrial state, show that biology is a crucial causal factor affecting our social nature, and the ways we behave are precisely those expected if selection acts to maximize the reproductive potential of the individual.

Combine all of this with what we know already, particularly about human biological nature and the importance of the epigenetic rules in moulding human conscious thought and action. What do we have? Certainly not a finished case for the evolution of the human moral capacity, even when it is agreed (as it must be) that we talk now only of

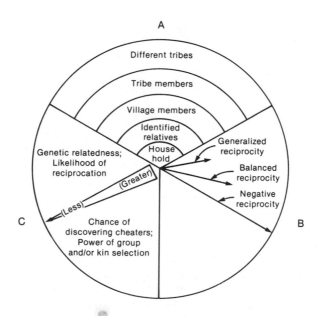

Figure 6.5 We have here a correlation between (A) social relationships, (B) patterns of reciprocity, and (C) factors influencing altruism in preliterate cultures. (After Alexander, 1975.)

the basic moral inclinations, leaving the full development to culture.[5] We are going beyond the evidence as we argue that (in the human case) the way in which selection spurs us into biologically advantageous social action is by infusing our pertinent innate dispositions, our epigenetic rules, with a sense of moral obligation. However, we do now have a strong hypothesis – an hypothesis made yet more plausible when we recollect that the incest barrier, undoubtedly of biological value, is backed by a forceful sense of right and wrong. It is not just that you do not want to sleep with your sister/brother, but that you feel you should not.

And now, with the scientific case laid before us, let us switch back to philosophical enquiry. Does the hand of biology, reaching up, in any way grasp the downward-reaching hand of philosophy, or do they pass each other by? If the hands do meet, then the naturalistic approach to philosophy is much advanced. We will begin by seeing if the product of the Darwinian bears any true correspondence to the moral picture sketched by philosophers (substantive ethics). Then, we will go on to the tough questions about status and justification. Do the findings of the Darwinian speak to meta-ethical concerns?

Substantive ethics reconsidered: utilitarianism

Running parallel to the discussion of the last chapter, substantival claims about happiness and fairness are to the moral philosopher what claims about simplicity and consilience were to the philosopher of science. Can we mesh what Darwinians would have us believe about the evolution and nature of human altruism with the substantival premises of moral philosophy, recognizing that (as with science) a certain amount of adjustment is almost to be expected?

Using our brief sketch of major substantival theories to guide us, let us start with utilitarianism. Does the willingness to help and co-operate, which the Darwinian sees as the result of evolution – assuming now that it makes itself felt via the epigenetic rules – bear any affinities to utilitarian ethics, with its emphasis on happiness as the end and guide to action? The obvious answer is that it does. Things which give us pleasure and things which give us pain, things which make us happy and things which make us unhappy, did not just happen by evolution-

---

[5] I shall leave relatively unexplored the ways in which cultures, under the influence of biology, actually develop. What happens to morality runs parallel to the case of science, discussed in the last chapter, with biology providing the underlying skeletal themes – to be considered in detail in the next sections – and culture putting on the flesh. In the Conclusion, I shall mention work which is trying to model gene-culture coevolution.

ary chance to be as they are. The fact that we enjoy sexual intercourse is not accidental, nor is the already noted fact that we are terrified of snakes (Lumsden and Wilson, 1981). As one perceptive writer has asked: why is sugar sweet? The answer is that pleasure and pain, wanting and fearing, are powerful guides to action (Barash, 1977). Consequently, natural selection has made us in such a way that we enjoy things which are biologically good for us and dislike things which are biologically bad for us.

This last statement obviously has to be modified somewhat to take into account many of the effects of modern civilization. We need sugars for energy, but as your dentist will tell you, you can have too much of a good thing. I presume, however, that the Darwinian can accept that short-term pleasures must be balanced against long-term happiness and pain. Also, it is clear that the Darwinian would not want to equate happiness (as a spur to action) simply with sensuous pleasure or short-term ecstasy. You might be in very dangerous or unpleasant circumstances (like a concentration camp). Suicide might seem like the most efficient way to minimize unhappiness. At the same time, you could have an overwhelming urge to go on living, no matter what the consequences. However, one doubts that utilitarians would necessarily take this kind of situation as a genuine counter to their position. Life in itself would be considered a happiness, thus outweighing present trials.

We can conclude, therefore, that the Darwinian agrees with the utilitarian that happiness is an important desired end in life. Indeed, when broadly conceived, it is virtually the only such end in life. As John Stuart Mill says:

> The only proof capable of being given that an object is visible, is that people actually see it. The only proof that a sound is audible, is that people hear it: and so of the other sources of our experience. In like manner, I apprehend, the sole evidence it is possible to produce that anything is desirable, is that people do actually desire it. If the end which the utilitarian doctrine proposes to itself were not, in theory and in practice, acknowledged to be an end, nothing could ever convince any person that it was so. (1910, p. 32)

(Mill then goes on to claim that 'each person's happiness is a good to that person, and the general happiness, therefore, a good to the aggregate of all persons.' This does not at all follow, nor is it an argument required by the Darwinian.)

This is not to say that evolution always promotes happiness. We have already seen Wilson (1975) saying: 'It is possible to be unhappy and very adaptive' (p. 255). The pain from fire is very unpleasant, and yet highly adaptive. What we are talking about is happiness and avoidance of unhappiness, as spurs to action. We could have been born without nerve endings, but we would (biologically speaking) be a lot worse off.

From the point of view of evolution and from the point of view of utilitarianism, what counts is happiness as a desired end. Because the pain from fire is so unpleasant, we are motivated to avoid it, thus minimizing unhappiness/maximizing happiness. This makes good sense both to the Darwinian and to the utilitarian.

Let us grant that the ends of sociobiology and utilitarianism broadly overlap. This is not yet to say that a Darwinian substantive ethics (i.e. that which is yielded by the epigenetic rules) is going to be the same as utilitarianism. The whole point about utilitarianism is that you are supposed to promote happiness, not just for yourself, but for everyone. The Greatest Happiness Principle makes the criterion of goodness that of making 'the greatest happiness for the greatest number'. It is not just a question of wanting happiness for yourself, but feeling that you *ought* promote the general happiness.

At this point, the Darwinian reminds you of the mechanisms promoting help and co-operation – kin selection and reciprocal altruism. We need something to get us moving, to give help and to show friendship and warmth to people other than ourselves. This is a biological imperative. Thus, we have epigenetic rules urging us to work in an altruistic manner with others. What sense of 'altruism' results here – metaphorical or literal? Both! Biology demands that we be 'altruistic' in its (metaphorical) sense. For ants, that is it. They are programmed to do what they do. In the case of humans, biology achieves its ends by making us altruistic in the literal sense. We are aware of dictates of morality – given through the epigenetic rules – which we should obey. (More on this point later.)

But what would be the precise content of these rules of obligation? Since happiness is something which we all crave, what is more natural than that we should have a sense that *we ought to promote the happiness of others?* Our general inclination is to look to our own ends. However, (unbeknown to us) our biological fitness is increased if we have urges to expend effort on promoting the ends that others (consciously) want. Since the ends of others are analogous to our ends – we are, after all, members of the same species – our urges are directed towards promoting the general happiness of our fellows, as well as ourselves. Given that the genes work through epigenetic rules – biases which incline (or, more precisely, direct) us towards or away from certain courses of action – the Darwinian argues that we have such rules to make us think that we have obligations to increase the happiness (and decrease the unhappiness) of all.

In broad outline, therefore, the utilitarian perspective on the nature of morality meshes comfortably with the Darwinian approach to such thought and behaviour. I admit fully that we are here pushing up to and beyond the bounds of proven science – claiming that something akin to the Greatest Happiness Principle is encoded in the human epigenetic rules. Moreover, only a total hypocrite would pretend that we have arrived at this conclusion independent of any prior knowledge of utilitarianism. In filling out the content of our sense of obligation, the Darwinian has obviously turned to the philosopher. But I argue that that is the very point of an enquiry such as this. As empirical scientists, who are we to turn to but the moral philosophers, if we are to discover the sorts of constraints which govern human thought and action?

As in epistemology, there is nothing dreadfully circular in any of this. There is (growing) independent evidence for such mechanisms as kin selection and reciprocal altruism, not to mention claims about the importance of the epigenetic rules. Moreover, the Darwinian, in his/her own right, has already centred on happiness as an importantly motivating factor in human affairs. The utilitarian merely helps the biologist to bring his/her position fully into the light. What is offered here is a hypothesis made plausible by the ready way in which biology and philosophy connect isomorphically together.

In broad outlines, Darwinism meshes happily with utilitarianism. Does it favour rule utilitarianism or act utilitarianism? One suspects perhaps the former, given that the human mind seems to work by rule, rather than by deciding each issue anew. This is probably a question for the philosopher, rather than the biologist. Yet our own work – at the interface of biology and philosophy – is not quite finished. There remain some obvious as yet undiscussed points of potential tension. These must now be considered to see if, in fact, there are genuine differences and, if so, how biology and philosophy can be adjusted to bring them into closer harmony. Let us begin with what must have struck many readers: the apparent disparity between the comparative weights the utilitarian and Darwinian put on our obligations to other people. (Apologies to Gerald Durrell for borrowing his title.)

My family and other animals

The utilitarian argues that each and every individual counts as an equal moral being, deserving of as much attention as any other. 'As between his own happiness and that of others, utilitarianism requires him to be as strictly impartial as a disinterested and benevolent spectator' (Mill, 1910, p. 16). Taken to the extreme, this means that towards the several billion people on this planet, of which I myself am one, I have an equal moral obligation. I have a moral obligation to take most of my salary, although I and my family will be moved to near poverty, and to send it to Oxfam or some like organization. However much I may equivocate and talk about levels of happiness and so forth, the comparative misery of several Ruses is surely outweighed by the life-saving effects on possibly several dozen Africans or Indians (Singer, 1972). What else can one mean by the 'Greatest Happiness for the Greatest Number'?

Without being categorical on a matter for which there is still little hard empirical evidence, I somewhat doubt that Darwinism points to so strong a conclusion. Take first the matter of your own relatives, particularly your own children. Thanks to kin selection, you have emotions leading you to want to give to them – and give and give again. Moreover, you have no expectations or feelings for return. This is just as well, because usually they are not in a position to return, nor are they mature moral beings that you could shame or coerce into return. You love your children because they are your children, and you want the best for them. And these emotions are backed up by moral sentiments. You do not just love your children, but you feel you have a duty towards them. After all, you brought them into the world, and they are helpless.

My sense is that biological feelings – including moral feelings – towards one's own children must be stronger than feelings towards the children of others, or to adults for that matter either. To the Darwinian, morality is an important factor in getting you to do what is in your evolutionary interests. I find it implausible that selection would fail to back up your parental emotions with an increased sense of moral obligation. Help from others may or may not prove useful. Saving the skin of close relatives is absolutely crucial. Thus I suggest that the Darwinian looks for a greater feeling of obligation to promote the happiness of your own children than those of anyone else. This is not to say that you have no obligations to the children of others. But it is to say that not only do your children most probably come first in your affections, but you feel that they *should* come first. Consequently, the Darwinian does not expect you to feel undue guilt about spending money on your children, rather than sending all to Oxfam. (No one denies that your present distribution of funds may be morally unacceptable.)

Pushing this line of argument, the Darwinian is probably inclined to conclude that we also get a gradation of moral sentiments between non-relatives. I doubt that natural selection would set up any strong sense of obligation towards people from whom there is absolutely no possibility of return, or who never were, are, or could reasonably be expected to be in my community, as it were. I would think rather that moral sentiments would be strongest between close neighbours, and then diminish as the circle broadens (Wilson, 1978). Note that I am talking now about morality and not just regular feelings. For this reason, we do not expect an exact correspondence between feelings of friendship and the sense of moral obligation. After all, if it costs you little enough (in biological terms) to help a total stranger, who knows but that there may be a possibility of return to yourself if ever you are in a like situation.

I suggest, therefore, that the Darwinian expects a stronger sense of moral obligation to those who are in the same moral pool as we, than to others. For instance, I as a Canadian have a stronger obligation *per se* to the poor of my own country than (say) to the poor of Chad. This is *not* to say that I have no obligations to the poor of foreign countries. Apart from anything else, given modern methods of communication and so forth, everyone in the world is brought into much closer contact, and thus each person's moral sphere has been made bigger. Here, you have technology affecting our culture which, although rooted in biology, rises up above it. Also, let us not forget that there might be other factors, biologically based or otherwise – like religion – that affect morality sensibilities. But even now, you would expect to find that much of our dealing with (say) the Third World will be more a question of expediency than the result of a moral urge.

Parenthetically, I suspect that the reason why we of the West behave so indifferently to the poor of the Third World is precisely because our technology has outstripped our biological nature. Until recently, our neglect of the poor of Africa was not a moral issue – we knew nothing of such poor and, even if we had done, we could not have helped. Now, apart from having compounded problems with our technology, even though we have the ability to help, we do not really have the required moral sentiments. It is interesting and surely significant that we can respond to a known individual, even though the masses go unhelped. This aspect of our biology is known and used by clever relief agencies, like the Foster Parents' Plan.

How do you compare and evaluate utilitarianism and the Darwinian position, as I have conceived it? You may complain that I am substituting (dubious) sociobiology for (good) philosophy. Even if we grant that our dealings with Africa are prompted more by a fear of Russian influence than morality, this is hardly to say how things ought to be. Utilitarianism, like any substantival moral theory, deals with right and wrong. Darwinism, like any scientific theory of humankind, deals with feelings. The point is not whether we have an urge to help the starving masses, but whether we should have such an urge. Or rather, whether we should help them whether we have an urge or not. In the case of the starving child, pictured in the Foster Parent's Plan advertisement, no one denies we feel an urge to help just that child. The point is whether or not we have a moral urge. And Darwinism says nothing to this.

But this criticism is off-target. The Darwinian is not merely talking of wants and dislikes. He/she is talking of a full-blown sense of moral obligation, conveyed to us through the epigenetic rules. The sense of obligation could well be and often is working against our basic selfish desires. Conversely, as Mill recognized, the bottom line for moral insight has to be our own personal awareness – whatever the ultimate source. We have seen how John Rawls (1971) has spoken of the need to achieve a state of 'relective equilibrium', where all of our insights and conclusions and everything else are brought into a coherent consistent whole. And this is true. But, ultimately, as noted in chapter 3, moral premises have to be rooted in what we feel is right and wrong. (This does not as such deny the possibility of an objectively based morality causing such moral feelings.)

The Darwinian and the utilitarian are talking of the same types of thing – human moral sensitivities. Therefore, in bringing the two into line, an empirical appeal is both proper and needed. You might tell me that I have a moral obligation to stand on my head every Friday afternoon, but I am not going to take you very seriously until you strike some responsive chord within my breast. Thus we can and must ask: which theory, Darwinism or utilitarianism, better accords with our moral feelings? And here, I suggest, Darwinism wins decisively. We do feel we have special obligations to our children. To deny this is to make total hypocrites of us all. And after our children come our neighbours and countrymen. In this context, I remind you of the writings of Charles Dickens, a sure guide to popular moral sentiment. Remember in *Bleak House* how there is a savage attack on Mrs Jellyby who neglects her husband and children to campaign for the benighted heathen in Borrioboola-Gha. Obligations begin at home, Dickens tells us. Then they spread to the poor of our own country, like Jo, the crossing-sweeper, from Tom-all-Alone's. Only, finally, do they reach out abroad.

If what I claim is true, why does traditional utilitarianism not pick up on it? The answer in major part seems to be that (as with biology) technology has taken utilitarianism by surprise. So long as one is dealing with a relatively tight little world, you can argue for treating most people more or less as equally deserving beings. (Although this does not speak to the question of intra-familial relations.) With a small, intimate group, all will benefit including yourself. But in the modern situation, to put utilitarianism into action simply leads to a never ending drain on your own resources, as you give everything away. And, somehow, there just does not seem to be the obligation to do this.

In this context, it is interesting to quote Mill's defence of the disinterestedness of the Greatest Happiness Principle. The pertinent passage, part of which was quoted earlier, is as follows:

> As between his own happiness and that of others, utilitarianism requires him to be as strictly impartial as a disinterested and benevolent spectator. In the golden rule of Jesus of Nazareth, we read the complete spirit of the ethics of utility. To do as you would be done by, and to love your neighbour as yourself, constitute the ideal perfection of utilitarian morality. (1910, p. 16)

To this, the Darwinian says 'Amen.' But what is the case when we are not dealing with neighbours? Here, Darwinism seems to fit more with our moral intuitions than does utilitarianism. We have a moral obligation to promote happiness, but this obligation weakens as the circle widens. If you doubt me, ask yourself the following: is your own government grossly immoral when it puts more of your tax money into social programmes benefitting the poor and needy of your own country, rather than into foreign aid? (I suspect, in fact, Darwinian and utilitarian usually agree on distribution of aid. You can do more good closer to home, because of practical factors. But there is still a difference in moral claim here.)

To give and not to count the cost

No doubt, the critic will still worry that the Darwinian fails to do justice to morality. Leave on one side the question of whether or not moral obligations do diminish as one moves to beings further away. There remains the major point, thus far ignored, that the mechanisms of evolution demand returns. It is certainly true that the returns of kin selection are sufficiently subtle as not to require a conscious expectation of reward. But, again and again, it has been emphasized that non-relatives acting under the influence of reciprocal altruism will be looking for returns. And, if such returns are not forthcoming, co-operation will break down. How can this be compatible with true morality? Utilitarianism demands that you promote happiness, not that you promote happiness so long as you get lots back in return.

This is an important objection, but can be handled readily by the Darwinian. There are at least two possible responses. Empirical enquiry will have to decide between them; but there is probably truth in both. First, you can point out that reciprocal altruism does not imply that all of our social interactions are moral – which is just as well, for obviously much which occurs is not moral at all. When dealing with other people (especially non-relatives), a great deal of conscious self-interest enters in. This is not necessarily immoral – there is nothing wrong about buying a kilo of potatoes, and paying ready cash – but certainly at times our thoughts and behaviours put us in active opposition to our moral sentiments. And it is selfishness which often wins. It is open to the Darwinian to argue that morality is but one of the urges promoted by reciprocal altruism. Non-moral, restricting feelings are also produced by the same mechanism. Morality gets us to help and co-operate, and the rest of us ensures that morality does not get out of hand and prove biologically disadvantageous. (In the case of relatives, perhaps non-moral love displaces the urge for return.)

Here, incidentally, the Darwinian finds a possible answer to the utilitarian who insists that he/she really does feel the same obligations to all humankind. Perhaps the epigenetic rules promote classical utilitarianism – all count equally – but other, non-moral forces keep our co-operative behaviour down, more or less to those in the same reciprocating pool as we. This is not the answer I accept, but it is plausible. The fact that different concerned people might have different feelings about obligations to the Third World is general support for the biological position. Selection left us without a definitive answer to the problem. It was not an issue for the Australopithecines. (As will be noted at the end of the chapter, a Darwinian analysis of human nature is surely a first step to an adequate policy on world poverty.)

The second response to the critic who worries that reciprocal altruism demands returns, centres on the fact that morality itself is not powerless in the face of selfishness. Suppose I help you, because I feel morally obliged to do so, but that you do not reciprocate, either by helping me or by throwing your help into the general pool. In the name of morality, I cannot demand help from you simply because I have helped you. However, in the name of morality, I can demand help from you because *it is right for you to help me*. My being a moral individual does not entail my being a sucker (Mackie, 1978). You should help me and others, because that is the moral thing to do, and I can demand this of you. I even have an obligation to keep you up to the mark. And note how quickly we move to isolate or otherwise change the individual who does not co-operate. We punish them ('for their own good'), or we declare them moral imbeciles and restrict their role in society.

I do emphasize that what has just been said is predicated on the assumption that interactions are between equals. We do not demand such reciprocation from children, especially our own. They are not yet fully responsible moral agents. Nor, on the same grounds that he/she could not return the help, would we refuse to help the paraplegic. That is the whole point about morality. It does push us out beyond immediate expectations of reward. Biologically speaking, it is an insurance policy, in case anything dreadful happens to us. However, when returns could be made, human nature has several ways of enforcing the balance – and none of these compromise the genuine nature of our moral feelings.

Parenthetically, we have in these last two paragraphs the complete answer to those who invoke the names of Jesus or a saintly follower, like Mother Teresa, as a counter to the naturalistic approach which I urge (Singer, 1981; Trigg, 1982). Jesus urges us to forgive seven times seventy times; but I suspect that long before we got to the limit, most people *in the name of morality* would insist that a stop be put to the transgressions. You may forgive the perpetual offender, but you have an obligation to take him out of society. Not to do so would be wrong. (See Wallwork, 1982, and Furnish, 1982, for discussions suggesting that Christianity would accept this conclusion.)

As far as the saint is concerned, given the variation which exists in all populations – especially populations where culture takes a major hand – one fully expects some people to be more sensitive to their moral urges than others. Even if sainthood takes you into the biologically maladaptive, the Darwinian would think this no more than the occasional price you pay for a first-class social-facilitating mechanism like morality (Wilson, 1978). Most of us admire saints, but feel no great pressure to follow them – nor do we think we should. Most would-be saints are thought dangerous fanatics – at least, more trouble than they are worth. I am reminded of Ghandi's whimsical comment: 'My friends tell me it costs them a great deal to keep me in poverty.'

I conclude, therefore, that the morality of the Darwinian is genuine. Moreover, although Darwinism and utilitarianism may not coincide precisely, with some adjustment they can be brought into mutual focus.[6]

Substantive ethics reconsidered: Kantianism

Let us turn now to the other great theme in philosophical writing on substantive ethics, that which focuses on the status and rights of the individual. 'Treat others as ends and not as means.' 'Justice as fairness.' And so forth. This position can as readily be given a Darwinian backing as can utilitarianism – subject to modifications of the kind we have just been discussing.

That Darwinism is sensitive to the Kantian emphasis on individual rights is obvious. From the biological viewpoint, we are all persons in society, interacting in such a way that aims to maximize our share of society's goods. But, for each and every one of us, there must be a point beyond which the price of the acquisition of society's goods becomes too high. It is just not worth the cost. And the bottom line clearly is when we are used merely for the benefit of others. Thus, as Darwinians we want to stop this happening to us. The most obvious way to prevent this happening, particularly when the chief underlying causal mechanism for social functioning is reciprocal altruism, is to agree that we will not use others as a means either. But how is this 'ideal' to be enforced? Natural selection serves it up under the guise of morality! We have the Categorical Imperative, or something very much like it, embedded in an epigenetic rule. We feel we ought to treat others as ends. They feel the same way about us. Hence, Darwinism and Kantianism are each satisfied.

[6] The implication might seem to be that utilitarianism must do all of the adjusting, but obviously we will have a dialogue. After all, the science only got to where it is now, because of the philosophy.

It cannot have escaped the reader's attention that the way in which Rawls presents his moral theory sounds almost as if it had been prepared by a Darwinian. (In fact, Wilson (1975) has some sharply critical things to say of Rawls, but these are based on total misreadings.) Remember how Rawls presents the initial case for 'justice as fairness'.

> The guiding idea is that the principles of justice for the basic structure of society are . . . . the principles that free and rational persons concerned to further their own interests would accept in an initial position of equality as defining the fundamental terms of their association. These principles are to regulate all further agreements; they specify the kinds of social cooperation that can be entered into and the forms of Government that can be established. This way of regarding the principles of justice I shall call justice as fairness. (Rawls, 1971, p. 11)

This all sounds like reciprocal altruism in action. Indeed, Wilson's words about such co-operation between non-relatives ('soft-core altruism') are virtually those of Rawls.

> In human beings soft-core altruism has been carried to elaborate extremes. Reciprocation among distantly related or unrelated individuals is the key to human society. The perfection of the social contract has broken the ancient vertebrate constraints imposed by rigid kin selection.
>
> Human beings appear to be sufficiently selfish and calculating to be capable of indefinitely [great] harmony and social homeostasis. This statement is not self-contradictory. True selfishness, if obedient to the other constraints of mammalian biology, is the key to a more nearly perfect social contract. (Wilson, 1978, pp. 156-7)

Note that 'true selfishness' does not imply that people are consciously selfish in their everyday social intercourse. The whole point is that they are not.

The strength of the Darwinian position is that it tells us why our sense of fairness arises in the first place. Everyone, including Rawls, always emphasizes the hypothetical nature of the original position – that which supposedly leads to the contract to enter into society, under conditions of fairness.

> In justice as fairness the original position of equality corresponds to the state of nature in the traditional theory of the social contract. This original position is not, of course, thought of as an actual historical state of affairs, much less as a primitive condition of culture. It is understood as a purely hypothetical situation characterized so as to lead to a certain conception of justice. (Rawls, 1971, p. 12)

But this just leaves us dangling. Through the process of reflective equilibrium we can check out our conclusions against our common-sense intuitions of morality. However, as we saw above, ultimately this is an internal process. There is still the question of why we take morality seriously. Perhaps morality is *as if* we had made a contract; but, if really we did not, then who cares? Or rather, why do we care? Was the contract made for us in heaven, or what? Since we ourselves did not sign it, why should we keep it – other than from expediency?

Darwinism gives us the answer. The contract was not made consciously. But it is simulated by natural selection – burned into our souls – because that is the way to maximize an individual's interests, in a group where everyone is trying to do the same. And we cannot (readily) drop out, because acceptance of the contract is part of our biological nature. Interestingly, Rawls himself senses the gap in his position, and even picks up on the relevance of reciprocal altruism.

> In arguing for the greater stability of the principles of justice I have assumed that certain psychological laws are true, or approximately so. I shall not pursue the question of stability beyond this point. We may note however that one might ask how it is that human beings have acquired a nature described by these psychological principles. The theory of evolution would suggest that it is the outcome of natural selection; the capacity for a sense of justice and the moral feelings is an adaption of mankind to its place in nature. (Rawls, 1971, pp. 502-3)

However, he does then rather spoil things by claiming: 'These remarks are not intended as justifying reasons for the contract view' (p. 504). My point is that the view needs such justification, and that the remarks gives us all of the justification we are going to get or need. (More on this point, especially on 'justifying reasons', when we get to meta-ethics.)

Concluding the direct discussion of the Kantian approach to the principles of right action, I confess as a Darwinian to the same sorts of reservations (about family and strangers) as expressed in the analysis of utilitarianism. Interestingly, Rawls for one is sensitive to some of my worries, recognizing that our sense of obligation to our immediate family will be different – stronger – than our sense of obligation to others. Discussing people in the 'original position', that is behind the 'veil of ignorance', trying to decide what they as rational self-interested beings should accept/demand as a condition of entry into society with others, Rawls asks about our obligations to our children.

> The question arises, however, whether the persons in the original position have obligations and duties to third parties, for example, to their immediate descendants . . . . I shall make a motivational assumption. The parties are thought of as representing continuing lines of claims, as being, so to speak, deputies for a kind of everlasting moral agent or institution . . . . It is not necessary to think of the parties as heads of families, although I shall generally follow this interpretation. What is essential is that each person in the original position should care about the well-being of some of those in the next generation, it being presumed that their concern is for different individuals in each case. (Rawls, 1971, pp. 128-9)

I am not sure that (in Rawlsian terms) this would give us a stronger sense of moral obligation to our children, since morality seems to arise as a consequence of the contract we have made with other people in the original position. But it is clear that our relations with our children will differ from relations with others. I should think, incidentally, that a Rawlsian might well argue that relations with people from other countries, particularly very deprived countries, call for somewhat different levels of moral obligation. Were the members of such countries really, even hypothetically, in an original position with us?[7]

Moral disagreements

This now completes what I have to say directly about substantive ethics, as viewed through the lens of Darwinism. As with science, the discussion at this level should have been reasonably non-threatening, even to those very suspicious of claims about the relevance of our biological nature to philosophy. The aim has not been revolutionary; but rather, to the contrary, to show that modern evolutionary thinking about humankind furnishes a ready base for the ideas articulated by the great moral philosophers – subject to some of the reservations discussed above. However, before we turn to the next phase of our analysis – discussion of the meta-ethical implications of Darwinism – one final question must be addressed. In our ecumenical rush to give equal time to both utilitarianism and Kantianism, have we not proven too much? Surely, Darwinism supports one or other substantival ethical approach, but not both.

I have warned already against taking too seriously the disagreements of professional philosophers. Utilitarians and Kantians agree nearly all of the time on moral matters. The utilitarian is against rape, no less than is the Kantian. The utilitarian thinks we have an obligation to the sick and poor in our society, no less than does the Kantian. The utilitarian values individual freedom and liberty. As noted, John Stuart Mill wrote the classic defence of liberty, on utilitarian grounds. The Kantian, as we have seen, thinks happiness of value, and certainly happiness must play an important role in Rawls's system – why else bother to be fair?

Thus, at worst, if we argue for the existence of epigenetic rules giving rise to both utilitarian and Kantian sentiments, no real violence will be done to moral philosophy. Of course, why those who analyse morality from a philosophical perspective are led to emphasize one position

[7] Rawls (1980) openly acknowledges that he deals only with a closed 'well-ordered' society, putting on one side 'questions of justice between societies', acknowledging that when we turn to this issue, 'to what extent the conception of justice for the basic structure will have to be revised in the process, cannot be foreseen in advance' (p. 524).

rather than the other is a nice question. You might argue that we have different alleles, balanced within populations. I am more inclined to look to culture, backed by a certain amount of imprinting. This certainly seems the reason why 'every little boy and girl who's born into this world alive, is either a little liberal or a little conservative.' Perhaps the same holds true of moral philosophies. (Although, for reasons to be countered later, Nozick (1981) denies the ultimate relevance of biology for ethics, he does toy with the idea of intra-group genetically caused variations in moral sensitivity. See pp. 712-13, n. 52; also, Ruse and Wilson, 1986.)

Nothing said thus far is to deny that, at times, you do get genuine failures in moral understanding. People simply fall out over what is right and what is wrong. As I have explained already, most of the disagreements are like disagreements in science. The trouble is not so much with the guide-lines given to us by natural selection. Difficulties arise in the application of the rules. Should pornography be banned? Much of the controversy is not about morality at all. No one wants small children corrupted. Nor does any morally healthy person want the police peering under the bed-sheets. Debate centres on empirical questions about the effects of pornography. Does looking at naked women turn men into rapists? Is the most erotic material that involving violence? And so forth. There are no moral issues at stake at all in these questions.

But what of those moral disagreements which do stem from a clash of basic principles? We have seen that utilitarian and Kantian divide on the respective merits of group needs and individual rights. Unfortunately, sometimes you do just get a clash between the overall benefits to society, and what an individual can reasonably expect in that society. Without the highway, traffic is dangerously delayed. Everyone suffers, in lost industry and potential accidents. With the highway, a small minority lose their lands and homes without any choice. I can well imagine utilitarian and Kantian deciding differently on this matter, and the difference being a direct function of individual moral insights.

Again, there are differences between utilitarians and Kantians on the relative merits of means and ends. For the utilitarian, the way things turn out has to be your deciding principle. Admittedly, the rule utilitarian generalizes over a number of cases, but the consequences are what count. For Kant, consequences are never the ultimate deciding factors. The good will is everything. If you sincerely do your best, then that is what counts, no matter how things turn out.

The usual course in moral philosophy, when faced with dilemmas like these, is to argue that one side or the other must be wrong (right), and then to think up ingenious fictitious examples to make your own case plausible. But deep down inside most of us can see the merits of both horns of any such dilemma. We do need the road; but it is surely wrong to tear people from their homes. The man who tried to murder his wife, but who bungled, is just as culpable as the man who succeeded. Yet, after all, things did not turn out quite so badly, and this surely has some bearing on the case. Would you execute the husband who gave his wife water to drink, even though he thought it was prussic acid?

I want to suggest that the trouble with conventional analyses is that we think there must be a uniquely right answer. As Darwinians, we are bound to be a lot less certain that this is necessarily so. Let me state what has been stated many times before. Evolution is not going anywhere. Evolution does not guarantee truth or, in this case, absolute knowledge of right and wrong. Moreover, evolution does not guarantee that our adaptations are going to work perfectly all of the time. Humans, like everything else, are bundles of compromises. It is advantageous to walk around. It is advantageous to have big heads. And for these virtues, human females have to bear greater risks in childbirth than do other female mammals.

Given that moral understanding is no less a part of human nature than are bipedalism and head-size, my hunch is that perhaps at times in moral activity there are simply insoluble dilemmas. Our moral capabilities break down, and any decision we may make means that in some respects we must do what we think is wrong. We have utilitarian yearnings and we have Kantian yearnings, and some phenomena bring both sets into (conflicting) play. Then we have the ethical equivalent of the maladaptive troubles faced by human females in childbirth. Closer to home, we have the equivalent of the troubles caused by such mind-stretching phenomena as electrons, which force us to revise our conventional thinking about the nature of reality. As far as the moral dilemmas are concerned, the only consolation is that not deciding at all is as equally – or perhaps more – wrong as opting for either utilitarianism or Kantianism.

I am not arguing that, as a methodological rule, we should cease philosophical enquiry as soon as we come to a thorny moral issue. Certainly, in everyday life there are answers to most problems. And let me again emphasize that normally our biologically backed moral sensitivities blend harmoniously together. Take the matter of means and ends. Usually, the best guide to sincerity is consequences, and vice versa. Remember the Jacques Tati film, *Jour de Fête*, where every action of the good-intentioned postman goes awry. Remember the Flashman novels, where every action of the bad-intentioned bounder turns out well. Why are these so funny? Precisely because this is not the way real life works. Usually, the best guide to good intentions is consequences, and the best guide to consequences is good intentions. That is why we value both, even though they sometimes get decoupled. And that is why we are not altogether sure what to do when they do get decoupled. So we laugh – or cry.

Fortunately, we can usually muddle through, and that is good enough for evolution.[8]

Darwinian meta-ethics

We come now to the fundamental questions about the ultimate ground of morality. The initial, and perhaps most pressing question of all, centres on the very nature or meaning of morality. Thanks most particularly to Hume, we realize that when we make a moral claim, we simply do not mean the same thing as when we make a non-moral claim. The statement 'I find the thought of sex with small children upsetting' is quite different from 'Paedophilic behaviour is morally wrong.' The second has a sense of obligation, of force about what you ought or ought not do, which the first does not have. I could have a real yen for sex with children, and yet think it grossly immoral.

Now, at once the critic will charge that the Darwinian approach glosses right over this point, and thus flounders on its own insensitivity. Let us grant the scientific case, that epigenetic rules influence our social intercourse, and that thanks to kin selection and reciprocal altruism human behaviour rebounds to the reproductive benefit of the actor. But this says nothing about morality! At most, we have wants, wishes, desires, hates, and associated actions. Moreover, these are all directed to individual self-gain. That is to say, they are selfish (Singer, 1981; Trigg, 1982). This is the very antithesis of morality. Huxley was right. Right action opposes the Darwinian course of nature. It does not complaisantly acquiesce in it.

By now, I trust you will agree with me that this objection misses the very essence of the Darwinian case. The Darwinian is the first to accept and stress the difference between 'is' and 'ought', between statements about matters of fact, like normal feelings, and statements about matters of obligation, as occur in morality. His/her point is that normal feelings alone would not be enough to get us interacting socially in ways that would benefit us biologically. It is true that normal feelings get us a long way. For instance, we feel an innate love for our children, which spurs us to action benefitting them – thereby improving our own reproductive efforts. Indeed, the Darwinian endorses Immanuel Kant's (1959) astute psychological perception that much that we do is (at best) only loosely

---

[8] Ross (1930) discusses the resolution of moral intuitions – prima-facie duties – which come into conflict, appealing ultimately to the moral consciousnesses of reasonably thoughtful and well-educated people. Perhaps something like this does happen (although there is more than a hint of circularity about such an appeal to the best people). Darwinism explains why all is not clear in the first place.

properly called 'good' or 'moral', because we do not do it from a call of duty but from sheer wish or desire. The mother breast-feeding her baby is doing so because she thereby feels happy, rather than from heeding the cry of the Categorical Imperative.

However, by their very nature, normal feelings and their effects are generally limited and restricted. They do tend to be (although are certainly not exclusively) selfish or immediate, in a fairly literal sense. I like fast cars, so I strive to buy one. I like respect and honour from my peers, so I labour long and hard at my work. I like sex and companionship, therefore I shower bounties on my mate. Moreover, for good evolutionary reasons, normal feelings have a negative side, making us wary of others and unwilling to do something for nothing.

It is precisely because of the limited potential of normal feelings alone that the Darwinian posits the need for morality – something which goes beyond such feelings to obligation. Biologically, we need to back up our normal feelings, and to help and co-operate with others. We need a spur to make us change a diaper in the middle of the night, or to coach for the spelling test. We need to push a make us aid our neighbour when his barn burns down. Our sense of morality, our sentiment of obligation, comes in here. We have evolved epigenetic rules which make us do things because they are right, and abstain from other things because they are wrong. These rules drive us into social action, above and beyond and perhaps despite our inclinations.

In this respect, the very last thing the Darwinian wants to do is break Hume's law by denying that there is a genuine 'is/ought' distinction. *The distinction is fundamental to his/her analysis of morality.* You may object that the Darwinian accounts inadequately for the evolution of morality. That is a separate question. It is one which we have now looked at in depth in this chapter, and I will say no more here. But insensitivity to the task at hand is not something on which you can fault the Darwinian. What we are talking of is 'right' and 'wrong', 'good' and 'bad', 'should' and 'ought'.

Grant now that the epigenetic rules do embody genuine moral sentiments, or rather give rise to genuine moral sentiments. Thanks to evolution, humans have innate dispositions to believe that we should promote the general happiness, and that we should treat people as ends rather than means. What then must we conclude about the status of morality, when viewed in this Darwinian light?

Many would respond: absolutely nothing! They would argue that a genetic account of the evolution of morality says nothing about the justificatory foundations of morality (Nozick, 1981; Flanagan, 1981; Ruse, 1979b). To pretend otherwise is indeed to violate Hume's law with a vengeance. If you deny the is/ought distinction, then at least you cannot be faulted for wanting to go from 'is' to 'ought'. But to affirm it, and then to go from one to the other is to compound the philosophical sins. One is put in mind of Mr Micawber, who thought he could cancel his debts by acknowledging them, and writing IOUs.

This is too fast. To argue in this way – as many (including my former self) would argue – is to miss what the Darwinian has given us. Once you agree that morality is a biological adaptation, you are directed to a meta-ethical conclusion about its status. Remember our earlier meta-ethical division of putative analyses of morality, into those which saw it as 'objective' and those which saw it as 'subjective'. We must ask whether, to the Darwinian, morality is – because of the science, must be taken as – something objective, in the sense of having an authority and existence of its own, independent of human beings? Or whether morality is – because of the science, must be taken as – subjective, being a function of human nature, and reducing ultimately to feelings and sentiments – feelings and sentiments of a type different from wishes and desires, but ultimately emotions of some kind?

I claim that, having accepted the natural evolution of morality, the Darwinian is forced to take the second option. The naturalistic approach, locating morality in the dispositions produced by the epigenetic rules, makes our sense of obligation a direct function of human nature. We feel that we ought to help others and to co-operate with them, because of the way that we are. That is the complete answer to the origins and status of morality. There is no need to invoke (and much against invoking) some Platonic world of values. Morality has neither meaning nor justification, outside the human context. Morality is subjective.

Now, this conclusion is little more than a statement of faith at the moment. Let me therefore go on to argue for it: first, by tackling an already mentioned general objection to subjectivist approaches, proving not only that Darwinism can handle the objection (indeed, gaining strength from the objection), but that it positively excludes objectivist approaches; second, by showing that no fallacies are involved in this naturalistic position; and, third, by demonstrating that such a biologically based approach does not have that within it which makes any true morality impossible.

Objectifying morality

We turn first to the major general query about any subjectivist approach to morality's foundation. As we know, the big weakness of traditional subjectivism is that it fails to account for the true nature of our moral experience. The whole point about morality is that it is binding, not open to individual choice. It is greater than and above any of us. In other words, it has all of the features that we associate with objectivity. If I say 'Killing is wrong', I do not mean simply that I do not like killing, nor yet (as traditional emotivism would have it) am I merely emoting against it: 'I hate killing, Goddam it!' I am saying that killing fails by certain standards, not up for decision or choice. Therefore, its prohibition is laid upon and fixed for us all. That is part of the import of 'ought'.

Darwinism can handle this point, and does so in such a manner that much strengthens its claim to be the key to a meta-ethical, correct approach to moral understanding. The Darwinian argues that morality simply does not work (from a biological perspective), unless we believe that it is objective. Darwinian theory shows that, in fact, morality is a function of (subjective) feelings; but it shows also that we have (and must have) the illusion of objectivity. In other words, we 'objectify' moral claims, to use an ugly but descriptive term (Mackie, 1977).

The point about morality (says the Darwinian) is that it is an adaptation to get us to go beyond regular wishes, desires and fears, and to interact socially with people. How does it get us to do this? By filling us full of thoughts about obligations and duties, and so forth. And the key to what is going on is that we are then moved to action, precisely because we think morality is something laid upon us. We may have choice about whether to do right and wrong, but we have no choice about right and wrong in themselves. If morality did not have this air of externality or objectivity, it would not be morality and (from a biological perspective) would fail to do what it is intended to do. Why should I care whether you are upset at my stealing your food and clothing?

In a sense, therefore, morality is a collective illusion foisted upon us by our genes. Note, however, that the illusion lies not in the morality itself, but in its sense of objectivity. I am certainly not saying that morality is unreal. Of course it is not! What is unreal is the apparent objective reference of morality. I hasten to add that I am not now suggesting that morality is in any way a sign of immaturity. Nor would I have those of us who see the illusory nature of morality's objectivity throw over moral thought, as suggested by Plato's Thrasymachus or Nietzche's Superman. Morality is part of human nature, and (subject to reservations to be made later) an effective adaptation. Why should we forego morality any more than we should put out our eyes? I would not say that we could not escape morality – presumably we could get into wholesale, anti-morality, genetic engineering – but I strongly suspect that a simple attempt to ignore it will fail. This is surely the (true) message of Dostoevsky in *Crime and Punishment*. Raskolnikov tries to go beyond conventional right and wrong, but finds ultimately that this is impossible.

In passing, I cannot forebear mentioning that Dostoevsky would have us find salvation through Christianity. I am certainly not suggesting this here as a necessary antidote to the terrors of Darwinism. But it is surely significant that morality in most people's minds is bound up with religion, in some way (Reynolds and Tanner, 1983). God supposedly endorses and enforces moral norms. I very much doubt that the traditional conception of God has much more connection with objective reality than has morality. He does, however, serve an extremely useful biological purpose, inasmuch as He backs up the objective, binding status of morality. Of course, God and religion serve other biological ends as well, not the least of which is giving life some purpose.

What if you do not feel quite so negatively as I about the traditional conception of God? What if you think that God really does exist, and that morality is His will? Or what if, as an objectivist, you locate morality in some other source, like Plato's Forms or non-natural properties? Could you not accept virtually everything the Darwinian claims about morality being a human phenomenon (after all, how could it not be), and yet argue that our human faculties are perceiving or intuiting objective truth? An analogy with mathematics springs at once to mind. (Nozick, 1981, makes this argument).

However, even if the case for mathematics be accepted (as you know, I would not accept it), the analogy with morality fails. At the least, the objectivist must agree that his/her ultimate principles are (given Darwinism) redundant. You would believe what you do about right and wrong, irrespective of whether or not a 'true' right and wrong existed! The Darwinian claims that his/her theory gives an entire analysis of our moral sentiments. Nothing more is needed. Given two worlds, identical except that one has an objective morality and the other does not, the humans therein would think and act in exactly the same ways.

Hence the objective foundation for morality is redundant. But, surely, the last thing that the objectivist can accept is that his/her principles are redundant. 'God wants us to be good, and that is the ultimate defining source of good, but it wouldn't matter whether He did or not!' If anything is ruled out by objectivism, it is this. Thus, we must conclude that not only is Darwinian ethics a subjectivist ethics, it is one which positively excludes the objectivist approach. If the empirical thesis of this chapter is right, there is no objective ethics. Nor can one readily see how the objectivist might patch up the situation, making his/her position compatible with evolutionism. At least, this seems impossible, so long as one locates the foundation of morality in some sort of extra-human existence, like God's will or non-natural properties. (I will speak later to the objectivism of the Kantian, who poses a rather different challenge.) To suppose that evolution will seek out the true morality is to revert right back to Spencerian progressionism. For the Darwinian, what works is what counts. Had evolution taken us down another path, we might well think moral that which we now find horrific, and conversely. This is not a conclusion acceptable to the traditional objectivist.

Finally, in this section, reverting again to general problems with subjectivism, note that the Darwinian's position does not plunge him/her into wholesale ethical relativism. If morality is just a question of feelings (albeit of a special kind), why should I not simply have one moral insight and you have another, and the one be as good as the other? Certain African tribes say female circumcision is a good thing. We in the West say it is a bad thing. That is the end of the matter. We have no right to criticize. Morality is probably little more than desires, and even if these desires be of funny kind, implying standards, the norms are personal.

Against this, the Darwinian recognizes that there are indeed differences from society to society, and also within societies, particularly across time. However, these are readily (and surely properly) explained in the way that most moral theorists would explain them, as secondary, modified consequences of shared primary moral imperatives (Taylor, 1978, chapter 2). Take the case of extra-marital sex mentioned earlier. In the past quarter of a century we have seen a great change within our own society, in attitudes towards it. In the 1950s nice girls said 'No!' and (I speak here with some feeling) this was a moral issue. Pregnancy spelled much unhappiness to the mother-to-be, to her family and, quite probably, to the child. Now, efficient contraception has removed the threat of pregnancy, and with it has gone much of the moral hand-wringing. Nice girls no longer have to say 'No!' – and they don't. But none of this represents a change in primary moral attitude. Wantonly causing unhappiness is still wrong. It is just that new technology has changed the ways in which we now can achieve the things we desire, and avoid those things we do not desire.

When it comes to general shared moral principles, the Darwinian stands firm. Humans share a common moral understanding. This universality is guaranteed by the shared genetic background of every member of *Homo sapiens*. The differences between us are far outweighed by the similarities. We (virtually) all have hands, eyes, ears, noses, and the same ultimate awareness. That is part of being human. There is, therefore, absolutely nothing arbitrary about morality, considered from the human perspective. I, like you, have forty-six chromosomes. I, like you, have a shared moral sense. People who do not have forty-six chromosomes are considered abnormal, and (probably) sick. People who do not have our moral sense are considered abnormal, and (probably) sick.

I did not choose my chromosome number. I did not choose my moral code. For the Darwinian, the very essence of morality is that it is shared and not relative. It does not work as a biological adaptation, unless we all join in. Unless there is this joint participation, the illusion of (objective) morality will not keep afloat. It is only in my biological interests to have moral sentiments if you likewise have such sentiments.

Otherwise, I will be moral; you will cheat; and I shall be left a loser.

Of course, all of this is said with the proviso that, notwithstanding the points just made, since the Darwinian does take a naturalistic approach, he/she must stand ready to revise in the face of new empirical findings. If one found that there were certain broad behavioural differences between races, this could extend to moral awareness. But, what we know already strongly suggests that any hypothetical differences will be strongly outweighed by similarities. (See Ruse and Wilson, 1986, for more on this point.)

Stepping around Hume's law

Grant that Darwinian subjectivism starts to look more plausible. We must now go back to the key problem of justification. Let it be said yet again. Moral claims are not of the same type as factual claims. This is one arm of Hume's law. But what about the other arm? Despite all the warnings, is it not being argued that, although there is a difference in type, moral claims can be derived from factual claims? And, as already stressed, is this not just as much of a violation of the law, as confusions between 'is' and 'ought'? The Darwinian claims that, on the basis of his/her factual theory about the nature and process of evolution, you can provide a total explanation of morality. Surely, indeed, this is a gross violation of the 'is/ought' barrier. You are acknowledging that there is a barrier; but, then, you are calmly walking right through it. The naturalistic fallacy is being committed in the grandest Spencerian fashion.

Not quite! Fallacies occur when you try to *deduce* moral claims from factual claims. 'This is what evolution has produced. Therefore, this is a morally good thing.' What the Darwinian would have us do is something rather different. He/she is trying to derive morality from a factual theory, in the sense of *explaining* our moral awareness, by means of the theory. More particularly, he/she is explaining away the apparent objective referent of morality, that which gives it its binding prescriptive nature, and which takes it in meaning beyond the merely factual. To use an American sporting metaphor, the Darwinian does an end-run around the is/ought barrier. He/she realizes that you cannot go through it, but argues that you can go around it, giving morality all of the justificatory insight possible.

Consider an analogy. During the First World War, many bereaved parents and wives turned to spiritualism for solace. They would try to communicate with the dead, thus numbing their sense of loss. And not a few felt they were successful in their efforts. Down through the ouija board would come reassuring messages: 'It's all right, Mum. I've gone to a far better place. I'll be waiting for you and Dad.' How do we analyse such messages as these? We can discount universally blatant fraud. I am sure that people (including many of the professional spiritualists) were genuine. I take it that readers will also agree with me that we can exclude the possibility that the fallen were indeed speaking to the survivors. You cannot justify 'Don't worry about me' by saying that it really was the late Private Higgins speaking from Beyond. How otherwise do you account for messages received from someone who turns out to be alive and well, but in a prison camp? The obviously correct answer is that the bereaved were subconsciously deceiving themselves, because of their extreme psychological anxiety. This is the answer you can give, and all the answer that you need give.

The Darwinian argues that we have a similar situation in ethics. You cannot justify 'Killing is wrong' in the sense of deducing if from factual premises. What you can do is explain why we hold this belief. This is all that can or need be offered. The difference between the spiritualism case and morality is that, in the former, most people recognize its deceptive nature and, therefore, we can quite comfortably and literally speak of 'illusion'. In the case of morality, we are all part of the game, and even those of us who realize this have no desire to drop out. Thus, literally, we would not speak of 'illusion'. Illusion in ethics means believing one has a moral obligation to be friendly to cabbages. But ethics is still what I have referred to as a 'collective illusion', in the sense that we all think it is something it really is not.

We have here the answer to those many people (again including my earlier self) who argue that the naturalist confuses 'causes' with 'reason' – that what is needed is reasoned justification of moral claims, and that all that is given is a genetic causal analysis (Nagel, 1980; Singer, 1981; Beatty, 1981; Ruse 1979b). To use an analogy, the mistake (according to critics) is akin to talking about Freud's own nature and Jewish heritage, when what is needed is rational proof (or disproof) of the Oedipus complex. In response, the Darwinian agrees that you should take reasoned justification as far as you can, but concludes in the case of morality that there comes a point where there are no further reasons. After you have achieved reflective equilibrium, you have gone about as far as you can go, within the moral game.

You must, as it were, step outside of morality itself, and then all you can do is give a causal analysis. There are no ultimate justifying reasons for: 'It's all right, Mum. I'm happy now.' Nor are there for 'Hurting people for fun is wrong.' This does not mean, of course, that the wise person pays equal attention to both claims, any more than does the fact that there are no ultimate justifying reasons for allowing three outs in a baseball (half) innings mean that it is silly to have such a rule.

The [Darwinian] may well agree . . . . that value judgments are properly defended in terms of other value judgments until we reach some that are fundamental. All of this, in a sense, is the giving of *reasons*. However, suppose we seriously raise the question of why these fundamental judgments are regarded as fundamental. There may be only a *causal* explanation for this! We reject simplistic utilitarianism because it entails consequences that are morally *counterintuitive*, or we embrace a Rawlsian theory of justice because it systematizes (places in 'reflective equilibrium') our *pretheoretical convictions*. But what is the status of those intuitions or convictions? Perhaps there is nothing more to be said for them than that they involve deep *preferences* (or patterns of preference) built into our biological nature. If this is so, then at a very fundamental point the reasons/causes (and the belief we ought/really ought) distinction breaks down, or the one transforms into the other. (Murphy, 1982, p. 112, n. 21)

Freedom of choice

By now, one query in particular must be troubling many readers. The Darwinian argues that the genes make a significant causal input to our moral awareness, and to our consequent decisions and actions. The implication, therefore, is that we do what we do because of our evolutionary heritage. But if this is so, then what place can there be for genuine morality? A major precondition for moral thought and action is that you have the freedom to choose between right and wrong. A banana is not a moral agent, because it has no such freedom or will of its own. Unfortunately, if we humans are mere genetic robots, then there seems little hope of making such choices. In which case, morality becomes a sham. At best, we are prisoners of our genes, watching the world go by in front of us, as if on a picture screen. Or, for those who like historical analogies, we are like chained prisoners in Plato's cave, watching the shadows flickering on the wall.

Moreover, when a prominent Darwinian writes as follows, all fears seem realized.

> The genes hold culture on a leash. The leash is very long, but inevitably values will be constrained in accordance with their effects on the human gene pool. The brain is a product of evolution. Human behaviour – like the deepest capacities for emotional response which drive and guide it – is the circuitous technique by which human genetic material has been and will be kept intact. Morality has no other demonstrable ultimate function. (Wilson, 1978, p. 167)

Despite Wilson's words, a quick conclusion that the Darwinian approach makes genuine ethics impossible is unwarranted. I am not going to pretend to solve here all of the problems to do with the will and its freedom, nor would I even claim that Darwinism unaided could solve them all. However, the approach being taken in this book certainly does not exacerbate the problems of the will, and perhaps in some respects throws light on them. Thus, worries to do with (what critics of the application of Darwinism to humanity like to call) 'genetic determinism' need not bother us (Lewontin, Rose and Kamin, 1984). (A good collection of essays on free will and determinism is Lehrer, 1966. Hudson, 1970, and Mackie, 1977, contain clear discussions of major issues.)

As a function of our biology, our moral ideas are thrust upon us, rather than being things needing or allowing decision at the individual level. This is the claim. Just as we have no choice about having four limbs, so we have no choice about the nature of our moral awareness. (I will ignore obvious questions about genetic manipulation.) But who, other than perhaps some of the existentialists, ever really pretended that we have choice in this respect anyway? Kant is surely right in arguing that the supreme principle of morality is *categorical* – it is laid upon us, without any 'ifs' and 'buts'. We are not free to choose what right and wrong are to be. Where the freedom comes, if it is to come at all, is in working within the given bounds of right and wrong: 'A free will and a will under moral laws are identical' (Kant, 1959, p. 65).

As one moral philosopher has written recently: 'It is one thing to choose to act from a certain principle. It is quite a different thing, and an impossible thing , to choose which principles will be the principles that determine the difference between right and wrong. Moral principles cannot be enacted, and neither can principles of justice' (Singer, 1977, p. 614). In fact, even the existentialists usually end up with much the same norms as the rest of us. Sartre (1965) argues that we must choose our ultimate principles, but the actual choices seem set within very familiar bounds – honour to country and family.

What then of freedom of choice, given genetically underpinned moral norms? I argue that precisely because Darwinian ethics does so strongly uphold the is/ought distinction, insisting that our sense of ethics is of a real demanding set of obligations, a dimension of human freedom is absolutely presupposed. If we had gone the route of the Hymenoptera, programmed to do blindly what we do, then there would be no true freedom. But we are conscious beings, aware of the dictates imposed by our epigenetic rules – aware of the prescriptions of morality. Far from Darwinism denying freedom, it demands it! And this demand is obviously met, for nothing has been said to negate our phenomenological awareness of ourselves as free beings. Furthermore, we do break sometimes (often) with our sense of morality. Indeed, as we have seen, the Darwinian rather expects this to happen.

None of this is to decide on whether or not, in some basic sense, all human thought and action lies within the causal nexus. My own presumption is that it does. Like many philosophers, I have difficulty in imagining what an uncaused thought/action would be like. I certainly cannot see how such would open up a presently missing opening for human freedom. Nor does my lack of insight at this point stem simply from boundary conditions on human reason, as discussed at the end of the last chapter. Freedom seems to imply responsibility, and this is ruled out by random thoughts and actions. If what I think and do just pops out of nowhere, then this is hardly the mark of a free person. It sounds more like the thought and action of a madman.

Remember that many of the strongest claims for freedom are predicated on ignorance. As we find out more about ourselves, particularly about the workings of the mind, the less inclined we are to believe in some absolute, beyond-causality freedom. Think, for instance, of the effects of Freud's *Essays on Sexuality* (1905) on our thinking about sexual responsibility. The fact that in everyday life we are unaware of the causal underpinnings of our thoughts and action, or even that we believe we transcend causality, is no more definitive proof of some ultimate metaphysical freedom than our belief in the objectivity of morality is proof of such objectively. Indeed, in both cases, the aim of selection is not to give us ultimate insight, but to make us function efficiently. This is not to say that freedom is a total illusion, any more than is morality – only that it may not be quite all we think it is. (Nor is it to say that becoming aware of what drives us simply turns us into amoral robots. As Freud himself – and before him, Spinoza – argued, knowledge of causes leads to the increased possibility of self-control.)

If we humans are indeed part of the world's causal network, then you might well wonder why selection bothered with morality at all. Why were we not made as the insects, with rigidly programmed patterns? I would hazard the guess that the reason why we humans interact socially through morality, rather than according to fixed dictates which are genetically wired into our brains (as are the social actions of ants), is because this gives us more flexibility as circumstances change. If something untoward occurs, we can try to handle it, rather than being destined to do that which would normally be the optimal thing to do. In large part because of our own intelligences, the realm in which we live is far more variable than that faced by ants. Hence, mechanisms like reciprocal altruism can function more efficiently by working through moral norms, as produced by the epigenetic rules.

If my guess is correct (one which does seem common among Darwinians), then perhaps we can say a little more about the dimension of freedom which is genuinely open to humans. There is no question but that such does exist. In an important sense there is nothing illusory about the personal awareness of freedom that we all have. Freedom lies in the fact that there is nothing in our external circumstances directly dictating between a number of routes from which we must each choose and take, and that there is nothing internal within us which rigidly predetermines that we must take one (or a limited option) of the routes, come what may.

A human's choice and action is a function of that person, as he/she interacts with the environment. This is not non-caused freedom. Given all of the information from outside and given the way that we work, then our thoughts and actions will follow necessarily. But it is a freedom denied the (obviously unfree) bound prisoner, and it is a freedom denied the (equally obviously unfree) rigidly programmed ant. Morality gives us standards which we feel the demand to follow; but there is nothing within or without us that alone determines that we must or must not follow these moral demands. We can respond to morality, and depending on circumstances we may or may not follow it. This is our freedom.[9]

The analogy I like is that of missiles zeroing in on a target. Ants are like those missiles which have their expected target position built in. Their social behaviour is firmly genetically controlled. There are benefits in doing things this way. It is simple and cheap (in whatever costs you have). Usually, such missiles/ants work just fine. But, of course, things do break down, particularly as conditions tend to complexity. Humans are like those missiles which have internal homing devices. They can respond to changes in target positions, because they can pick up information and modify their courses. Their social behaviour is not firmly genetically controlled. However, the genes through morality influence behaviour, as do programmes put into the missile's homing device. Neither humans nor missiles have to figure out everything, right from scratch. Neither is programmed to work blindly, but each is programmed to respond to certain guides. Again, there are benefits in doing things this way. But it is more costly and more prone to internal problems.

One can push this analogy in ways that a biologist rather likes. Note, for instance, that any sensible defence minister will want missiles of both kinds. This corresponds to the Darwinian's conviction that there is no uniquely 'best' way of doing things. Ants and humans are both biological success stories. The point I make here, however, is that humans (unlike ants) have a dimension of freedom, just as do missiles with homing devices (unlike fixed-direction missiles).

With this discussion of freedom, the basic outlines of the Darwinian approach to meta-ethics loom into focus. We can start to draw our discussion towards its close. We have yet to turn briefly to history, and this we should do. As with epistemology, my interest is not so much in history for its own sake. Rather, the hope is to dig a little more deeply into the Darwinian's naturalistic approach to ethics.

[9] My aim at the moment is to find a sense of freedom which meshes smoothly with Darwinism, showing how the morality of the human differs from the blind rigidity of the ant. As will be acknowledged shortly, the position itself is hardly that new. It is known technically as 'soft determinism' or 'compatibilism'. The hard determinist denies that one can have determinism and any genuine sense of freedom, and hence of moral responsibility.

Possible precursor: Kant?

In seeking the precise nature of the epigenetic rules which guide our thinking about substantive ethics, we relied openly and heavily on claims and results of thinkers from the past 300 years. In fact, virtually all of the great moral philosophers have acknowledged the intrinsic worth of promoting happiness, and at the same time have stressed the need for justice and fairness. We have seen that this was true of Kant and Mill, and it was true also of others. With reason, David Hume (1978) is often taken as an important forerunner of utilitarianism, for he made the promotion of happiness a central part of his (substantival) ethical theory. But happiness alone was not enough for Hume. He too was sensitive to the demands of justice, and devoted a major section of his *Treatise* to this and related topics (Harrison, 1981).

What of meta-ethics? Is there an important philosopher (or tradition) of the past, who foreshadowed the Darwinian approach to morality? Drawing on the discussion of the last chapter, since our approach to morality is very much part of a general attitude towards the problems of philosophy, including those of epistemology, the familiar names of Kant and Hume spring at once to mind. Nevertheless, you might be inclined to dismiss the claims of Kant, without further argument. Darwinism yields the paradigm of meta-ethical subjectivism, and yet Kant is one that we have seen placed in the objectivist column.

However, such a dismissal would be a little hasty, for (as with epistemology) there is certainly that in Kant's philosophy which attracts the Darwinian. Kant did not locate the source of moral insight in some external phenomenon, like non-natural properties or the will of God. Rather, for Kant, morality lay in the conditions which obtain automatically when rational beings interact socially. Moreover, as we saw in passing, Kant's proof of his substantival position – the grounds be gave for the necessity of the Categorical Imperative – rested on showing that the Imperative's violation leads to 'contradictions'. These are hardly literal logical contradictions, but are instead the kinds of maladaptive interactions that the Darwinian would think eliminated by selection. Hence, in Kant's moral philosophy there is much in spirit which makes it a plausible pre-evolutionary precursor to the meta-ethics of Darwinism.

The same is true also of today's distinguished Kantian, John Rawls. Commending 'justice as fairness' he writes:

> What justifies a conception of justice is not its being true to an order antecedent to and given to us, but its congruence with our deeper understanding of ourselves and our aspirations, and our realization that, given our history and the traditions embedded in our public life, it is the most reasonable doctrine for us. (Rawls, 1980, p. 519)

And

> This [Kantian] rendering of objectivity implies that, rather than think of
> the principles of justice as true, it is better to say that they are the
> principles most reasonable for us, given our conception of persons as free
> and equal, and fully cooperating members of a democratic society. (Rawls,
> 1980, p. 554)

Nevertheless, as with epistemology, ultimately we must deny Kant
(and the Kantians) genuine precursor (or fellow-traveller) status – and
for much the same reasons as before. Kant aimed to resecure the
certainty that those like David Hume put in doubt. He desired a
foundation that is alien to Darwinism. In particular, he wanted a
necessity to knowledge that Darwin forbids, and likewise he wanted a
necessity to moral imperatives foreign to the modern evolutionist. Kant
thought the Categorical Imperative necessarily binding on all interacting
rational beings. Likewise, Rawls sees his position on justice operating in
all 'well-ordered' societies of free and equal 'moral persons' (1980,
p. 520). The Darwinian, however, ties morality tightly to contingent
human nature. Perhaps, as much as we will ever know rationality, the
Imperative (and like dictates) will in fact be binding on all such beings,
here on earth and elsewhere in the universe. But there is certainly no
necessity why this must be so.

Certainly, there is that in Darwinism which makes him/her very
uncomfortable with the strong stand of Kant and the Kantian. We are
what we are because we are recently evolved from savannah-dwelling
primates. Suppose that we had evolved from cave-dwellers, or some
such thing. We might have as our highest principle of moral obligation
the imperative to eat each others' faeces. Not simply the desire, but the
obligation. Before you dismiss this as a rather disgusting fancy,
remember that faeces eating is far from uncommon in the animal world.
Termites, for instance, must eat each others' body waste in order to pick
up certain parasites necessary for cellulose digestion. (The parasites are
lost at each moulting – Wilson, 1971.)

Perhaps, however, Kant and the Kantian would object at this point.
What has been overlooked is the distinction between our contingent
human nature and our essential being as free moral individuals (Rawls,
1980, p. 535). No one denies that, had human nature been otherwise,
we should be subject to different (lower-order) imperatives. But the
ultimate Categorical Imperative would remain the same. The need to eat
faeces is covered by the general prohibition against suicide, which Kant
sees as coming from the Imperative.

> One immediately sees a contradiction in a system of nature whose law
> would be to destroy life by the feeling whose special office is to impel the

improvement of life. In this case it would not exist as nature; hence that maxim cannot obtain as a law of nature, and thus it wholly contradicts the supreme principle of all duty. (Kant, 1959, p. 40)

But, even now, the Kantian falls before the Darwinian. Apart from anything else, Darwinism shows how incomplete is any position with contractarian leanings (as Kant's is at least implicitly, and Rawls's is explicitly). As asked before, why should we take seriously the belief that people are in society as if for their mutual benefit? Or, even if it be conceded that people are 'as if' for mutual benefit, then still pressing is the query about how everything started. I take it that no one today believes in the idea of an actual pact between early or proto-humans.

Darwinism explains why we are *moral*, which is always a problem for the theorist who sees morality arising out of the inter-personal relations within society. To take Rawls's case: why should we not be impersonal non-moral calculating machines, who simply behave as if life were a consequence of a rational deal? Darwinism explains that morality – a real sense of right and wrong – comes about because this was a cost-effective way of making humans co-operative. Biologically, it is certainly possible that we be non-moral beings with super-brains. (Remember: this point was made earlier in the chapter. No one is now saying that total rationality is a better biological strategy for us humans, than is the illusion of objective morality.)

Unfortunately, the position is even worse than thus stated for Kant and Kantians, since Darwinism surely opens the possibility of our being free moral persons, whose highest dictates flatly contradict the Categorical Imperative and like norms. It is biologically plausible to suggest that reciprocal altruism might have yielded a kind of reverse imperative, where our highest obligation is to hate our neighbours. We do not simply dislike them. We are aware of a prescription to hate them and to love ourselves. However, we recognize that they feel the same way, and so we enter into cautious balanced co-operative enterprises. But all of the time we are looking out for ourselves, because we feel we should – and we know they feel the same duties to themselves. If this all seems a little far-fetched, I would remind you of the way in which today's so-called 'Super-powers' conduct business.

Whatever else, in such a case as this we are certainly not treating others as ends. We are treating them as means to our own ends. Nor does it help Kant much if we switch to other formulations of the Imperative. At least, there is no help if you take the Imperative as affirming more than merely those formal conditions of reciprocation allowed by the Darwinian. Consider the appeal to universal law: 'Act only according to that maxim by which you can at the same time will that it should become a universal law' (Kant, 1959, p. 39). As Kant himself realized, at one level – the level the Darwinian seizes on – you can get a well-functioning society, without any morality as we would recognize it. You get the required reciprocation.

> [Consider a] man, for whom things are going well, sees that others (whom he could help) have to struggle with great hardships, and he asks, 'What concern of mine is it? Let each one be as happy as heaven wills, or as he can make himself; I will not take anything from him or even envy him; but to his welfare or to his assistance in time of need I have no desire to contribute.' If such a way of thinking were a universal law of nature, certainly the human race could exist, and without doubt even better than in a state where everyone talks of sympathy and good will, or even exerts himself occasionally to practice them while, on the other hand, he cheats when he can and betrays or otherwise violates the rights of man. (Kant, 1959, p. 41)

However, Kant then goes on to point out that, given the way that we are, we cannot *will* such a situation as this.

> Now although it is possible that a universal law of nature according to that maxim could exist, it is nevertheless impossible to will that such a principle should hold everywhere as a law of nature. For a will which resolved this would conflict with itself, since instances can often arise in which he would need the love and sympathy of others, and in which he would have robbed himself, by such a law of nature springing from his own will, of all hope of the aid he desires. (Kant, 1959, p. 41)

Kant is surely correct in this. However, had we evolved in such a way that we did not need love and sympathy, then there seems no reason at all why we should not will such a situation as this; which being so, we get an altogether different morality from anything Kant endorsed. (Kant might respond that at least we now have the Categorical Imperative applying, whatever the evolution. To which I counter that – as a purely formal condition – this may be so. But, as Kant himself shows, in order to get any moral content, you simply have to go on beyond and invoke our knowledge of human nature. In which case, the Darwinian can properly claim that the morality we have is certainly not binding on all rational beings.)

The spirit of Kantianism is antithetical to the spirit of Darwinism. The non-progressionism of Darwinism – pulling so much into the realm of the possible, including rational beings with altogether different senses of morality from us – destroys even that modified objectivity to morality demanded by the Kantian. We must therefore look elsewhere for our potential predecessors. (Deliberately, I have said nothing about the morality (or 'morality') of beings whose thinking is quite incommensurable with ours. It is enough here to show the difficulties of objective ethics, given our own understanding of the evolutionary process. But see Ruse, 1985.)

Possible precursor: Hume?

The choice is obvious. We turn again to David Hume. Darwinian epistemology is a modern-day extension of Hume's theory of knowledge. Can we say the same of Darwinian ethics and Humean ethics? We should indeed expect so, given that Darwinian epistemology and ethics are part and parcel of the same approach to philosophy, and that there is very good reason to think that Hume's epistemology was spurred by his excursions into ethics (Kemp Smith, 1941).

There is no need to be coy. The Darwinian meta-ethics presented in this chapter is almost exactly what one would expect from the pen of Hume, were he writing today. In fact, we can make yet stronger the historical continuity, for Hume himself writes in a tradition which goes back to Thomas Hobbes. More than two centuries before the *Origin*, Hobbes argued that morality must be explained in a materialistic way, starting with selfish individual motives, and making 'good' and 'bad' relative to human nature, and not to some distinct objective reality.

> Whatsoever is the object of any man's appetite or desire; that is it which he for his part calleth *good*: and the object of his hate, and aversion, *evil*; and of his contempt, *vile* and *inconsiderable*. For these words of good, evil, and contemptible, are ever used with relation to the person that useth them: there being nothing simply and absolutely so; nor any common rule of good and evil, to be taken from the nature of the objects themselves. (Raphael, 1969, p. 25, quoted by Mackie, 1980, p. 7)

Like Hobbes, Hume candidly took our own personal well-being as the ultimate motivation for action. In speaking of the laws of justice, he makes no bones about this: 'Tis self-love which is their real origin; and as the self-love of one person is naturally contrary to that of another, these several interested passions are oblig'd to adjust themselves after such a manner as to concur in some system of conduct and behaviour' (Hume, 1978, p. 529).

For this reason, Hume spoke of justice as an 'artificial' virtue, meaning that it was something which at some point people had actually to adopt. (In other words, he thought something akin to Rawls's original position was real, and not just hypothetical.) However, Hume embedded this in a view of human nature which showed that justice and like virtues would arise naturally from living together – because of what we are, we would devise principles of justice. (For this reason, Hume denied that justice is arbitrary.)

Most particularly, Hume linked our ability and wish to co-operate to a general feeling or sentiment. From our own nature and desires, we develop a kind of empathy or sympathy for the desires and well-being of others. This leads into morality, as we feel we ought to care about our fellow humans and, as these feelings dictate, that the best way to promote self-interest comes through justice. But what this all means is that there is not and cannot be any objective, extra-human morality. In a much-quoted aphorism, Hume stated : 'Reason is, and ought only to be the slave of the passions' (Hume, 1978, p. 415). What motivates us, and leads us to make moral judgements, necessarily has to start with emotions or sentiments.

Explaining his philosophy, Hume wrote:

> Vice and virtue . . . . may be compar'd to sounds, colours, heat and cold, which . . . . are not qualities in objects, but perceptions in the mind. (p. 469)

> Morality, therefore, is more properly felt than judg'd of. (p. 470)

> To have the sense of virtue, is nothing but to feel a satisfaction of a particular kind from the contemplation of a character. The very *feeling* constitutes our praise or admiration . . . . We do not infer a character to be virtuous, because it pleases. But in feeling that it pleases after such a particular manner, we in effect feel that it is virtuous. The case is the same as in our judgments concerning all kinds of beauty, and tastes, and sensations. (p. 471)

> . . . . virtue is distinguished by the pleasure, and vice by the pain, that any action, sentiment or character gives us by the mere view and contemplation. (p. 475. All of these passages are quoted in Mackie, 1980, p. 64)

Hume's 'sentimentalist' theory of morality is precisely that which one would expect as the precursor of Darwinism. The evolutionary approach carries us forward in crucial respects. Thanks to natural selection, we can sort out the true relationship between individual interests and virtues like justice. There is no need to think of us as all literally selfish. Nor (going beyond Hume) is there need to think of justice as artificial, implying that it required conscious decisions. Justice, like other aspects of morality, is linked to biological interests, and thus becomes as natural as any other part of us.

But, having said this, the connection between the Humean and Darwinian perspectives is incredibly strong. The Darwinian, like the Humean, makes morality entirely a function of human nature. Furthermore, the Darwinian follows Hume in recognizing moral sentiments as being of a type different from mere feelings. They carry a sense of obligation. This is what motivates us to action. Expectedly, we find Hume sensitive to the fact that, in some way, we think of morality as objective – laid upon us as it were. Note how Hume has said that vice and virtue are like colours. These (to Hume) are 'perceptions in the mind'. Yet this does not stop us from thinking of colours as objectively real. The same goes for morality. In the *Enquiry*, speaking of the difference between reason and taste, Hume wrote:

> The former conveys the knowledge of truth and falsehood: the latter gives the sentiment of beauty and deformity, vice and virtue. The one discovers objects as they really stand in nature, without addition or diminution: the other has a productive faculty, and gilding or staining all natural objects with the colours, borrowed from internal sentiment, raises in a manner a new creation. (Hume, 1975, p. 294, quoted by Mackie, 1980, p. 72)

Clearly, in morality Hume saw the manifestation of a process of objectification, akin to that which happens when we think about causality.

Relatedly, readers versed in the history of philosophy will have appreciated, already, that the solution to the free-will problem that I have recommended to Darwinians is Humean to the core. It was he who pointed out that an absence of causality does not spell freedom, but total chaos. Therefore, an adequate conception of freedom must centre on the absence of constraints, and not upon some imagined escape from causal necessity. (Which again takes us back to Hobbes (1839), for whom liberty is 'the absence of all impediments to action that are not contained in the nature and intrinsical quality of the agent.')

Finally, remember how the Darwinian worries about the range of any particular person's moral sentiments, concluding that for total strangers with whom there is no genuine interaction, (or possibility of such), there is probably less obligation than for those sharing one's own moral pool. Let me draw your attention to the fact that Hume likewise worried about the problem of moral sentiments weakening as we move away from any specified individual. He admitted candidly that:'In general, all sentiments of blame or praise are variable, according to our situation of nearness or remoteness, with regard to the person blam'd or prais'd, and according to the present disposition of our mind' (Hume, 1978, p. 582). Hume got around the problem by suggesting that where immediate sentiment fails, we keep up the sense of moral urgency by looking at matters from a 'steady and general point of view' – if we were close to strangers, how would we feel? Hence, moral norms can be applied 'disinterestedly'.

Whether, given his particular understanding of human psychology, Hume properly thus extricated himself is a question we need not address here. It is enough to note that, with respect to our own society, the Darwinian also argues that (particularly in this day and age) morality spreads beyond our closest circle of acquaintances. How evenly morality spreads is another matter. As also is the question of obligations to close kin. Without comment, I will quote an uncanny presentiment by Hume of the effect of kin selection on morality.

> A man naturally loves his children better than his nephews, his nephews

better than his cousins, his cousins better than strangers, where every thing else is equal. Hence arise our common measures of duty, in preferring one to the other. Our sense of duty always follows the common and natural course of our passions. (Hume, 1978, pp. 483-4)

Looking forward

The case for a Darwinian approach to morality is now concluded. Rather belatedly drawing attention to what I am sure many readers have spotted already, there is a close parallelism between the thesis of this chapter and that of the last – they are, in fact, different sides of the same coin. We are prepared for this, for we have seen the parallels between traditional (i.e. Spencerian) evolutionary epistemology and traditional (i.e. Spencerian) evolutionary ethics, and how they both came crashing down because of their illicit progressionism.

Now, what we have in the case of Darwinian epistemology is a denial of metaphysical reality – the world of the thing-in-itself, not to mention Platonic forms and eternal mathematical truths just waiting to be discovered – and an affirmation of common-sense reality, in which the enquiring subject plays an active, creative part. What we have in the case of Darwinian ethics is a denial of objectivity, which is surely a denial of metaphysical reality by another name, and an affirmation of subjectivity, which is no less a commitment to common sense, in which the moral subject plays an active creative part. If anything is common sense, it is that rape is simply, totally, wrong.

As Hume points out, analogously to epistemology, where things like atoms set up responses in us which lead us to read colours into the world, so things like human interactions set up responses in us which lead us to read values into the world. (Remember, incidentally, how intimately colours, like values, are linked to our distinctively primate nature.) I am not now, in one final fling, violating Hume's law, claiming that values are simply properties like colours, bearing the same relationship to elementary particles. But the parallels are there. A point, of course, that G. E. Moore noted, when, having firmly drawn the fact/value distinction, he spoke of goodness as a simple non-natural property, and used yellowness to show what he meant. (As you will have gathered from my discussion, I see the truths of ethics more closely paralleling truths like those of mathematics, rather than claims about colours. Mathematics and morality both come from the *secondary* epigenetic rules.)

And in both epistemology and ethics we seem (for biological reasons) to have a process of objectification – which leads to all kinds of difficulties if, in philosophical enquiry, its results are taken at face value. In epistemology, we normally think that the reality of common sense, the reality which we have truly had a role in creating (not choosing!), is the human-independent reality of the metaphysician. In ethics, we normally think the morality of common sense, the reality which we have truly had a role in creating (not choosing!), is the human-independent morality of the objectivist. But they are not.

This resonance between Darwinian epistemology and Darwinian ethics strikes echoes from the history of philosophy. Plato, for instance, located the ultimate form, the Good, in the super-sensible world, to which belong the objects of mathematics. That world is denied, in all its aspects, by the Darwinian, as is that domain perhaps somewhat closer to home, the home of the Kantian thing-in-itself, what Kant called the noumenal world (as opposed to the more familiar phenomenal world). Pertinently, we find Kant - whose ethical objectivism is denied by the Darwinian - arguing that the noumenal world plays a crucial role in morality, for it is only in that sphere that humans are truly free.

But enough of clarification and history. Deliberately, I have kept apart the arguments for epistemology and for ethics. If - mistakenly - you persist in being a metaphysical realist, you might still embrace the Darwinian position on morality. If you are persuaded by argument, that is. Given the ferocity that any such naturalistic attitude towards right and wrong almost always elicits, one suspects that many people find it deeply threatening. Somehow, it is felt that we are degraded to dirty brutes, with no more nobility than the pig. As Darwin's good friend, the geologist Charles Lyell, wrote worriedly in his common place book:

> It is small comfort or consolation to me, who feels that Lamarck or Darwin have lessened the dignity of their ancestry, making them out to be without souls, to be told, 'Never mind, you will be succeeded in unbroken lineal descent by angels who, like Superior Beings spoken of by Pope, "Will show a Newton as we show an ape".' (Wilson, 1970, p. 382)

I do not myself feel this way. To the contrary, I find it incredibly thrilling that we are now able to peer, albeit dimly and inadequately, at the true outlines of human nature. In such understanding, poor though it may be, we achieve a far greater status than would be conferred by a quasi-Spencerian insight into a pseudo-ultimate objective truth and reality, be this in epistemology or ethics. But emotion is no true substitute for argument - at least, not in philosophy. Therefore, I recommend the approach to you on its merits, and will say no more, as advocate or defender.

I will conclude this chapter by raising (but hardly answering) a question which all must have. If the major ethical claims of the Darwinian are correct, then what difference does this (could this) make to us humans, as intelligent moral beings? I can imagine at least two extreme conclusions. On the one hand, in a renewal of Nietzschian-like frenzy, you might argue that everything is now open to change, improvement, or even elimination. Through social and genetic manipulation, our whole moral sense could be altered. On the other hand, in a reversion to nineteenth-century Social Darwinism, you might argue that biology shows that you really need not bother about others, particularly the poor of the Third World. Our moral sentiments do not extend that far, so who cares?

I trust you will not be surprised to learn that I reject both options as mistaken. On the one hand, I would remind you that we all have moral sentiments, and simply breaking with them would cause great internal tensions. Moreover, I really cannot see any point to wholesale proposals for change. Are we to stop living socially? On the other hand, modern-day Darwinism is anything but a gospel for the extreme conservative. Apart from anything else, no one is saying that there are humans towards whom we have no sense of moral obligation whatsoever. Furthermore, the pretence that we need not bother about the Third World is self-refuting. If we ignore it, then through such effects as overpopulation, we shall soon find that it raises all sorts of difficult moral issues which do directly impinge on us.

Without giving the book-length treatment which this topic merits in its own right, my hunch is that Darwinism opens up the prospect for new thinking about morality, much in the way that we have the prospect for new thinking about science. Such biologically inspired thought would be based on an extension of already accepted substantive ethics – an extension in respects analogous to the way in which science has grown. For a moment, briefly reconsider quantum mechanics. As technology developed, we came up against entities like electrons, which called for a rethinking of such everyday notions as causality. Unreformed common sense failed us, and we had to fall back and rethink. Perhaps something similar occurs, or will occur, in ethics.

For instance, I suspect that most of us find highly repugnant the Chinese policy of insisting that married couples restrict their off-spring number to one, particularly when the policy is backed by forcible (or near-forcible) abortions. This is a gross violation of our sense of liberty. However, given present conditions, there are also good reasons – including good moral reasons – for such a policy. Are we all to die in a few years, from disease and starvation?

Darwinism helps us to understand what happened in physics, and why a break with everyday notions was needed, and was not necessarily a sign of intellectual hara-kiri. Perhaps analogously, Darwinism can help in ethics. We are not abandoning our moral sentiments, but we can see how the Chinese dilemma pushes us to limits for which our biology has not prepared us. This will, perhaps, not make us feel any better about forcing people to restrict family size, but we will recognize our feeling for the mammalian legacy that it is. We will, indeed, see the need for some sort of moral equivalent to Heisenberg's Uncertainty Principle, which will enable us most successfully to harmonize all of our sentiments, given the way in which technology and other aspects of human culture have taken us humans into realms undreamt of in our primate past.

If I were to say more, then I would have to say much more. My only hope is to have shown that a Darwinian approach to morality does not call for a repudiation of standards and values cherished by decent people of all nations. As with epistemology, Darwinism tells us much about ethics. It does not call upon us to repeat the fallacies of the past, or to provide new ones for the future.

Conclusion

Philosophy is the most important of enquiries. After all, what else is there? Despite cynics and the ignorant, it is possible to make progress in both epistemology and ethics. I would not for a moment suggest that we are wiser or cleverer men and women than Plato and Aristotle; but we do know much more about ourselves and about the world than they. I argue that Darwinism, brought literally and fully into philosophy, marks a significant step in the forward advance of understanding. Once we grasp the full import of the epigenetic rules – innate constraints rooted in the genes and put in place by natural selection – powerful light is thrown on human knowledge and morality.

I confess that even I feel somewhat uncomfortable about a declaration as immodest as this. In these concluding remarks, let me therefore make three brief points. They are not intended to weaken the main thesis. Indeed, I trust they will strengthen it and make it even more plausible. At the same time, I hope to soften any sense you might have that I am simply blowing my own trumpet, or fanatically preaching yet another, pathetically unreal, total world-system, like Christian Science or theosophy.

First, movement forward in philosophy is often, if not indeed usually, a function of movement forward in science. This should not surprise us. After all, philosophy is 'meta-physics' – talk about physics – and, conversely, science is 'natural philosophy'.[1] The exact way in which science affects philosophy varies. Sometimes, the science functions as a model or metaphor. Perhaps Kant's 'Copernican revolution' was such an instance. Kant wanted to turn around the relationship between

---

[1] Historically, Metaphysics was so-called because it was the book *after* Physics, in the Aristotelean *corpus*.

subject and object, in a way akin to Copernicus' turning around the relationship between sun and earth. Sometimes the science acts critically, showing that a particular philosophical thesis is untenable or redundant. It is hard to see vitalism, the belief in special life-forces, as a workable thesis against the background of modern biology (Hempel, 1966; Graham, 1981). Sometimes the science inspires and informs the philosophy. Descartes' *Discourse on Method* draws on Harvey's work on the heart. And sometimes the science simply moves in and takes over the philosophy. Plato's *Timaeus* deals with the origin and nature of the universe. Today, an astronomer would do this work. John Locke's *Essay Concerning Human Understanding* (1975) would now be written, in part, by a psychologist and, in part, perhaps, by an expert in linguistics.

I certainly do not mean to imply that philosophy is a mere epiphenomenal pimple on the backside of science, waiting to be scratched or lanced at its owner's whim. Indeed, just as science affects philosophy, an equally strong case can be made for the influence on, and importance of, philosophy for science. Newtonian mechanics, for instance, was made possible only by some drastic metaphysical rethinking about the very possibility and meaning of the notion of action at a distance (Hesse, 1961). However, my concern here is not with the full science/philosophy relationship for its own sake, but with emphasizing the extent to which progress in philosophy is linked to progress in empirical science.

Now, if you look at the history of science, two revolutions stand out above all others. First, there is the so-called 'Scientific Revolution', with the great names of Copernicus at the fore and of Newton at the rear. Second, there is the Darwinian Revolution. Some might add Freud's name to this list; but whatever the intrinsic merits of Freud's work, I am inclined to agree with recent historical assessment that really Freud's contributions should be considered part of the biology of man, rather than something quite independent (Sulloway, 1979a).

The importance of the Scientific Revolution for philosophy is beyond question. Modern philosophy – the work of both rationalists and empiricists – would have been impossible without the great advances in physics. Analogously, therefore, we should anticipate that the Darwinian Revolution will have important implications for philosophy. Indeed, I would go further and say that we might expect Darwin's work to have even greater implications for philosophy than those of physics. The theory of evolution through natural selection impinges so directly on our own species. It is not just that we are on a speck of dust whirling around in the void, but that we ourselves are no more than transformed apes. If such a realization is not to affect our views of epistemology and ethics, I do not know what is. As I said in the Preface, I find it inconceivable that it is irrelevant to the foundations of philosophy whether we are the end result of a slow natural evolutionary process, or made miraculously in God's own image on a Friday, some 6,000 years ago.

My second point is that the naturalistic philosophy which I advocate is not that original anyway! It is, I am afraid, all too true that Anglo-Saxon philosophy in this century has paid scant attention to Darwinism, and the same goes even more for Continental philosophy. However, we have seen that the Darwinian approach to epistemology and to ethics finds a deep response in the history of philosophy. Furthermore, this response is at its deepest precisely where we might expect to find it, namely in the finest flowering of British empiricism, the work of David Hume. His philosophy, which in its own right has attracted many people, is given a whole new validity when set against the background of evolution through natural selection. Conversely, Darwinian-infused philosophy is made that much more plausible when its pretensions to being some wholly new approach to understanding are thus dropped. Darwinism is vitally important, but it represents an advance on the past, not a sharp break.

We know that, after the publication of Darwin's *Origin*, people tried to extract a philosophy from claims about the process and product of evolution (Russett, 1976; Oldroyd, 1980). But, as we also know, such efforts were generally predicated either on a false understanding of the evolutionary process, or an inadequate grasp of the proper relationship between the world of facts and the world of philosophy. There were, however, some thinkers who explored ideas somewhat along the lines endorsed in this book, arguing that our thought and action are direct functions of adaptations brought by evolution. Most notably, one thinks of the American pragmatists, who argued that truth must be related to its worth to human beings, and how best we can fit everything together. 'Ideas (which themselves are but parts of our experience) become true just insofar as they help us to get into satisfactory relation with other parts of our experience' (James, 1907, p. 58, in italics in original).

Yet in certain crucial respects I would deny that the pragmatists generally stand in a direct ancestral relationship to the philosophy defended in this book. Apart from anything else, even though they became enthusiastic evolutionists, the leading pragmatists often felt somewhat uncomfortable with the Darwinian mechanism of natural selection. Charles Sanders Peirce, arguably the greatest of all American philosophers, always distrusted what he saw as the purposelessness of Darwinism, himself inclining rather to a quasi-Lamarckian directed evolutionary process (Weiner, 1949; Russett, 1976; Bowler, 1984). Even more strongly, Peirce loathed what he took to be the only possible applications of Darwinism to the moral sphere, speaking of selection as encouraging the 'greed-philosophy'. Darwin, remarked Peirce, should have taken as his slogan: 'Every individual for himself, and the Devil take the hindmost!' (Hartshorne and Weiss, 1931-5, 6, p. 293, quoted by Russett, 1976, p. 64).

William James responded more favourably to Darwin's ideas, although sometimes the direct use he made of them was hardly either that intended by Darwin or that pursued in this book. He seized upon the randomness of new variation and – ignoring natural selection – proclaimed that it demonstrates the possibility of freewill in a supposedly deterministic universe. Admittedly, in his analysis of the way in which we think, James was closer to the theses expounded in the last two chapters, for he did argue that there are certain controlling ideas in the mind that direct and inform human thought and action.

But, even here, at least when he was developing his pragmatic philosophy, James was no true Darwinian, for instead of relating these directing ideas to the effects of natural selection, he argued rather that their origin is purely cultural. Certain great men in the past have thought up these ideas, and they are now passed on down to us as part of our human heritage, which we unconsciously take up and use (James, 1907). From our perspective, this constitutes something of a regression, for (as noted in the fifth chapter) when James had earlier been expounding his psychology, explicitly he linked the mental dispositions standing behind the thought processes of logic, mathematics, and science, with a biological origin rooted in natural selection. (See James, 1890.)

Jumping from the nineteenth century down through the twentieth century, we do in recent years start to see encouraging signs that perhaps, at long last, Darwinism will come into its own philosophical right. For instance, the doyen of American philosophers, W.V.O. Quine, has long spoken of the need for a naturalistic approach to philosophy, and has even shown that he thinks such an approach must be Darwinian in major part (especially Quine, 1969a,b, and page 162 above).[2]

Quine has said little about the nature of morality, but his few comments suggest that here also he would favour a Darwinian approach (Quine, 1978). As also should a good many other philosophers, for although traditional evolutionary ethics has been anathema for a long time, many moral philosophers in this century have adopted a neo-Humean approach. Most notably, one thinks of the so-called 'emotivists', who (as we saw) argued that ethics is all a matter of feelings – that when you say something is right or wrong, you are not expressing

---

[2] Campbell (1974) contains a full bibliography of philosophical writings in this century which take seriously evolutionary ideas. In fairness, I must note that Popper (1962) toys with some of the epistemological ideas which I explore in chapter 5, although the main thrust of his Darwinism is the thesis criticized earlier. Indeed, eclectic as always, Herbert Spencer (1855) suggests that great men thought up good ideas, which get embedded in our consciousness through a form of Lamarckism.

a matter of objective fact, but are rather emoting (Ayer, 1946; Stevenson, 1944).

Although I have had critical things to say about emotivism, I suspect nevertheless that its spirit is close to the meta-ethics developed in the last chapter. The emotivist is on the right track in thinking that it is feelings which are at the heart of morality. The problem with emotivism lies in being incomplete to the point of immoral implausibility. Darwinism advances beyond emotivism by showing why we have our special kinds of moral feelings. Also, Darwinism makes absolutely crucial what is often not fully stressed by emotivists, and what – by its ommission – thus makes emotivism so wrong in the eyes of so many. Darwinism shows that, although morality may be all a question of feelings or sentiments, we humans project it into a prescriptively binding, supposedly objective status. We 'objectify' morality. And because – and only because – we do this, morality functions as an efficient social facilitating mechanism.

One who saw all of this, and who was (at the time of his death) relating it to evolutionary biology, was the late John Mackie (1977; 1978; 1980). He endorsed a neo-Humean type of moral philosophy and connected it to underlying genetic mechanisms, albeit without having available the full power of Wilsonian epigenetic rules. Another contemporary moral philosopher who has seen that the case for evolution needs reopening is Jeffrie Murphy (1982). I have already acknowledged my own debt to his work. But it is not my intention here simply to give a list of those people whose thoughts run parallel to mine. My aim is to show that the Darwinian approach to philosophy has its roots deep in the history of my subject, and that today it is starting to attract attention, even from those who (unlike myself) are not constantly immersed in the logic of biological science. The brief discussion of the past few paragraphs has surely shown this.

I will make a third and final point about the significance of Darwinism for philosophy, tempering (but not denying) my earlier grandiose claims. Although the main lines of the Darwinian approach have now been sketched, there remains far more work to be done than has yet been attempted. Given the nature of the main thesis, one which straddles biology and philosophy, such work clearly must come in both of the two pertinent fields. In the realm of science, I hope I have left you with the impression that evolutionary biology is moving ahead today as never before. Yet, even now, we can only dimly grasp some of the main issues. The application of Darwinism to human beings, as it tackles some of the questions to do with the relations between genes and culture, has far to go.

Several different models of 'gene/culture coevolution' have been proposed, but none yet has significantly established itself above all others (Durham, 1976; Richerson and Boyd, 1978; Cavalli-Sforza and

Feldman, 1981; Plotkin and Odling-Smee, 1981). For this reason, I have been careful not to endorse any one specific approach, nor do my philosophical claims depend on the success of one model over another. This is true especially of E.O. Wilson's own theorizing, even though I have made much of the epigenetic rules on which his own work rests (Lumsden and Wilson, 1981). Truly, the rules in some form are presupposed by all types of gene/culture investigation and, therefore, were Wilson's own work to collapse, my philosophizing would emerge unscathed.

Nevertheless, although I have thus been able to sketch the outlines of a full Darwinian philosophy, without committing myself to any specific way in which biology affects, controls, and in turn is modified by culture, my claims are necessarily thereby impoverished. As we explore the full extent of human evolutionary biology, and learn how it can reach right up to our epistemology and our ethics, our philosophical understanding will be accordingly enriched and extended. For instance, in the theory of knowledge we might hope to learn more about the exact nature of the pertinent epigenetic rules, and about which rules take precedence over others. Do some rules necessarily stand behind any scientific claims whatsoever, and why must it be these rules and not others? Relatedly, in scientific revolutions do we find that the epigentic rules generally provide a stable background for such changes, or are the rules themselves actively involved in the revolutions, with their very own status at stake? A well-confirmed model of coevolution would throw valuable light on this question.

Our understanding of morality likewise depends on advance in empirical science. I have been treating the human species (*qua* morality) as if it were composed of absolutely identical members. But, as has been conceded, perhaps this is an oversimplification. Perhaps different people have different genes affecting moral sensibility, or perhaps the genes of the same people affect them differently in different circumstances or at different stages of their lives. I do not say that this possibility of genetically controlled moral variation is necessarily true. Indeed, as you will have gathered from my discussion of the last chapter, I am rather inclined to dismiss its great importance. My point here is that the existence of genetically based moral conflict is not something which can be decided a priori. Its proof or disproof demands further empirical enquiry. Furthermore, if it were found to hold and to be widespread, then it is something of an understatement to say that its existence would disrupt traditional philosophical thinking about morality.

I have written thus far of the need for further empirical enquiry. There is a parallel need for further philosophical enquiry. Much work is needed on epistemology and ethics, exploring and exploiting the

---

[3] The reader might be interested also in some of the work relating co-operation to game theory. (See especially Axelrod and Hamilton, 1981.)

Darwinian perspective. I look upon the philosopher as being, in a sense, an applied scientist. This may or may not be elevating. It certainly carries responsibilities. The task of identifying the epigenetic rules falls as much to the philosopher as to the scientist. Effort is required from the theoretical end of knowledge and morality, no less than from the more applied quarters.

For instance, one question which I, as a philosopher, find particularly absorbing is whether different areas of science demand different epigenetic rules. Like many others, I have long suspected that biology demands a teleological or functional organizing element, absent from the physical sciences (Wright, 1976; Ruse, 1977). We see organic phenomena as organized towards ends, and thus understand them in these goal-oriented terms. We ask about the purpose served by the dimetrodon's back fin, and how the trilobite eye functions. We speak of the perfect 'design' of the camel's adaptations for desert life (whether or not we be Believers). And we do not use such modes of thought when dealing with the inorganic world. Mount Everest has no function, and Mars serves no purpose.

Could the end-directed understanding of the biologist be a consequence of our basic thought patterns? Did natural selection find it advantageous to have us regard organisms as if they were designed or planned? Is the analogy between organisms and artefacts rooted in an epigenetic rule, which simply does not apply when we look at rocks or mountains or planets? Only enquiry will tell, and this enquiry must be, at least in part, philosophical. The philosopher can identify and highlight the way we do think, as the empirical scientist gropes for underlying empirical understanding of this thought. The philosopher can pick out our way of thinking functionally, as the Darwinian scientist speculates on the reasons why it would be selectively advantageous to think of organisms as if consciously planned.

Apart from extending discussions already started in this book, attention must be paid to related philosophical problems that I have barely touched on. I have in mind here such problems as those raised by the body–mind relationship and the nature of free will. Necessarily, I have made some comments on these matters; but the comments are hardly adequate and certainly not very original. I have said nothing at all about other vital questions, like the nature and reasons for our feelings of beauty. My sense is that, thanks to Darwinism, we are feeling our way towards an overall coherent picture of human nature. But, at the moment, this is no more than a sense spiced with optimism. The Darwinian Revolution has only barely started to work its charm on philosophy.

The case is made. Further elaboration and qualification would seem like retreat. Therefore, I leave you with the main theme. The point is clear. A century and a quarter after the first appearance of *On the Origin of Species*, the time has surely come to take Darwin seriously.

References

Alexander, R. D. 1975. The search for a general theory of behavior. *Behavioral Science*, 20, 77–100.
—. 1977. Evolution, human behavior, and determinism. *PSA 1976*, ed. F. Suppe and P. Asquith (East Lansing: Philosophy of Science Association), 3–21.
—. 1979. *Darwinism and Human Affairs* (Seattle: University of Washington Press).
Allen, E. *et al.* 1977. Sociobiology: a new biological determinism. In Sociobiology Study Group of Boston (eds). *Biology as a Social Weapon* (Minneapolis: Burgess).
Allison, A. C. 1964. Polymorphism and natural selection in human populations. *C S H Symposium in Quantitative Biology* 29.
Alvarez, L. W. *et al.* 1980. Extraterrestrial cause for the Cretaceous-Tertiary extinction. *Science*, 208, 1095–1108.
Aquinas, St T. 1968. *Summa Theologica, 43, Temperance* (2a, 2ae, 141-54). Trans. T. Gilby (London: Blackfriars).
Axelrod, R. and W.D. Hamilton. 1981. The evolution of cooperation. *Science*, 211, 1390–6.
Ayala, F. J. and J. Kiger. 1984. *Modern Genetics*. 2nd edn (Reading, Mass.: Addison-Wesley).
Ayala, F. and J. Valentine. 1979. *Evolving* (Menlo Park: Benjamin Cummings).
Ayer, A. J. 1946. *Language, Truth and Logic*. 2nd edn (London: Gollancz)
Baker, R. and F. Elliston, eds. 1984. *Philosophy and Sex*. 2nd edn (Buffalo: Prometheus).
Bannister, R. 1973. William Graham Sumner's 'Social Darwinism'. *History of Political Economy*, 5, 89–109.
Barash, D. P. 1977. *Sociobiology and Behavior*. (New York: Elsevier).
—. 1982. *Sociobiology and Behavior*. 2nd edn (New York: Elsevier).
Barnes, J. 1984. *The Complete Works of Aristotle* (Princeton: Princeton University Press).
Barry, B. 1973. *The Liberal Theory of Justice: A Critical Examination of the Principal Doctrines in A Theory of Justice by John Rawls* (Oxford: Oxford University Press).
Beatty, J. 1981. Hopes, fears, and sociobiology. *Queen's Quarterly*, 88, 607–19.
Bechtel, W. 1984. The evolution of our understanding of the cell: a study in the dynamics of scientific progress. *Studies in History and Philosophy of Science*, 15, 309–56.

Beck, L. W. 1960. *A Commentary on Kant's Critique of Practical Reason* (Chicago: University of Chicago Press).

Benn, A. W. 1906. *The History of British Rationalism in the Nineteenth Century* (New York: Russell and Russell, 1969 reprint).

Berlin, B. and P. Kay. 1969. *Basic Color Terms: Their Universality and Evolution* (Berkeley: University of California Press).

Black, M. 1968. *The Labyrinth of Language.* (New York: Praeger).

Bochenski, I. 1961. *History of Formal Logic.* Trans. I. Thomas (Notre Dame, Ind.: Notre Dame University Press).

Bornstein, M. H. 1979. Perceptual development: stability and change in feature perception. In M. H. Bornstein and W. Kessen eds. *Psychological development from Infancy: Image to Intention* (Hillsdale: Lawrence Erlbaum), 37-81.

Bornstein, M. H., W. Kessen and S. Weiskopf. 1976. The categories of hue in infancy. *Science*, 191, 201-2.

Bowler, P. J. 1976. *Fossils and Progress* (New York: Science History Publications).

—. 1984. *Evolution: The History of an Idea.* (Berkeley: University of California Press).

Boyd, R. 1981. Scientific realism and naturalistic epistemology. In P. Asquith and R. Giere eds. *PSA 1980* (East Lansing: Philosophy of Science Association), 2, 613-62.

Bradie, M. 1986. Assessing evolutionary epistemology. *Biology and Philosophy*, forthcoming.

Braithwaite, R. B. 1953. *Scientific Explanation* (Cambridge: Cambridge University Press).

Brandon, R. N. and R. M. Burian, eds. 1984. *Genes, Organisms, Populations: Controversies Over the Units of Selection* (Cambridge, Mass.: MIT Press).

Brown, R. 1973. *A First Language: The Early Stages* (Cambridge, Mass.: Harvard University Press).

Bunn, H. 1981. Archaeological evidence for meat-eating by Plio-Pleistocene hominids from Koobi Fora and Olduvai Gorge. *Nature*, 291, 574-7.

Bunn, H., J. W. K. Harris, G. L. Isaac, Z. Kaufulu, E. Kroll, K. Schick, N. Toth, and A. K. Behrensmeyer. 1980. Fx Jj 50: an early Pleistocene site in northern Kenya. *World Archaeology*, 12, 109-36.

Burchfield, J. D. 1975. *Lord Kelvin and the Age of the Earth* (New York: Science History Publications).

Burkhardt, R. W. 1977. *The Spirit of System: Lamarck and Evolutionary Biology* (Cambridge: Harvard University Press).

Burret, C., ed. 1967. *L. W. Wittgenstein: Lectures and Conversations* (Berkeley: University of California Press).

Cain, A. J. 1979. Reply to Gould and Lewontin. *Proceedings of the Royal Society, Series B*, 205, 599-604.

Campbell, D. T. 1974a. Evolutionary epistemology. In P. A. Schilpp ed., *The Philosophy of Karl Popper* (LaSalle, Ill. Open Court Publishing), 1, 413-463.

—. 1974b. Unjustified variation and selective rentention in scientific discovery. In F. J. Ayala and Th. Dobzhansky eds., *Studies in the Philosophy of Biology* (London, Macmillan), 179-86.

—. 1977. *Descriptive Epistemology: Psychological, Sociological, and Evolutionary* (unpublished William James lectures, given at Harvard University).

Caplan, A. 1977. Tautology, circularity, and biological theory. *American Naturalist*, 111, 390-3.

Carnap, R. 1950. *Logical Foundations of Probability* (Chicago: University of Chicago Press).

282 *References*

—. 1967. Pseudoproblems in philosophy. In *The Logical Structure of the World and Pseudoproblems in Philosophy*. (Berkeley: University of California Press), 301–43.

Cavalli-Sforza, L. and M. Feldman. 1981. *Cultural Transmission: A Quantitative Approach* (Princeton: Princeton University Press).

Chagnon, N. A. 1980. Kin-selection theory, kinship, marriage and fitness among the Yanomamo Indians. In G. W. Barlow and J. Silverberg eds. *Sociobiology: Beyond Nature/Nurture?* (Boulder, Col.: Westview), 545–72.

Chomsky, N. 1957. *Syntactic Structures* (The Hague: Mouton).

—. 1965. *Aspects of the Theory of Syntax* (Cambridge, Mass.: MIT Press).

—. 1966. *Cartesian Linguistics* (New York: Harper and Row).

—. 1980a. Initial states and steady states. In M. Piattelli-Palmarini ed. *Language and Learning: The Debate between Jean Piaget and Noam Chomsky* (Cambridge, Mass.: Harvard University Press), 107–30.

—. 1980b. Rules and representations. *Behavioral and Brain Sciences*, 3, 1–61.

Churchland, P. 1984. *Matter and Consciousness* (Cambridge, Mass.: MIT Press).

Ciochon, R. L. and R. S. Corruccini, eds. 1983. *New Interpretations of Ape and Human Ancestry* (New York: Plenum).

Clark, G. 1977. *World Prehistory*, 3rd edn (Cambridge: Cambridge University Press).

Clarkson, E. N. K. and R. Levi-Setti. 1975. Trilobite eyes and the optics of Descartes and Huygens. *Nature*, 254, 663–7.

Cloud, P. 1974. Evolution of ecosystems. *American Scientist*, 62, 54–66.

Clutton-Brock, T. H. 1983. Selection in relation to sex. In D. S. Bendall ed. *Evolution from Molecules to Men* (Cambridge: Cambridge University Press), 457–810.

Clutton-Brock, T. H., F. E. Guinness and S. D. Abon, 1982. *Red Deer: Behavior and Ecology of Two Sexes.* (Chicago: University of Chicago Press).

Cohen, L. J. 1973. Is the progress of science evolutionary? *British Journal for the Philosophy of Science*, 24, 41–61.

Cohen, M. R. and E. Nagel. 1934. *An Introduction to Logic and Scientific Method* (New York: Harcourt Brace).

Colbert, E. H. 1969. *Evolution of Vertebrates* (New York: John Wiley).

Copi, I. 1973. *Symbolic Logic*, 4th edn (New York: Macmillan).

Cox A. ed. 1973. *Plate Tectonics and Geomagnetic Reversals* (San Francisco: Freeman).

Darwin, C. 1859. *On the Origin of Species* (London: John Murray).

—. 1871. *The Descent of Man* (London: John Murray).

Darwin, F. ed. 1887. *The Life and Letters of Charles Darwin, Including an Autobiographical Chapter* (London: Murray).

Darwin, F. and A. C. Seward, eds. 1903. *More Letters of Charles Darwin* (London: Murray).

Dawkins, R. 1976. *The Selfish Gene* (Oxford: Oxford University Press).

de Beer, G. *et al.*, eds. 1960–7. Darwin's notebooks on transmutation of species. *Bulletin of the British Museum (Natural History)*, Historical Series, 2, 27-200; 3, 129–76.

de Luce, J. and H. T. Wilder, eds. 1983. *Language in Primates: Perspectives and Implications* (New York: Springer-Verlag).

Descartes, R. 1912. *A Discourse on Method.* Trans. J. Veitch (London: Dent).

—. 1951. *Meditations on First Philosophy.* Trans L. J. Lafleur (Indianapolis: Bobbs-Merrill).

de Waal, F. 1982. *Chimpanzee Politics: Power and Sex Among Apes* (London: Collins).

Dobzhansky, T. 1937. *Genetics and the Origin of Species* (New York: Columbia University Press).

—. 1951. *Genetics and the Origin of Species*, 3rd edn (New York: Columbia University Press).

—. 1962. *Mankind Evolving* (New Haven: Yale University Press).

—. 1970. *Genetics of the Evolutionary Process* (New York : Columbia University Press).

Dobzhansky, T., F. Ayala, G. Stebbins, and J. Valentine. 1977. *Evolution* (San Francisco: Freeman).

Durham, W. H. 1976. The adaptive significance of cultural behavior. *Human Ecology*, 4, 89–121.

Eddington, A. 1929. *The Nature of the Physical World* (Cambridge: Cambridge University Press).

Eldredge, N. and S. J. Gould. 1972. Punctuated equilibria: an alternative to phyletic gradualism. In T. J. M. Schopf ed. *Models in Paleobiology* (San Francisco: Freeman Cooper).

Feduccia, A. 1980. *The Age of Birds* (Cambridge, Mass.: Harvard University Press).

Findlay, A. 1948. *A Hundred Years of Chemistry*, 2nd edn (London: Duckworth).

Flanagan, O. J. 1981. Is morality epiphenomenal? *Philosophical Forum*, 2/3, 207–225.

Flew, A. G. N. 1967. *Evolutionary Ethics* (London: Macmillan).

Fobes, J. L. and J. E. King. 1982. Vision: the dominant primate modality. In J. L. Fobes and J. E. King eds. *Primate Behavior* (New York: Academic Press), 219–43.

Foster, M. H. and M. Martin. 1966. *Probability, Confirmation, and Simplicity* (New York: Odyssey).

Fox, R. 1980. *The Red Lamp of Incest* (New York: Dutton).

Fox, S. W. and K. Dose. 1977. *Molecular Evolution and the Origin of Life*, rev. edn (New York: Marcel Dekker).

Frankel, H. 1981. The non-Kuhnian nature of the recent revolution in the earth sciences. In P. Asquith and I. Hacking eds. *P.S.A., 1978* (East Lansing, Mich.: Philosophy of Science Association), 2, 197–214.

Freeman, D. 1974. The evolutionary theories of Charles Darwin and Herbert Spencer. *Current Anthropology*, 15, 221.

Freud, S. 1905. *Three Essays on the Theory of Sexuality.* In J. Strachey ed. *Collected Works of Freud*, 7 (London: Hogarth, 1953), 125–243.

Friedman, M. 1975. *There's No Such Thing as a Free Lunch* (LaSalle, Ill.: Open Court).

Furnish, V. P. 1982. Love of neighbor in the New Testament. *The Journal of Religious Ethics*, 10(2), 327–34.

Futuyma, D. 1979. *Evolutionary Biology* (Sunderland, Mass.: Sinauer).

—. 1983. *Science on Trial* (New York: Pantheon).

Gardner, M. 1980. Monkey business. *The New York Review of Books*, 20 March, 3–6.

Gardner, R. A. and B. T. Gardner. 1969. Teaching sign language to a chimpanzee. *Science*, 165, 664–72.

Gelman, R. 1980. What young children know about numbers. *Educational Psychologist*, 15, 54–68.

Gelman, R. and C. R. Gallistel. 1978. *The Child's Understanding of Number* (Cambridge, Mass.: Harvard University Press).

Geschwind, N. 1974. *Language and the Brain* (Dordrecht: Reidel).

—. 1979. Specializations of the human brain. *Scientific American*, 241(3), 180–99.

Ghiselin, M. T. 1966. On psychologism in the logic of taxonomic controversies. *Systematic Zoology*, 15, 207–15.

—. 1973. Darwin and evolutionary psychology. *Science*, 179, 964–8.

Giere, R. 1979. *Understanding Scientific Reasoning* (New York: Holt, Rinehart and Winston).

Gillan, D. J. 1981. Reasoning in the chimpanzee: 2 Transitive inference. *Journal of Experimental Psychology: Animal Behavior Processes*, 7, 150–64.

Gillan, D. J., D. Premack, and C. Woodruff. 1981. Reasoning in the chimpanzee: 1 Analogical reasoning. *Journal of Experimental Psychology: Animal Behavior Processes*, 7, 1–17.

Gingerich, P. D. 1976. Paleontology and phylogeny: patterns of evolution at the species level in early Tertiary mammals. *American Journal of Science*, 276, 1–28.

—. 1977. Patterns of evolution in the mammalian fossil record. In A. Hallam, ed. *Patterns of Evolution As Illustrated by the Fossil Record* (Amsterdam: Elsevier), 469–500.

Gish, D. T. 1972. *Evolution: The Fossils Say No!* (San Diego: Creation-Life).

—. 1973. Creation, evolution, and the historical evidence. *American Biology Teacher*, 35, 132–40.

Glymour, C. 1980. *Theory and Evidence* (Princeton: Princeton University Press).

Goldman, A. I. 1967. A causal theory of knowing. *Journal of Philosophy*, 64, 357–72.

Goodall, J. V. L. 1971. *In The Shadow of Man* (London: Collins).

Goodman, N. 1955. *Fact, Fiction, and Forecast* (Cambridge, Mass.: Harvard University Press).

Goudge, T. 1973. Evolutionism. In *Dictionary of the History of Ideas* (New York: Scribners).

Gould, S. J. 1977. *Ontogeny and Phylogeny* (Cambridge, Mass.: Harvard University Press).

—. 1979. Episodic change versus gradualist dogma. *Science and Nature*, 2, 5–12.

—. 1980a. Is a new and general theory of evolution emerging? *Paleobiology*, 6, 119–30.

—.1980b. *The Panda's Thumb* (New York: Norton).

—. 1982a. Darwinism and the expansion of evolutionary theory. *Science*, 216, 380–7.

—. 1982b. Punctuated equilibrium – a different way of seeing. In J. Cherfas ed. *Darwin Up to Date* (London: IPC Magazines), 26–30.

Gould, S. J. and N. Eldredge. 1977. Punctuated equilibria: the tempo and mode of evolution reconsidered. *Paleobiology*, 3, 115–51.

Gould, S. J. and R. C. Lewontin. 1979. The spandrels of San Marco and the panglossian paradigm: a critique of the adaptationist programme. *Proceedings of the Royal Society, Series B*, 205, 581–98.

Graham, L. R. 1981. *Between Science and Values* (New York: Columbia University Press).

Grant, V. 1981. *Plant Speciation*. 2nd edn (New York: Columbia University Press).

Green, J. C. 1959. *The Death of Adam* (Ames: Iowa State University Press).

Griffin, D. R. 1981. *The Question of Animal Awareness: Evolutionary Continuity of Mental Experience*. 2nd edn (New York: Rockerfeller University Press).

—. 1984. *Animal Thinking* (Cambridge, Mass.: Harvard University Press).

Gruber, H. E. and P. H. Barrett. 1974. *Darwin on Man* (New York: Dutton).

Grünbaum, A. 1973. *Philosophical Problems of Space and Time*. 2nd edn (Dordrecht: Reidel).

Hacking, I. 1983. *Representing and Intervening: Introductory Topics in the Philosophy of Natural Science* (Cambridge: Cambridge University Press).

Hallam, A. 1973. *A Revolution in the Earth Sciences: From Continental Drift to Plate Tectonics* (Oxford: Clarendon Press).

Halstead, L. B. 1984. Evolution – the fossils say yes! In A. Montagu ed. *Science and Creationism* (New York: Oxford University Press), 240–54.

Hamilton, W. D. 1964a. The genetical evolution of social behaviour: I. *Journal of Theoretical Biology*, 7, 1–16.

—. 1964b. The genetical evolution of social behaviour. II. *Journal of Theoretical Biology*, 7, 17–32.

Hampshire, S. 1978. The illusion of sociobiology. *New York Review of Books*, 25, 15 (12 October), 64–9.

Hanson, N. R. 1958. *Patterns of Discovery* (Cambridge: Cambridge University Press).

Hardin, C. L. and A. Rosenberg. 1982. In defense of convergent realism. *Philosophy of Science*, 49, 604–15.

Harding, S. and M. B. Hintikka. 1983. *Discovering Reality: Feminist Perspectives on Epistemology, Metaphysics, Methodology, and Philosophy of Science* (Dordrecht: Reidel).

Hare, R. M. 1952. *The Language of Morals* (Oxford: Oxford University Press).

—. 1963. *Freedom and Reason* (Oxford: Oxford University Press).

Harris, M. 1971. *Culture, Man, and Nature: An Introduction to General Anthropology* (New York: Crowell).

Harrison, J. 1981. *Hume's Theory of Justice* (Oxford: Oxford University Press).

Hartshorne, C. and P. Weiss, eds. 1931–5. *Collected Papers of Charles Sanders Peirce* (Cambridge, Mass.: Harvard University Press).

Hempel, C. G. 1966. *Philosophy of Natural Science* (Englewood Cliffs: Prentice-Hall).

Herbert, S. 1974. The place of man in the development of Darwin's theory of transmutation. Part 1. To July 1837. *Journal of the History of Biology*, 7, 217–58.

—. 1977. The place of man in the development of Darwin's theory of transmutation. Part 2. *Journal of the History of Biology*, 10, 155–227.

Hesse, M. 1961. *Forces and Fields* (London: Nelson).

—. 1966. *Models and Analogies in Science* (Notre Dame, Ind.: University of Notre Dame Press).

Hilton, B. *et al.* 1973. *Ethical Issues in Human Genetics* (New York: Plenum).

Hobbes, T. 1839. *The English Works of Thomas Hobbes*. W. Molesworth ed. (London: John Bohn).

Hoyle, F. 1957. *The Black Cloud* (Harmondsworth: Penguin).

Hrdy, S. B. 1977. *The Langurs of Abu* (Cambridge, Mass.: Harvard University Press, 1977).

—. 1981. *The Woman That Never Evolved*. (Cambridge, Mass.: Cambridge University Press).

Hudson, W. D. 1970. *Modern Moral Philosophy* (London: Macmillan).

Hughes, G. E. and M. J. Cresswell. 1968. *An Introduction to Modal Logic* (London: Methuen).

Hull, D. L. 1973. *Darwin and His Critics* (Cambridge, Mass.: Harvard University Press).

—. 1983. Exemplars and scientific change. In P. Asquith and R. Giere eds. *PSA 1982* (East Lansing: Philosophy of Science Association), 2, 479–503.

Hume, D. 1779. *Dialogues Concerning Natural Religion*. Reprinted in R. Wollheim ed. *Hume on Religion* (London: Collins, 1963).

—. 1975. *Enquiries Concerning Human Understanding and Concerning the Principles of Morals*. 3rd edn P. H. Nidditch ed. (Oxford: Oxford University Press).

—. 1978. *A Treatise of Human Nature*. L. A. Selby-Bigge ed. 2nd edn P. H. Nidditch ed. (Oxford: Oxford University Press).

Huntley, W. B. 1972. David Hume and Charles Darwin. *Journal of the History of Ideas*, 33, 457–70.

Huxley, J. S. 1942. *Evolution: The Modern Synthesis* (London: Allen and Unwin).

Huxley, L. 1900. *Life and Letters of Thomas Henry Huxley* (London: Murray).

Huxley, T. H. 1893. The coming of age of The Origin of Species. In *Darwiniana: Collected Essays* (London: Macmillan), 2, 227–43.

—. 1894. *Evolution and Ethics, and Other Essays*. Collected Essays 9 (London: Macmillan).

—. 1901. *Evidence as to Man's Place in Nature* (London: Williams and Norgate). First published 1863.

Huxley, T. H. and J. S. Huxley. 1947. *Evolution and Ethics* (London: Pilot Press).

Isaac, G. L. 1978. Food sharing and human evolution: archaeological evidence from the Plio-Pleistocene of East Africa. *Journal of Anthropological Research*, 34, 311–25.

—. 1980. Casting the net wide: a review of archaeological evidence for early hominid land-use and ecological relations. In L.-K. Konigsson ed. *Current Argument on Early Man* (Oxford: Pergamon), 226–53.

—. 1981. Archaeological tests of alternative models of early hominid behaviour: excavation and experiments. *Philosophical Transactions of the Royal Society, London B*, 292, 177–88.

—. 1983. Aspects of human evolution. In D. S. Bendall ed. *Evolution from Molecules to Men* (Cambridge: Cambridge University Press), 509–43.

James, W. 1890. *The Principles of Psychology* (New York: Holt).

—. 1907. *Pragmatism: A New Name for Some Old Ways of Thinking* (New York: Longmans, Green).

Johanson, D. C. and M. Edey. 1981. *Lucy: The Beginnings of Humankind* (New York: Simon and Schuster).

Johanson, D. C. and T. D. White. 1979. A systematic assessment of early African hominids. *Science*, 203, 321–30.

Jones, J. S. 1981. Models of speciation – the evidence from *Drosophila*. *Nature*, 289, 743-4.

Kant, I. 1929. *Critique of Pure Reason*. Trans. N. Kemp Smith (London: Macmillan).

—. 1949. *Critique of Practical Reason*. Trans. L. W. Beck (Chicago: University of Chicago Press).

—. 1959. *Foundations of the Metaphysics of Morals*. Trans. L.W. Beck (Indianapolis: Bobbs-Merrill).

—. 1963. *Lectures on Ethics*. Trans. L. Infield. (New York: Harper and Row).

Keil, F. C. 1979. *Semantic and Conceptual Development: An Ontological Perspective* (Cambridge, Mass.: Harvard University Press).

—. 1981. Constraints on knowledge and development. *Psychological Review*, 88, 197–227.

Kellogg, D. E. 1975. The role of phyletic change in the evolution of *Pseudocubus vema* (Radiolaria). *Paleobiology*, 1, 359–70.

—. 1983. Phenology of morphologic change in radiolarian lineages from deep-sea cores: implications for macroevolution. *Paleobiology*, 9, 355–62.

Kemp Smith, N. 1923. *A Commentary to Kant's Critique of Pure Reason* (London: Macmillan).

—. 1941. *The Philosophy of David Hume* (London: Macmillan).

Kierkegaard, S. 1936. *Philosophical Fragments.* Trans. D. F. Swenson (Princeton: Princeton University Press).

Kimura, M. 1983. *The Neutral Theory of Molecular Evolution* (Cambridge: Cambridge University Press).

King, J. E. and J. L. Fobes. 1982. Complex learning by primates. In J. L. Fobes and J. E. King eds. *Primate Behavior* (New York: Academic Press), 327–60.

King, M. C. and A. C. Wilson. 1975. Evolution at two levels: molecular similarities and biological differences between humans and chimpanzees. *Science,* 188, 107–16.

Kitcher, P. 1981. Explanatory unification. *Philosophy of Science,* 48, 507–31.

—.1983a. *Abusing Science* (Cambridge, Mass.: MIT Press).

—. 1983b. *The Nature of Mathematical Knowledge.* (Oxford: Oxford University Press).

Kitts, D. B. 1974. Continental drift and scientific revolution. *Bulletin of the American Association of Petroleum Geologists,* 58, 2490–6.

Konigsson, L.-K. ed. 1980. *Current Argument on Early Man* (Oxford: Pergamon Press).

Körner, S. 1960. *Philosophy of Mathematics* (London: Hutchinson).

—. 1966. *Experience and Theory: An Essay in the Philosophy of Science* (London: Routledge and Kegan Paul).

Kropotkin, P. 1902. *Mutual Aid: A Factor of Evolution.* (London: Heinemann).

Kuhn, T. S. 1957. *The Copernican Revolution* (Cambridge, Mass.: Harvard University Press).

—. 1962. *The Structure of Scientific Revolutions.* (Chicago: University of Chicago Press).

Laitman, J. T. 1983. The evolution of the hominid upper respiratory system and implications for the origins of speech. In E. de Grolier ed. *Proceedings of the Transdisciplinary Symposium on Glosso-genetics, Paris, 1981* (Paris: Harwood Academic Press).

Laitman, J. T. and R. C. Heimbuch. 1982. The basicranium of Plio-Pleistocene hominids as an indicator of their upper respiratory systems. *American Journal of Physical Anthropology,* 59, 323–44.

Laitman, J. T., R. C. Heimbuch and E. S. Crelin. 1979. The basicranium of fossil hominids as an indicator of their upper respiratory systems. *American Journal of Physical Anthropology,* 51, 15–34.

Lakatos, I. and A. Musgrave, eds. 1970. *Criticism and the Growth of Knowledge* (Cambridge: Cambridge University Press).

Lamarck, J. B. 1809. *Philosophie Zoologique* (Paris). Trans. as *Zoological Philosophy* by H. Elliot (London: Macmillan, 1914).

Landau, M. 1984. Human evolution as narrative. *American Scientist,* 72(3), 262–8.

Lande, R. 1980. Review of Stanley's *Macroevolution. Paleobiology,* 6, 233–8.

Laudan, L. 1971. William Whewell on the consilience of inductions. *The Monist,* 55, 368–91.

—. 1977. *Progress and its Problems: Towards a Theory of Scientific Growth* (Berkeley: University of California Press).

—. 1981. A confutation of convergent realism. *Philosophy of Science,* 48, 1–49.

Laudan, R. 1981. The recent revolution in geology and Kuhn's theory of scientific change. In P. Asquith and I. Hacking eds. *PSA 1978* (East Lansing, Mich.: Philosophy of Science Association), 2, 227–39.

Lehrer, K. ed. 1966. *Freedom and Determinism* (New York: Random House).

Levins, R. and R. C. Lewontin. 1985. *The Dialectical Biologist* (Cambridge, Mass.: Harvard University Press).

Levitan, M. and A. Montagu. 1977. *Textbook of Human Genetics* (New York: Oxford University Press).

Lewontin, R. C. 1974. *The Genetic Basis of Evolutionary Change* (New York: Columbia University Press).

—. 1977. Sociobiology – a caricature of Darwinism. In F. Suppe and P. Asquith eds. *PSA 1976* (East Lansing, Mich.: Philosophy of Science Association), 2, 22–31.

—. 1978. Adaptation. *Scientific American*, 239, 3, 212–30.

Lewontin, R. C., S. Rose, and L. J. Kamin. 1984. *Not in Our Genes: Biology, Ideology, and Human Nature* (New York: Pantheon).

Li, C. C. 1955. *Population Genetics* (Chicago: Chicago University Press).

Lieberman, P. 1975. *On the Origins of Language: An Introduction to the Evolution of Human Speech* (New York: Macmillan)

—. 1984. *The Biology and Evolution of Language* (Cambridge, Mass.: Harvard University Press).

Lieberman, P. and E. S. Crelin. 1971. On the speech of Neanderthal man. *Linguistic Inquiry*, 2, 203–22.

Limoges, C. 1970. *La Sélection Naturelle* (Paris: Universitaires de France).

Livingstone, F. B. 1967. *Abnormal Hemoglobins in Human Populations* (Chicago: Aldine).

—. 1971. Malaria and human polymorphisms. *Annual Review of Genetics*, 5, 33–64.

Locke, J. 1975. *An Essay Concerning Human Understanding*. P. H. Nidditch ed. (New York: Oxford University Press).

Lorenz, K. 1941. Kant's Lehre von apriorischen im Lichte geganwartiger Biologie. *Blatter fur Deutsche Philosophie*, 15, 94-125. Translated and reprinted as: Kant's doctrine of the a priori in the light of contemporary biology. In H. C. Plotkin ed. *Learning, Development, and Culture: Essays in Evolutionary Epistemology* (Chichester: John Wiley, 1982), 121–43.

Lovejoy, O. 1981. The origin of man. *Science*, 211, 341–50.

Lucas, J. R. 1979. Wilberforce and Huxley: a legendary encounter. *Historical Journal*, 22: 313–330.

Lumsden, C. and E. O. Wilson. 1981. *Genes, Mind, and Culture* (Cambridge, Mass.: Harvard University Press).

—. 1983. *Promethean Fire* (Cambridge, Mass.: Harvard University Press).

Luria, S. E., S. J. Gould, and S. Singer. 1981. *A View of Life* (Menlo Park, Calif.: Benjamin/Cummings).

Lyell, C. 1830-3. *Principles of Geology*. (London: Murray).

Lyell, K. ed. 1881. *Life, Letters and Journals of Sir Charle Lyell, Bart*. (London: Murray).

Lyons, D. 1965. *Forms and Limits of Utilitarianism* (Oxford: Oxford University Press).

Macbeth, N. 1971. *Darwin Retried* (Boston: Gambit).

Mackie, J. L. 1955. Evil and omnipotence. *Mind*, 64, 200–12.

—. 1977. *Ethics: Inventing Right and Wrong* (Harmondsworth: Penguin).

—. 1978. The law of the jungle. *Philosophy*, 53, 553–73.

—. 1980. *Hume's Moral Theory* (London: Routledge and Kegan Paul).

Maller, O. and J. A. Desor. 1974. Effect of taste on ingestion by human newborns. In J. Bosma ed. *Fourth Symposium on Oral Sensation and Perception:*

Development in the Fetus and Infant. (Washington, DC: Government Printing Office), 279–311.

Malthus, T. R. 1963. *An Essay on the Principle of Population*. 1st edn 1798. 6th edn 1826. 6th edn reprinted 1963 (Homewood, Ill.: Irwin).

Manier, E. 1978. *The Young Darwin and His Cultural Circle* (Dordrecht: Riedel).

Manser, A. R. 1965. The concept of evolution. *Philosophy*, 40, 18–34.

Marchant, J. 1916. *Alfred Russel Wallace: Life and Reminiscences* (New York: Harper).

Marks, I. M. 1969. *Fears and Phobias* (New York: Academic Press).

Marr, D. 1984. *Vision: A Computational Investigation into the Human Representation and Processing of Visual Information*. (San Francisco: W. H. Freeman).

Marvin, V. B. 1973. *Continental Drift: The Evolution of a Concept* (Washington, D.C. : Smithsonian Institution Press).

Maynard Smith, J. 1975. *The Theory of Evolution*. 3rd edn (Harmondsworth: Penguin).

—. 1978. The evolution of behavior. *Scientific American*, 239, September, 176–92.

—. 1981. Did Darwin get it right? *London Review of Books*, 3 (11), 10–11.

—. 1982. *Evolution and the Theory of Games* (Cambridge: Cambridge University Press).

Mayr, E. 1963. *Animal Species and Evolution* (Cambridge, Mass.: Harvard University Press).

—. 1969. *Principles of Systematic Zoology* (New York: McGraw-Hill).

—. 1982. *The Growth of Biological Thought: Diversity, Evolution, and Inheritance*. (Cambridge, Mass.: Harvard University Press).

McCloskey, H. J. 1960. God and evil. *Philosophical Quarterly*, 10, 97-114.

McDonald, J. F. *et al*. 1977. Adaptive responses due to changes it gene regulation: a study with Drosophila. *Proceedings of the National Academy of Sciences USA*, 74, 4562–6.

Menzel, E. W. 1972. Spontaneous invention of ladders in a group of young chimpanzees. *Folia Primatologica*, 17, 87–106.

Michalos, A. C. 1969. Analytic and other dumb guides of life. *Analysis*, 30, 121–2.

Midgley, M. 1978. *Beast and Man*. (Ithaca: Cornell University Press).

Mill, J. S. 1884. *System of Logic*, 8th edn (London: Longman).

—. 1910. *Utilitarianism, Liberty and Representative Government* (London: Dent).

Miller, H. 1847. *Footprints of the Creator, or the Asterolepis of Stromness* (Edinburgh: Constable).

Mills, S. K. and J. H. Beatty. 1979. The propensity interpretation of fitness. *Philosophy of Science*, 46, 263–86.

Moore, G. E. 1903. *Principia Ethica* (Cambridge: Cambridge University Press).

Moore, J. R. 1979. *The Post-Darwinian Controversies: A Study of the Protestant Struggle to Come to Terms with Darwin in Great Britain and America, 1870–1900*. (Cambridge: Cambridge University Press).

Morris, H. M. ed. 1974. *Scientific Creationism* (San Diego: Creation-Life).

Murphy, J. G. 1982.*Evolution, Morality, and the Meaning of Life* (Totowa, NJ: Rowman and Littlefield).

Nagel, E. 1961. *The Structure of Science* (New York: Harcourt, Brace and World).

Nagel, T. 1980. Ethics as an autonomous theoretical subject. In G. Stent ed. *Morality as a Biological Phenomenon* (Berkeley: University of California Press), 196–205.

Negus, V. E. 1949. *The Comparative Anatomy and Physiology of the Larynx* (New York: Hafner).

Newman, J. R. and E. Nagel. 1958. *Gödel's Proof* (New York: New York University Press).

Nickles, T. ed. 1980a. *Scientific Discovery: Logic and Rationality* (Dordrecht: Reidel).
—. ed. 1980b. *Scientific Discovery: Case Studies* (Dordrecht: Reidel).
Nozick, R. 1981. *Philosophical Explanations* (Cambridge, Mass.: Harvard University Press).
Oakley, K. P. 1964. The problem of man's antiquity, *Bulletin of the British Museum (Natural History), Geological Series, 9*, 5.
Ospovat, D. 1981. *The Development of Darwin's Theory* (Cambridge: Cambridge University Press).
Overton, W. R. 1982. Creationism in schools: the decision in McLean versus the Arkansas Board of Education. *Science, 215*, 934–43.
Pais, A. 1982. *'Subtle is the Lord . . .' The Science and the Life of Albert Einstein* (Oxford: Oxford University Press).
Paton, H. J. 1946. *The Categorical Imperative: A Study in Kant's Moral Philosophy* (London: Hutchinson).
Peirce, C. S. 1931–35. *Collected Papers.* C. Hartshorne and P. Weiss, eds (Cambridge, Mass.: Harvard University Press).
Peters, R. H. 1976. Tautology in evolution and ecology. *American Naturalist, 110*, 1–12.
Pilbeam, D. 1984. The descent of Hominoids and Hominids. *Scientific American, 250/3*, 84–97.
Plato. 1941. *The Republic.* Trans. F. Cornford (Oxford: Oxford University Press).
—. 1948. *Euthyphro.* Trans F. J. Church (Indianapolis: Bobbs-Merrill).
Plotkin, H. C. and F. J. Odling-Smee. 1981. A multiple-level model of evolution and its implications for sociobiology. *Behavioral and Brain Sciences, 4*, 225–68.
Popper, K. R. 1959. *The Logic of Scientific Discovery.* (London: Hutchinson).
—. 1962. *Conjectures and Refutations* (London: Routledge and Kegan Paul).
—. 1963. *The Open Society and its Enemies.* 4th edn (Princeton, NJ: Princeton University Press).
—. 1970. Normal science and its dangers. In I. Lakatos and A. Musgrave eds. *Criticism and the Growth of Knowledge* (Cambridge: Cambridge University Press).
—. 1972. *Objective Knowledge: An Evolutionary Approach* (Oxford: Oxford University Press).
—. 1974. Darwinism as a metaphysical research programme. In P. A. Schilpp ed. *The Philosophy of Karl Popper* (LaSalle, Ill.: Open Court), 1, 133–43.
—. 1978. Natural selection and the emergence of mind. *Dialectica, 32*, 339–55.
Potts, R. and P. Shipman. 1981. Cutmarks made by stone tools on bones from Olduvai Gorge, Tanzania. *Nature, 291*, 577–80.
Premack, D. 1972. Language in chimpanzees. *Science, 172*, 808–22.
—. 1976. *Intelligence in Ape and Man* (Hillsdale, NJ: Lawrence Erlbaum).
Premack, D. and G. Woodruff. 1978. Does the chimpanzee have a theory of mind? *The Behavioral and Brain Sciences, 1* (4), 515–26.
Putnam, H. 1981. *Reason, Truth and History* (Cambridge: Cambridge University Press).
—. 1982. Why reason can't be naturalized. *Synthese, 52*, 3–23.
Quine, W.V.O. 1953. *From a Logical Point of View* (Cambridge, Mass.: Harvard University Press).
—. 1964. *Word and Object* (Cambridge, Mass.: MIT Press).
—. 1969a. Epistemology naturalized. In *Ontological Relativity and Other Essays* (New York: Columbia University Press), 69–90.
—. 1969b. Natural kinds. In *Ontological Relativity and Other Essays* (New York: Columbia University Press), 114–38.

—. 1970. *Philosophy of Logic*. (Englewood Cliffs: Prentice–Hall).

—. 1978. On the nature of moral values. In A. I. Goldman and J. Kim eds. *Values and Morals* (Dordrecht: Reidel).

Raper, A. B. 1960. Sickling and malaria. *Transactions of the Royal Society of Tropical Medicine and Hygiene, 54*, 503–4.

Raphael, D. D. 1958. Darwinism and ethics. In S. A. Barnett ed. *A Century of Darwin* (London: Heinemann), 334–59.

—. 1969. *British Moralists, 1650–1800*. (Oxford: Oxford University Press).

Raup, D. M. and S. M. Stanley. 1978. *Principles of Paleontology*. 2nd edn (San Francisco: Freeman).

Rawls, J. 1971. *A Theory of Justice* (Harvard: Harvard University Press).

—. 1980. Kantian constructivism in moral theory. *Journal of Philosophy, 77*, 515–72.

Rescher, N. 1977. *Methodological Pragmatism* (Oxford: Basil Blackwell).

—. 1978. *Scientific Progress*. (Pittsburgh: University of Pittsburgh Press).

Reynolds, V. and R. E. S. Tanner. 1983. *The Biology of Religion* (London: Longman).

Richards, R. J. 1977. The natural selection model of conceptual evolution. *Philosophy of Science, 44*, 494–501.

Richerson, P. J. and R. Boyd. 1978. A dual inheritance model of the human evolutionary process: I. Basic postulates and a simple model. *Journal of Social and Biological Structures, 1* (2), 127–54.

Riedl, R. 1980. *Biologie der Erkenntnis*. Written in collaboration with R. Kaspar. (Berlin-Hamburg: P. Parey). Translated as *Biology of Knowledge* (Chichester: Wiley, 1984).

Riesen, A. H. 1982. Primate perceptual processes. In J. L. Fobes and J. E. King eds. *Primate Behavior* (New York: Academic Press), 271–86.

Rorty, R. 1980. *Philosophy and the Mirror of Nature* (Oxford: Basil Blackwell).

Rosch, E. H. 1973. Natural categories. *Cognitive Psychology, 4*, 328–50.

Rose, S. 1982. *Towards a Liberatory Biology* (London: Allison and Busby).

Rosenthal, R. ed. 1965. *Clever Hans (The Horse of Mr. von Osten), by Oskar Pfungst* (New York: Holt, Rinehart and Winston).

Ross, W. D. 1930. *The Right and the Good* (Oxford: Clarendon Press).

Rudwick, M. J. S. 1972. *The Meaning of Fossils* (London: Macdonald).

Rumbaugh, D. M., E. S. Savage-Rumbaugh, and J. L. Scanlon. 1982. The relationship between language in apes and human beings. In J. L. Fobes and J. E. King eds. *Primate Behavior* (New York: Academic Press), 361–85.

Ruse, M. 1969. Confirmation and falsification of theories of evolution, *Scientia*, CIV, 329–57.

—. 1973a. *The Philosophy of Biology* (London: Hutchinson).

—. 1973b. The value of analogical models in science. *Dialogue, 12*, 246–53.

—. 1975a. Charles Darwin's theory of evolution: an analysis. *Journal of the History of Biology, 8*, 219–41.

—. 1975b. The relationship between science and religion in Britain, 1830–1870. *Church History, 44*, 505–22.

—. 1975c. Charles Darwin and artificial selection. *Journal of the History of Ideas, 36*, 339–50.

—. 1975d. Darwin's debt to philosophy: an examination of the influence of the philosophical ideas of John F. W. Hershel and William Whewell on the development of Charles Darwin's theory of evolution. *Studies in History and Philosophy of Science, 6*, 159–81.

—. 1976. Reduction in genetics. In A. C. Michalos *et al.* eds. *PSA 1974* (Dordrecht: Reidel), 633–52.

—. 1977. Is biology different from physics? In R. G. Colodny ed. *Logic, Laws, and Life* (Pittsburgh: University of Pittsburgh Press), 89–127.

—. 1979a. *The Darwinian Revolution: Science Red in Tooth and Claw* (Chicago: University of Chicago Press).

—. 1979b. *Sociobiology: Sense or Nonsense?* (Dordrecht: Reidel).

—. 1980a. Charles Darwin and group selection. *Annals of Science*, 37, 615–30.

—. 1980b. Genetics and the quality of life. *Social Indicators Research*, 7, 419–441.

—. 1980c. Ought philosophers consider scientific discovery? A Darwinian case study. In T. Nickles ed. *Scientific Discovery: Case Studies* (Dordrecht: Reidel), 131–50.

—. 1981a. Are there gay genes? Sociobiology and homosexuality. *Journal of Homosexuality*, 6 (4), 5–34.

—. 1981b. *Is Science Sexist? and Other Problems in the Biomedical Sciences* (Dordrecht: Reidel).

—. 1981c. What kind of revolution occurred in geology? P. Asquith and I. Hacking eds. *PSA 1978* (East Lansing: PSA), 2, 240–73.

—. 1982a. A philosopher at the monkey trial. *New Scientist*, 93, 317–19.

—. 1982b. Creation-science is not science. *Science, Technology, and Human Values*, 40, 72–8.

—. 1982c. *Darwinism Defended: A Guide to the Evolution Controversies* (Reading, Mass.: Addison-Wesley).

—. 1984a. The morality of homosexuality. In R. Baker and F. Elliston eds. *Philosophy and Sex*. 2nd edn (Buffalo: Prometheus), 370–90.

—. 1984b. Is there a limit to our knowledge of evolution? *BioScience*, 34 (2), 100–104.

—. 1984c. A philosopher's day in court. In A. Montagu ed. *Science and Creationism*. (New York: Oxford University Press), 311–42.

—. 1985. Is rape wrong on Andromeda? In E. Regis ed. *Extraterrestrials* (Cambridge: Cambridge University Press), 43–78.

Ruse, M. and E. O. Wilson. 1986. Ethics as applied science. *Philosophy*.

Russell, B. 1937. *The Principles of Mathematics* 2nd ed. (London: Allen and Unwin).

Russell, E. S. 1916. *Form and Function* (London: Murray).

Russett, C. 1976. *Darwin in America: The Intellectual Response. 1865–1912* (San Francisco: Freeman).

Ryle, G. 1949. *The Concept of Mind* (London: Hutchinson).

Sahlins, M. D. 1965. On the sociology of primitive exchange. In M. Banton ed. *The Relevance of Models for Social Anthropology* (London: Tavistock), 139–236.

—. 1976. *The Use and Abuse of Biology* (Ann Arbor: University of Michigan Press).

Salmon, W. C. 1968. The justification of inductive rules of inference. In I. Lakatos ed. *The Problem of Inductive Logic* (Amsterdam: North Holland), 24–43.

—. 1973. *Logic* 2nd edn (Englewood Cliffs: Prentice-Hall).

Sartre, J.-P. 1965. *The Humanism of Existentialism*. Trans. B. Frechtman. In W. Baskin ed. *J.-P. Sartre, The Philosophy of Existentialism*. (New York: Philosophical Library).

Savage-Rumbaugh, E. S., D. M. Rumbaugh, and S. Boysen. 1978. Linguistically mediated tool use and exchange by chimpanzees. *The Behavioral and Brain Sciences*, 1 (4), 539–54.

—. 1980. Do apes use language? *American Scientist*, 68, 49–61.

Schaffner, K. F. 1969. The Watson-Crick model and reductionism. *British Journal for the Philosophy of Science*. 20, 325–48.

—. 1976. Reductionism in biology: prospects and problems. In A. C. Michalos *et al*. eds. *PSA 1974* (Dordrecht: Reidel), 613–32.

Scheffler, I. *The Anatomy of Inquiry* (New York: Knopf).

Schilcher, F. V. and N. Tennant. 1984. *Philosophy, Evolution and Human Nature* (London: Routledge and Kegan Paul).

Sebeok, T. A. and J. Umiker-Sebeok. 1979. Performing animals: secrets of the trade. *Psychology Today*, 13 (November), 78–91.

—. eds. 1980. *Speaking of Apes* (New York: Plenum Press).

Seemanova, E. 1971. A study of children of incestuous matings. *Human Heredity*, 21 (1), 108–28.

Seligman, M. E. P. 1972. Phobias and preparedness. In M. E. P. Seligman and J. L. Hager eds. *Biological Boundaries of Learning* (New York: Appleton-Century-Crofts), 451–60.

Sen, A. and B. Williams, eds. 1982. *Utilitarianism and Beyond* (Cambridge: Cambridge University Press).

Shepher, J. 1979. *Incest: The Biosocial View* (Cambridge, Mass.: Harvard University Press).

Shimony, A. 1971. Perception from an evolutionary point of view. *Journal of Philosophy*, 68, 571–83.

Sibley, C. G. and J. E. Ahlquist. 1984. The phylogeny of the Hominoid primates, as indicated by DNA-DNA hybridization. *Journal of Molecular Evolution*, 20, 2–15.

Simpson, G. G. 1951. *Horses* (New York: Oxford University Press).

—. 1953. *The Major Features of Evolution* (New York: Columbia University Press).

Singer, M. G. 1977. Justice, theory, and a theory of justice. *Philosophy of Science*, 44, 594–618.

Singer, P. 1972. Famine, affluence, and morality. *Philosophy and Public Affairs*, 1 (3), 229–43.

—. 1981. *The Expanding Circle: Ethics and Sociobiology* (New York: Farrar, Straus, and Giroux).

Skagestad, P. 1978. Taking evolution seriously: critical comments on D. T. Campbell's evolutionary epistemology. *The Monist*, 61, 611–21.

Smart, J. J. C. 1963. *Philosophy and Scientific Realism*. (London: Routledge and Kegan Paul).

—. 1968. *Between Science and Philosophy* (New York: Random House).

Smart, J. J. C. and B. Williams. 1973. *Utilitarianism: For and Against* (Cambridge: Cambridge University Press).

Sober, E. 1975. *Simplicity* (Oxford: Oxford University Press).

—. 1981. The evolution of rationality. *Synthese*, 46, 95–120.

—. 1984. *Conceptual Issues in Evolutionary Biology*. (Cambridge, Mass.: MIT Press).

Spencer, H. 1852. A theory of population, deduced from the general law of animal fertility. *Westminster Review*, n.s. 1, 468–501.

—. 1855. *Principles of Psychology* (London: Williams and Norgate).

—. 1857. Progress: its law and cause. *Westminster Review* Reprinted in *Essays: Scientific, Political, and Speculative* (London, Williams and Norgate, 1868), 1, 1–73.

—. 1864. *Principles of Biology* (London: Williams and Norgate).

—. 1874. *The Study of Sociology* (London: Williams and Norgate).

—. 1879. *The Data of Ethics* (London: Williams and Norgate).

—. 1892. *Principles of Ethics* (London: Williams and Norgate).

Staal, J. F. 1967. Indian logic. In A. N. Prior ed. History of logic. In P. Edwards ed. *Encyclopedia of Philosophy* (New York: Collier Macmillan), 4, 520–3.

Stanley, S. M. 1979. *Macroevolution: Pattern and Process* (San Francisco: Freeman).

Stebbins, G. L. and F. J. Ayala. 1981. Is a new evolutionary synthesis necessary? *Science*, 213, 967–71.

Stern, C. 1973. *Principles of Human Genetics*. 3rd edn (San Francisco: Freeman).

Stevenson, C. 1944. *Ethics and Language* (New Haven: Yale University Press).

Strawson, P. F. 1952. *Introduction to Logical Theory* (London: Methuen).

Stroud, B. 1977. *Hume* (London: Routledge and Kegan Paul).

—. 1984. *The Significance of Philosophical Scepticism* (Oxford: Oxford University Press).

Sulloway, F. 1979a. *Freud: Biologist of the Mind* (New York: Basic Books).

—. 1979b. Geographic isolation in Darwin's thinking: the vicissitudes of a crucial idea. *Studies in the History of Biology*, 3, 23–65.

Sumner, W. G. 1883. *What Social Classes Owe to Each Other* (New York: Harper and Brothers).

—. 1914. *The Challenge of Facts and Other Essays*. A. G. Keller ed. (New Haven: Yale University Press).

—. 1918. *The Forgotten Man and Other Essays*. A. G. Keller. ed. (New Haven: Yale University Press).

Suppe, F. ed. 1974. *The Structure of Scientific Theories* (Urbane: University of Illinois Press).

Symons, D. 1979. *The Evolution of Human Sexuality* (New York: Oxford University Press).

Taylor, G. R. 1983. *The Great Evolution Mystery* (New York: Harper and Row).

Taylor, P. W. ed. 1978. *Problems of Moral Philosophy* (Belmont, Calif.: Wadsworth).

Terrace, H. S. 1979. *Nim* (New York: Knopf).

—. 1983. Apes who talk: language or protection of language by their teachers? In J. de Luce and H. T. Wilder eds. *Language in Primates* (New York: Springer-Verlag), 19–42.

Terrace, H. S., L. A. Petitto, R. J. Sanders, and T. G. Bever. 1979. Can an ape create a sentence? *Science*, 206, 891–902.

Thagard, P. 1980. Against evolutionary epistemology. In P. Asquith and R. Giere eds. *PSA 1980* (East Lansing, Mich.: Philosophy of Science Association), 1, 187–96.

Toulmin, S. 1967. The evolutionary development of natural science. *American Scientist*, 57, 456–71.

—. 1972. *Human Understanding* (Oxford: Oxford University Press).

—. 1981. Evolution, adaptation, and human understanding. In M. B. Brewer and B. E. Collins eds. *Scientific Inquiry and the Social Sciences: A Volume in Honor of Donald T. Campbell* (San Francisco: Jossey – Bass), 18–36.

Trigg, R. 1982. *The Shaping of Man* (Oxford: Blackwell).

Trinkaus, E. and W. W. Howells. 1979. The Neanderthals. *Scientific American*, 241, 118–33.

Trivers, R. L. 1971. The evolution of reciprocal altruism. *Quarterly Review of Biology*, 46, 35–57.

—. 1976. Foreword to R. Dawkins, *The Selfish Gene* (Oxford: Oxford University Press), v–vii.

Turner, J. 1984. Why we need evolution by jerks. *New Scientist*, 101 (1396), 9 February, 34–5.

Valentine, J. W. 1978. The evolution of multicellular plants and animals. *Scientific American*, 239, September, 140–58.

van den Berghe, P. 1979. *Human Family Systems* (New York: Elsevier).

—. 1983. Human inbreeding avoidance: culture–nature. *The Behavioral and Brain Sciences*, 6, 91–124.

van Fraassen, B. 1980. *The Scientific Image* (Oxford: Oxford University Press).

Wald, G. 1969. The molecular basis of color vision. In B. R. Straatsma *et al.* eds. *The Retina: Morphology, Function, and Clinical Characteristics* (Berkeley: University of California Press), 281–95.

Walker, S. 1983. *Animal Thought* (London: Routledge and Kegan Paul).

Wallwork, E. 1982. Thou shalt love thy neighbor as thyself: the Freudian critique. *The Journal of Religious Ethics*, 10 (2) 264–319.

Watson, J. D. 1968. *The Double Helix* (New York: Atheneum).

Watson, J. D. and F. H. C. Crick. 1953. Molecular structure of nucleic acids. *Nature*, 171, 737–8.

Weiner, P. 1949. *Evolution and the Founders of Pragmatism* (Cambridge, Mass.: Harvard University Press).

Weinrich, J. D. 1982. Is homosexuality biologically natural? In W. Paul, J. D. Weinrich, J. C. Gonsiorek, and M. E. Matvedt eds. *Homosexuality: Social, Psychological, and Biological Issues* (Beverly Hills: Sage), 197–208.

Weitzenfeld, J. S. 1984. Valid reasoning by analogy. *Philosophy of Science*, 51, 137–49.

Wellman, C. 1963. The ethical implications of cultural relativity. *Journal of Philosophy*, 60, 169–84.

Westermarck, E. 1891. *The History of Human Marriage* (London: Macmillan).

Westfall, R. S. 1971. *Force in Newton's Physics: The Science of Dynamics in the Seventeenth Century* (London: Macdonald).

—. 1981. *Never at Rest: A Biography of Isaac Newton* (Cambridge: Cambridge University Press).

Whewell, W. 1840. *Philosophy of the Inductive Sciences.* (London: Parker).

—. 1860. *The Philosophy of Discovery* (London: Parker).

Whitcomb, J. C. and H. M. Morris. 1961. *The Genesis Flood.* (Nutley, NJ: Presbyterian and Reformed Publishing Co.).

Williams, B. A. O. *Descartes: The Project of Pure Enquiry* (Harmondsworth: Penguin).

—. 1980. Conclusion. In G. Stent ed. *Morality as a Biological Phenomenon* (Berkeley: University of California Press), 275–85.

Williams, G. C. 1966. *Adaptation and Natural Selection: A Critique of some Current Evolutionary Thought* (Princeton: Princeton University Press).

—. 1975. *Sex and Evolution* (Princeton: Princeton University Press).

Wilson, E. O. 1971. *The Insect Societies* (Cambridge, Mass.: Harvard University Press).

—. 1975. *Sociobiology: The New Synthesis* (Cambridge, Mass.: Harvard University Press).

—. 1978. *On Human Nature* (Cambridge, Mass.: Harvard University Press).

—. 1984. *Biophilia* (Cambridge, Mass.: Harvard University Press).

Wilson, L. 1970. *Sir Charles Lyell's Scientific Journals on the Species Question* (New Haven: Yale University Press).

—. 1972. *Charles Lyell, the Years to 1841: The Revolution in Geology* (New Haven: Yale University Press).

Wolff, R. P. 1960. Hume's theory of mental activity. *Philosophical Review*, 49, 289–310.

—. 1963. *Kant's Theory of Mental Activity* (Cambridge, Mass.: Harvard University Press).

—. 1977. *Understanding Rawls* (Princeton: Princeton University Press).

Wood, B. A. 1981. Tooth size and shape and their relevance to studies of hominid evolution. *Philosophical Transactions of the Royal Society London B*, 292, 65–76.

Woodruff, G., D. Premack, and K. Kennel. 1978. Conservation of liquid and solid quantity by the chimpanzee. *Science*, 202, 991–4.

Wright, J. P. 1983. *The Sceptical Realism of David Hume* (Minneapolis: University of Minnesota Press).

Wright, L. 1976. *Teleological Explanations* (Berkeley: University of California Press).

Wuketits, F. J. 1978. *Wissenschafts theoretische Probleme der Modernen Biologie* (Berlin: Duncker and Humblot).

—. 1981. *Biologie und Kausalität. Biologische Ausatze zur Kausalität, Determination und Freiheit* (Berlin-Hamburg: P. Parey).

—. ed. 1983. *Concepts and Approaches in Evolutionary Epistemology* (Dordrecht: Reidel).

Young, R. M. 1971. Darwin's metaphor: does nature select? *Monist*, 55, 442–503.

Yunis, J. J. *et al.* 1980. The striking resemblance of high resolution G-banded chromosomes of man and chimpanzee. *Science*, 208, 1145–8.

Index